Fixed Point Theory and Fractals

Fixed Point Theory and Fractals

Guest Editors

María A. Navascués
Bilel Selmi
Cristina Serpa

MDPI

Basel • Beijing • Wuhan • Barcelona • Belgrade • Novi Sad • Cluj • Manchester

Guest Editors
María A. Navascués
Department of Applied Mathematics
University of Zaragoza
Zaragoza
Spain

Bilel Selmi
Department of Mathematics
University of Monastir
Monastir
Tunisia

Cristina Serpa
Center for Mathematical Studies
Academia Militar at Portuguese Army
Amadora
Portugal

Editorial Office
MDPI AG
Grosspeteranlage 5
4052 Basel, Switzerland

This is a reprint of the Special Issue, published open access by the journal *Fractal and Fractional* (ISSN 2504-3110), freely accessible at: https://www.mdpi.com/journal/fractalfract/special_issues/K2X7V77KSM.

For citation purposes, cite each article independently as indicated on the article page online and as indicated below:

Lastname, A.A.; Lastname, B.B. Article Title. *Journal Name* **Year**, *Volume Number*, Page Range.

ISBN 978-3-7258-5403-5 (Hbk)
ISBN 978-3-7258-5404-2 (PDF)
https://doi.org/10.3390/books978-3-7258-5404-2

Contents

Preface

Currently, the power of the theoretical and practical contents of fractal and fractional theories is undeniable. The fields of application of Fractal Theory vary from SIR (Susceptible-Infectious-Removed) dynamics to the resolution of fractional differential and integral equations modelling all kinds of physical phenomena.

Fractal Theory creates a bridge between classical geometry and applied mathematics. The static models of the old geometry and analysis are enriched with the dynamics of an infinite iterative process, where the outputs are not merely points but more sophisticated geometric objects and structures.

A fractal set can be described in very different ways, but the current mathematical research defines a fractal as the fixed point of a map on the space of compact subsets of a metric or topological space. The theory of iterated function systems by Barnsley and Hutchinson provides a way to define an operator on the space of compact sets, along with an algorithm to approach the fractal. Thus the relationships between Fixed Point Theory, Fractals and Fractional Calculus are deep and increasingly intricate.

This Reprint is aimed at emphasizing the relationships between these fields, including their theoretical and applied aspects.

Some articles push forward the classical conditions of existence of a fixed point (a contraction on a complete metric space), considering wider structures on the underlying set and more general contractive conditions for the map. For instance, the mappings can be nonexpansive instead of contractive and multi-valued instead of single-valued. Some papers deal with fuzzy metric spaces and fuzzy contractions whose results find applications in SIR dynamics.

The text presents applications of the theories to the solution of certain fractional differential equations, fuzzy fractional differential equations, integral equations and fractional boundary value problems. An article reviews the properties of the intriguing cosmic web.

For fractal functions, defined as fixed points of the Read-Bajraktarević operator, some articles consider non-standard functional spaces and Matkowski and Rakotch maps instead of the classical Banach contractions.

The text deepens in abstract structures of the theory as Hausdorff measures and the degree of multi-valued mappings as well.

Novel iterative methods for the approximation of common fixed points to several maps, common attractors and fractals of different iterated function systems are also presented. The convergence and stability of the algorithms are analyzed.

In summary, the text collects a sample of interesting advanced approaches by prominent mathematicians to the current research on Fractals, Fixed Point Theory, their relationships and their applications.

María A. Navascués, Bilel Selmi, and Cristina Serpa
Guest Editors

fractal and fractional

MDPI

Article

An Effective Iterative Process Utilizing Transcendental Sine Functions for the Generation of Julia and Mandelbrot Sets

Khairul Habib Alam [1,*], Yumnam Rohen [2], Anita Tomar [3], Naeem Saleem [4,5,*], Maggie Aphane [5] and Asima Razzaque [6,7]

1 Department of Mathematics, National Institute of Technology Manipur, Imphal 795004, Manipur, India
2 Department of Mathematics, Manipur University, Imphal 795003, Manipur, India
3 Pt. L. M. S. Campus, Sridev Suman Uttarakhand University, Rishikesh 249201, Uttarakhand, India
4 Department of Mathematics, University of Management and Technology, Lahore 54770, Pakistan
5 Department of Mathematics and Applied Mathematics, Sefako Makgatho Health Sciences University, Pretoria 0204, South Africa
6 Department of Basic Sciences, Preparatory Year, King Faisal University, Al-Ahsa 31982, Saudi Arabia; arazzaque@kfu.edu.sa
7 Department of Mathematics, College of Science, King Faisal University, Al-Ahsa 31982, Saudi Arabia
* Correspondence: alamkh@nitmanipur.ac.in (K.H.A.); naeem.saleem2@gmail.com (N.S.)

Abstract: This study presents an innovative iterative method designed to approximate common fixed points of generalized contractive mappings. We provide theorems that confirm the convergence and stability of the proposed iteration scheme, further illustrated through examples and visual demonstrations. Moreover, we apply s-convexity to the iteration procedure to construct orbits under convexity conditions, and we present a theorem that determines the condition when a sequence diverges to infinity, known as the escape criterion, for the transcendental sine function $\sin(u^m) - \alpha u + \beta$, where $u, \alpha, \beta \in \mathbb{C}$ and $m \geq 2$. Additionally, we generate chaotic fractals for this orbit, governed by escape criteria, with numerical examples implemented using MATHEMATICA software. Visual representations are included to demonstrate how various parameters influence the coloration and dynamics of the fractals. Furthermore, we observe that enlarging the Mandelbrot set near its petal edges reveals the Julia set, indicating that every point in the Mandelbrot set contains substantial data corresponding to the Julia set's structure.

Keywords: efficiency; stability; escape criterion; fractals; Julia set; Mandelbrot set; s-convexity

MSC: 28A10; 31E05; 37C25; 37F46; 47H10; 47J25

1. Introduction

Fixed point theory, a growing branch of mathematics, combines functional analysis and topology (see [1,2]). Specific iterative methods, such as those by Picard [3], Mann [4], Ishikawa [5], and Noor [6], are commonly employed to approximate fixed points of contractive mappings. Recent advancements include the application of Fibonacci–Ishikawa iteration for solving Caputo-type nonlinear fractional differential equations involving monotone asymptotically non-expansive mappings by Alam et al. [7] and their study [8] addressing nonlinear integral equations with two delays in hyperbolic spaces. Furthermore, Alam [9] introduced an efficient iterative approach for fractional Volterra–Fredholm integro-differential equations. Ofem et al. [10] proposed the AI iteration method, which improves the speed of fixed-point approximations.

Furthermore, numerous researchers have proposed the use of s-convexity in their studies (see, [11–15]). These diverse iteration processes can be examined from two perspectives. Firstly, they generally achieve faster convergence compared to traditional iterative methods. Secondly, each iteration method displays distinct dynamics and behaviors, which are valuable from both application and graphical viewpoints.

Fractals, characterized by their self-similar structures across scales, have had a profound impact on fields like art, physics, biology, and finance [16–19]. The advent of computational graphics during the "Fractals Era" at the end of the 20th century brought fractals, such as the Mandelbrot set [20,21] and the Julia set [22,23], into prominence. These sets are generated using iterative processes on complex numbers, revealing intricate visual patterns. The applications of fractals extend to image compression [24], signal processing [25], data compression [26], and human body organs [27], and their aesthetic appeal has inspired the field of fractal art [28]. Theoretical studies of fractals continue in geometry, dynamical systems, and topology [14].

The Mandelbrot set has been generalized using functions like $u^m + \beta$ instead of quadratic polynomials [29,30] and further expanded to include elliptic, transcendental, and rational functions, as well as extensions to systems like octonions [31], bicomplex numbers, and quaternions. Cyclical techniques, such as superfractals [32], inversion fractals, v-variable fractals, and biomorphs [33], have been used to identify fixed points and construct fractals via fixed-point theory. Iterative methods, such as Mann [34], Ishikawa [35], and Jungck–Mann [36], have been applied to visualize Julia and Mandelbrot sets, often incorporating s-convexity to enhance these techniques [12,37]. Recently, Alam et al. [38] investigated the escape criterion for generating fractals as Julia and Mandelbrot sets via s-convex AI iteration for functions of the type $\cos(u^m) - \alpha u + \beta$.

Building on this foundation, we introduce the Jungck–AI iteration process, demonstrating its convergence and stability through examples and visualizations. We incorporate s-convexity into this process to generate fractals based on the transcendental sine function $\sin(u^m) - \alpha u + \beta$, establishing an escape criterion for this function and the associated orbit under convexity conditions. Using MATHEMATICA, we analyze the chaotic properties of these fractals and illustrate the effects of various parameters on their dynamics. The ability of fractal geometry to capture intricate real-world structures has transformative potential in fields like textile design (e.g., Batik and Kalamkari). Fractal-based design automation supports scalability, reduces errors, promotes global collaboration, and lowers costs, driving industry growth and sustainability.

Section 2 outlines key definitions and concepts essential for the analysis. Section 3 proves that iterative methods Jungck–S, Jungck–CR, and Jungck–DK converge slower than the proposed Jungck–AI iteration. A numerical example validates this and shows that the weak compatibility condition ensures a unique common fixed point for both contractions, where our iteration converges. Section 4 explores the escape criterion of the Jungck–AI orbit using s-convex combinations for transcendental sine functions in the complex plane. Using MATHEMATICA 12.3, we generate chaotic fractals, including Julia and Mandelbrot sets, on a system with an 11th Gen Intel i3-1115G4 processor, 8 GB RAM, and Windows 11. Section 5 concludes the study.

2. Preliminaries

This section provides key definitions and discusses related concepts that will be useful in our analysis. Let $T : A \longrightarrow A$ be a self-mapping within a Banach space A. The AI iteration process, as outlined in [10], is described as

$$\begin{cases} u_{n+1} = Tv_n \\ v_n = Tw_n \\ w_n = Tx_n \\ x_n = a_n Tu_n + (1 - a_n)u_n, \;\; n \in \mathbb{N}, \end{cases}$$

for random choice, $u_1 \in A$, where $\{a_n\} \subset [0,1]$.

For two non-self mappings $S, T : B \longrightarrow A$, defined on a nonempty subset B of a Banach space A, where $T(A) \subseteq S(A)$, Jungck [39] introduced an iterative process satisfying the contraction condition:

$$d(Tu, Tv) \leq \lambda d(Su, Sv), \;\; \lambda \in [0,1).$$

Chugh et al. [40] proposed the Jungck–SP iterative scheme, which is described as follows:

$$\begin{cases} Su_{n+1} = a_n Tv_n + (1 - a_n)Sv_n \\ Sv_n = b_n Tw_n + (1 - a_n)Sw_n \\ Sw_n = c_n Tu_n + (1 - c_n)Su_n, \;\; n \in \mathbb{N}, \end{cases} \tag{1}$$

for random choice, $u_1 \in B$, where $\{a_n\}, \{b_n\}, \{c_n\} \subset [0,1]$.

Definition 1 ([41]). *Two non-self mappings $S, T : A \longrightarrow A$ on a nonempty Banach space A, with $T(A) \subseteq S(A)$, are said to satisfy a general contractive condition if*

$$||Tu - Tv|| \leq \varphi(||Su - Tu||) + \lambda ||Su - Sv||, \;\; \forall \; u, v \in A$$

where $\lambda \in [0,1)$ and $\varphi : (0, +\infty) \rightarrow (0, +\infty)$ is a monotonic function with $\varphi(0) = 0$.

Building on the general contractive condition outlined in [41], Hussain et al. [42] developed the Jungck–CR iteration process for sequences $\{a_n\}, \{b_n\}, \{c_n\} \subset [0,1]$ as

$$\begin{cases} Su_{n+1} = a_n Tv_n + (1 - a_n)Sv_n \\ Sv_n = b_n Tw_n + (1 - a_n)Tu_n \\ Sw_n = c_n Tu_n + (1 - c_n)Su_n, \;\; n \in \mathbb{N}, \end{cases} \tag{2}$$

for random choice, $u_1 \in B$.

In recent work, Guran et al. [43] introduced the Jungck–DK iterative method for sequences $\{a_n\}, \{b_n\} \subset [0,1]$ as

$$\begin{cases} Su_{n+1} = a_n Tv_n + (1 - a_n)Sw_n \\ Sv_n = b_n Tw_n + (1 - b_n)Su_n \\ Sw_n - Tu_n, \;\; n \in \mathbb{N}, \end{cases} \tag{3}$$

for random choice, $u_1 \in B$, and analyzed its efficiency compared to the iterative methods proposed by Chugh et al. [40] and Hussain et al. [42], as well as its stability and the escape criterion used for generating Mandelbrot and Julia sets.

Motivated by these considerations, we propose a new iteration procedure, referred to as the Jungck–AI, which demonstrates a faster convergence rate compared to the iterations introduced by Chugh et al. [40], Hussain et al. [42], and Guran et al. [43].

Our Jungck–AI iteration procedure is given by

$$\begin{cases} u_1 \in B \\ Su_{n+1} = Tv_n \\ Sv_n = Tw_n \\ Sw_n = Tx_n \\ Sx_n = a_n Tu_n + (1-a_n)Su_n, \ \forall n \in \mathbb{N}, \end{cases} \tag{4}$$

for sequence $\{a_n\} \subseteq (0,1)$.

Definition 2 ([44]). *Let $S, T : A \longrightarrow A$ be two mappings such that $Su = Tu$ for some $u \in A$. In this case, u is referred to as a coincidence point, and $Su = Tu = v$ is called a point of coincidence. If $Su = Tu = u$, then u is termed a common fixed point. Additionally, if $TSu = STu$ at a coincidence point u, the pair (S, T) is said to be weakly compatible.*

Definition 3 ([45]). *In any nonempty convex Banach space A, given a function F, a converging iteration procedure $Su_{n+1} = F(u_n, T)$ with $T(A) \subseteq S(A)$, which converges to a point of coincidence u, is said to be stable with respect to S and T or (S,T)¯stable if*

$$\lim_{n \to +\infty} ||S\gamma_n - F(\gamma_n, T)|| = 0 \Leftrightarrow \lim_{n \to +\infty} S\gamma_n = u,$$

for a chosen sequence $\{S\gamma_n\}$ in A.

Lemma 1 ([46]). *If for two real non-negative sequences $\{\gamma_n\}$ and $\{\delta_n\}$, we have $\gamma_{n+1} \leq (1-\eta_n)\gamma_n + \delta_n$, where $0 < \eta_n < 1$, for all $n \in \mathbb{N}$, with $\sum\limits_{n=0}^{\infty} \eta_n = \infty$ and $\lim\limits_{n \to +\infty} \frac{\delta_n}{\eta_n} = 0$, then $\lim\limits_{n \to +\infty} \gamma_n = 0$.*

Definition 4 ([22,23]). *A collection of complex numbers such that an orbit does not converge to an infinite point is a filled Julia set. If $T : \mathbb{C} \longrightarrow \mathbb{C}$ is a polynomial of degree $m (\geq 2)$, then the boundary set ∂F_T of the set $F_T = \{u \in \mathbb{C} : \{|T\ u_n|\} \text{ is bounded}\}$ is known as the Julia set.*

Definition 5 ([20,21]). *All of the parameter values β for which the filled-in Julia set of $T(u) = u^2 + \beta$ is connected to comprise the Mandelbrot set M. That is, $M = \{u \in \mathbb{C} : \partial F_T \text{ is connected}\}$ or $M = \{u \in \mathbb{C} : \{|T\ u_n|\} \nrightarrow +\infty \text{ whenever } n \to +\infty\}$.*

There are several generalizations of the convex combination in the literature; the s-convex combination is one example of such generalizations.

Definition 6 ([47]). *For a finite set of complex numbers $u_1, u_2, \ldots, u_n \in \mathbb{C}$, the s-convex combination is presented as $a_1^s u_1 + a_2^s u_2 + \cdots + a_n^s u_n$, where $0 \leq a_i \leq 1$ and $i \in \{1, 2, \ldots, n\}$ so that $\sum\limits_{i=1}^{n} a_i = 1$.*

Let us observe that, for $s = 1$, the s-convex combination simplifies to the conventional convex combination.

3. Efficiency, Stability, and Convergence in an Arbitrary Banach Space

This section provides an analytical proof showing that the iterative sequences generated by Equations (1)–(3) converge at a slower rate compared to our Jungck–AI iteration procedure (4). We also include a numerical example to support our theoretical results. First, we demonstrate that the weak compatibility condition ensures the existence of a unique common fixed point for both contractions, to which our iteration (4) converges.

Theorem 1. *Let A be a Banach space, and $S, T : B \longrightarrow A$ be two non-self mappings that satisfy the general contractive condition, defined on a non-empty subset B such that $T(B) \subseteq S(B)$ and $S(B)$ is complete in A. Then, the Jungck–AI iteration procedure $\{Su_n\}$ defined in (4) converges strongly to the unique common fixed point $Sv = Tv = u$ (denoted as u) if S and T are weakly compatible and $A = B$.*

Proof. Initially, we show that the Jungck–AI iterative procedure (4) converges to u. Based on the definition of the Jungck–AI iteration procedure in (4), we derive four inequalities:

$$\begin{aligned} ||Su_{n+1} - u|| &= ||Tv_n - u|| \\ &= ||Tv_n - Tv|| \\ &\leq \varphi(||Sv - Tv||) + \lambda||Sv_n - Sv|| \\ &\leq \lambda||Sv_n - Sv|| \\ &= \lambda||Sv_n - u||, \end{aligned}$$

$$\begin{aligned} ||Sv_n - u|| &= ||Tw_n - u|| \\ &= ||Tw_n - Tv|| \\ &\leq \varphi(||Sv - Tv||) + \lambda||Sw_n - Sv|| \\ &\leq \lambda||Sw_n - Sv|| \\ &= \lambda||Sw_n - u||, \end{aligned}$$

$$\begin{aligned} ||Sw_n - u|| &= ||Tx_n - u|| \\ &= ||Tx_n - Tv|| \\ &\leq \varphi(||Sv - Tv||) + \lambda||Sx_n - Sv|| \\ &\leq \lambda||Sx_n - Sv|| \\ &= \lambda||Sx_n - u|| \end{aligned}$$

and

$$\begin{aligned} ||Sx_n - u|| &= ||a_n Tu_n + (1 - a_n)Su_n - u|| \\ &\leq a_n||Tu_n - u|| + (1 - a_n)||Su_n - u|| \\ &= a_n||Tu_n - Tv|| + (1 - a_n)||Su_n - u|| \\ &\leq a_n(\varphi(||Sv - Tv||) + \lambda||Su_n - Sv||) + (1 - a_n)||Su_n - u|| \\ &\leq a_n\lambda||Su_n - Sv|| + (1 - a_n)||Su_n - u|| \\ &= a_n\lambda||Su_n - u|| + (1 - a_n)||Su_n - u|| \\ &= (1 - a_n(1 - \lambda))||Su_n - u||. \end{aligned}$$

Hence,

$$\begin{aligned} ||Su_{n+1} - u|| &\leq \lambda||Sv_n - u|| \\ &\leq \lambda^2||Sw_n - u|| \\ &\leq \lambda^3||Sx_n - u|| \\ &\leq \lambda^3(1 - a_n(1 - \lambda))||Su_n - u||. \end{aligned}$$

Since $1 - a_n(1 - \lambda) < 1$, we obtain

$$\begin{aligned} ||Su_{n+1} - u|| &\leq \lambda^3||Su_n - u|| \\ &\leq \lambda^6||Su_{n-1} - u|| \\ &\leq \lambda^{3n}||Su_1 - u||. \end{aligned}$$

Again, $0 < \lambda < 1$ implies $\lim_{n\to+\infty} ||Su_{n+1} - u|| = 0$; that is, the iteration procedure $\{Su_n\}$ defined in (4) converges to $Sv = Tv = u$.

We now prove that u is the unique common fixed point of S and T. Let u^* also be considered a point of coincidence. Consequently, v^* satisfies $Sv^* = Tv^* = u^*$. However, from the general contractive condition of S and T, we obtain the following

$$\begin{aligned} 0 \le ||u - u^*|| &= ||Tv - Tv^*|| \\ &\le \varphi(||Sv - Tv||) + \lambda||Sv - Sv^*|| \\ &\le \lambda||Sv - Sv^*|| \\ &= \lambda||u - u^*||. \end{aligned}$$

This implies that $u = u^*$ as $\lambda \in [0,1)$. Again, by the weak compatibility condition of S, T, from $Tu = TSv = TTv$, we obtain Tu as a point of coincidence of S and T. By the uniqueness of the point of coincidence, we have $u = Tu$. Consequently, $Su = u = Tu$; that is, S and T have a unique common fixed point, at which our Jungck–AI iterative procedure (4) converges. □

We provide the following theorem to demonstrate our iterative process (4) is stable.

Theorem 2. *Let A be a Banach space, and $S, T : B \longrightarrow A$ be two non-self mappings that satisfy the general contractive condition, defined on a non-empty subset B such that $T(B) \subseteq S(B)$ and $S(B)$ is complete in A. Then, the Jungck–AI iteration procedure $\{Su_n\}$ defined in (4) is (S,T)-stable if $\{a_n\}$ is bounded away from 0.*

Proof. Suppose the iteration procedure $\{Su_n\}$ defined in (4) is given by $Su_{n+1} = F(u_n, T)$, for some function F and converges to a point of coincidence $Sv = Tv = u$, for some $v \in B$.

Now, let the sequence $\{Sz_n\}$ be arbitrary; then,

$$||Sz_{n+1} - u|| \le ||Sz_{n+1} - F(z_n, T)|| + ||F(z_n, T) - u||,$$

where

$$\begin{cases} F(z_n, T) = Tv_n \\ Sv_n = Tw_n \\ Sw_n = Tx_n \\ Sx_n = a_n Tz_n + (1 - a_n)Sz_n, \ n \in \mathbb{N}. \end{cases}$$

Proceeding similar to Theorem 1, we have

$$||Sz_{n+1} - u|| \le ||Sz_{n+1} - F(z_n, T)|| + \lambda^3(1 - a_n(1 - \lambda))||Sz_n - u||.$$

On setting $\delta_n = ||Sz_{n+1} - F(z_n, T)||$, $\eta_n = a_n(1 - \lambda)$ and $\gamma_n = ||Sz_n - u||$, we see, if $\lim_{n\to+\infty} ||Sz_{n+1} - F(z_n, T)|| = 0$ and as $\{a_n\}$ is a bounded away sequence from 0, i.e., a non-negative sequence, then, by Lemma 1, $\lim_{n\to+\infty} \gamma_n = 0$, i.e., $\lim_{n\to+\infty} ||Sz_n - u|| = 0$, i.e., $\lim_{n\to+\infty} Sz_n = u$.

Conversely, let $\lim_{n\to+\infty} Sz_n = u$, i.e., $\lim_{n\to+\infty} ||Sz_n - u|| = 0$ and $\lim_{n\to+\infty} ||Sz_{n+1} - u|| = 0$. Then, $||Sz_{n+1} - F(z_n, T)||$

$$\begin{aligned} &\le ||Sz_{n+1} - u|| + ||F(z_n, T) - u|| \\ &\le ||Sz_{n+1} - u|| + \lambda^3(1 - a_n(1 - \lambda))||Sz_n - u||. \end{aligned}$$

which implies $\lim\limits_{n \to +\infty} ||Sz_{n+1} - F(z_n, T)|| = 0$. That is, the iteration procedure $\{Su_n\}$ defined in (4) is stable with respect to S, T or (S, T)-stable. □

Remark 1. *In the following numerical calculations for the iterative procedure $\{Su_n\}$ defined in (4), we utilize the sequence outlined below:*

- *Start with an initial point $u_1 \in B$.*
- *Compute a value $Sv_2 = F(u_1, T)$, which is approximately equal to Su_2 ($Sv_2 \approx Su_2$) rather than an exact representation of Su_2 due to computational limitations.*
- *Next, compute $Sv_3 = F(u_2, T) \approx Su_3$ using the next term in the sequence, $Su_3 = F(u_2, T)$.*

Ultimately, we obtain a numerically approximated sequence $\{Sv_n\}$ corresponding to the conceptual sequence $\{Su_n\}$. At each iteration, if Sv_n remains sufficiently close to Su_n and continues to converge to the common fixed point u of S and T, the fixed point reached by the iterations will be considered numerically stable or stable.

We now demonstrate numerically that our Jungck–AI iterative method (4) converges faster than the three previous iteration methods introduced by Chugh et al. [40], Hussain et al. [42], and Guran et al. [43].

Example 1. *Let $S, T : [1, 3] \longrightarrow [1, 27]$ be two mappings defined as $Su = u^3$, $Tu = 3u + 2$. Then, from Figure 1 below and for $\lambda = \frac{3}{4}, \varphi(t) = 2t$, S, T satisfies the general contractive condition.*

Now, for sequences $\left\{a_n = \frac{1}{n^2}\right\}, \left\{b_n = \frac{1}{2}\right\}, \left\{c_n = \frac{1}{n+1}\right\} \subseteq (0, 1)$ and the initial guess $u_1 = 1$, Table 1 and Figure 2 below represent the iterations of Chugh et al. [40], Hussain et al. [42] and Guran et al. [43] and our Jungck–AI iteration (4) converging to the point of coincidence 8 of S, T with the stop criterion $||u_n - u|| < 10^{-5}$.

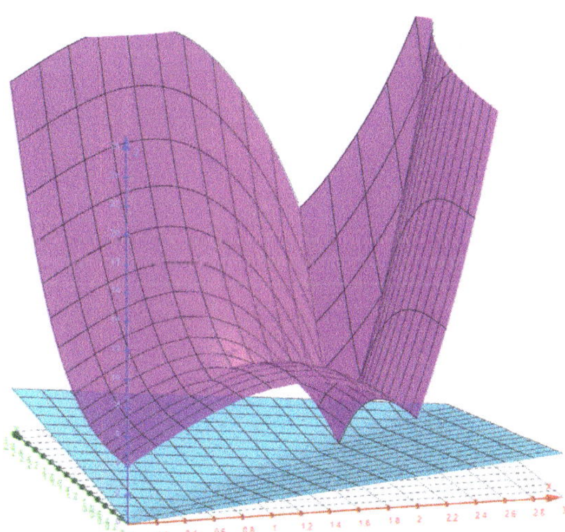

Figure 1. The surface above illustrates the right-hand-side term, while the surface below represents the left-hand-side term of the inequality in the general contractive condition.

Remark 2. *It is important to note that in Example 1, the mappings S and T are not weakly compatible. As a result, the iteration converges to a point of coincidence rather than a common fixed point.*

In the following example, we not only showcase the faster convergence of our iteration to a unique common fixed point but also explore and compare the effect of different parameters on the initial points.

Example 2. *In the Banach space* $([3,+\infty), d_u)$, *let* $S,T:[3,+\infty)\longrightarrow[3,+\infty)$ *be two mappings described as* $Su=\frac{u^4}{16}-75,\ \ Tu=u^2-6u+6$, *where* d_u *is the usual metric of* $\mathbb{R}$. *Then for* $\lambda=\frac{1}{5}$ *and* $\varphi(t)=3t$, *Figure 3 below shows that* S,T *satisfies the general contractive condition.*

Now, for sequences $\left\{a_n=\frac{1+n}{2+n^2}\right\},\left\{b_n=\frac{1}{1+n}\right\},\left\{c_n=\frac{i}{2n+3}\right\}\subseteq(0,1)$, *the initial value* $u_1=4$, *and the stop criterion* $||u_n-u||<10^{-5}$, *Table 2 and Figure 4 below show the iterations of Chugh et al. [40], Hussain et al. [42], and Guran et al. [43] and our Jungck–AI iteration (4) converging to a unique common fixed point* $S6=T6=6$.

Table 1. Comparison of iterations.

Steps	Jungck–SP (1)	Jungck–CR (2)	Jungck–DK (3)	Jungck–AI (4)
0	1	1	1	1
1	7.0121	7.3474	6.7878	7.9430
2	7.6188	7.8809	7.7186	7.9993
3	7.8218	7.9751	7.9325	8
4	7.9096	7.9945	7.9836	8
5	7.9520	7.9988	7.9960	8
6	7.9738	7.9997	7.9990	8
7	7.9854	7.9999	7.9998	8
8	7.9917	8	7.9999	8
9	7.9953	8	8	8
⋮	⋮	⋮	⋮	⋮
17	7.9999	8	8	8
18	8	8	8	8

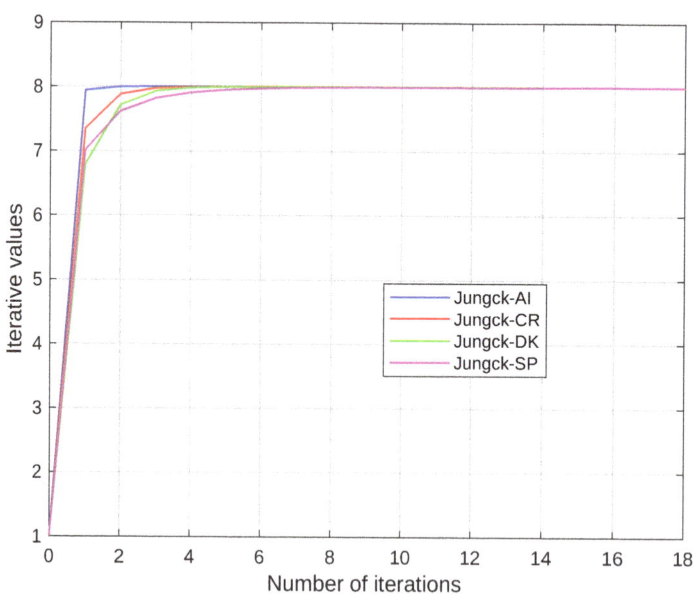

Figure 2. Convergence of iterations.

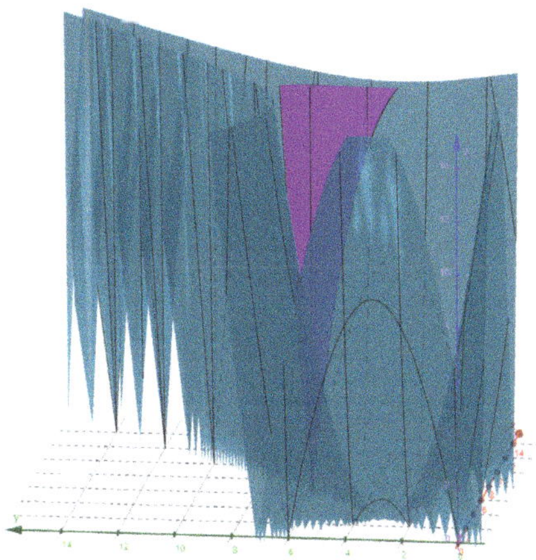

Figure 3. The surface above illustrates the right-hand-side term, while the surface below represents the left-hand-side term of the inequality in the general contractive condition.

Table 2. Comparison of iterations.

Steps	Jungck–SP (1)	Jungck–CR (2)	Jungck–DK (3)	Jungck–AI (4)
0	9	9	9	9
1	63.705	16.100	25.194	6.1473
2	22.654	6.5624	7.7380	6.0001
3	12.152	6.0391	6.1753	6
4	8.5756	6.0031	6.0184	6
5	7.1583	6.0003	6.0020	6
6	6.5449	6	6.0002	6
7	6.2642	6	6	6
8	6.1309	6	6	6
9	6.0659	6	6	6
⋮	⋮	⋮	⋮	⋮
20	6.0001	6	6	6
21	6	6	6	6

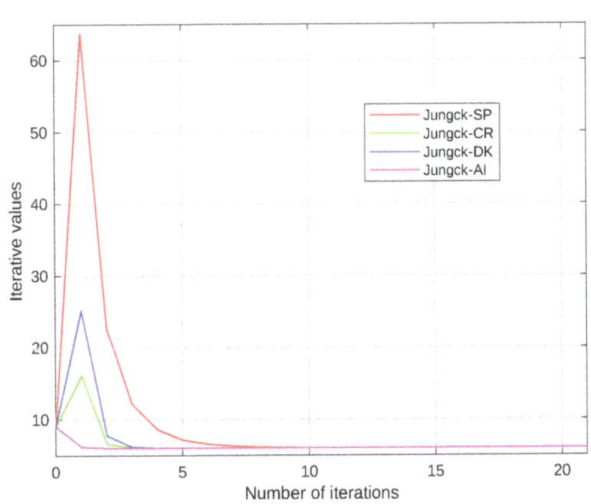

Figure 4. Convergence of iterations.

Table 3 below shows the effect of the initial value and parameters in comparison to the other methods. Numerically, we observe that the sequence generated by (4) converges more rapidly to a unique common fixed point of S and T when compared to the other iterations given by (1)–(3).

Table 3. Impact of parameters on the initial points for different iteration procedures.

Initial Points	0	5	11	265	688	1721	3264
$a_n = \frac{4n}{n^2+5}, b_n = \frac{n}{2n+7}, c_n = \frac{n+3}{(7n+1)^3}$							
Jungck–SP (1)	14	13	17	33	39	44	47
Jungck–CR (2)	5	6	7	9	10	10	10
Jungck–DK (3)	6	6	7	9	9	10	10
Jungck–AI (4)	2	2	3	3	3	3	3
$a_n = \frac{n+2}{4n+1}, b_n = \frac{3n}{(3n+8)^2}, c_n = \frac{1}{n^2+1}$							
Jungck–SP (1)	42	40	50	93	106	119	127
Jungck–CR (2)	5	7	8	10	10	10	10
Jungck–DK (3)	7	7	8	10	10	10	10
Jungck–AI (4)	2	2	3	3	4	4	4
$a_n = \frac{5}{7}, b_n = \frac{3}{4}, c_n = \frac{89}{90}$							
Jungck–SP (1)	3	4	4	6	7	7	8
Jungck–CR (2)	3	4	4	6	6	6	6
Jungck–DK (3)	5	5	6	8	8	8	8
Jungck–AI (4)	2	2	3	3	3	4	4
$a_n = \frac{13}{14}, b_n = \frac{n+1}{n+4}, c_n = \frac{n+2}{n+9}$							
Jungck–SP (1)	5	5	6	9	10	10	11
Jungck–CR (2)	4	4	4	6	6	6	6
Jungck–DK (3)	5	5	6	8	8	8	8
Jungck–AI (4)	2	2	2	3	3	3	3

4. Generation of Fractals as Julia and Mandelbrot Sets

The general escape criterion of the Jungck–AI orbit with an s-convex combination connected to transcendental sine functions in the complex plane is examined in this section. Using MATHEMATICA 12.3, we generate non-traditional chaotic fractals, specifically Julia and Mandelbrot sets, within the Jungck–AI orbit, incorporating s-convexity. The range of the area extends from $[-0.3, 0.3] \times [-0.3, 0.3]$ to $[-7, 7] \times [-7, 7]$. The computations were conducted on a system with an 11th Gen Intel(R) Core(TM) i3-1115G4 (Realme Book, DLF Cyber City, Gurgaon, India) processor operating at 3.00 GHz, equipped with 8 GB of DDR3 RAM, running Microsoft Windows 11 Home Single Language (64-bit), Version 24H2, OS build 26063.1, and Feature Experience Pack 1000.26063.1.0.

In the Jungck–AI iteration, we now substitute the concept of s-convex combination to obtain the Jungck–AI orbit with s-convexity.

Definition 7. *In the complex plane $\mathbb{C}$, let $S, T : \mathbb{C} \longrightarrow \mathbb{C}$ be two self-mappings. Then, the Jungck–AI orbit with s-convexity is described as*

$$\begin{cases} Su_{n+1} = Tv_n \\ Sv_n = Tw_n \\ Sw_n = Tx_n \\ Sx_n = a^s Tu_n + (1-a)^s Su_n, \ \forall n \in \mathbb{N} \cup \{0\}, \end{cases} \tag{5}$$

for random choice $u_0 \in \mathbb{C}$, where $a, s \in (0,1]$.

Remark 3. *The reason for selecting the Jungck–AI iteration with s-convexity in generating Julia and Mandelbrot fractals lies in the property that all iterations—Chugh et al. [40], Hussain et al. [42], Guran et al. [43] and all Jungck-type iterative procedures (including Singh et al. [45], Olatinwo et al. [41], Kang et al. [11], Antal et al. [37], and many more)—converge to a coincidence point. But the Jungck–AI iteration with s-convexity demonstrates faster convergence compared to Chugh et al. [40], Hussain et al. [42], Guran et al. [43] and all Jungck-type iterative procedures (including Singh et al. [45], Olatinwo et al. [41], Kang et al. [11], Antal et al. [37], and many more).*

Since the Jungck–AI iteration involves two mappings, the number of mappings employed in the iteration should be considered when substituting the Jungck–AI orbit for other well-known orbits. We employ a certain process to deal with this.

Here, we consider transcendental sine functions of the type $\sin(u^m) - \alpha u + \beta$, for $u, \alpha, \beta \in \mathbb{C}, m \geq 2$, which can be written as $Tu - Su$, where $Su = \alpha u$ and $Tu = \sin(u^m) + \beta$. Apart from the reconstruction, where S is one-to-one, it is also necessary to create a new escape criterion and the iteration procedure (5).

For the function $\sin(u^m)$, we know that

$$|\sin(u^m)| = \left| u^m - \frac{u^{3m}}{3!} + \frac{u^{5m}}{5!} - \cdots \right| = |u^m| \left| 1 - \frac{u^{2m}}{3!} + \frac{u^{4m}}{5!} - \cdots \right|,$$

for all $u \in \mathbb{C}$.

Now consider $\mathbb{A}$ as the set of all $u \in \mathbb{C}$ so that $\sin(u^m) \neq 0$. Then, we can write

$$\frac{|\sin(u^m)|}{|u^m|} = \left| 1 - \frac{u^{2m}}{3!} + \frac{u^{4m}}{5!} - \cdots \right|, \text{ for all } u \in \mathbb{A}.$$

For fixed $u \in \mathbb{A}$, let $\gamma_u = \min\left\{1, \frac{|\sin(u^m)|}{|u^m|}\right\}$, then $0 < |\gamma_u| \leq 1$ and $|\sin(u^m)| \geq |\gamma_u||u^m|$. Again, let $u_0 \in \mathbb{A}$ and $\mathbb{A}_{u_0} = \{u \in \mathbb{A} : |u| > |u_0|\}$; then, we can define a number $\gamma = \inf\{\gamma_u : u \in \mathbb{A}\}$ so that $0 < |\gamma| \leq 1$ and $|\sin(u^m)| \geq |\gamma||u^m|$, for all $u \in \mathbb{A}_{u_0}$.

For the defined orbit, the following is an escape criterion.

Theorem 3. *The Jungck–AI orbit $\{u_n\}$ with s-convexity defined in (5) is so that $|u_n| \to +\infty$ whenever $n \to +\infty$, if*

$$|u| \geq |\beta| \geq \left(\frac{2|\alpha|}{|\gamma_1|}\right)^{\frac{1}{m-1}}, |u| \geq |\beta| \geq \left(\frac{2|\alpha|}{|\gamma_2|}\right)^{\frac{1}{m-1}},$$

$$|u| \geq |\beta| \geq \left(\frac{2|\alpha|}{|\gamma_3|}\right)^{\frac{1}{m-1}} \text{ and } |u| \geq |\beta| \geq \left(\frac{2(|\alpha|+1)}{as|\gamma_4|}\right)^{\frac{1}{m-1}}.$$

Proof. For $n = 0$, let $u_0 = u$. Then, from the Jungck–AI iteration procedure with s-convexity, we have

$$\begin{aligned} |Sx_0| &= |a^s Tu_0 + (1-a)^s Su_0| \\ &= |a^s Tu + (1-a)^s Su| \\ &= |a^s[\sin(u^m) + \beta] + (1-a)^s \alpha u| \\ &\geq |a^s|[|\sin(u^m)| - |\beta|] - |(1-a)^s \alpha u|. \end{aligned}$$

Now, there exists $\gamma_4 \in \mathbb{C}$ with $|\gamma_4| \in (0,1]$ so that $|\sin(u^m)| \geq |\gamma_4||u^m|$, for all $u \in \mathbb{C}$ but for which $|\gamma_4| = 0$. Also, $a, s \in (0,1]$ implies $a^s \geq as$, and from the binomial expansion of $(1-a)^s$, we have $(1-a)^s \leq 1 - as < 1$. Hence, utilizing $|u| \geq |\beta|$, we obtain

$$\begin{aligned} |\alpha||x_0| &\geq as[|\gamma_4||u^m| - |u|] - |\alpha||u| \\ &\geq as|\gamma_4||u^m| - |u| - |\alpha||u|, \text{ since } as < 1 \\ &= |u|(|\alpha|+1)\left(\frac{as|\gamma_4||u^{m-1}|}{|\alpha|+1} - 1\right). \end{aligned}$$

Since $|\alpha| + 1 > \alpha$ and $|u| \geq \left(\frac{2(|\alpha|+1)}{as|\gamma_4|}\right)^{\frac{1}{m-1}}$, we have $|x_0| \geq |u| \geq |\beta|$.
This brings us to the next iteration of the Jungck–AI procedure for $x_0 = x$:

$$\begin{aligned} |Sw_0| &= |Tx_0| \\ &= |Tx| \\ &= |\sin(x^m) + \beta| \\ &\geq |\sin(x^m)| - |\beta|. \end{aligned}$$

Now, there exists $\gamma_3 \in \mathbb{C}$ with $|\gamma_3| \in (0,1]$ so that $|\sin(x^m)| \geq |\gamma_3||x^m|$, for all $x \in \mathbb{C}$ but for which $|\gamma_3| = 0$. Hence, utilizing $|x| \geq |u| \geq |\beta|$, we obtain

$$\begin{aligned} |\alpha||w_0| &\geq |\gamma_3||x^m| - |x| \\ &= |x|(|\gamma_3||x^{m-1}| - 1) \\ \Rightarrow |w_0| &\geq |x|\left(\frac{|\gamma_3||x^{m-1}|}{|\alpha|} - 1\right). \end{aligned}$$

Since $|x| \geq \left(\frac{2|\alpha|}{|\gamma_3|}\right)^{\frac{1}{m-1}}$, we have $|w_0| \geq |x| \geq |u| \geq |\beta|$.
This brings us to the next iteration of the Jungck–AI procedure for $w_0 = w$:

$$\begin{aligned} |Sv_0| &= |Tw_0| \\ &= |Tw| \\ &= |\sin(w^m) + \beta| \\ &\geq |\sin(w^m)| - |\beta|. \end{aligned}$$

Now, there exists $\gamma_2 \in \mathbb{C}$ with $|\gamma_2| \in (0,1]$ so that $|\sin(w^m)| \geq |\gamma_2||w^m|$, for all $w \in \mathbb{C}$ but for which $|\gamma_2| = 0$. Hence, utilizing $|w| \geq |x| \geq |u| \geq |\beta|$, we obtain

$$\begin{aligned} |\alpha||v_0| &\geq |\gamma_2||w^m| - |w| \\ &= |w|(|\gamma_3||w^{m-1}| - 1) \\ \Rightarrow |v_0| &\geq |w|\left(\frac{|\gamma_3||w^{m-1}|}{|\alpha|} - 1\right). \end{aligned}$$

Since $|w| \geq \left(\frac{2|\alpha|}{|\gamma_2|}\right)^{\frac{1}{m-1}}$, we have $|v_0| \geq |w| \geq |x| \geq |u| \geq |\beta|$.
This brings us to the next iteration of the Jungck–AI procedure for $v_0 = v$

$$\begin{aligned} |Su_1| &= |Tv_0| \\ &= |Tv| \\ &= |\sin(v^m) + \beta| \\ &\geq |\sin(v^m)| - |\beta|. \end{aligned}$$

Now, there exists $\gamma_1 \in \mathbb{C}$ with $|\gamma_1| \in (0,1]$ so that $|\cos(v^m)| \geq |\gamma_1||v^m|$, for all $v \in \mathbb{C}$ but for which $|\gamma_1| = 0$. Hence, utilizing $|v| \geq |w| \geq |x| \geq |u| \geq |\beta|$, we obtain

$$\begin{aligned} |\alpha||u_1| &\geq |\gamma_1||v^m| - |v| \\ &= |v|(|\gamma_1||v^{m-1}| - 1) \\ \Rightarrow |u_1| &\geq |u|\left(\frac{|\gamma_1||v^{m-1}|}{\alpha} - 1\right). \end{aligned}$$

Consequently, for $n = 1$, we have

$$\begin{aligned} |u_2| &\geq |u_1|\left(\frac{|\gamma_1||v^{m-1}|}{\alpha} - 1\right) \\ &\geq |u|\left(\frac{|\gamma_1||v^{m-1}|}{\alpha} - 1\right)^2. \end{aligned}$$

Continuing the iteration, we have

$$\begin{aligned} |u_3| &\geq |u|\left(\frac{|\gamma_1||v^{m-1}|}{\alpha} - 1\right)^3, \\ |u_4| &\geq |u|\left(\frac{|\gamma_1||v^{m-1}|}{\alpha} - 1\right)^4, \\ &\vdots \\ |u_n| &\geq |u|\left(\frac{|\gamma_1||v^{m-1}|}{\alpha} - 1\right)^n. \end{aligned}$$

Since $|u| \geq \left(\frac{2|\alpha|}{|\gamma_1|}\right)^{\frac{1}{m-1}}$, we have $|u_n| \to +\infty$ as $n \to +\infty$. □

Now we present subsequent corollaries that offer exploration methods for Julia and Mandelbrot sets.

Corollary 1. *The Jungck–AI orbit $\{u_n\}$ with s-convexity defined in (5) escapes to infinity if*

$$|u| \geq |\beta| \geq \max\left\{\left(\frac{2|\alpha|}{|\gamma_1|}\right)^{\frac{1}{m-1}}, \left(\frac{2|\alpha|}{|\gamma_2|}\right)^{\frac{1}{m-1}}, \left(\frac{2|\alpha|}{|\gamma_3|}\right)^{\frac{1}{m-1}}, \left(\frac{2(|\alpha|+1)}{as|\gamma_4|}\right)^{\frac{1}{m-1}}\right\}.$$

Corollary 2. *The Jungck–AI orbit $\{u_n\}$ with s-convexity defined in (5) escapes to infinity if*

$$|u| \geq \max\left\{|\beta|, \left(\frac{2|\alpha|}{|\gamma_1|}\right)^{\frac{1}{m-1}}, \left(\frac{2|\alpha|}{|\gamma_2|}\right)^{\frac{1}{m-1}}, \left(\frac{2|\alpha|}{|\gamma_3|}\right)^{\frac{1}{m-1}}, \left(\frac{2(|\alpha|+1)}{as|\gamma_4|}\right)^{\frac{1}{m-1}}\right\}.$$

While fractal geometry and complex numbers are foundational to both Julia sets and Mandelbrot sets, these are distinct mathematical constructs with key differences, as illustrated by the algorithms in Tables 4 and 5. For the Julia set algorithm, typically presented in Table 4, various initial values of u_0 are used with a fixed parameter β to observe which points remain bounded and which diverge to infinity. In contrast, the Mandelbrot set algorithm in Table 5 consistently starts with $u_0 = 0$ for each iteration.

Table 4. Algorithm for the generation of fractals as Julia sets.

1.	Setup:
(i)	Define the functions $Su = \alpha u$ and $Tu = \sin(u^m) + \beta$.
(ii)	Consider a complex number $\beta = p + iq$
(iii)	Set the variables $\alpha, a, \gamma_1, \gamma_2,, \gamma_3, \gamma_4, m, n, s, p, q$ to their initial values
(iv)	Take into account the initial iteration $u_0 = x + iy$
2.	Iterate:
	$Su_{n+1} = Tv_n$ $Sv_n = Tw_n$ $Sw_n = Tx_n$ $Sx_n = a^s Tu_n + (1-a)^s Su_n$
3.	Stop:
	$\lvert u\rvert \geq \max\left\{\lvert\beta\rvert, \left(\frac{2\lvert\alpha\rvert}{\lvert\gamma_1\rvert}\right)^{\frac{1}{m-1}}, \left(\frac{2\lvert\alpha\rvert}{\lvert\gamma_2\rvert}\right)^{\frac{1}{m-1}}, \left(\frac{2\lvert\alpha\rvert}{\lvert\gamma_3\rvert}\right)^{\frac{1}{m-1}}, \left(\frac{2(\lvert\alpha\rvert+1)}{as\lvert\gamma_4\rvert}\right)^{\frac{1}{m-1}}\right\}$
4.	Count:
	The number of attempts made to escape.
5.	Colour:
	In accordance with the number of escape repetitions required.

Table 5. Algorithm for the generation of fractals as Mandelbrot sets.

1.	Setup:
(i)	Define the functions $Su = \alpha u$ and $Tu = \sin(u^m) + \beta$.
(ii)	Consider a complex number $\beta = x + iy$
(iii)	Set the variables $\alpha, a, \gamma_1, \gamma_2,, \gamma_3, \gamma_4, m, n, s$ to their initial values
(iv)	Take into account $u = \beta$
2.	Iterate:
	$Su_{n+1} = Tv_n$ $Sv_n = Tw_n$ $Sw_n = Tx_n$ $Sx_n = a^s Tu_n + (1-a)^s Su_n$
3.	Stop:
	$\lvert u\rvert \geq \max\left\{\lvert\beta\rvert, \left(\frac{2\lvert\alpha\rvert}{\lvert\gamma_1\rvert}\right)^{\frac{1}{m-1}}, \left(\frac{2\lvert\alpha\rvert}{\lvert\gamma_2\rvert}\right)^{\frac{1}{m-1}}, \left(\frac{2\lvert\alpha\rvert}{\lvert\gamma_3\rvert}\right)^{\frac{1}{m-1}}, \left(\frac{2(\lvert\alpha\rvert+1)}{as\lvert\gamma_4\rvert}\right)^{\frac{1}{m-1}}\right\}$
4.	Count:
	The number of attempts made to escape.
5.	Colour:
	In accordance with the number of escape repetitions required.

4.1. *Fractals as Julia Sets*

This subsection demonstrates the behavior changes in Julia set fractals generated by the transcendental sine function within the Jungck–AI orbit, incorporating s-convexity. Notably, even slight adjustments to any parameter lead to substantial changes in the fractals' structure. Therefore, we systematically vary almost every parameter to produce fractals for our orbit, as illustrated in the images below.

The primary fractals created by adjusting the parameter m (as detailed in Table 6), while keeping other parameters constant, are shown in Figure 5. As m increases, the number of chaotic attractors in the fractals grows, and the fractals become increasingly circular. Each Julia set contains $2m$ spokes. An interesting color shift is observed, with a grey tone at $m = 3$ and a yellow tone at $m = 7$, forming a visually appealing pattern. Additionally, the Julia fractal shape becomes progressively circular as m increases.

Table 6. Changes in parameter m for generating fractals as a Julia set.

	m	α	β	a	s	γ_1	γ_2	γ_3	γ_4
(i)	2	-2	$-1.4i$	0.936	0.928	0.056	0.012	0.003	0.006
(ii)	3	-2	$-1.4i$	0.936	0.928	0.056	0.012	0.003	0.006
(iii)	4	-2	$-1.4i$	0.936	0.928	0.056	0.012	0.003	0.006
(iv)	5	-2	$-1.4i$	0.936	0.928	0.056	0.012	0.003	0.006
(v)	6	-2	$-1.4i$	0.936	0.928	0.056	0.012	0.003	0.006
(vi)	7	-2	$-1.4i$	0.936	0.928	0.056	0.012	0.003	0.006

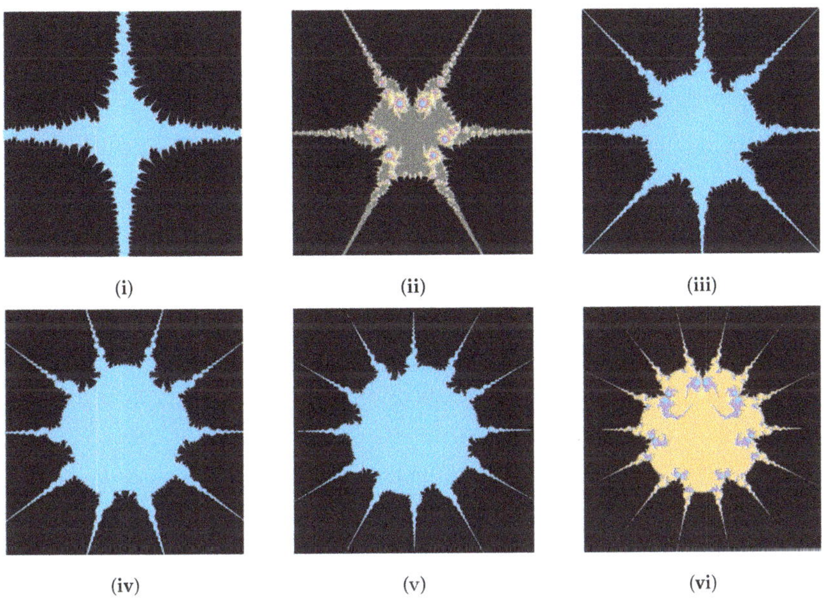

Figure 5. (**i–vi**) Effect of m on fractals as a Julia set.

Parameter α adds visual appeal to the fractals. A segment of the Julia set begins to separate as α changes from -1 to 0.8 (Figure 6i–iv). Distinct purple chaotic fractals emerge when the parameter α has a negative complex component (Table 7), as shown in Figure 6ii–v. Higher modulus values of α cause the fractal to distort.

Table 7. Changes in parameter α for generating fractals as a Julia set.

	m	α	β	a	s	γ_1	γ_2	γ_3	γ_4
(i)	4	-1	$-0.6 - 0.01i$	0.736	0.928	0.034	0.021	0.002	0.001
(ii)	4	$-0.4 - 0.7i$	$-0.6 - 0.01i$	0.736	0.928	0.034	0.021	0.002	0.001
(iii)	4	$1.1i$	$-0.6 - 0.01i$	0.736	0.928	0.034	0.021	0.002	0.001
(iv)	4	0.8	$-0.6 - 0.01i$	0.736	0.928	0.034	0.021	0.002	0.001
(v)	4	$0.7 + 0.3i$	$-0.6 - 0.01i$	0.736	0.928	0.034	0.021	0.002	0.001
(vi)	4	$0.6 - 0.5i$	$-0.6 - 0.01i$	0.736	0.928	0.034	0.021	0.002	0.001

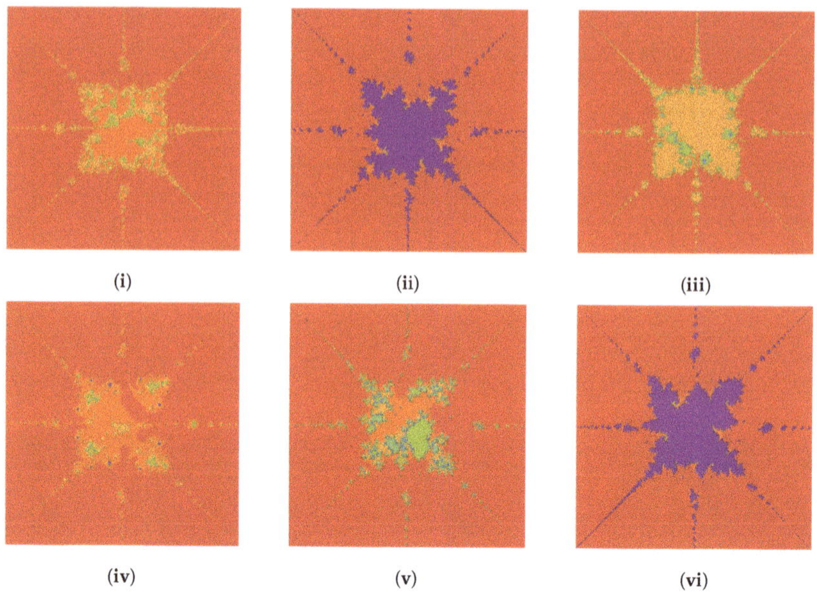

Figure 6. (**i–vi**) Effect of α on fractals as Julia sets.

Variations in color and form appear in Figure 7 for different values of β (Table 8), showing a resemblance to Rangoli patterns.

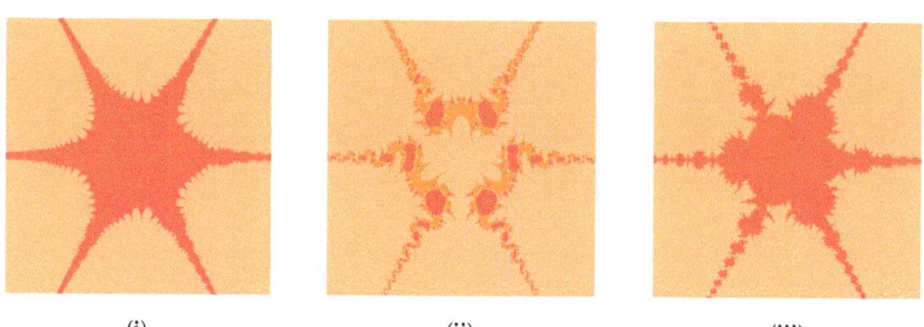

Figure 7. (**i–iii**) Effect of β on fractals as Julia sets.

Table 8. Changes in parameter β for generating fractals as Julia sets.

	m	α	β	a	s	γ_1	γ_2	γ_3	γ_4
(i)	3	-2	$-0.542 + 0.245i$	0.963	0.828	0.056	0.012	0.003	0.006
(ii)	3	-2	$2i$	0.963	0.828	0.056	0.012	0.003	0.006
(iii)	3	-2	$1 - i$	0.963	0.828	0.056	0.012	0.003	0.006

Changes in the basic shape occur as the convexity parameter increases, though colors remain the same. Larger values enhance the Julia set's aesthetic and make it suitable for textile design. With increasing values of the convex parameter s (Table 9), Figure 8 shows an increase in symmetrical chaotic forms within the fractals.

Table 9. Changes in parameter s for generating fractals as Julia sets.

	m	α	β	a	s	γ_1	γ_2	γ_3	γ_4
(i)	4	$1-1.3i$	$-0.4+1.5i$	0.017	0.26	0.056	0.078	0.095	0.063
(ii)	4	$1-1.3i$	$-0.4+1.5i$	0.017	0.56	0.056	0.078	0.095	0.063
(iii)	4	$1-1.3i$	$-0.4+1.5i$	0.017	0.96	0.056	0.078	0.095	0.063

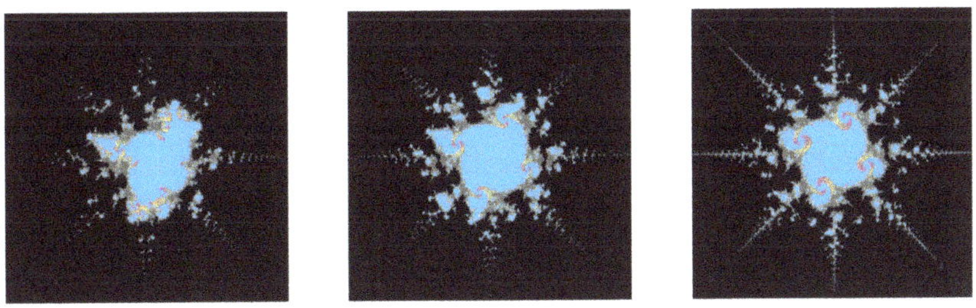

(i) (ii) (iii)

Figure 8. **(i–iii)** Effect of s on fractals as Julia sets.

The basic shape also transforms with higher values of the parameter a, while color saturation increases at higher a values. In Figure 9, more red appears in the center of the fractals as a increases (Table 10).

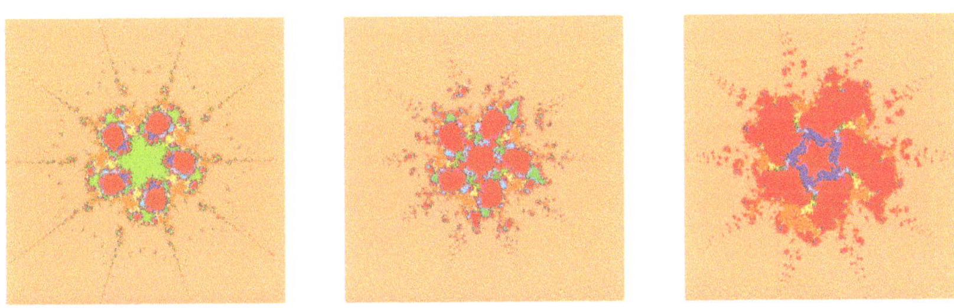

(i) (ii) (iii)

Figure 9. **(i–iii)** Effect of a on fractals as Julia sets.

Table 10. Changes in parameter a for generating fractals as Julia sets.

	m	α	β	a	s	γ_1	γ_2	γ_3	γ_4
(i)	5	$1.2i$	$-0.2+0.82i$	0.001	0.96	0.256	0.378	0.595	0.463
(ii)	5	$1.2i$	$-0.2+0.82i$	0.048	0.96	0.256	0.378	0.595	0.463
(iii)	5	$1.2i$	$-0.2+0.82i$	0.123	0.96	0.256	0.378	0.595	0.463

Only minimal changes occur in the fractals shown in Figure 10 as the parameters $\gamma_1, \gamma_2, \gamma_3$, and γ_4 vary (Table 11).

Table 11. Changes in parameters $\gamma_1, \gamma_2, \gamma_3, \gamma_4$ for generating fractals as Julia sets.

	m	α	β	a	s	γ_1	γ_2	γ_3	γ_4
(i)	2	-2.1	$1.7-1.6i$	0.001	0.99	0.004	0.002	0.001	0.003
(ii)	2	-2.1	$1.7-1.6i$	0.001	0.99	0.294	0.192	0.391	0.293
(iii)	2	-2.1	$1.7-1.6i$	0.001	0.99	0.94	0.92	0.91	0.93

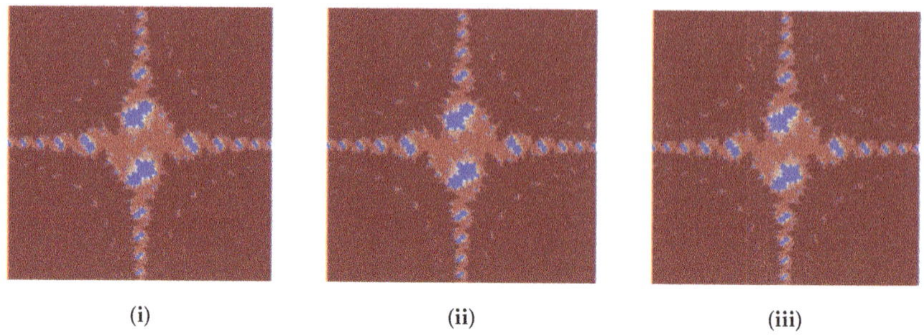

Figure 10. (i–iii) Effect of $\gamma_1, \gamma_2, \gamma_3, \gamma_4$ on fractals as Julia sets.

The fractals displayed in Figure 11 are derived from randomly selected parameters (Table 12).

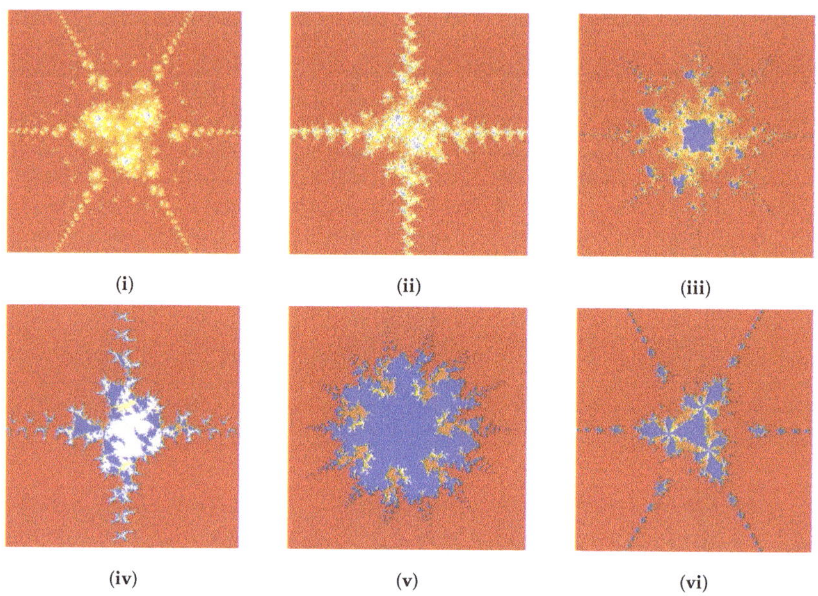

Figure 11. (i–vi) Effect of random choice of parameters on fractals as Julia sets.

Table 12. Random changes in parameters for generating fractals as Julia sets.

	m	α	β	a	s	γ_1	γ_2	γ_3	γ_4
(i)	3	-2.2	$1.8-1.5i$	0.002	0.89	0.034	0.042	0.074	0.98
(ii)	2	$-2.2-0.8i$	$-1.8+2i$	0.012	0.49	0.064	0.072	0.094	0.028
(iii)	4	$-2.4i$	$2.8i$	0.035	0.872	0.566	0.457	0.873	0.867
(iv)	2	-2.7	$1.3-1.8i$	0.007	0.086	0.435	0.568	0.657	0.874
(v)	7	$3.4i$	$-1+2.8i$	0.061	0.784	0.023	0.065	0.098	0.054
(vi)	3	$0.8+0.7i$	0.9	0.999	0.961	0.263	0.152	0.542	0.123

4.2. Fractals as Mandelbrot Sets

This section also explores behavior shifts in fractals as Mandelbrot sets generated by the transcendental sine function within the Jungck–AI orbit with s-convexity. Small parameter modifications cause significant changes in the fractals. Thus, we altered each parameter to generate the fractals in the images below.

Adjusting m (Table 13) while keeping other parameters fixed produces the fractals shown in Figure 12. As m increases, the number of chaotic attractors grows, and each Mandelbrot set has $2m$ major blue attractors.

Table 13. Parameters for generating fractals as Mandelbrot sets.

	m	α	a	s	γ_1	γ_2	γ_3	γ_4
(i)	2	2	0.076	0.036	0.035	0.068	0.057	0.056
(ii)	3	2	0.076	0.036	0.035	0.068	0.057	0.056
(iii)	4	2	0.076	0.036	0.035	0.068	0.057	0.056
(iv)	5	2	0.076	0.036	0.035	0.068	0.057	0.056
(v)	6	2	0.076	0.036	0.035	0.068	0.057	0.056
(vi)	7	2	0.076	0.036	0.035	0.068	0.057	0.056

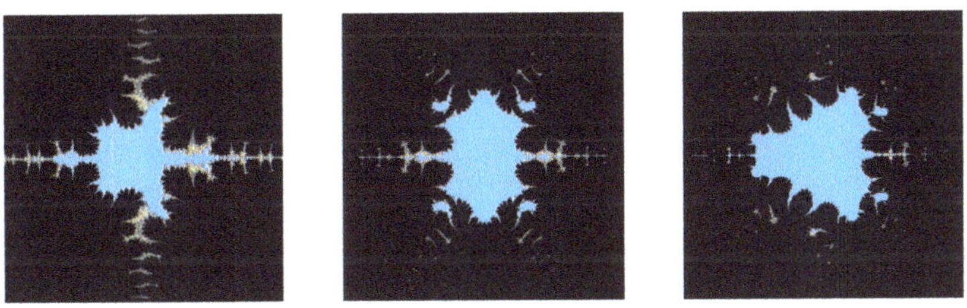

(i) (ii) (iii)

(iv) (v) (vi)

Figure 12. (**i–vi**) Effect of m on fractals as Mandelbrot sets.

Parameter α enhances the aesthetic quality of the fractals. Visually appealing fractals appear in Figure 13, while other parameters are kept constant (Table 14). Complex values of α emphasize the central region.

Table 14. Changes in parameter α for generating fractals as Mandelbrot sets.

	m	α	a	s	γ_1	γ_2	γ_3	γ_4
(i)	3	$2.5+i$	0.001	0.704	0.867	0.897	0.567	0.765
(ii)	3	$6-1.5i$	0.001	0.704	0.867	0.897	0.567	0.765
(iii)	3	$-1+i$	0.001	0.704	0.867	0.897	0.567	0.765
(iv)	3	-0.3	0.001	0.704	0.867	0.897	0.567	0.765
(v)	3	0.6	0.001	0.704	0.867	0.897	0.567	0.765
(vi)	3	$1.1i$	0.001	0.704	0.867	0.897	0.567	0.765

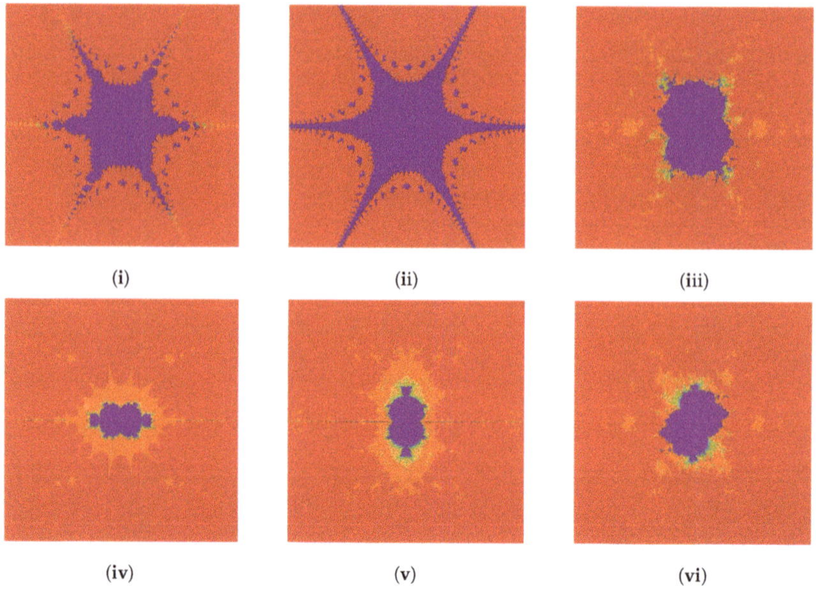

Figure 13. (i–vi) Effect of α on fractals as Mandelbrot sets.

Figure 14 (Table 15) demonstrates that small changes in the convex parameter s significantly affect the fractals. Lower s values brighten the Mandelbrot set's perimeter.

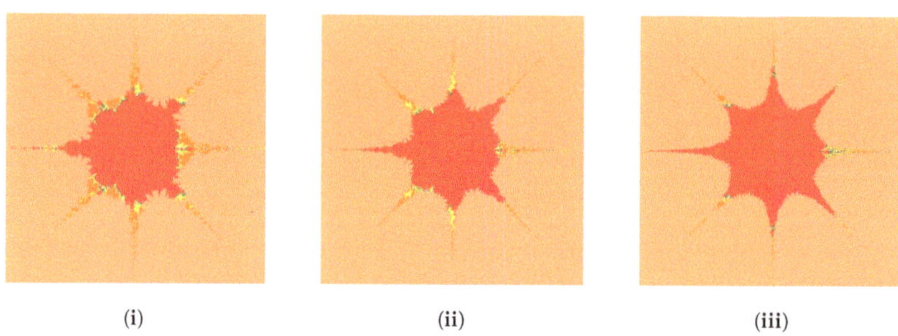

Figure 14. (i–vi) Effect of s on fractals as Mandelbrot set.

Table 15. Changes in parameter s for generating fractals as Mandelbrot sets.

	m	α	a	s	γ_1	γ_2	γ_3	γ_4
(i)	4	−2	0.534	0.054	0.078	0.075	0.065	0.057
(ii)	4	−2	0.534	0.454	0.078	0.075	0.065	0.057
(iii)	4	−2	0.534	0.954	0.078	0.075	0.065	0.057

The fractals in Figure 15 turn blue with increasing values of parameter a (Table 16), and the shape transforms as a increases.

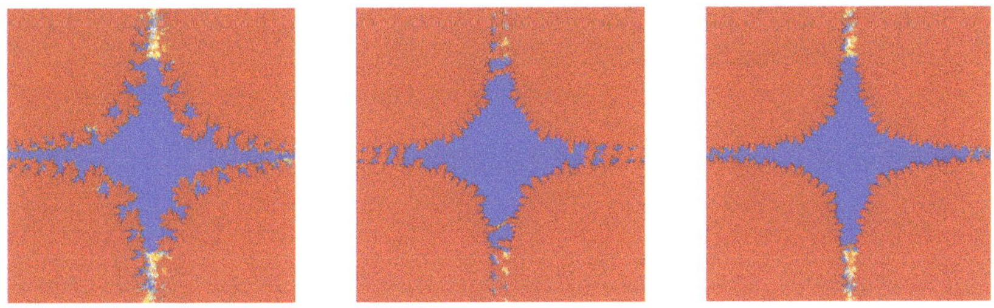

(i) (ii) (iii)

Figure 15. (i–iii) Effect of a on fractals as Mandelbrot sets.

Table 16. Changes in parameter a for generating fractals as Mandelbrot sets.

	m	α	a	s	γ_1	γ_2	γ_3	γ_4
(i)	2	$-3i$	0.034	0.999	0.021	0.013	0.043	0.023
(ii)	2	$-3i$	0.634	0.999	0.021	0.013	0.043	0.023
(iii)	2	$-3i$	0.934	0.999	0.021	0.013	0.043	0.023

As with Julia sets, Mandelbrot fractals show minimal variation with changes to parameters $\gamma_1, \gamma_2, \gamma_3, \gamma_4$.

Remark 4. *These generated fractals have broad applications in fabric design, such as in Batik, Kalamkari, Tie and Dye, and other textile prints (e.g., Figures 5, 8, 10, 12, 14 and 15). They revolutionize textile design by providing intricate patterns, streamlining processes to save time and resources, enabling scalable designs across different fabric types, and allowing digital previews to minimize waste. This promotes global collaboration, fosters creativity, cuts costs, supports sustainability, and boosts competitiveness in the textile industry.*

5. Conclusions

Our study presented a novel iterative approach, namely the Jungck–AI iteration procedure, for approximating unique common fixed points of general contractive mappings. We provided theorems to demonstrate the convergence and stability of this iteration process with examples and graphs. Additionally, we established that Jungck–AI(4) converges to the point of coincidence more quickly than Jungck–SP, Jungck–CR, Jungck–DK, and other similar methods. With s-convexity, and for the subsequent orbit, we generated fractals as Julia and Mandelbrot sets for the transcendental sine function $T_{\alpha,\beta}(u) = \sin(u^m) - \alpha u + \beta$, for $u, \alpha, \beta \in \mathbb{C}$ and $m \geq 2$. We provided a theorem to demonstrate the escape criterion for the sine function and the orbit with the convexity condition. Additionally, we explored the following impacts of the involved parameters on the color deviance, appearance, and dynamics of generated chaotic fractals.

- It is unexpected to observe that, given the same set of values, even little changes in one parameter have a significant influence on how the resulting fractal appears during the generation process. As a result, choosing the right parameters is crucial to obtaining the desired fractal pattern.
- In both Julia and Mandelbrot fractals, the number of outer spokes is twice the value of the parameter m.
- The majority of fractals exhibit symmetry about the initial line.

- In the case of both Julia and Mandelbrot fractals, a small change in the convex parameter s is highly effective.
- The number of colors is typically limited in almost all fractals, and there exists a hollow portion in each of them.
- We notice that when we enlarge the Mandelbrot set at its petal edges, we encounter the Julia set, indicating that every Mandelbrot set point contains a significant amount of Julia set image data.

Fractal geometry is widely recognized for its ability to depict the intricacy of many complex forms found in our environment. The chaotic behaviors of fractals, in reality, are able to depict surfaces and forms that conventional Euclidean geometry is unable to convey (Figures 16 and 17).

```
(*Program Source Used for Generating the Julia Sets*)

T[u_] := Sin[u^m] + β;
iter[x_, y_, Lim_] := Block[{β, z, m, α, p, q, a, s, i, j, k, l, ct},
  β = p + q I; z = x + y I; m = 2; α = -2.7; p = 1.3; q = -1.8; a = 0.006;
  s = 0.086; i = 0.435; j = 0.568; k = 0.657; l = 0.874;|ct = 0;
  While[
   (Abs[z] < Max[Abs[β], ((2 * Abs[α]) / (Abs[i]))^(1 / (m - 1)),
       ((2 * Abs[α]) / (Abs[j]))^(1 / (m - 1)),
       ((2 * Abs[α]) / (Abs[k]))^(1 / (m - 1)),
       (2 * (Abs[α] + 1) / (a * s * Abs[l]))^(1 / (m - 1))]) && (ct ≤ Lim), ++ct;
   g = (((1 - a)^s) * α * z + (a^s) * T[z]) / α;
   w = T[g] / α;
   h = T[w] / α;
   v = T[h] / α;
   z = v;
  ];
  Return[ct];
 ]
DensityPlot[-iter[x, y, 10], {x, -5, 5}, {y, -5, 5}, PlotPoints → 200,
 ColorFunction → "TemperatureMap", PlotLegends → Automatic,
 FrameStyle → None, Frame → None]
```

Figure 16. The Figure shows a source code for generating Julia set.

```
(*Program Source Used for Generating the Mandelbrot Sets*)

T[u_] := Sin[u^m] + β;
iter[x_, y_, Lim_] := Block[{β, z, m, α, a, s, i, j, k, l, ct},
  β = x + y I; z = β; m = 5; α = 1 + 2 I; a = 0.004; s = 0.009;
  i = 0.021; j = 0.013; k = 0.043; l = 0.023; ct = 0;
  While[
   (Abs[z] < Max[Abs[β], ((2 * Abs[α]) / (Abs[i]))^(1 / (m - 1)),
       ((2 * Abs[α]) / (Abs[j]))^(1 / (m - 1)),
       ((2 * Abs[α]) / (Abs[k]))^(1 / (m - 1)),
       (2 * (Abs[α] + 1) / (a * s * Abs[l]))^(1 / (m - 1))]) && (ct ≤ Lim), ++ct;
   g = (((1 - a)^s) * α * z + (a^s) * T[z]) / α;
   w = T[g] / α;
   h = T[w] / α;
   v = T[h] / α;
   z = v;
  ];
  Return[ct];
 ]
DensityPlot[-iter[x, y, 10], {x, -6, 6}, {y, -6, 6}, PlotPoints → 200,
 ColorFunction → "ThermometerColors", PlotLegends → Automatic,
 FrameStyle → None, Frame → None]
```

Figure 17. The Figure shows a source code for generating Mandelbrot set.

Author Contributions: Conceptualization, N.S., K.H.A. and Y.R.; methodology, N.S., K.H.A. and Y.R.; validation, A.T., Y.R. and M.A.; formal analysis, N.S., Y.R. and A.T.; resources, M.A.; writing—original draft preparation, K.H.A. and N.S.; writing—review and editing, N.S. and A.R.; visualization, K.H.A., Y.R. and M.A.; funding acquisition, N.S. and M.A. All the authors discussed the results and contributed to the final manuscript. All authors have read and agreed to the published version of the manuscript.

Funding: This work was supported by the Deanship of Scientific Research, Vice Presidency for Graduate Studies and Scientific Research, King Faisal University, Saudi Arabia [KFU250082].

Institutional Review Board Statement: Not applicable.

Data Availability Statement: No new data were created or analyzed in this study. Data sharing is not applicable to this article.

Acknowledgments: The first author expresses gratitude to the University Grants Commission (UGC), New Delhi, India.

Conflicts of Interest: The authors declare that they have no conflicts of interest.

References

1. Alam, K.H.; Rohen, Y.; Tomar, A. (α,F)-Geraghty type generalized F-contractions on non-Archimedean fuzzy metric-unlike spaces. *Demonstr. Math.* **2024**, *57*, 20240046. [CrossRef]
2. Alam, K.H.; Rohen, Y.; Tomar, A.; Sajid, M. On geometry of fixed figures via φ-interpolative contractions and application of activation functions in neural networks and machine learning models. *Ain Shams Eng. Journal* **2025**, *16*, 103182. [CrossRef]
3. Berinde, V. Picard iteration converges faster than Mann iteration for a class of quasi-contractive operators. *Fixed Point Theory Appl.* **2004**, *2*, 97–105. [CrossRef]
4. Mann, W.R. Mean value methods in iteration. *Proc. Amer. Math. Soc.* **1953**, *4*, 506–510. [CrossRef]
5. Ishikawa, S. Fixed points by a new iteration method. *Proc. Am. Math. Soc.* **1974**, *44*, 147–150. [CrossRef]
6. Noor, M.A. New approximation schemes for general variational inequalities. *J. Math. Anal. Appl.* **2000**, *251*, 217–229. [CrossRef]
7. Alam, K.H.; Rohen, Y.; Saleem, N.; Aphane, M.; Razzaque, A. Convergence of Fibonacci–Ishikawa iteration procedure for monotone asymptotically non-expansive mappings. *J. Inequalities Appl.* **2024**, *2024*, 81. [CrossRef]
8. Alam, K.H.; Rohen, Y. An efficient iterative procedure in hyperbolic space and application to non-linear delay integral equation. *J. Appl. Math. Comput.* **2024**, *70*, 429–4317. [CrossRef]
9. Alam, K.H.; Rohen, Y. Convergence of a refined iterative method and its application to fractional Volterra–Fredholm integro-differential equations. *Comput. Appl. Math.* **2025**, *44*, 2. [CrossRef]
10. Ofem, A.E.; Igbokwe, I.D. An efficient Iterative method and its applications to a nonlinear integral equation and delay differential equation in Banach space. *Turk. J. Inequalities* **2020**, *4*, 79–107.
11. Kang, S.; Nazeer, W.; Tanveer, M.; Shahid, A. New fixed point results for fractal generation in Jungck Noor orbit with s-convexity. *J. Funct. Spaces* **2015**, *2015*, 963016. [CrossRef]
12. Nazeer, W.; Kang, S.; Tanveer, M.; Shahid, A. Fixed point results in the generation of Julia and Mandelbrot sets. *J. Inequalities Appl.* **2015**, *2015*, 298. [CrossRef]
13. Mishra, M.; Ojha, D.; Sharma, D. Some common fixed point results in relative superior Julia sets with Ishikawa iteration and s-convexity. *Int. J. Adv. Eng. Sci. Technol.* **2011**, *2*, 175–180.
14. Cho, S.; Shahid, A.; Nazeer, W.; Kang, S. Fixed point results for fractal generation in Noor orbit and s-convexity. *SpringerPlus* **2016**, *5*, 1843. [CrossRef]
15. Kumari, S.; Kumari, M.; Chugh, R. Generation of new fractals via SP orbit with s-convexity. *Int. J. Eng. Technol.* **2017**, *9*, 2491–2504. [CrossRef]
16. Gdawiec, K.; Shahid, A. Fixed point results for the complex fractal generation in the S-iteration orbit with s-convexity. *Open J. Math. Sci.* **2018**, *2*, 56–72. [CrossRef]
17. Orsucci, F. *Complexity Science, Living Systems, and Reflexing Interfaces: New Models and Perspectives*; IGI Global: Hershey, PA, USA, 2012.
18. Sreenivasan, K.R. Fractals and multifractals in fluid turbulence. *Annu. Rev. Fluid Mech.* **1991**, *23*, 539–604. [CrossRef]
19. Kenkel, N.C.; Walker, D.J. Fractals in the biological sciences. *Coenoses* **1996**, *11*, 77–100.
20. Devaney, R.L. *A First Course in Chaotic Dynamical Systems: Theory and Experiment*, 2nd ed.; Addison-Wesley: Boston, MA, USA, 1992.
21. Mandelbrot, B.B. *The Fractal Geometry of Nature*; W. H. Freeman: New York, NY, USA, 1982.
22. Barnsley, M. *Fractals Everywhere*, 2nd ed.; Academic Press: San Diego, CA, USA, 1993.
23. Julia, G. Mémoire sur l'itération des fonctions rationnelles. *J. Math. Pures Appl.* **1918**, *8*, 47–745.

24. Fisher, Y. Fractal image compression. *Fractals* **1994**, *2*, 347–361. [CrossRef]
25. Cohen, N. Fractal antenna applications in wireless telecommunications. In Proceedings of the Professional Program Proceedings. Electronic Industries Forum of New England, Boston, MA, USA, 6–8 May 1997; pp. 43–49.
26. Liu, S.A.; Bai, W.L.; Liu, G.C.; Li, W.H.; Srivastava, H.M. Parallel fractal compression method for big video data. *Complexity* **2018**, *2018*, 2016976. [CrossRef]
27. King, C.C. Fractal and chaotic dynamics in nervous systems. *Prog. Neurobiol.* **1991**, *36*, 279–308. [CrossRef]
28. Martinez, F.; Manriquez, H.; Ojeda, A.; Olea, G. Organization Patterns of Complex River Networks in Chile: A Fractal Morphology. *Mathematics* **2022**, *10*, 1806. [CrossRef]
29. Dhurandhar, S.V.; Bhavsar, V.C.; Gujar, U.G. Analysis of z-plane fractal images from $z \rightarrow z\alpha + c$ for $\alpha < 0$. *Comput. Graph.* **1993**, *17*, 89–94.
30. Adhikari, N.; Sintunavarat, W. Exploring the Julia and Mandelbrot sets of $z^p + \log c^t$ using a four-step iteration scheme extended with s-convexity. *Math. Comput. Simul.* **2024**, *220*, 357–381. [CrossRef]
31. Griffin, C.; Joshi, G. Octonionic Julia sets. *Chaos Solitons Fractals* **1992**, *2*, 11–24. [CrossRef]
32. Singh, S.; Jain, S.; Mishra, S. A new approach to superfractals. *Chaos Solitons Fractals* **2009**, *42*, 3110–3120. [CrossRef]
33. Kumari, S.; Gdawiec, K.; Nandal, A.; Postolache, M.; Chugh, R. A novel approach to generate Mandelbrot sets, Julia sets and biomorphs via viscosity approximation method. *Chaos, Solitons Fractals* **2022**, *163*, 112540. [CrossRef]
34. Rani, M.; Kumar, V. Superior Julia set. *J. Korea Soc. Math. Educ. Ser. D Res. Math. Educ.* **2004**, *8*, 261–277.
35. Chauhan, Y.S.; Rana, R.; Negi, A. New Julia sets of Ishikawa iterates. *Int. J. Comput. Appl.* **2010**, *7*, 34–42. [CrossRef]
36. Li, D.; Tanveer, M.; Nazeer, W.; Guo, X. Boundaries of filled Julia sets in generalized Jungck-Mann orbit. *IEEE Access* **2019**, *7*, 76859–76867. [CrossRef]
37. Antal, S.; Tomar, A.; Prajapati, D.J.; Sajid, M. Variants of Julia and Mandelbrot sets as fractals via Jungck-Ishikawa fixed point iteration system with s-convexity. *AIMS Math.* **2022**, *7*, 10939–10957. [CrossRef]
38. Alam, K.H.; Rohen, Y.; Saleem, N.; Aphane, M.; Razzaque, A. On escape criterion of an orbit with s-convexity and illustrations of the behavior shifts in Mandelbrot and Julia set fractals. *PLoS ONE* **2025**, *20*, e0312197, *in press*. [CrossRef]
39. Jungck, G. Commuting mappings and fixed points. *Am. Math. Mon.* **1976**, *83*, 261–263. [CrossRef]
40. Chugh, R.; Kumar, V. Strong Convergence and Stability results for Jungck–SP iterative scheme. *Int. J. Comput. Appl.* **2011**, *36*, 40–46.
41. Olatinwo, M.O.; Imoru, C.O. Some convergence results for the Jungck–Mann and the Jungck–Ishikawa iteration processes in the class of generalized Zamfirescu operators. *Acta Math. Univ. Comen. New Ser.* **2008**, *27*, 299–304.
42. Hussain, N.; Kumar, V.; Kutbi, M.A. On rate of convergence of Jungck-type iterative schemes. *Abstr. Appl. Anal.* **2013**, *2013*, 132626. [CrossRef]
43. Guran, L.; Shabbir, K.; Ahmad, K.; Bota, M.F. Stability, Data Dependence, and Convergence Results with Computational Engendering of Fractals via Jungck–DK Iterative Scheme. *Fractal Fract.* **2023**, *7*, 418. [CrossRef]
44. Jungck, G.; Hussain, N. Compatible maps and invariant approximations. *J. Math. Anal. Appl.* **2007**, *325*, 1003–1012. [CrossRef]
45. Singh, S.L.; Bhatnagar, C.; Mishra, S.N. Stability of Jungck-type iterative procedures. *Int. J. Math. Math. Sci.* **2005**, *19*, 3035–3043. [CrossRef]
46. Weng, X. Fixed point iteration for local strictly pseudo contractive mapping. *Proc. Amer. Math. Soc.* **1991**, *113*, 727–731. [CrossRef]
47. Pinheiro, M. s-convexity: Foundations for analysis. *Differ. Geom. Dyn. Syst.* **2008**, *10*, 257–262.

fractal and fractional

MDPI

Article

A Study of Fuzzy Fixed Points and Their Application to Fuzzy Fractional Differential Equations

Nawal Alharbi [1,*] and Nawab Hussain [2]

[1] Department of Mathematics, College of Science, Qassim University, Buraydah 51452, Saudi Arabia
[2] Department of Mathematics, King Abdulaziz University, P.O. Box 80203, Jeddah 21589, Saudi Arabia; nhusain@kau.edu.sa
* Correspondence: 3590@qu.edu.sa

Abstract: This study investigates fuzzy fixed points and fuzzy best proximity points for fuzzy mappings within the newly introduced framework θ-fuzzy metric spaces that extends various existing fuzzy metric spaces. We establish novel fixed-point and best proximity-point theorems for both single-valued and multivalued mappings, thereby broadening the scope of fuzzy analysis. Furthermerefore, we have for aore, we apply one of our key results to derive conditions, ensuring the existence and uniqueness of a solution to Hadamard Ψ-Caputo tempered fuzzy fractional differential equations, particularly in the context of the SIR dynamics model. These theoretical advancements are expected to open new avenues for research in fuzzy fixed-point theory and its applications to hybrid models within θ-fuzzy metric spaces.

Keywords: θ-fuzzy metric space; fuzzy mapping; fuzzy fixed point; fuzzy best proximity point; Hadamard Ψ-Caputo tempered fractional derivative

MSC: 54E15; 54H25; 03B52; 47H10; 34A08

1. Introduction

One of the fundamental challenges in the mathematical modeling of real-world phenomena is to address the uncertainty caused by the imprecision in categorizing events. Classical mathematics has historically faced difficulties in effectively managing imprecise or vague information. To address this limitation, in 1965, Zadeh [1] introduced the concept of fuzzy sets (FSs), providing a framework for modeling uncertainty that aligns with practical applications in fields such as engineering, life sciences, economics, medicine, and linguistics. Over the years, the foundational ideas of FSs have been significantly extended and developed. In particular, Heilpern [2] pioneered the concept of a fuzzy mapping and extended the fixed-point theorem for contraction mappings, making it applicable to fuzzy sets. Since then, various researchers have explored and applied fuzzy fixed-point (FFP) results in numerous contexts (see, for example, [3–7]).

It is worth noting that the fuzzy mappings involved in these studies are predominantly self-mappings. In a complete metric space $(\mathcal{X}, d)$, the presence of the two nonempty subsets $\mathcal{U}$ and $\mathcal{V}$ does not necessarily imply that a contractive mapping $\mathcal{T} : \mathcal{U} \to \mathcal{V}$ will have a fixed point (FP). This lack of certainty has led researchers to explore points ξ that achieve the minimum distance $d(\xi, \mathcal{T}\xi)$. Specifically, the aim is to find a ξ for which $d(\xi, \mathcal{T}\xi)$ reaches the lowest possible value, which corresponds to the distance $d(\mathcal{U}, \mathcal{V})$ separating the two subsets. This point ξ is termed the best proximity point (BPP). As a result, a BPP theorem provides sufficient conditions that guarantee an approximate optimal solution ξ satisfying $d(\xi, \mathcal{T}\xi) = d(\mathcal{U}, \mathcal{V})$, see [8–11].

Numerous authors in the literature have examined the existence and the convergence of FPs and BPPs under contractive conditions within distance metric spaces (see, for instance, [7,12–14]). However, these investigations have largely focused on mappings in classical or fuzzy metric spaces (FMSs) without considering the optimal proximity of fuzzy mappings. On the other hand, Amir et al. [15] defined the Hadamard Ψ-Caputo tempered fractional derivative (Ψ-CTFD), which is used as a mathematical tool in fuzzy calculus to measure the rate of change of a fuzzy function over time. It is considered a generalization of the classical derivative and can be applied to model systems with imprecise or uncertain data. For more studies, see [16,17]. In this research, we address a significant gap by exploring FFPs and fuzzy best proximity points (FBPPs) for fuzzy mappings within θ-FMSs and by elucidating their interconnections. This comprehensive framework encompasses multiple spaces, such as FMSs and non-Archimedean FMSs, broadening the applicability of current findings in the field. Consequently, we derive pertinent theorems for FPs and BPPs, which apply to both multivalued and single-valued mappings. In addition, one of the derived results is utilized to examine the conditions for solving fuzzy fractional differential equation problems, especially concerning the Susceptible-Infectious-Removed (SIR) dynamics model. It is important to mention that these results could be further refined and expanded upon when examined within other generalized hybrid models in the larger field of fuzzy mathematics. The remainder of this paper is organized as follows: Section 2 provides fundamental definitions, lemmas, and theorems related to θ-FMSs. Section 3 introduces the FFP theorem and its implications within θ-FMSs. Furthermore, Section 4 focuses on FBPPs for fuzzy mappings and explores their consequences. Lastly, Section 5 presents an application that demonstrates the validity of the theoretical findings.

2. Preliminaries

This section gathers crucial definitions and findings related to the completion of θ fuzzy metrics, which are vital to the continuation of the article.

Definition 1 ([18]). *A binary operation $* : [0,1] \times [0,1] \to [0,1]$ is called a continuous t-norm (CtN) if $*$ is commutative, associative, $a * 1 = a$ and for all $a, b, c, d \in [0,1]$, if $a \leq c$ and $b \leq d$ then $a * b \leq c * d$.*

Example 1.

1. $*(a,b) = a{\cdot}b\,;$
2. $*(a,b) = \min\{a,b\}\,;$
3. $*(a,b) = \max\{a+b-1, 0\}\,.$

Definition 2 ([19]). *Let $\mathcal{X}$ be a non-empty set and $*$ represents a CtN. Furthermore, let $\mathcal{M} : \mathcal{X} \times \mathcal{X} \times (0,+\infty) \to [0,1]$ be a fuzzy set. A triple $(\mathcal{X}, \mathcal{M}, *)$ is called a fuzzy metric space over $\mathcal{X}$ if the following conditions hold for any $\xi, \eta, \gamma \in \mathcal{X}$ and $t, \iota > 0$:*

(M1) $\mathcal{M}(\xi,\eta,t) > 0$;

(M2) $\mathcal{M}(\xi,\eta,t) = 1$ *if and only if* $\xi = \eta$;

(M3) $\mathcal{M}(\xi,\eta,t) = \mathcal{M}(\eta,\xi,t)$;

(M4) $\mathcal{M}(\xi,\eta,t+\iota) \geq \mathcal{M}(\xi,\gamma,t) * \mathcal{M}(\gamma,\eta,\iota)$;

(M5) $\mathcal{M}(\xi,\eta,.) : (0,+\infty) \to [0,1]$ *is continuous and* $\lim_{t\to+\infty} \mathcal{M}(\xi,\eta,t) = 1$.

Definition 3 ([20]). *Let $\theta : [0, +\infty) \times [0, +\infty) \to [0, +\infty)$ be a continuous mapping with respect to both variables. The image of θ is denoted by $Im(\theta) = \{\theta(\xi, \eta) : \xi \geq 0, \eta \geq 0\}$. The mapping θ is called an $\mathcal{B}$-action if and only if it satisfies the following conditions:*

($\mathcal{B}1$) *$\theta(0,0) = 0$ and $\theta(\xi, \eta) = \theta(\eta, \xi)$ for all $\xi, \eta \geq 0$;*

($\mathcal{B}2$)

$$\theta(\xi, \eta) < \theta(u, v) \text{ implies } \begin{cases} \text{either } \xi < u, \eta \leq v, \\ \text{or } \xi \leq u, \eta < v; \end{cases}$$

($\mathcal{B}3$) *For each $r \in Im(\theta)$ and for each $s \in [0, r]$, there exists $t \in [0, r]$ such that $\theta(t, s) = r$;*

($\mathcal{B}4$) *$\theta(\xi, 0) \leq \xi$ for all $\xi > 0$.*

The set of all $\mathcal{B}$-actions is denoted by Θ.

Example 2 ([20]). *The following functions serve as examples of $\mathcal{B}$-actions on $[0, +\infty) \times [0, +\infty)$:*

1. $\theta_1(\xi, \eta) = \xi + \eta$;
2. $\theta_2(\xi, \eta) = k(\xi + \eta + \xi\eta); k \in [0, 1)$
3. $\theta_3(\xi, \eta) = (\xi + \eta)(1 + \xi\eta)$;
4. $\theta_4(\xi, \eta) = \xi + \eta + \sqrt{\xi\eta}$;
5. $\theta_5(\xi, \eta) = \sqrt{\xi^2 + \eta^2}$;
6. $\theta_6(\xi, \eta) = \max\{\xi, \eta\}$.

Definition 4 ([1,2]). *In the set $\mathcal{X}$, a fuzzy set (FS) is characterized by a function $\mathcal{A} : \mathcal{X} \to [0, 1]$, which assigns each element $\xi \in \mathcal{X}$ a membership value $\mathcal{A}(\xi)$ within the interval $[0, 1]$. The collection of all fuzzy sets in $\mathcal{X}$ is denoted by $I^{\mathcal{X}}$. The α-level set of $\mathcal{A}$, indicated as $[\mathcal{A}]_\alpha$, is defined as follows:*

$$[\mathcal{A}]_\alpha = \{\xi \in \mathcal{X} : \mathcal{A}(\xi) \geq \alpha\}, \quad \text{for} \quad \alpha \in (0, 1],$$
$$[\mathcal{A}]_0 = \overline{\{\xi \in \mathcal{X} : \mathcal{A}(\xi) \geq 0\}}.$$

Definition 5 ([21]). *Let $\mathcal{X}$ be a non-empty set, and $*$ represents a CtN. Furthermore, let $\mathcal{N} : \mathcal{X} \times \mathcal{X} \times (0, +\infty) \to [0, 1]$ be a fuzzy set. There exists $\theta \in \Theta$ such that a quadruple $(\mathcal{X}, \mathcal{N}, *, \theta)$ is called a θ-fuzzy metric space (θ-FMS) over $\mathcal{X}$ if the following conditions hold for any $\xi, \eta, \gamma \in \mathcal{X}$ and $t, \iota > 0$:*

(N1) $\mathcal{N}(\xi, \eta, t) > 0$;

(N2) $\mathcal{N}(\xi, \eta, t) = 1$ *if and only if* $\xi = \eta$;

(N3) $\mathcal{N}(\xi, \eta, t) = \mathcal{N}(\eta, \xi, t)$;

(N4) $\mathcal{N}(\xi, \eta, \theta(t, \iota)) \geq \mathcal{N}(\xi, \gamma, t) * \mathcal{N}(\gamma, \eta, \iota)$;

(N5) $\mathcal{N}(\xi, \eta, .) : (0, +\infty) \to [0, 1]$ *is continuous and* $\lim_{t \to +\infty} \mathcal{N}(\xi, \eta, t) = 1$.

Example 3. *Let $\mathcal{X} = \mathbb{R}$. Define $a * b = a \cdot b$, $\theta \in \Theta$ and $\mathcal{N} : \mathcal{X} \times \mathcal{X} \times (0, +\infty) \to [0, 1]$ by*

$$\mathcal{N}(\xi, \eta, t) = \exp\left(-\frac{|\xi - \eta|}{t}\right). \tag{1}$$

Then $(\mathcal{X}, \mathcal{N}, *, \theta)$ is a θ-FMS over $\mathcal{X}$. Our goal is to show condition (N4) from Definition 5, as the other assumptions, can be verified more straightforwardly.

$$\begin{aligned} \mathcal{N}(\xi,\eta,\theta(t,\iota)) = \exp\Big(-\tfrac{|\xi-\eta|}{\theta(t,\iota)}\Big) &\geq \exp\Big(-\tfrac{|\xi-\gamma|+|\gamma-\eta|}{\theta(t,\iota)}\Big) \\ &\geq \exp\Big(-\tfrac{|\xi-\gamma|}{\theta(t,\iota)}\Big)\cdot \exp\Big(-\tfrac{|\gamma-\eta|}{\theta(t,\iota)}\Big) \\ &\geq \exp\Big(-\tfrac{|\xi-\gamma|}{t}\Big)\cdot \exp\Big(-\tfrac{|\gamma-\eta|}{\iota}\Big) \\ &= \mathcal{N}(\xi,\gamma,t) * \mathcal{N}(\gamma,\eta,\iota), \end{aligned}$$

for all $\xi, \eta, \gamma \in \mathcal{X}$ and $t, \iota > 0$.

Example 4. *Let $\mathcal{X} = \mathbb{R}$. Define $a * b = a \cdot b$, $\theta \in \Theta$ and $\mathcal{N} : \mathcal{X} \times \mathcal{X} \times (0, +\infty) \to [0,1]$ by*

$$\mathcal{N}(\xi,\eta,t) = \frac{t}{t+|\xi-\eta|}. \tag{2}$$

Then $(\mathcal{X}, \mathcal{N}, *, \theta)$ is a θ-FMS over $\mathcal{X}$. Our goal is to show that condition (N4) from Definition 5, as the other assumptions, can be verified more straightforwardly for all $\xi, \eta, \gamma \in \mathcal{X}$ and $t, \iota > 0$. Utilizing the characteristics of θ, we obtain

$$\begin{aligned} \mathcal{N}(\xi,\gamma,t) * \mathcal{N}(\gamma,\eta,\iota) &= \tfrac{t}{t+|\xi-\gamma|}\cdot\tfrac{\iota}{\iota+|\gamma-\eta|} \\ &= \tfrac{1}{1+\frac{|\xi-\gamma|}{t}}\cdot\tfrac{1}{1+\frac{|\gamma-\eta|}{\iota}} \\ &\leq \tfrac{1}{1+\frac{|\xi-\gamma|}{\theta(t,\iota)}}\cdot\tfrac{1}{1+\frac{|\gamma-\eta|}{\theta(t,\iota)}} \\ &\leq \tfrac{1}{1+\frac{|\xi-\gamma|+|\gamma-\eta|}{\theta(t,\iota)}} \\ &\leq \tfrac{\theta(t,\iota)}{\theta(t,\iota)+|\xi-\gamma|+|\gamma-\eta|} \\ &\leq \tfrac{\theta(t,\iota)}{\theta(t,\iota)+|\xi-\eta|} \\ &= \mathcal{N}(\xi,\eta,\theta(t,\iota)). \end{aligned}$$

Hence, (N4) is satisfied.

Definition 6 ([21]). *Let $(\mathcal{X}, \mathcal{N}, *, \theta)$ be a θ-FMS.*

1. *A sequence $\{\xi_n\} \subset \mathcal{X}$ is considered to converge to a point $\xi \in \mathcal{X}$ if $\mathcal{N}(\xi_n, \xi, t) \to 1$ as $n \to +\infty$ for every $t > 0$. The point ξ is called the limit of the sequence $\{\xi_n\}$.*
2. *A sequence $\{\xi_n\} \subseteq$in $\mathcal{X} \subseteq\subseteq$ is called a Cauchy sequence if there exists $n_0 \in \mathbb{N}$ such that $\mathcal{N}(\xi_n, \xi_m, t) \to 1$ as $n, m \to +\infty$, for every $n, m \geq n_0$, $t > 0$.*
3. *A subset $\mathcal{Y}$ of $\mathcal{X}$ is said to be closed if the limit of a convergent sequence of $\mathcal{Y}$ always belongs to $\mathcal{Y}$.*
4. *A subset $\mathcal{Y}$ of $\mathcal{X}$ is said to be complete if every Cauchy sequence in $\mathcal{Y}$ is a convergent and its limit is in $\mathcal{Y}$.*
5. *The mapping $\mathcal{T} : \mathcal{X} \to \mathcal{X}$ is called continuous at a point $\xi_0 \in \mathcal{X}$ if for every sequence $\{\xi_n\} \subseteq \mathcal{X}$ with $\xi_n \to \xi$ as $n \to +\infty$ we have $\mathcal{T}(\xi_n) \to \mathcal{T}(\xi)$ in $\mathcal{X}$ as $n \to +\infty$.*

Definition 7 ([22]). *Let $\mathcal{X}$ be an arbitrary set and $\mathcal{Y}$ a metric space. A mapping $\mathcal{T}$ from $\mathcal{X}$ to $\mathcal{Y}$ is called a fuzzy mapping, which is a fuzzy subset of $\mathcal{X} \times \mathcal{Y}$ with the membership function $\mathcal{T}(\xi)(\eta)$ representing the degree of membership of η in $\mathcal{T}(\xi)$. For convenience, we denote the α-level set of $\mathcal{T}(\xi)$ by $[\mathcal{T}\xi]_\alpha$ instead of $[\mathcal{T}(\xi)]$.*

3. Fuzzy Contractions

In what follows, we will use specific assumptions and definitions within the framework of θ-FMS $(\mathcal{X}, \mathcal{N}, *, \theta)$. Let the set of all nonempty bounded proximal sets in $\mathcal{X}$ be denoted by $\mathcal{P}(\mathcal{X})$, the set of all nonempty compact subsets of $\mathcal{X}$ be presented by $C(2^{\mathcal{X}})$, and the set of all nonempty closed and bounded subsets of $\mathcal{X}$ be denoted by $CB(\mathcal{X})$. Since every compact set is proximal and any proximal set is closed, the following are included:

$$C\left(2^{\mathcal{X}}\right) \subseteq \mathcal{P}(\mathcal{X}) \subseteq CB(\mathcal{X}). \tag{3}$$

For $\mathcal{U}, \mathcal{V} \in C(2^{\mathcal{X}})$, we define the following:

- $\mathcal{N}(\xi, \mathcal{U}, t) = \sup\{\mathcal{N}(\xi, \eta, t) : \eta \in \mathcal{U}, t > 0\}$.
- $\mathcal{N}(\mathcal{U}, \mathcal{V}, t) = \sup\{\mathcal{N}(\xi, \eta, t) : \xi \in \mathcal{U}, \eta \in \mathcal{V}, t > 0\}$.
- We induce the Hausdorff fuzzy metric $\mathcal{H}$ on $C(2^{\mathcal{X}})$ by the fuzzy θ-metric $\mathcal{N}$, for all $t > 0$ is defined as

$$\mathcal{H}(\mathcal{U}, \mathcal{V}, t) = \begin{cases} \min\left\{ \inf\limits_{\xi \in \mathcal{U}} \mathcal{N}(\xi, \mathcal{V}, t), \inf\limits_{\eta \in \mathcal{V}} \mathcal{N}(\eta, \mathcal{U}, t) \right\}, & \text{if it exists,} \\ 1, & \text{otherwise.} \end{cases} \tag{4}$$

Definition 8. *Let $(\mathcal{X}, \mathcal{N}, *, \theta)$ be a θ-FMS. A subset $\mathcal{U}$ being a subset of $\mathcal{X}$ is called proximal, if for each $\xi \in \mathcal{X}$, there exists $\eta \in \mathcal{U}$ such that $\mathcal{N}(\xi, \eta, t) = \mathcal{N}(\xi, \mathcal{U}, t)$, for all $t > 0$.*

Definition 9. *Let $(\mathcal{X}, \mathcal{N}, *, \theta)$ be a θ-FMS and $\mathcal{T} : \mathcal{X} \to I^{\mathcal{X}}$ be a fuzzy mapping. Then a point $\xi \in \mathcal{X}$ is called an FFP of $\mathcal{T}$ if there exists $\alpha \in (0,1]$ such that $\mathcal{N}(\xi, [\mathcal{T}\xi]_\alpha, t) = 1$ for all $t > 0$, i.e., $\xi \in [\mathcal{T}\xi]_\alpha$.*

We will initially present a series of lemmas concerning θ-FMSs.

Lemma 1. *If $[\mathcal{T}\xi]_{\alpha_\mathcal{T}(\xi)} \in C(2^{\mathcal{X}}), \alpha_\mathcal{T}(\xi) \in (0,1], \xi \in \mathcal{X}$, then $\xi \in [\mathcal{T}\xi]_{\alpha_\mathcal{T}(\xi)}$ if and only if $\mathcal{N}\left([\mathcal{T}\xi]_{\alpha_\mathcal{T}(\xi)}, \xi, t\right) = 1$ for all $t > 0$.*

Proof. Assume $\mathcal{N}\left(\xi, [\mathcal{T}\xi]_{\alpha_\mathcal{T}(\xi)}, t\right) = \sup\left\{\mathcal{N}(\xi, \eta, t) : \eta \in [\mathcal{T}\xi]_{\alpha_\mathcal{T}(\xi)}, t > 0\right\} = 1$ for all $t > 0$. Then, there exists a sequence $\{\eta_n\} \in [\mathcal{T}\xi]_{\alpha_\mathcal{T}(\xi)}$ such that $\mathcal{N}(\xi, \eta_n, t) \geq 1 - \frac{1}{n}$. Since $[\mathcal{T}\xi]_{\alpha_\mathcal{T}(\xi)} \in C(2^{\mathcal{X}})$, $\alpha_\mathcal{T}(\xi) \in (0,1]$, and $\xi \in \mathcal{X}$, it follows that $\xi \in [\mathcal{T}\xi]_{\alpha_\mathcal{T}(\xi)}$. Conversely, if $\xi \in [\mathcal{T}\xi]_{\alpha_\mathcal{T}(\xi)}$, we have for all $t > 0$

$$\mathcal{N}\left([\mathcal{T}\xi]_{\alpha_\mathcal{T}(\xi)}, \xi, t\right) = \sup\left\{\mathcal{N}(\xi, \eta, t) : \eta \in [\mathcal{T}\xi]_{\alpha_\mathcal{T}(\xi)}\right\} \geq \mathcal{N}(\xi, \xi, t) = 1.$$

Thus, $\mathcal{N}\left([\mathcal{T}\xi]_{\alpha_\mathcal{T}(\xi)}, \xi, t\right) = 1$ for all $t > 0$. □

Lemma 2. *Let $(\mathcal{X}, \mathcal{N}, *, \theta)$ be a complete θ-FMS , where $(C(2^{\mathcal{X}}), \mathcal{H}, *)$ forms a Hausdorff FMS on $C(2^{\mathcal{X}})$. Let $\mathcal{T}$ be a fuzzy mapping assuming, for every $[\mathcal{T}\xi_1]_{\alpha_\mathcal{T}(\xi_1)}$ and $[\mathcal{T}\xi_2]_{\alpha_\mathcal{T}(\xi_2)}$ in $C(2^{\mathcal{X}})$, that for each $\xi \in [\mathcal{T}\xi_1]_{\alpha_\mathcal{T}(\xi_1)}$, there exists an $\eta \in [\mathcal{T}\xi_2]_{\alpha_\mathcal{T}(\xi_2)}$ satisfying $\mathcal{N}\left(\xi, [\mathcal{T}\xi_1]_{\alpha_\mathcal{T}(\xi_1)}, t\right) = \mathcal{N}(\xi, \eta, t)$, $t > 0$; then the following inequality holds:*

$$\mathcal{H}\left([\mathcal{T}\xi_1]_{\alpha_\mathcal{T}(\xi_1)}, [\mathcal{T}\xi_2]_{\alpha_\mathcal{T}(\xi_2)}, t\right) \leq \mathcal{N}(\xi, \eta, t).$$

Proof. Since

$$\mathcal{H}\Big([\mathcal{T}\xi_1]_{\alpha_{\mathcal{T}}(\xi_1)},[\mathcal{T}\xi_2]_{\alpha_{\mathcal{T}}(\xi_2)},t\Big) = \min\{ \inf_{\xi\in[\mathcal{T}\xi_1]_{\alpha_{\mathcal{T}}(\xi_1)}} \Big\{\mathcal{N}\Big(\xi,[\mathcal{T}\xi_2]_{\alpha_{\mathcal{T}}(\xi_2)},t\Big)\Big\}, \inf_{\eta\in[\mathcal{T}\xi_2]_{\alpha_{\mathcal{T}}(\xi_2)}} \Big\{\mathcal{N}\Big(\eta,[\mathcal{T}\xi_1]_{\alpha_{\mathcal{T}}(\xi_1)},t\Big)\}\Big\},$$

then we have two cases:

Case 1: If

$$\mathcal{H}\Big([\mathcal{T}\xi_1]_{\alpha_{\mathcal{T}}(\xi_1)},[\mathcal{T}\xi_2]_{\alpha_{\mathcal{T}}(\xi_2)},t\Big) = \inf_{\xi\in[\mathcal{T}\xi_1]_{\alpha_{\mathcal{T}}(\xi_1)}} \Big\{\mathcal{N}\Big(\xi,[\mathcal{T}\xi_2]_{\alpha_{\mathcal{T}}(\xi_2)},t\Big)\Big\},$$

implies that

$$\mathcal{H}\Big([\mathcal{T}\xi_1]_{\alpha_{\mathcal{T}}(\xi_1)},[\mathcal{T}\xi_2]_{\alpha_{\mathcal{T}}(\xi_2)},t\Big) \leq \mathcal{N}\Big(\xi,[\mathcal{T}\xi_2]_{\alpha_{\mathcal{T}}(\xi_2)},t\Big), \tag{5}$$

then, by assumption, for each $\xi \in [\mathcal{T}\xi_1]_{\alpha_{\mathcal{T}}(\xi_1)}$ and for $t > 0$, there exists $\eta \in [\mathcal{T}\xi_2]_{\alpha_{\mathcal{T}}(\xi_2)}$, satisfying

$$\mathcal{N}(\xi,\eta,t) = \mathcal{N}\Big(\xi,[\mathcal{T}\xi_2]_{\alpha_{\mathcal{T}}(\xi_2)},t\Big). \tag{6}$$

Therefore, based on (5) and (6), we can conclude that

$$\mathcal{H}\Big([\mathcal{T}\xi_1]_{\alpha_{\mathcal{T}}(\xi_1)},[\mathcal{T}\xi_2]_{\alpha_{\mathcal{T}}(\xi_2)},t\Big) \leq \mathcal{N}(\xi,\eta,t).$$

Case 2: If

$$\mathcal{H}\Big([\mathcal{T}\xi_1]_{\alpha_{\mathcal{T}}(\xi_1)},[\mathcal{T}\xi_2]_{\alpha_{\mathcal{T}}(\xi_2)},t\Big) = \inf_{\eta\in[\mathcal{T}\xi_2]_{\alpha_{\mathcal{T}}(\xi_2)}} \Big\{\mathcal{N}\Big(\eta,[\mathcal{T}\xi_1]_{\alpha_{\mathcal{T}}(\xi_1)},t\Big)\Big\},$$

then

$$\mathcal{H}\Big([\mathcal{T}\xi_1]_{\alpha_{\mathcal{T}}(\xi_1)},[\mathcal{T}\xi_2]_{\alpha_{\mathcal{T}}(\xi_2)},t\Big) \leq \mathcal{N}(\eta,\mathcal{T}\xi_1]_{\alpha_{\mathcal{T}}(\xi_1)},t), \tag{7}$$

again, since there exists $\eta \in [\mathcal{T}\xi_2]_{\alpha_{\mathcal{T}}(\xi_2)}$ satisfying

$$\mathcal{N}(\xi,\eta,t) = \mathcal{N}\Big(\eta,[\mathcal{T}\xi_1]_{\alpha_{\mathcal{T}}(\xi_1)},t\Big). \tag{8}$$

Hence, from (7) and (8), we obtain

$$\mathcal{H}\Big([\mathcal{T}\xi_1]_{\alpha_{\mathcal{T}}(\xi_1)},[\mathcal{T}\xi_2]_{\alpha_{\mathcal{T}}(\xi_2)},t\Big) \leq \mathcal{N}(\xi,\eta,t).$$

□

Theorem 1. *Let $(\mathcal{X},\mathcal{N},*,\theta)$ be a complete θ-FMS. Let $\mathcal{T} : \mathcal{X} \to I^{\mathcal{X}}$ be a fuzzy mapping. Assume that, for every $\xi \in \mathcal{X}$, there exists an $\alpha_{\mathcal{T}}(\xi) \in (0,1]$ such that $[\mathcal{T}\xi]_{\alpha_{\mathcal{T}}(\xi)} \in C(2^{\mathcal{X}})$. Additionally, suppose that the following condition holds:*

$$\mathcal{H}\Big([\mathcal{T}\xi_1]_{\alpha_{\mathcal{T}}(\xi_1)},[\mathcal{T}\xi_2]_{\alpha_{\mathcal{T}}(\xi_2)},kt\Big) \geq \mathcal{N}(\xi_1,\xi_2,t), \tag{9}$$

for all $\xi_1,\xi_2 \in \mathcal{X}, k \in (0,1)$ and $t > 0$. Then $\mathcal{T}$ has an FFP.

Proof. Let $\xi_0 \in \mathcal{X}$ be arbitrary. We choose a sequence $\{\xi_n\}$ in $\mathcal{X}$ as follows: By hypothesis, there exists $\alpha_{\mathcal{T}}(\xi_0) \in (0,1]$ such that $[\mathcal{T}\xi_0]_{\alpha_{\mathcal{T}}(\xi_0)} \in C(2^{\mathcal{X}})$. Since $[\mathcal{T}\xi_0]_{\alpha_{\mathcal{T}}(\xi_0)} \in C(2^{\mathcal{X}})$ is a nonempty compact subset of $\mathcal{X}$, there exists $\xi_1 \in [\mathcal{T}\xi_0]_{\alpha_{\mathcal{T}}(\xi_0)}$ such that $\mathcal{N}(\xi_0, \xi_1, t) = \mathcal{N}\Big(\xi_0, [\mathcal{T}\xi_0]_{\alpha_{\mathcal{T}}(\xi_0)}, t\Big)$. By Lemma 2, we can choose $\xi_2 \in [\mathcal{T}\xi_1]_{\alpha_{\mathcal{T}}(\xi_1)}$ such that

$$\mathcal{N}(\xi_1, \xi_2, t) \geq \mathcal{H}\Big([\mathcal{T}\xi_0]_{\alpha_{\mathcal{T}}(\xi_0)}, [\mathcal{T}\xi_1]_{\alpha_{\mathcal{T}}(\xi_1)}, t\Big)$$

for all $t > 0$. By induction, we have that $\xi_{n+1} \in \mathcal{T}\xi_n$, which satisfies the following inequality:

$$\mathcal{N}(\xi_n, \xi_{n+1}, \theta(t,s)) \geq \mathcal{H}\Big([\mathcal{T}\xi_n]_{\alpha_{\mathcal{T}}(\xi_n)}, [\mathcal{T}\xi_{n+1}]_{\alpha_{\mathcal{T}}(\xi_{n+1})}, \theta(t,s)\Big), \tag{10}$$

for all $t > 0$. Now, by (9) and (10) together with Lemma 2, we have,

$$\begin{aligned}
\mathcal{N}(\xi_n, \xi_{n+1}, t) &\geq \mathcal{H}\Big([\mathcal{T}\xi_n]_{\alpha_{\mathcal{T}}(\xi_n)}, [\mathcal{T}\xi_{n+1}]_{\alpha_{\mathcal{T}}(\xi_{n+1})}, t\Big) \\
&\geq \mathcal{N}(\xi_n, \xi_{n+1}, \tfrac{t}{k}) \\
&\geq \mathcal{H}\Big([\mathcal{T}\xi_{n-1}]_{\alpha_{\mathcal{T}}(\xi_{n-1})}, [\mathcal{T}\xi_n]_{\alpha_{\mathcal{T}}(\xi_n)}, \tfrac{t}{k}\Big) \\
&\geq \mathcal{N}\Big(\xi_{n-1}, \xi_n, \tfrac{t}{k^2}\Big) \\
&\;\;\vdots \\
&\geq \mathcal{H}\Big([\mathcal{T}\xi_0]_{\alpha_{\mathcal{T}}(\xi_0)}, [\mathcal{T}\xi_1]_{\alpha_{\mathcal{T}}(\xi_1)}, \tfrac{t}{k^{n-1}}\Big) \\
&\geq \mathcal{N}(\xi_0, \xi_1, \tfrac{t}{k^n}).
\end{aligned} \tag{11}$$

Let $m > n$, then, by (N4) and (11). We have for all $t \in Im(\theta)$, which means by ($\mathcal{B}$3), there exists $s_i \leq t$ for all $r_i \leq t, i = 1, 2, \cdots, m-n-1$ such that

$$\begin{aligned}
\mathcal{N}(\xi_n, \xi_m, t) &\geq \mathcal{N}(\xi_n, \xi_n, s_1) * \mathcal{N}(\xi_{n+1}, \xi_m, r_1) \\
&\geq \mathcal{N}(\xi_n, \xi_{n+1}, s_1) * \mathcal{N}(\xi_{n+1}, \xi_{n+2}, s_2) * \mathcal{N}(\xi_{n+2}, \xi_m, r_2) \\
&\geq \mathcal{N}(\xi_n, \xi_{n+1}, s_1) * \mathcal{N}(\xi_{n+1}, \xi_{n+2}, s_2) * \cdots * \mathcal{N}(\xi_{m-1}, \xi_m, s_{m-n-1}) \\
&\geq \mathcal{N}\Big(\xi_0, \xi_1, \tfrac{s_1}{k^{n-1}}\Big) * \cdots * \mathcal{N}\Big(\xi_0, \xi_1, \tfrac{s_{m-n-1}}{k^{m-n-1}}\Big).
\end{aligned}$$

By taking the limit as $n \to +\infty$, we obtain $\mathcal{N}(\xi_n, \xi_m, t) = 1$. This shows that $\{\xi_n\}$ is a Cauchy sequence. Hence, the completeness of $(\mathcal{X}, \mathcal{N}, *, \theta)$ implies that there exists $\eta \in \mathcal{X}$ such that $\xi_n \to \eta$ as $n \to +\infty$. Now, we have to prove $\eta \in [\mathcal{T}\eta]_{\alpha_{\mathcal{T}}(\eta)}$

$$\begin{aligned}
\mathcal{N}\Big(\eta, [\mathcal{T}\eta]_{\alpha_{\mathcal{T}}(\eta)}, t\Big) &\geq \mathcal{N}(\eta, \xi_{n+1}, t) \\
&\geq \mathcal{H}\Big([\mathcal{T}\eta]_{\alpha_{\mathcal{T}}(\eta)}, [\mathcal{T}\xi_n]_{\alpha_{\mathcal{T}}(\xi_n)}, t\Big) \\
&\geq \mathcal{N}(\eta, \xi_n, \tfrac{t}{k}) \\
&\to 1 \text{ as } n \to +\infty.
\end{aligned}$$

By Lemma 1, we have $\eta \in [\mathcal{T}\eta]_{\alpha_{\mathcal{T}}(\eta)}$. Hence, η is an FFP for $\mathcal{T}$. □

Example 5. *Let $\mathcal{X} = [0, +\infty)$. Define $\mathcal{N} : \mathcal{X} \times \mathcal{X} \times (0, +\infty) \to [0,1]$ as in Example 4, as follows:*

$$\mathcal{N}(\xi, \eta, t) = \frac{t}{t + |\xi - \eta|}.$$

Let $\alpha \in (0,1]$ and consider a fuzzy mapping $\mathcal{T} : \mathcal{X} \to I^{\mathcal{X}}$ defined as follows:

(i) If $\xi = 0$

$$\mathcal{T}(\xi)(\eta) = \begin{cases} 1 & , \eta = 0, \\ 0 & , \eta \neq 0. \end{cases}$$

(ii) If $0 < \xi < \infty$

$$\mathcal{T}(\xi)(\eta) = \begin{cases} \alpha & , 0 \leq \eta < \frac{\xi}{3}, \\ \frac{\alpha}{3} & , \frac{\xi}{3} < \eta \leq \frac{\xi}{2}, \\ \frac{\alpha}{6} & , \frac{\xi}{2} \leq \eta < \frac{2\xi}{3}, \\ \frac{\alpha}{18} & , \frac{2\xi}{3} \leq \eta < \infty. \end{cases}$$

It is clear that, for $\frac{\alpha}{3}$, *we have*

$$[\mathcal{T}\xi]_{\frac{\alpha}{3}} = \{\eta \in \mathcal{X} : \mathcal{T}(\xi)(\eta) \geq \frac{\alpha}{3}\} = \left[0, \frac{\xi}{2}\right].$$

Thus, for every $\xi \in \mathcal{X}$, *there exists* $\frac{\alpha}{3}_{\mathcal{T}}(\xi) \in (0,1]$ *such that* $[\mathcal{T}\xi]_{\frac{\alpha}{3}_{\mathcal{T}}(\xi)} \in C(2^{\mathcal{X}})$. *Then,*

$$\begin{aligned} \mathcal{H}\Big([\mathcal{T}\xi_1]_{\frac{\alpha}{3}_{\mathcal{T}}(\xi_1)}, [\mathcal{T}\xi_2]_{\frac{\alpha}{3}_{\mathcal{T}}(\xi_2)}, kt\Big) &= \mathcal{H}\Big(\left[0, \frac{\xi_1}{2}\right], \left[0, \frac{\xi_2}{2}\right], kt\Big) \\ &= \frac{kt}{kt + |\frac{\xi_1}{2} - \frac{\xi_2}{2}|} \\ &\geq \frac{t}{t + |\xi_1 - \xi_2|} \\ &= \mathcal{N}(\xi_1, \xi_2, t), \end{aligned}$$

for all $\xi_1, \xi_2 \in \mathcal{X}, k = \frac{1}{2}$ *and* $t > 0$. *Consequently, all the conditions of Theorem 1 are satisfied to find* $0 \in [\mathcal{T}0]_{\frac{\alpha}{3}_{\mathcal{T}}(0)}$.

Corollary 1. *Let* $(\mathcal{X}, \mathcal{N}, *, \theta)$ *be a complete* θ*-FMS. Let* $\mathcal{S} : \mathcal{X} \to C(2^{\mathcal{X}}) \setminus \phi$ *be a multivalued mapping. Assume for every* $\xi \in \mathcal{X}$. *Suppose that the following condition holds:*

$$\mathcal{H}(\mathcal{S}\xi_1, \mathcal{S}\xi_2, kt) \geq \mathcal{N}(\xi_1, \xi_2, t), \tag{12}$$

for all $\xi_1, \xi_2 \in \mathcal{X}, k \in (0,1)$ *and* $t > 0$. *Then there exists* $\xi \in \mathcal{X}$ *such that* $\xi \in \mathcal{S}(\xi)$.

Proof. Let $\alpha_{\mathcal{T}} : \mathcal{X} \to (0,1]$ be a mapping, and consider a fuzzy mapping $\mathcal{T} : \mathcal{X} \to \mathcal{I}^{\mathcal{X}}$ defined as follows:

$$\mathcal{T}(\xi)(u) = \begin{cases} \alpha_{\mathcal{T}}(\xi), & \text{if } u \in \mathcal{T}\xi, \\ 0, & \text{if } u \notin \mathcal{T}\xi. \end{cases} \tag{13}$$

Then, for all $\xi \in \mathcal{X}$, we have

$$[\mathcal{T}\xi]_{\alpha_{\mathcal{T}}} = \{u \in \mathcal{X} : \mathcal{T}(\xi)(u) \geq \alpha_{\mathcal{L}}(\xi)\} = \mathcal{S}\xi. \tag{14}$$

As a result,

$$\mathcal{H}\Big([\mathcal{T}\xi_1]_{\alpha_{\mathcal{T}}(\xi_1)}, [\mathcal{T}\xi_2]_{\alpha_{\mathcal{T}}(\xi_2)}, kt\Big) = \mathcal{H}(\mathcal{S}\xi_1, \mathcal{S}\xi_2, kt) \geq \mathcal{N}(\xi_1, \xi_2, t), \tag{15}$$

for all $\xi_1, \xi_2 \in \mathcal{X}, k \in (0,1)$ and $t > 0$. Hence, Theorem 1 is applicable; then $\mathcal{S}$ has an FP. □

Corollary 2. *Let* $(\mathcal{X}, \mathcal{N}, *, \theta)$ *be a complete* θ*-FMS. Let* $\mathcal{S} : \mathcal{X} \to \mathcal{X}$ *be a mapping. Assume that the following condition holds:*

$$\mathcal{N}(\mathcal{S}\xi_1, \mathcal{S}\xi_2, kt) \geq \mathcal{N}(\xi_1, \xi_2, t), \tag{16}$$

for all $\xi_1, \xi_2 \in \mathcal{X}$ *and* $t > 0$, *where* $k \in (0,1)$. *Then* $\mathcal{S}$ *has a unique FP.*

Proof. Let $\alpha_{\mathcal{T}} : \mathcal{X} \to (0,1]$ be an arbitrary mapping, and consider a fuzzy mapping $\mathcal{T} : \mathcal{X} \to \mathcal{I}^{\mathcal{X}}$ defined as follows:

$$\mathcal{T}(\xi)(u) = \begin{cases} \alpha_{\mathcal{T}}(\xi), & \text{if } u = \mathcal{S}\xi, \\ 0, & \text{if } u \neq \mathcal{S}\xi. \end{cases} \tag{17}$$

Then, for all $\xi \in \mathcal{X}$, we have

$$[\mathcal{T}\xi]_{\alpha_{\mathcal{T}}} = \{u \in \mathcal{X} : \mathcal{T}(\xi)(u) \geq \alpha_{\mathcal{T}}(\xi)\} = \{\mathcal{S}\xi\}. \tag{18}$$

Notice that, in this case, for all $\xi_1, \xi_2 \in \mathcal{X}, k \in (0,1)$ and $t > 0$, we have

$$\mathcal{H}\Big([\mathcal{T}\xi_1]_{\alpha_{\mathcal{T}}}, [\mathcal{T}\xi_2]_{\alpha_{\mathcal{T}}}, t\Big) = \mathcal{N}(\mathcal{S}(\xi_1), \mathcal{S}(\xi_2), t) \geq \mathcal{N}(\xi_1, \xi_2, t). \tag{19}$$

Therefore, Theorem 1 can be applied to find $\xi \in \mathcal{X}$ such that $\xi \in \{\mathcal{S}\xi\}$; that is, ξ is an FP.

Uniqueness: Suppose that there exist two fixed points $u, v \in \mathcal{X}$; then by the contraction condition, we obtain

$$\begin{aligned} \mathcal{N}(\mathcal{T}u, \mathcal{T}v, t) = \mathcal{N}(u, v, t) \ & \geq \mathcal{N}(u, v, \tfrac{t}{k}) \\ & \geq \mathcal{N}(\mathcal{T}u, \mathcal{T}v, \tfrac{t}{k}) \\ & \geq \mathcal{N}\Big(u, v, \tfrac{t}{k^2}\Big) \\ & \ \vdots \\ & \geq \mathcal{N}(u, v, \tfrac{t}{k^n}) \to 1, \text{as } n \to +\infty, \end{aligned}$$

which implies $u = v$. □

4. Proximal Contractions

4.1. Proximal Fuzzy Contraction

This section introduces a new concept called k-proximal fuzzy contraction related to $\mathcal{U}_\circ$. For $\mathcal{U}, \mathcal{V} \in C(2^{\mathcal{X}})$, we define the following:

- $\mathcal{U}_\circ = \{\xi \in \mathcal{U} : \mathcal{N}(\xi, \eta, t) = \mathcal{N}(\mathcal{U}, \mathcal{V}, t), \text{ for some } \eta \in \mathcal{V}\}$.
- $\mathcal{V}_\circ = \{\eta \in \mathcal{V} : \mathcal{N}(\xi, \eta, t) = \mathcal{N}(\mathcal{U}, \mathcal{V}, t), \text{ for some } \xi \in \mathcal{U}\}$.

Definition 10. *Let $\mathcal{U}$ and $\mathcal{V}$ be nonempty subsets of a θ-FMS $(\mathcal{X}, \mathcal{N}, *, \theta)$ and $\mathcal{T} : \mathcal{U} \to I^{\mathcal{V}}$ be a fuzzy mapping. Then a point $\xi \in \mathcal{X}$ is called an FBPP of $\mathcal{T}$ if there exists $\alpha \in (0,1]$ such that $\mathcal{N}(\xi, [\mathcal{T}\xi]_\alpha, t) = \mathcal{N}(\mathcal{U}, \mathcal{V}, t)$, for all $t > 0$.*

Definition 11. *Let $\mathcal{U}$ and $\mathcal{V}$ be non-empty subsets of a θ-FMS $(\mathcal{X}, \mathcal{N}, *, \theta)$. A fuzzy mapping $\mathcal{T} : \mathcal{U} \to I^{\mathcal{V}}$ is said to be a k-proximal fuzzy contraction with respect to $\mathcal{U}_\circ$ if there exists $k \in (0,1)$, such that, for each $\xi_1, \xi_2 \in \mathcal{U}_\circ, \alpha_{\mathcal{T}}(\xi_1), \alpha_{\mathcal{T}}(\xi_2) \in (0,1]$,*

$$\mathcal{V}_{\xi_1} = \Big\{\eta \in \mathcal{U}_0 : \mathcal{N}\Big(\eta, [\mathcal{T}\xi_1]_{\alpha_{\mathcal{T}}(\xi_1)}, t\Big) = \mathcal{N}(\mathcal{U}, \mathcal{V}, t), t > 0\Big\},$$

and

$$\mathcal{V}_{\xi_2} = \Big\{\eta \in \mathcal{U}_0 : \mathcal{N}\Big(\eta, [\mathcal{T}\xi_2]_{\alpha_{\mathcal{T}}(\xi_2)}, t\Big) = \mathcal{N}(\mathcal{U}, \mathcal{V}, t), t > 0\Big\}$$

are nonempty, closed, and bounded sets and

$$\mathcal{H}(\mathcal{V}_{\xi_1}, \mathcal{V}_{\xi_2}, kt) \geq \mathcal{N}(\xi_1, \xi_2, t). \tag{20}$$

Lemma 3. *Let $(\mathcal{U}, \mathcal{V})$ be a pair of nonempty subsets of a θ-FMS $(\mathcal{X}, \mathcal{N}, *, \theta)$ with $\mathcal{U}_\circ \neq \phi$. Let $\mathcal{T} : \mathcal{U} \to I^{\mathcal{V}}$ be a fuzzy mapping such that, for every $\xi \in \mathcal{U}_\circ$, $[\mathcal{T}\xi]_{\alpha_\mathcal{T}(\xi)} \cap \mathcal{V}_\circ$ is nonempty, and there exists $\alpha_\mathcal{T}(\xi) \in (0,1]$ with $[\mathcal{T}\xi]_{\alpha_\mathcal{T}(\xi)} \in C(2^{\mathcal{X}})$,then,*

1. *For all $\xi \in \mathcal{U}_\circ$, the set $\mathcal{V}_\xi$ is nonempty.*
2. *If $\mathcal{U}_\circ$ is closed and $\xi \in \mathcal{U}_\circ$, then $\mathcal{V}_\xi$ is closed.*

Proof. (1) Let $\xi \in \mathcal{U}_\circ$; since $[\mathcal{T}\xi]_{\alpha_\mathcal{T}(\xi)} \cap \mathcal{V}_\circ$ is nonempty, there exists $\eta \in [\mathcal{T}\xi]_{\alpha_\mathcal{T}(\xi)} \cap \mathcal{V}_\circ$, which implies that there exists $\zeta \in \mathcal{U}_\circ$ such that $\mathcal{N}(\zeta, \eta, t) = \mathcal{N}(\mathcal{U}, \mathcal{V}, t)$, for all $t > 0$. Therefore, $\mathcal{N}\left(\zeta, [\mathcal{T}\xi]_{\alpha_\mathcal{T}(\xi)}, t\right) = \mathcal{N}(\mathcal{U}, \mathcal{V}, t)$, proving that $\mathcal{V}_\xi$ is not empty.

(2) To prove that $\mathcal{V}_\xi$ is closed, consider a sequence $\{\eta_n\}$ in $\mathcal{V}_\xi$ that converges to a limit η. Since $\eta_n \in \mathcal{U}_\circ$ and satisfies

$$\mathcal{N}\left(\eta_n, [\mathcal{T}\xi]_{\alpha_\mathcal{T}(\xi)}, t\right) = \mathcal{N}(\mathcal{U}, \mathcal{V}, t), \quad \forall t > 0.$$

The continuity of $\mathcal{N}$ guarantees that

$$\mathcal{N}\left(\eta, [\mathcal{T}\xi]_{\alpha_\mathcal{T}(\xi)}, t\right) = \mathcal{N}(\mathcal{U}, \mathcal{V}, t), \quad \forall t > 0.$$

Since $\mathcal{U}_\circ$ is closed so $\eta \in \mathcal{U}_\circ$, it follows that $\eta \in \mathcal{V}_\xi$. Therefore, $\mathcal{V}_\xi$ must also be closed. □

Theorem 2. *Let $(\mathcal{U}, \mathcal{V})$ be a pair of nonempty subsets of a complete θ-FMS $(\mathcal{X}, \mathcal{N}, *, \theta)$ such that $\mathcal{U}_\circ$ is nonempty and closed. Assume that $\mathcal{T} : \mathcal{U} \to I^{\mathcal{V}}$ is a fuzzy mapping such that, for every $\xi \in \mathcal{U}$, there exists $\alpha_\mathcal{T}(\xi) \in (0,1]$ such that $[\mathcal{T}\xi]_{\alpha_\mathcal{T}(\xi)} \in C(2^{\mathcal{V}})$. Assume that the following conditions are also satisfied:*

1. *$\mathcal{T}$ is an k-proximal fuzzy contraction with respect to $\mathcal{U}_\circ$;*
2. *for each $\xi \in \mathcal{U}_\circ$, $[\mathcal{T}\xi]_{\alpha_\mathcal{T}(\xi)} \cap \mathcal{V}_\circ$ is nonempty.*

Then there exist $\xi \in \mathcal{U}$ such that $\mathcal{N}\left(\xi, [\mathcal{T}\xi]_{\alpha_\mathcal{T}(\xi)}, t\right) = \mathcal{N}(\mathcal{U}, \mathcal{V}, t)$.

Proof. Let $\xi_0 \in \mathcal{U}_\circ$. By Lemma 3 (1), we see that $\mathcal{V}_{\xi 0}$ is a nonempty set. Let $\xi_1 \in \mathcal{V}_{\xi_0}$. Then $\xi_1 \in \mathcal{U}_\circ$, which implies that $\mathcal{V}_{\xi_1}$ is nonempty. $\mathcal{U}_\circ$ is closed, and by Lemma 3 (2), for each $\xi \in \mathcal{U}_\circ$, we get that $\mathcal{V}_\xi$ is closed and therefore is a compact subset of $[\mathcal{T}\xi]_{\alpha_\mathcal{T}(\xi)}$, so we can choose $\xi_2 \in \mathcal{V}_{\xi_1}$ such that

$$\mathcal{N}(\xi_1, \xi_2, t) \geq \mathcal{H}(\mathcal{V}_{\xi_0}, \mathcal{V}_{\xi_1}, t).$$

Continuing this process, we obtain a sequence $\{\xi_n\}$ in $\mathcal{U}_\circ$ such that $\mathcal{N}(\xi_{n+1}, \xi_n, t) = \mathcal{N}(\mathcal{U}, \mathcal{V}, t)$ and, by Lemma 2, we have

$$\mathcal{N}(\xi_{n+1}, \xi_n, t) \geq \mathcal{H}(\mathcal{V}_{\xi_n}, \mathcal{V}_{\xi_{n-1}}, t) \text{ for all } n \in \mathbb{N}.$$

Next, we show that $\{\xi_n\}$ is a Cauchy sequence in $\mathcal{U}_\circ$, and its limit is a BPP of $\mathcal{T}$. Now, by (20) together with Lemma 2, for every $t > 0$, we find that

$$\begin{aligned}\mathcal{N}(\xi_n, \xi_{n+1}, t) &\geq \mathcal{H}(\mathcal{V}_{\xi_n}, \mathcal{V}_{\xi_{n-1}}, t)\\ &\geq \mathcal{N}(\xi_{n-1}, \xi_n, \tfrac{t}{k})\\ &\geq \mathcal{H}(\mathcal{V}_{\xi_{n-1}}, \mathcal{V}_{\xi_{n-2}}, \tfrac{t}{k})\\ &\geq \mathcal{N}\Big(\xi_{n-2}, \xi_{n-1}, \tfrac{t}{k^2}\Big)\\ &\vdots\\ &\geq \mathcal{H}\Big(\mathcal{V}_{\xi_0}, \mathcal{V}_{\xi_1}, \tfrac{t}{k^{n-1}}\Big)\\ &\geq \mathcal{N}(\xi_0, \xi_1, \tfrac{t}{k^n}).\end{aligned} \tag{21}$$

Using (N4) and (21), let $m > n$, for all $t \in Im(\theta)$, which means that there exists $s_i \leq t$ for all $r_i \leq t, i = 1, 2, \cdots, m-n-1$ such that

$$\begin{aligned}\mathcal{N}(\xi_n, \xi_m, t) &\geq \mathcal{N}(\xi_n, \xi_{n+1}, s_1) * \mathcal{N}(\xi_{n+1}, \xi_m, r_1)\\ &\geq \mathcal{N}(\xi_n, \xi_{n+1}, s_1) * \mathcal{N}(\xi_{n+1}, \xi_{n+2}, s_2) * \mathcal{N}(\xi_{n+2}, \xi_m, r_2)\\ &\geq \mathcal{N}(\xi_n, \xi_{n+1}, s_1) * \mathcal{N}(\xi_{n+1}, \xi_{n+2}, s_2) * \cdots * \mathcal{N}(\xi_{m-1}, \xi_m, s_{m-n-1})\\ &\geq \mathcal{N}\Big(\xi_0, \xi_1, \tfrac{s_1}{k^{n-1}}\Big) * \cdots * \mathcal{N}\Big(\xi_0, \xi_1, \tfrac{s_{m-n-1}}{k^{m-n-1}}\Big).\end{aligned}$$

It follows that $\{\xi_n\}$ is a Cauchy sequence in $\mathcal{U}_\circ$. Since $\mathcal{U}_\circ$ is closed, there exists $\xi \in \mathcal{U}_\circ$ such that $\{\xi_n\}$ converges to ξ as $n \to +\infty$. By Lemma 3, it follows that $\mathcal{V}_\xi$ is nonempty and closed. Thus, there exists $\xi'_n \in \mathcal{V}_\xi$ such that

$$\mathcal{N}(\xi_{n+1}, \xi'_n, t) \geq \mathcal{H}(\mathcal{V}_{\xi_n}, \mathcal{V}_\xi, t) \geq \mathcal{N}\Big(\xi_n, \xi, \frac{t}{k}\Big),$$

which implies $\lim_{n\to+\infty} \mathcal{N}(\xi_{n+1}, \xi'_n, t) = 1$. Therefore, $\{\xi'_n\}$ converges to ξ, and since $\mathcal{V}_\xi$ is closed, it follows $\xi \in \mathcal{V}_\xi$, that is, $\mathcal{N}\Big(\xi, [\mathcal{T}\xi]_{\alpha_\mathcal{T}(\xi)}, t\Big) = \mathcal{N}(\mathcal{U}, \mathcal{V}, t)$. □

Example 6. *Consider $\mathcal{X} = \mathbb{R}^2$. Define $a * b = a \cdot b$, $\theta \in \Theta, \theta(t,s) = t + s + ts, t, s \geq 0$ and $\mathcal{N} : \mathcal{X} \times \mathcal{X} \times (0, +\infty) \to (0, 1]$ by*

$$\mathcal{N}((a_1, a_2), (b_1, b_2), t) = \exp\Big(-\frac{|a_1 - b_1| + |a_2 - b_2|}{t}\Big). \tag{22}$$

Suppose $\mathcal{U} = \{(1, \xi) : \xi \in [0,1]\}$ and $\mathcal{V} = \{(0, \eta), \eta \in [0,1]\}$. Let $\alpha \in (0,1]$; $\mathcal{T} : \mathcal{U} \to I^{\mathcal{V}}$ is defined by

(i) If $\xi = 0$

$$\mathcal{T}((1,0))((0,u)) = \begin{cases} 1, & \text{if } u = 0,\\ 0, & \text{if } u \neq 0.\end{cases}$$

(ii) If $\xi \neq 0$

$$\mathcal{T}(1,\xi)(0,u) = \begin{cases} \alpha, & \text{if } 0 < u < \frac{\xi}{4},\\ \frac{\alpha}{2}, & \text{if } \frac{\xi}{4} \leq u \leq \frac{\xi}{2},\\ \frac{\alpha}{4}, & \text{if } \frac{\xi}{2} < u \leq \xi.\end{cases}$$

$\mathcal{N}(\mathcal{U},\mathcal{V},t) = e^{\frac{-1}{t}}, t > 0$. *As* $\mathcal{U}_\circ = \mathcal{U}, \mathcal{V}_\circ = \mathcal{V}$, *for every* $(1,\xi) \in \mathcal{U}$, *there exists* $\frac{\alpha}{2}_{\mathcal{T}}(\xi) \in (0,1]$; *we obtain*

$$[\mathcal{T}(1,\xi)]_{\frac{\alpha}{2}} = \{(0,\eta) \in \mathcal{V} : \mathcal{T}((1,\xi))((0,\eta)) \geq \tfrac{\alpha}{2}\} = \{0\} \times \left[0,\tfrac{\xi}{2}\right] \in C(2^{\mathcal{V}}).$$

We can see for each $\xi \in \mathcal{U}_\circ$ *we have that* $[\mathcal{T}\xi]_{\alpha_{\mathcal{T}}(\xi)} \cap \mathcal{V}_\circ$ *is nonempty. Now, we show that the fuzzy mapping* $\mathcal{T} : \mathcal{U} \to I^{\mathcal{V}}$ *is a k-proximal fuzzy contraction with respect to* $\mathcal{U}_\circ$. *Let* $\xi_1, \xi_2 \in \mathcal{U}_\circ$; *then we have* $\mathcal{V}_{\xi_1} = \left\{\left(1, \frac{\xi_1}{2}\right)\right\}$, *and* $\mathcal{V}_{\xi_2} = \left\{\left(1, \frac{\xi_2}{2}\right)\right\}$ *are non-empty, closed, and bounded, and the condition*

$$\mathcal{H}(\mathcal{V}_{\xi_1}, \mathcal{V}_{\xi_2}, kt) \geq \mathcal{N}(\xi_1, \xi_2, t) \tag{23}$$

holds with $k = \frac{1}{2} \in (0,1)$. *Consequently, all the conditions of Theorem 2 are satisfied to find an* $\frac{\alpha}{2} \in (0,1]$ *such that* $\mathcal{N}((1,0), [\mathcal{T}(1,0)]_{\frac{\alpha}{2}}, t) = \mathcal{N}(\mathcal{U},\mathcal{V},t)$, *for all* $t > 0$.

4.2. Multivalued Proximal Mappings

Definition 12. *Let* $\mathcal{U}$ *and* $\mathcal{V}$ *be non-empty subsets of a θ-FMS* $(\mathcal{X},\mathcal{N},*,\theta)$. *The multivalued mapping* $\mathcal{S} : \mathcal{U} \to 2^{\mathcal{V}} \setminus \phi$ *is said to be a k-proximal multivalued contraction with respect to* $\mathcal{U}_\circ$ *if there exists* $k \in (0,1)$, *such that, for each* $\xi_1, \xi_2 \in \mathcal{U}_\circ$,

$$\mathcal{V}_{\xi_1} = \{\eta \in \mathcal{U}_0 : \mathcal{N}(\eta, \mathcal{S}\xi_1, t) = \mathcal{N}(\mathcal{U},\mathcal{V},t), t > 0\},$$

and

$$\mathcal{V}_{\xi_2} = \{\eta \in \mathcal{U}_0 : \mathcal{N}(\eta, \mathcal{S}\xi_2, t) = \mathcal{N}(\mathcal{U},\mathcal{V},t), t > 0\},$$

two sets are non-empty, closed, bounded, and

$$\mathcal{H}(\mathcal{V}_{\xi_1}, \mathcal{V}_{\xi_2}, kt) \geq \mathcal{N}(\xi_1, \xi_2, t). \tag{24}$$

Corollary 3. *Let* $(\mathcal{U},\mathcal{V})$ *be a pair of nonempty subsets of a complete θ-FMS* $(\mathcal{X},\mathcal{N},*,\theta)$ *such that* $\mathcal{U}_\circ$ *is nonempty and closed. Assume that* $\mathcal{S} : \mathcal{U} \to 2^{\mathcal{V}} \setminus \varnothing$ *is a multivalued mapping satisfying the following conditions:*

1. $\mathcal{S}$ *is a k-proximal fuzzy contraction with respect to* $\mathcal{U}_\circ$.
2. *For each* $\xi \in \mathcal{U}_\circ, \mathcal{T}\xi \cap \mathcal{V}_\circ$ *is nonempty.*

Then there exists some $\xi \in \mathcal{U}$ *such that* $\mathcal{U}$ *such that* $\mathcal{N}(\xi, \mathcal{T}\xi, t) = \mathcal{N}(\mathcal{U},\mathcal{V},t)$.

Proof. Let $\alpha_{\mathcal{T}} : \mathcal{X} \to (0,1]$ be an arbitrary mapping, and consider a fuzzy mapping $\mathcal{T} : \mathcal{U} \to \mathcal{I}^{\mathcal{V}}$ defined as follows:

$$\mathcal{T}(\xi)(u) = \begin{cases} \alpha_{\mathcal{T}}(\xi), & \text{if } u \in \mathcal{S}\xi, \\ 0, & \text{if } u \notin \mathcal{S}\xi. \end{cases} \tag{25}$$

Then, for all $\xi \in \mathcal{U}$, we have

$$[\mathcal{T}\xi]_{\alpha_{\mathcal{T}}} = \{u \in \mathcal{U} : \mathcal{T}(\xi)(u) \geq \alpha_{\mathcal{T}}(\xi)\} = \mathcal{S}\xi. \tag{26}$$

Thus, for each $\xi_1, \xi_2 \in \mathcal{U}_\circ$,

$$\mathcal{V}_{\xi_1} = \left\{\eta \in \mathcal{U}_0 : \mathcal{N}(\eta, \mathcal{S}\xi_1, t) = \mathcal{N}\left(\eta, [\mathcal{T}\xi_1]_{\alpha_{\mathcal{T}}}, t\right) = \mathcal{N}(\mathcal{U},\mathcal{V},t), t > 0\right\},$$

and

$$\mathcal{V}_{\xi_2} = \left\{ \eta \in \mathcal{U}_0 : \mathcal{N}(\eta, \mathcal{S}\xi_2, t) = \mathcal{N}\left(\eta, [\mathcal{T}\xi_2]_{\alpha_\mathcal{T}}, t\right) = \mathcal{N}(\mathcal{U}, \mathcal{V}, t), t > 0 \right\},$$

two sets are non-empty, closed, bounded, and

$$\mathcal{H}(\mathcal{V}_{\xi_1}, \mathcal{V}_{\xi_2}, kt) \geq \mathcal{N}(\xi_1, \xi_2, t). \tag{27}$$

As a result, Theorem 2 is applicable. □

4.3. Single-Valued Proximal Contraction

Definition 13. *Let $\mathcal{U}$ and $\mathcal{V}$ be non-empty subsets of a θ-FMS $(\mathcal{X}, \mathcal{N}, *, \theta)$. A single-valued mapping $\mathcal{T} : \mathcal{U} \to \mathcal{V}$ is said to be a k-proximal contraction concerning $\mathcal{U}_\circ$ if there exists $k \in (0,1)$, such that, for each $\xi_1, \xi_2, \eta_1, \eta_2 \in \mathcal{U}_\circ$,*

$$\begin{cases} \mathcal{N}(\eta_1, \mathcal{T}\xi_1, t) = \mathcal{N}(\mathcal{U}, \mathcal{V}, t), \\ \mathcal{N}(\eta_2, \mathcal{T}\xi_2, t) = \mathcal{N}(\mathcal{U}, \mathcal{V}, t), \end{cases}$$

implies that

$$\mathcal{N}(\eta_1, \eta_2, kt) \geq \mathcal{N}(\xi_1, \xi_2, t). \tag{28}$$

Corollary 4. *Let $(\mathcal{U}, \mathcal{V})$ be a pair of nonempty subsets of a complete θ-FMS $(\mathcal{X}, \mathcal{N}, *, \theta)$ such that $\mathcal{U}_\circ$ is nonempty and closed. Let $\mathcal{S} : \mathcal{U} \to \mathcal{V}$ be a single-valued mapping. Assume that the subsequent conditions are also met, as follows:*

1. *$\mathcal{S}$ is a k-proximal contraction with respect to $\mathcal{U}_\circ$.*
2. *For each $\xi \in \mathcal{U}_\circ, \mathcal{S}\xi \in \mathcal{V}_\circ$.*

Then there exists $\xi \in \mathcal{U}$ such that $\mathcal{N}(\xi, \mathcal{S}\xi, t) = \mathcal{N}(\mathcal{U}, \mathcal{V}, t)$.

Proof. Let $\alpha_\mathcal{S} : \mathcal{X} \to (0,1]$ be an arbitrary mapping, and consider a fuzzy mapping $\mathcal{S} : \mathcal{U} \to \mathcal{I}^\mathcal{V}$ defined as follows:

$$\mathcal{T}(\xi)(u) = \begin{cases} \alpha_\mathcal{T}(\xi), & \text{if } u = \mathcal{S}\xi, \\ 0, & \text{if } u \neq \mathcal{S}\xi. \end{cases} \tag{29}$$

Then, for all $\xi \in \mathcal{U}$, we have

$$[\mathcal{T}\xi]_{\alpha_\mathcal{T}} = \{u \in \mathcal{U} : \mathcal{T}(\xi)(u) \geq \alpha_\mathcal{L}(\xi)\} = \{\mathcal{S}\xi\}. \tag{30}$$

For each $\xi_1, \xi_2 \in \mathcal{U}_\circ$, we have

$$\mathcal{V}_{\xi_1} = \left\{ \eta_1 \in \mathcal{U}_0 : \mathcal{N}(\eta_1, \{\mathcal{S}\xi_1\}, t) = \mathcal{N}\left(\eta_1, [\mathcal{T}\xi_1]_{\alpha_\mathcal{T}}, t\right) = \mathcal{N}(\mathcal{U}, \mathcal{V}, t), t > 0 \right\} = \{\eta_1\},$$

and

$$\mathcal{V}_{\xi_2} = \left\{ \eta_2 \in \mathcal{U}_0 : \mathcal{N}(\eta_2, \{\mathcal{S}\xi_2\}, t) = \mathcal{N}\left(\eta_2, [\mathcal{T}\xi_2]_{\alpha_\mathcal{T}}, t\right) = \mathcal{N}(\mathcal{U}, \mathcal{V}, t), t > 0 \right\} = \{\eta_2\},$$

are two sets non-empty, closed, bounded, and

$$\mathcal{H}(\mathcal{V}_{\xi_1}, \mathcal{V}_{\xi_2}, kt) = \mathcal{N}(\eta_1, \eta_2, kt) \geq \mathcal{N}(\xi_1, \xi_2, t). \tag{31}$$

Therefore, Theorem 1 can be applied to find $\xi \in \mathcal{U}$ such that $\xi \in \{\mathcal{T}(\xi)\}$, which further implies $\mathcal{N}(\xi, \mathcal{T}(\xi), t) = \mathcal{N}(\mathcal{U}, \mathcal{V}, t)$, for all $t > 0$. □

Corollary 5. *Theorem 1 implies Theorem 2.*

Proof. Define $\mathcal{G} : \mathcal{U}_\circ \to C(2^{\mathcal{U}_\circ})$ by

$$[\mathcal{G}\xi]_{\alpha_{\mathcal{G}}(\xi)} = \left\{\eta \in \mathcal{U}_\circ : \mathcal{N}\left(\eta, [\mathcal{T}\xi]_{\alpha_{\mathcal{T}}(\xi)}, t\right) = \mathcal{N}(\mathcal{U}, \mathcal{V}, t), t > 0\right\},$$

for $\xi \in \mathcal{U}_\circ, \alpha_{\mathcal{G}}(\xi) \in (0,1]$. It follows from Lemma 3 that $[\mathcal{G}\xi]_{\alpha_{\mathcal{G}}(\xi)}$ is a nonempty, closed, and bounded subset of $\mathcal{U}_\circ$ for each $\xi \in \mathcal{U}_\circ$ and so $[\mathcal{G}\xi]_{\alpha_{\mathcal{G}}(\xi)}$ is well defined. Since $\mathcal{T}$ is a k-proximal fuzzy contraction with respect to $\mathcal{U}_\circ$,

$$\mathcal{H}\left([\mathcal{G}\xi]_{\alpha_{\mathcal{G}}(\xi)}, [\mathcal{G}\eta]_{\alpha_{\mathcal{G}}(\eta)}, kt\right) = \mathcal{H}(\mathcal{V}_\xi, \mathcal{V}_\eta, kt) \geq \mathcal{N}(\xi, \eta, t),$$

for all $\xi, \eta \in \mathcal{U}_\circ$. It now follows from Theorem 1 that there exists $\zeta \in \mathcal{U}_\circ$ such that $\zeta \in [\mathcal{G}\zeta]_{\alpha_{\mathcal{T}}(\zeta)}$. By the definition of the mapping $[\mathcal{G}\zeta]_{\alpha_{\mathcal{G}}(\xi)}$, the point ζ satisfies $\mathcal{N}\left(\zeta, [\mathcal{T}\zeta]_{\alpha_{\mathcal{T}}(\zeta)}, t\right) = \mathcal{N}(\mathcal{U}, \mathcal{V}, t)$, and this completes the proof that Theorem 1 implies Theorem 2. □

5. Application to Fuzzy Fractional Differential Equations

The fuzzy Hadamard Ψ-CTFD was introduced by Abdou Amir et al. [15] as a comprehensive generalization, established through the integration of various fractional operators, including tempered Riemann–Liouville,Ψ-Riemann–Liouville–Hadamard, Riemann–Liouville, Caputo, and Ψ-Caputo. This unification provides a cohesive framework for understanding their applications across different mathematical settings, offering a systematic perspective on these operators and expanding their potential uses in various research fields and mathematical analysis.

Definition 14 ([15])**.** *Let ξ be a fuzzy number-valued function $n-1 < \alpha < n, n \in \mathbb{N}, \gamma, p, q \geq 0$ and $\Psi \in C^n([a,b], \mathbb{R})$ such that $\Psi'(t) > 0, \forall t \in [a,b]$. The design of the generalized Hadamard Ψ-CTFD of level α of the function ξ is defined by*

$$\begin{aligned} {}^{CH}\mathcal{D}_0^{\alpha,\gamma,p,q,\Psi}\xi(t) = \; & \frac{E_{p,q}(-\gamma\ln(\Psi(t)))}{\Gamma(n-\alpha)} \odot \int_a^t \frac{\Psi'(s)}{\Psi(s)}\left[\ln\left(\frac{\Psi(t)}{\Psi(s)}\right)\right]^{n-\alpha-1} \\ & \odot \left[\frac{\Psi(s)}{\Psi'(s)}\frac{d}{ds}\right]^n (E_{p,q}(\gamma\ln(\Psi(s))) \odot \xi(s)ds, \end{aligned} \tag{32}$$

where $E_{p,q}(s) = \sum\limits_{k=0}^{+\infty} \frac{s^k}{\Gamma(pk+q)}, p, q > 0, Re(s) > 0.$

First of all, we should consider the multiplication of a fuzzy number by a scalar in its level-wise form.

Suppose that $k \in \mathbb{R}$ is a scalar, and M is a fuzzy number. Then, in level-wise form, we have

$$k \odot M[r] = \begin{cases} [k\cdot M_l(r),\ k\cdot M_u(r)] & \text{if } k \geq 0, \\ \cdot M_u(r),\ k\cdot M_l(r)] & \text{if } k < 0, \end{cases} \quad \text{for all } r \in [0,1].$$

For any two arbitrary fuzzy numbers M and N, and any fixed $r \in [0,1]$, if $M \odot N = K$, then we have

$$K[r] = [K_l(r), K_u(r)] = M[r] \odot N[r] = [M_l(r), M_u(r)] \odot [N_l(r), N_u(r)].$$

Then,

$$K_l(r) = \min\left\{\begin{array}{l} M_l(r)\cdot N_l(r), \\ M_l(r)\cdot N_u(r), \\ M_u(r)\cdot N_l(r), \\ M_u(r)\cdot N_u(r) \end{array}\right\}, \quad K_u(r) = \max\left\{\begin{array}{l} M_l(r)\cdot N_l(r), \\ M_l(r)\cdot N_u(r), \\ M_u(r)\cdot N_l(r), \\ M_u(r)\cdot N_u(r) \end{array}\right\}.$$

As an application, we extend the SIR dynamics model investigated by Subramanian et al. [23] to include the fuzzy Hadamard Ψ-CTFD. Here, the susceptible population $S(t)$, the infected population $I(t)$, and the removed population $R(t)$ compose the overall population $N(t)$, structured as follows:

$$\left\{\begin{array}{l} {}^{CH}\mathcal{D}_0^{\alpha,\gamma,p,q,\Psi} S(t) = (1-p)\pi - \widetilde{\beta} SI - \mu S, \\ {}^{CH}\mathcal{D}_0^{\alpha,\gamma,p,q,\Psi} I(t) = \widetilde{\beta} SI - (\widetilde{\gamma} + \mu) I, \\ {}^{CH}\mathcal{D}_0^{\alpha,\gamma,p,q,\Psi} R(t) = p\pi + \widetilde{\gamma} I - \mu R, \end{array}\right. \tag{33}$$

where $\mu, \pi, p, \widetilde{\beta}, \widetilde{\gamma}$ represent natural death rate, birth date, fraction of the vaccinated population at birth, contact rate of susceptible individuals, and infected individuals who recover at a rate, respectively. Now, the right-hand side of (33) becomes

$$\left\{\begin{array}{l} A(t, S(t)) = (1-p)\pi - \widetilde{\beta} SI - \mu S, \\ B(t, I(t)) = \widetilde{\beta} SI - (\widetilde{\gamma} + \mu) I, \\ D(t, R(t)) = p\pi + \widetilde{\gamma} I - \mu R. \end{array}\right. \tag{34}$$

where A, B, D are fuzzy functions. Then, for $r \in [0,1]$, the model in Equation (33) is expressed as

$$\left\{\begin{array}{l} {}^{CH}\mathcal{D}_0^{\alpha,\gamma,p,q,\Psi} S(t) = A(t, S(t)), \\ {}^{CH}\mathcal{D}_0^{\alpha,\gamma,p,q,\Psi} I(t) = B(t, I(t)), \\ {}^{CH}\mathcal{D}_0^{\alpha,\gamma,p,q,\Psi} R(t) = D(t, R(t)), \end{array}\right. \tag{35}$$

with fuzzy initial conditions

$$\begin{array}{l} \widetilde{S}(0,r) = \left[\underline{S}(0,r), \overline{S}(0,r)\right], \\ \widetilde{I}(0,r) = \left[\underline{I}(0,r), \overline{I}(0,r)\right], \\ \widetilde{R}(0,r) = \left[\underline{R}(0,r), \overline{R}(0,r)\right]. \end{array} \tag{36}$$

Let us put

$$G(t) = \left\{\begin{array}{l} S(t), \\ I(t), \\ R(t), \end{array}\right. \tag{37}$$

$$G(0,r) = \left\{\begin{array}{l} \widetilde{S}(0,r), \\ \widetilde{I}(0,r), \\ R(0,r) \end{array}\right. \tag{38}$$

$$F(t,G(t)) = \begin{cases} A(t,S(t)), \\ B(t,I(t)), \\ D(t,R(t)). \end{cases} \tag{39}$$

Then, problem (33) can be reformulated as

$$\begin{aligned} {}^{CH}\mathcal{D}_0^{\alpha,\gamma,p,q,\Psi} \quad & G(t) = F(t,G(t)), t \in [0,a], 0 < \alpha < 1. \\ & G(0,r) = G_0 \in E^1, \end{aligned} \tag{40}$$

where ${}^{CH}\mathcal{D}_0^{\alpha,\gamma,p,q,\Psi}$ design the generalized Hadamard Ψ-CTFD of level α and $F \in C([0,a] \times E^1, E^1)$, Ψ is a continuously differentiable, increasing function on the interval $[0,\infty)$ with $\Psi(0) = 0, \Psi'(t) > 0$ for all $t \in (0,+\infty)$, $\lim_{t\to+\infty} \Psi(t) = +\infty$.

A complete fuzzy θ-metric on $C([0,a] \times E^1, E^1)$ is defined as follows:

$$\mathcal{N}(G_1(t), G_2(t), \tau) = \exp\left(-\frac{\| G_1(t) - G_2(t) \|}{\tau}\right), \tau > 0, \tag{41}$$

where $\| G_1(t) - G_2(t) \| = \max_{t\in[0,a]}\{|S_1(t) - S_2(t)| + |I_1(t) - I_2(t)| + |R_1(t) - R_2(t)|\}$ and $\theta(r,s) = \sqrt{r^2+s^2}, a * b = a\cdot b$.

Lemma 4 ([15]). *Let $G(t)$ represent the solution to Equation* (40).

- *If $G(t)$ is Caputo (i)-gH differentiable,*

$$\begin{aligned} G(t) = \;& E_{p,q}(-\gamma \ln(\Psi(t))) \odot \xi(0) + \frac{1}{\Gamma(\alpha)} \\ & \odot \int_0^t \frac{\Psi'(s)}{\Psi(s)} \left[\ln\left(\frac{\Psi(t)}{\Psi(s)}\right)\right]^{\alpha-1} E_{p,q}\left(-\gamma \ln\left(\frac{\Psi(t)}{\Psi(s)}\right)\right) \odot f(s,\xi(s))ds. \end{aligned} \tag{42}$$

- *If $G(t)$ is Caputo (ii)-gH differentiable,*

$$\begin{aligned} G(t) = \;& E_{p,q}\left(-\gamma \ln(\Psi(t))\right) \odot \xi(0) \ominus \frac{-1}{\Gamma(\alpha)} \\ & \odot \int_0^t \frac{\Psi'(s)}{\Psi(s)} \left[\ln\left(\frac{\Psi(t)}{\Psi(s)}\right)\right]^{\alpha-1} E_{p,q}\left(-\gamma \ln\left(\frac{\Psi(t)}{\Psi(s)}\right)\right) \odot f(s,\xi(s))ds. \end{aligned} \tag{43}$$

Theorem 3. *Assume that $F \in C([0,a] \times E^1, E^1)$ is bounded such that*

$$\| F(t,G_1(t)) - F(t,G_1(t)) \| \le M \| G_1(t) - G_1(t) \|, \text{ for all } t \in [0,a] \tag{44}$$

such that $\frac{M}{\gamma^\alpha} < 1$. Then by Theorem 1, Equation (35) has a unique solution for two cases in Lemma 4.

Proof. WOLG, assume that $G(t)$ is Caputo (i)-gH differentiable. Consider a closed convex subset $\mathcal{X} = \{G \in C([0,a] \times E^1, E^1) : \| G(t) - E_{p,q}(-\gamma \ln(\Psi(t))) \odot G(0) \| \le R\}$, where $R = \frac{N}{\gamma^\alpha}, N = \| f(t,G(t)) \|$. Additionally, consider a mapping $\mathcal{P}_G(t)$ over $\mathcal{X}$ such that

$$\begin{aligned} \mathcal{P}_G(t) = \;& E_{p,q}(-\gamma \ln(\Psi(t))) \odot G(0) + \frac{1}{\Gamma(\alpha)} \\ & \odot \int_0^t \frac{\Psi'(s)}{\Psi(s)} \left[\ln\left(\frac{\Psi(t)}{\Psi(s)}\right)\right]^{\alpha-1} E_{p,q}\left(-\gamma \ln\left(\frac{\Psi(t)}{\Psi(s)}\right)\right) \odot f(s,G(s))ds. \end{aligned} \tag{45}$$

First, we show $\mathcal{P}_G(t)$ maps $\mathcal{X}$ into $\mathcal{X}, as follows:$

$$\begin{aligned}
&\| \mathcal{P}_G(t) - E_{p,q}(-\gamma \ln(\Psi(t))) \odot G(0) \| \\
&\leq \frac{1}{\Gamma(\alpha)} \int_0^t \frac{\Psi'(s)}{\Psi(s)} \left[\ln\left(\frac{\Psi(t)}{\Psi(s)}\right)\right]^{\alpha-1} E_{p,q}\left(-\gamma \ln\left(\frac{\Psi(t)}{\Psi(s)}\right)\right) \odot \| f(s, G(s)) \| ds \\
&\leq \frac{N}{\Gamma(\alpha)} \int_0^t \frac{\Psi'(s)}{\Psi(s)} \left[\ln\left(\frac{\Psi(t)}{\Psi(s)}\right)\right]^{\alpha-1} E_{p,q}\left(-\gamma \ln\left(\frac{\Psi(t)}{\Psi(s)}\right)\right) ds.
\end{aligned}$$

Let us make a change to variables by putting $u = \ln\left(\frac{\Psi(t)}{\Psi(s)}\right)$, which implies that $ds = \frac{-\Psi(s)}{\Psi'(s)} du$. Thus,

$$\begin{aligned}
\| \mathcal{P}_G(t) - E_{p,q}(-\gamma \ln(\Psi(t))) \odot G(0) \| \quad &\leq \frac{N}{\Gamma(\alpha)} \int_0^t \frac{\Psi'(s)}{\Psi(s)} \left[\ln\left(\frac{\Psi(t)}{\Psi(s)}\right)\right]^{\alpha-1} E_{p,q}\left(-\gamma \ln\left(\frac{\Psi(t)}{\Psi(s)}\right)\right) ds \\
&\leq \frac{N}{\Gamma(\alpha)} \int_0^{\ln \Psi(t)} \frac{\Psi'(s)}{\Psi(s)} u^{\alpha-1} E_{p,q}(-\gamma u)) du \\
&\leq \frac{N}{\Gamma(\alpha)} \int_0^{\ln \Psi(t)} \frac{\Psi'(s)}{\Psi(s)} u^{\alpha-1} \exp(-\gamma u)) du \\
&\leq \frac{N}{\Gamma(\alpha)} \int_0^{+\infty} \frac{\Psi'(s)}{\Psi(s)} u^{\alpha-1} \exp(-\gamma u)) du \\
&= \frac{N}{\gamma^\alpha} = R.
\end{aligned}$$

Let $\beta : C([0,a] \times E^1, E^1) \to [0,1]$ be a mapping. Consider a fuzzy mapping $\mathcal{T} : \mathcal{X} \to \mathcal{I}^{\mathcal{X}}$, defined by

$$\mu_{\mathcal{T}(G)} r = \begin{cases} \beta(G), & \text{if } r(t) = \mathcal{P}_G(t), \\ 0, & \text{otherwise.} \end{cases} \tag{46}$$

Therefore, we have

$$[\mathcal{T}G]_{\beta(G)} = \{r(t) \in \mathcal{X} : (\mathcal{T}(G)(t) \geq \beta(G)\} = \{\mathcal{P}_G(t)\}. \tag{47}$$

Therefore, we have for all $\tau > 0$,

$$\begin{aligned}
&\mathcal{H}\left([\mathcal{T}G_1]_{\beta(G_1)}, [\mathcal{T}G_2]_{\beta(G_2)}, k\tau\right) \\
&= \min\left\{ \inf_{G_1 \in [\mathcal{T}G_1]_{\beta(G_1)}} \mathcal{N}\left(G_1, [\mathcal{T}G_2]_{\beta(G_2)}, k\tau\right), \inf_{G_2 \in [\mathcal{T}G_2]_{\beta(G_2)}} \mathcal{N}\left(G_2, [\mathcal{T}G_1]_{\beta(G_1)}, k\tau\right) \right\} \\
&= \inf_{t \in [0,a]} \mathcal{N}(\mathcal{P}_{G_1}(t), \mathcal{P}_{G_2}(t), k\tau) \\
&\geq \inf_{t \in [0,a]} \exp\left(\frac{-\frac{1}{\Gamma(\alpha))} \odot \int_0^t \frac{\Psi'(s)}{\Psi(s)} [\ln(\frac{\Psi(t)}{\Psi(s)})]^{\alpha-1} E_{p,q}(-\gamma \ln(\frac{\Psi(t)}{\Psi(s)})) \odot \| F(s, G_1(s)) - F(s, G_2(s)) \| ds}{k\tau}\right) \\
&\geq \inf_{t \in [0,a]} \exp\left(\frac{-\frac{M\|G_1 - G_2\|}{\Gamma(\beta)} \odot \int_0^t \frac{\Psi'(s)}{\Psi(s)} [\ln(\frac{\Psi(t)}{\Psi(s)})]^{\alpha-1} E_{p,q}(-\gamma \ln(\frac{\Psi(t)}{\Psi(s)})) ds}{k\tau}\right) \\
&\geq \inf_{t \in [0,a]} \exp\left(\frac{-\frac{M\|G_1 - G_2\|}{\Gamma(\alpha)} \odot \int_0^{\ln \Psi(t)} u^{\alpha-1} E_{p,q}(-\gamma u) du}{k\tau}\right) \\
&\geq \exp\left(\frac{-\frac{M\|G_1 - G_2\|}{\Gamma(\alpha)} \odot \int_0^{+\infty} u^{\alpha-1} E_{p,q}(-\gamma u) du}{k\tau}\right) \\
&\geq \exp\left(\frac{-M\|G_1 - G_2\|}{\gamma^\alpha \tau}\right) \\
&= \exp\left(\frac{-M\|G_1 - G_2\|}{\gamma^\alpha k\tau}\right) \\
&= \mathcal{N}(G_1, G_2, \tau), k = \frac{M}{\gamma^\alpha} < 1.
\end{aligned}$$

Consequently, the requirements of Theorem 1 are satisfied, resulting in (35) possessing a unique type 1 solution; similar results are obtained when $G(t)$ is Caputo (ii)-gH differentiable. □

6. Conclusions and Future Works

This article addresses five key aspects. First, introducing θ-FMSs provides a unifying framework that generalizes various existing spaces. Second, it establishes FFP and FBPP theorems within θ-FMSs, deriving corresponding results for both single-valued and multivalued mappings. Third, it explores the intrinsic relationship between FFP and FBPP theorems, offering deeper insights into their interplay. From an application perspective, one of our main results is to establish existence conditions for solutions to the SIR dynamics model using the fuzzy Hadamard Ψ-Caputo tempered fractional derivative (Ψ-CTFD). To our knowledge, these findings are novel and fundamental in the study of θ-FMSs and fuzzy set theory. In future studies, these ideas could be expanded to more extensive areas like L-fuzzy mappings, intuitionistic fuzzy mappings, soft set-valued maps, and other diverse hybrid models within fuzzy mathematics.

Author Contributions: Conceptualization, N.A. and N.H.; methodology, N.H.; formal analysis, N.H.; investigation, N.A.; resources, N.A.; data curation, N.A.; writing—original draft preparation, N.A.; writing—review and editing, N.H.; visualization, N.H.; supervision, N.H.; project administration, N.H.; funding acquisition, N.A. All authors have read and agreed to the published version of the manuscript.

Funding: The researchers would like to thank the Deanship of Graduate Studies and Scientific Research at Qassim University for the financial support (QU-APC-2025).

Data Availability Statement: Data are contained within the article.

Conflicts of Interest: The authors declare no conflicts of interest.

Abbreviations

The following abbreviations are used in this manuscript:

θ-FMS	θ-fuzzy metric space
FSVM	fuzzy set-valued mapping
FS	fuzzy set
FFP	fuzzy fixed-point
CtN	continuous triangular norm
FP	fixed point
BCT	Banach contraction theorem
FSVMs	fuzzy set-valued mappings
BPP	best proximity point
BPFP	best proximity fuzzy point
SIR	Susceptible-Infectious-Removed dynamics
Hadamard Ψ-CTFD	Hadamard Ψ-Caputo tempered fractional derivative
WOLG	without loss of generality

References

1. Zadeh, L. Fuzzy sets. *Inf. Control* **1965**, *8*, 338–353. [CrossRef]
2. Heilpern, S. Fuzzy mappings and fixed point theorem. *J. Math. Anal. Appl.* **1981**, *83*, 566–569. [CrossRef]
3. Alamgir, N.; Kiran, Q.; Aydi, H.; Gaba, Y. Fuzzy fixed point results of generalized almost F-contractions in controlled metric spaces. *Adv. Differ. Equ.* **2021**, *2021*, 476. [CrossRef]
4. Alansari, M.; Mohammed, S.; Azam, A. Fuzzy Fixed Point Results in F-Metric Spaces with Applications. *J. Funct. Spaces* **2020**, *2020*, 5142815. [CrossRef]
5. Kumam, W.; Sukprasert, P.; Kumam, P.; Shoaib, A.; Shahzad, A.; Mahmood, Q. Some fuzzy fixed point results for fuzzy mappings in complete b-metric spaces. *Cogent Math. Stat.* **2018**, *5*, 1458933. [CrossRef]
6. Muhammad, R.; Shagari, M.; Azam, A. On interpolative fuzzy contractions with applications. *Filomat* **2023**, *37*, 207–219. [CrossRef]

7. Sagheer, D.; Rahman, Z.; Batul, S.; Aloqaily, A.; Mlaiki, N. Existence of Fuzzy Fixed Points and Common Fuzzy Fixed Points for FG-Contractions with Applications. *Mathematics* **2023**, *11*, 3981. [CrossRef]
8. Shayanpour, H.; Nematizadeh, A. Some results on common best proximity point in fuzzy metric spaces. *Bol. Soc. Parana. Mat.* **2017**, *35*, 177–194. [CrossRef]
9. Ali, G.; Hussain, N.; Moussaoui, A. Best Proximity Point Results via Simulation Function with Application to Fuzzy FractionalDifferential Equations. *Symmetry* **2024**, *16*, 627. [CrossRef]
10. Pragadeeswarar, V.; Gopi, R. Existence and Uniqueness of a Common Best Proximity Point on Fuzzy Metric Space. *Fuzzy Inf. Eng.* **2019**, *11*, 54–63. [CrossRef]
11. Saleem, N.; Raazzia, M.T.; Hussain, N.; Asiri, A. Geraghty–Pata–Suzuki-Type Proximal Contractions and Related CoincidenceBest Proximity Point Results. *Symmetry* **2023**, *15*, 1572. [CrossRef]
12. De la Sen, M.; Abbas, M.; Saleem, N. On optimal fuzzy best proximity coincidence points of proximal contractions involving cyclic mappings in non-Archimedean fuzzy metric spaces. *Mathematics* **2017**, *5*, 22. [CrossRef]
13. Vetro, C.; Salimi, P. Best proximity point results in non-Archimedean fuzzy metric spaces. *Fuzzy Inf. Eng.* **2013**, *5*, 417–429. [CrossRef]
14. Ishtiaq, U.; Jahangeer, F.; Kattan, D.A.; De la Sen, M. Generalized common best proximity point results in fuzzy multiplicative metric spaces. *AIMS Math.* **2023**, *8*, 25454–25476. [CrossRef]
15. Amir, F.I.A.; Moussaoui, A.; Shafqat, R.; El Omari, M.; Melliani, S. The Hadamard Ψ-Caputo tempered fractional derivative in various types of fuzzy fractional differential equations. *Soft Comput.* **2024**, *28*, 9253–9270. [CrossRef]
16. Zhao, K. Study on the stability and its simulation algorithm of a nonlinear impulsive ABC-fractional coupled system with a Laplacian operator via F-contractive mapping. *Adv. Contin. Discret. Model.* **2024**, *2024*, 5. [CrossRef]
17. Abouelregal, A.E.; Alhassan, Y.; Alsaeed, S.S.; Marin, M.; Elzayady, M.E. MGT Photothermal Model Incorporating a Generalized Caputo Fractional Derivative with a Tempering Parameter: Application to an Unbounded Semiconductor Medium. *Contemp. Math.* **2024**, *5*, 6556–6581. [CrossRef]
18. Schweizer, B.; Sklar, A. Statistical metric spaces. *Pac. J. Math.* **1960**, *10*, 313–334. [CrossRef]
19. George, A.; Veeramani, P. On some results in fuzzy metric spaces. *Fuzzy Sets Syst.* **1994**, *64*, 395–399. [CrossRef]
20. Khojasteh, F.; Karapınar, E.; Radenović, S. θ-Metric Space: A Generalization. *Math. Probl. Eng.* **2013**, *2013*, 504609. [CrossRef]
21. Alharbi, N.; Hussain, N. Fixed-point results with application to solving fuzzy boundary value problems. *Res. Math.* **2025**, *12*, 2479226. [CrossRef]
22. Azam, A.; Beg, I. Common fixed points of fuzzy maps. *Math. Comput. Model.* **2009**, *49*, 1331–1336. [CrossRef]
23. Subramanian, S.; Kumaran, A.; Ravichandran, S.; Venugopal, P.; Dhahri, S.; Ramasamy, K. Fuzzy Fractional Caputo Derivative of Susceptible-Infectious-Removed Epidemic Model for Childhood Diseases. *Mathematics* **2024**, *12*, 466. [CrossRef]

fractal and fractional

MDPI

Article

Topological Degree for Operators of Class $(S)_+$ with Set-Valued Perturbations and Its New Applications

Evgenii S. Baranovskii * and Mikhail A. Artemov

Department of Applied Mathematics, Informatics and Mechanics, Voronezh State University, 394018 Voronezh, Russia; artemov_m_a@mail.ru
* Correspondence: esbaranovskii@gmail.com

Abstract: We investigate the topological degree for generalized monotone operators of class $(S)_+$ with compact set-valued perturbations. It is assumed that perturbations can be represented as the composition of a continuous single-valued mapping and an upper semicontinuous set-valued mapping with aspheric values. This allows us to extend the standard degree theory for convex-valued operators to set-valued mappings whose values can have complex geometry. Several theoretical aspects concerning the definition and main properties of the topological degree for such set-valued mappings are discussed. In particular, it is shown that the introduced degree has the homotopy invariance property and can be used as a convenient tool in checking the existence of solutions to corresponding operator inclusions. To illustrate the applicability of our approach to studying models of real processes, we consider an optimal feedback control problem for the steady-state internal flow of a generalized Newtonian fluid in a 3D (or 2D) bounded domain with a Lipschitz boundary. By using the proposed topological degree method, we prove the solvability of this problem in the weak formulation.

Keywords: topological degree; generalized monotone operators; set-valued mappings; aspheric set; fractals; fixed point; coincidence set; generalized Navier–Stokes system; shear-thickening fluids; optimal feedback control

MSC: 47H11; 47H04; 47H05

1. Introduction

Fixed point theory is a very important and emerging scientific branch, which lies at the intersection of pure and applied mathematics [1–8]. It provides effective methods for solving numerous complex (both linear and nonlinear) problems arising in diverse fields such as physics, chemistry, biology, engineering, game theory, and mathematical economics. An interesting deep connection has been discovered between fixed point theory and fractal geometry [9–17]. In particular, fractals, which are intuitively understood as highly irregular sets with fractional dimension and self-similarity properties, can be realized as fixed points of special operators on the space of compact subsets of a metric-type space. Using the formalism of iterated function systems, one can provide a way of constructing such operators and a scheme for the approximation of their fixed points [18–20], as well as obtain sharp results on the Hausdorff dimension in terms of fractal structures [21].

A natural generalization of the fixed point problem is the coincidence problem. Recall that for given nonempty sets X, Y and mappings $\phi, \psi\colon X \to Y$, a point $x \in X$ satisfying the equality $\phi(x) = \psi(x)$ is said to be a *coincidence point* of the mappings ϕ and ψ in the set X. Clearly, if ϕ (or ψ) is a one-to-one operator, then finding a coincidence point is reduced to finding a fixed point of the mapping $\phi^{-1} \circ \psi$ (or $\psi^{-1} \circ \phi$, respectively). However, in applications, it is very often needed to deal with mappings that are not bijective. Interesting results from the coincidence theory (the study of coincidence points) can be found in the works [22–29].

The further development of this theory is related to the consideration of the case where one of the mappings in a pair (ϕ, ψ) is set-valued. For the sake of being definite, let the single-valued mapping $\psi\colon X \to Y$ be replaced by a set-valued mapping $\Psi\colon X \multimap Y$. The passing from the equation $\phi(x) = \psi(x)$ to the inclusion $\phi(x) \in \Psi(x)$ produces significant difficulties in handling the corresponding "set-valued" coincidence problem. To overcome these difficulties, various coincidence point principles were developed by introducing and applying the topological degree for different classes of set-valued perturbations of single-valued operators [30–38]. The proposed approaches and abstract results are successfully used to solve complex problems arising in various real-world applications (see, for example, [39–41]).

The present paper continues and extends the results of the PhD thesis [37] of the first author, in which a variant of the topological degree theory for set-valued perturbations of monotone-like operators between a reflexive Banach space and its dual has been proposed. Our aim is to discuss the definition, some properties and new applications of the topological degree for set-valued mappings that can be represented in the form $T - \Phi$, where T is a single-valued $(S)_+$-operator [42–44], while Φ is a compact set-valued operator with not necessarily convex values. More precisely, unlike conventional approaches that require the convexity values property for the definition of topological degree [25,45–47], we use set-valued operators with aspheric values. This allows us to consider set-valued mappings with values having complex geometry, in particular, with values that are fractal-type contractible sets. We present the construction of the degree mapping, which is based on the principle of continuous single-valued approximations [26,47] and essentially uses the monotonicity arguments that are appropriate for $(S)_+$-operators [48]. It is shown that the introduced topological degree can be used as a tool for checking the existence of a solution to the inclusion $T(x) \in \Phi(x)$.

The remainder of this paper is organized as follows. The next section is entirely devoted to the necessary preliminaries. In Section 3, we construct the topological degree for $(S)_+$-operators with compact set-valued perturbations (Definition 13) and show that this degree is well defined. Section 4 is devoted to studying the main properties of the introduced degree (Theorems 1–3) and obtaining sufficient conditions for the existence of solutions to the inclusion $T(x) \in \Phi(x)$ (Theorem 4). Finally, in Section 5, we apply our abstract results to the analysis of the solvability of an optimal control problem for a model of incompressible fluid dynamics with shear-dependent viscosity (Theorem 6).

2. Preliminaries

This section provides the notions and statements that will be needed to obtain our main results.

2.1. Topological Degree for Operators of Class $(S)_+$

Let X be a real reflexive Banach space. X^* denotes its dual space.

For any $x \in X$ and $\ell \in X^*$, by $\langle \ell, x \rangle_{X^* \times X}$ we denote the value of the functional ℓ on the element x. For brevity, we will sometimes write $\langle \ell, x \rangle$ instead of $\langle \ell, x \rangle_{X^* \times X}$ when it is clear from the context that a duality pairing is meant.

The symbol $\to$ ($\rightharpoonup$, resp.) denotes strong (weak, resp.) convergence.

Let $\mathcal{D}$ be an arbitrary open set in X and let $\overline{\mathcal{D}}$ be its closure.

Definition 1. *An operator $A\colon \overline{\mathcal{D}} \to X^*$ is called strong-to-weak continuous (or demicontinuous) on $\overline{\mathcal{D}}$, if, for any sequence $\{u_n\}_{n=1}^{\infty} \subset \overline{\mathcal{D}}$ and $u_0 \in \overline{\mathcal{D}}$, from $u_n \to u_0$ in X it follows that $A(u_n) \rightharpoonup A(u_0)$ in X^* as $n \to \infty$.*

Definition 2. *An operator $B\colon \overline{\mathcal{D}} \to X^*$ is called weak-to-strong continuous (or completely continuous) on $\overline{\mathcal{D}}$, if, for any sequence $\{u_n\}_{n=1}^{\infty} \subset \overline{\mathcal{D}}$ and $u_0 \in \overline{\mathcal{D}}$, from $u_n \rightharpoonup u_0$ in X it follows that $B(u_n) \to B(u_0)$ in X^* as $n \to \infty$.*

Definition 3. *An operator $M\colon \overline{\mathcal{D}} \to X^*$ is called monotone if the following inequality holds:*

$$\langle M(u) - M(v), u - v \rangle \geq 0, \quad \forall u, v \in \overline{\mathcal{D}}.$$

Moreover, if there exists a positive constant c such that

$$\langle M(u) - M(v), u - v \rangle \geq c\|u - v\|_X^2, \quad \forall u, v \in \overline{\mathcal{D}},$$

then the operator M is said to be strongly monotone.

The monotonicity property, in conjunction with some other conditions, makes it possible to obtain existence theorems for solutions to operator equations and these theorems have applications to various boundary value problems of partial differential equations, to differential equations in Banach spaces, and to integral equations [48–50].

Let us recall the definitions of three frequently used classes of generalized monotone mappings in Banach spaces (see [48]).

Definition 4. *Let $T_1, T_2, T_3\colon \overline{\mathcal{D}} \to X^*$ be operators.*

- *An operator T_1 is said to be pseudo-monotone if it is bounded and if, for any sequence $\{u_n\}_{n=1}^{\infty} \subset \overline{\mathcal{D}}$, from $u_n \rightharpoonup u_0$ in X and*

$$\limsup_{n\to\infty} \langle T_1(u_n), u_n - u_0 \rangle \leq 0$$

it follows that

$$\liminf_{n\to\infty} \langle T_1(u_n), u_n - x \rangle \geq \langle T_1(u_0), u_0 - x \rangle, \quad \forall x \in X.$$

- *We say that an operator T_2 satisfies the condition $\alpha_0(\mathcal{F})$, where $\mathcal{F}$ is a subset $\overline{\mathcal{D}}$, if, for any sequence $\{u_n\}_{n=1}^{\infty} \subset \mathcal{F}$, from $u_n \rightharpoonup u_0$ in X, $T_2(u_n) \rightharpoonup 0$ in X^*, and*

$$\limsup_{n\to\infty} \langle T_2(u_n), u_n - u_0 \rangle \leq 0$$

it follows that $u_n \to u_0$ in X as $n \to \infty$.

- *We say that the operator T_3 satisfies the condition $(S)_+$ if, for any sequence $\{u_n\}_{n=1}^{\infty} \subset \overline{\mathcal{D}}$, from $u_n \rightharpoonup u_0$ in X and*

$$\limsup_{n\to\infty} \langle T_3(u_n), u_n - u_0 \rangle \leq 0$$

it follows that $u_n \to u_0$ in X as $n \to \infty$.

Mappings that satisfy the condition $(S)_+$ are sometimes called *$(S)_+$-operators* or *operators of class $(S)_+$*.

The following proposition gives an important example of $(S)_+$-operators.

Proposition 1. *Suppose that*

- *$M_1\colon \overline{\mathcal{D}} \to X^*$ is a strongly monotone operator;*
- *$M_2\colon \overline{\mathcal{D}} \to X^*$ is a monotone operator;*
- *$B\colon \overline{\mathcal{D}} \to X^*$ is a weak-to-strong continuous operator.*

Then the operator $T := M_1 + M_2 + B$ is an $(S)_+$-operator.

The proof of this statement can be found in [40].

Skrypnik has developed the theory of topological degree for operators satisfying the condition $(S)_+$ (or the condition α_0) and has considered its applications to the study of nonlinear elliptic boundary value problems [48].

Here, we give a scheme of the construction of the topological degree for $(S)_+$-operators.

By $\mathscr{F}(X)$ denote the set of all finite-dimensional subspaces of X. Let $E \in \mathscr{F}(X)$ and $\mathcal{D}_E := \mathcal{D} \cap E$. We introduce the projection $\pi_E : X^* \to E$ by

$$\pi_E(h) := \sum_{i=1}^{m} \langle h, v_i \rangle v_i, \quad \forall h \in X^*, \tag{1}$$

where $v_1, \ldots, v_m$ is a basis of the space E.

Lemma 1. *Let $T : \overline{\mathcal{D}} \to X^*$ be an operator such the following two conditions hold:*

- *T is strong-to-weak continuous and satisfies the condition $(S)_+$;*
- *$T(x) \neq 0$ for any $x \in \partial\mathcal{D}$, where $\partial\mathcal{D}$ denotes the boundary of the set $\mathcal{D}$.*

Then there exists a subspace $E_0 \in \mathscr{F}(X)$ such that, for any $E \in \mathscr{F}(X)$ satisfying the containment $E_0 \subset E$, we have

$$(\pi_E \circ T)(x) \neq 0, \quad \forall x \in \partial\mathcal{D}_E,$$

and

$$\deg(\pi_E \circ T, \overline{\mathcal{D}}_E, 0) = \deg(\pi_{E_0} \circ T, \overline{\mathcal{D}}_{E_0}, 0),$$

where "deg" denotes the topological degree for a finite-dimensional mapping (Brouwer's degree [51]).

Consider the triplet $(T, \overline{\mathcal{D}}, 0)$, where $0 \in X^*$. Taking into account Lemma 1, one can define the topological degree of this triplet as follows

$$\mathrm{Deg}(T, \overline{\mathcal{D}}, 0) := \deg(\pi_{E_0} \circ T, \overline{\mathcal{D}}_{E_0}, 0).$$

The numerical characteristic $\mathrm{Deg}(T, \overline{\mathcal{D}}, 0)$ introduced in this way is well defined and has all the natural properties of the Brouwer degree. In particular, the following existence result holds.

Proposition 2. *Suppose a strong-to-weak continuous operator $T : \overline{\mathcal{D}} \to X^*$ satisfies the condition $(S)_+$ and $T(x) \neq 0$ for any $x \in \partial\mathcal{D}$. Moreover, suppose that*

$$\mathrm{Deg}(T, \overline{\mathcal{D}}, 0) \neq 0.$$

Then the equation $T(x) = 0$ has at least one solution in the domain $\mathcal{D}$.

2.2. Set-Valued Mappings of C-ASV-Type

Let us give the definition of one class of set-valued mappings, denoted by C-ASV. First, we recall some concepts and facts (see [26,52]).

Let $\mathscr{X}$, $\mathscr{X}'$, and $\mathscr{Y}$ be metric spaces.

Definition 5. *A set-valued mapping $\Sigma : \mathscr{X} \multimap \mathscr{Y}$ is called compact-set-valued if the $\Sigma(x)$ is compact in $\mathscr{Y}$ for all $x \in \mathscr{X}$.*

Below, we will consider only compact-set-valued mappings.

Definition 6. *A nonempty compact set $\mathcal{M}$ in $\mathscr{X}$ is called aspheric if, for any $\varepsilon > 0$, there exists a number δ, $0 < \delta < \varepsilon$, such that, for each $n \in \mathbb{N} \cup \{0\}$, any continuous mapping $\xi : \mathcal{S}^n \to O_\delta(\mathcal{M})$ can be extended to a continuous mapping $\widetilde{\xi} : \mathcal{B}^{n+1} \to O_\varepsilon(\mathcal{M})$, where*

$$\mathcal{S}^n := \{\vec{r} \in \mathbb{R}^{n+1} : \|\vec{r}\|_{\mathbb{R}^{n+1}} = 1\},$$
$$\mathcal{B}^{n+1} := \{\vec{r} \in \mathbb{R}^{n+1} : \|\vec{r}\|_{\mathbb{R}^{n+1}} \leq 1\},$$
$$O_\varepsilon(\mathcal{M}) := \{x \in \mathscr{X} : \mathrm{dist}(x, \mathcal{M}) < \varepsilon\}.$$

Three examples of aspheric sets in $\mathbb{R}^2$ are given in Figure 1.

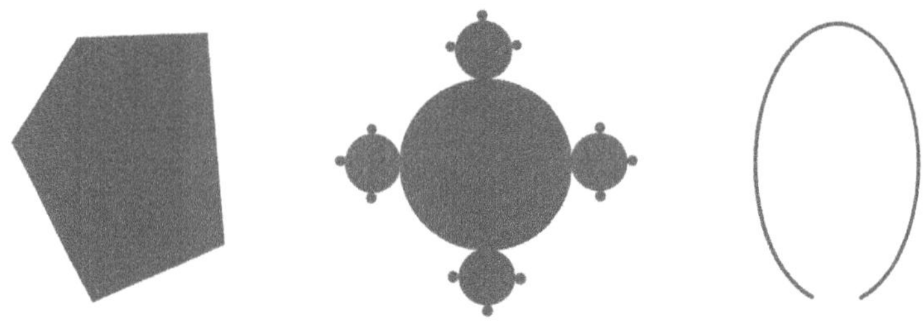

Figure 1. Examples of aspheric sets: one convex non-smooth set and two non-convex smooth sets.

Definition 7. *A set-valued mapping* $\Sigma : \mathscr{X} \multimap \mathscr{Y}$ *is called* ASV*-mapping if* $\Sigma(x)$ *is an aspheric set for any* $x \in \mathscr{X}$.

Of course, the initialism ASV stands for "Aspheric-Set-Valued".

If $\Sigma\colon \mathscr{X} \multimap \mathscr{Y}$ is an upper semicontinuous ASV-mapping, we write $\Sigma \in \mathrm{ASV}(\mathscr{X}, \mathscr{Y})$. By C-ASV$(\mathscr{X}, \mathscr{X}')$ denote the set of all set-valued mappings $\Phi\colon \mathscr{X} \multimap \mathscr{X}'$ representable in the form $\Phi = \psi \circ \Sigma$, where $\Sigma \in \mathrm{ASV}(\mathscr{X}, \mathscr{Y})$ and $\psi\colon \mathscr{Y} \to \mathscr{X}'$ is a continuous single-valued mapping.

In order to demonstrate how wide the C-ASV-class of set-valued mappings is, we recall the following definitions and statements (see [26,53] for details).

Definition 8. *A metric space* $\mathscr{Y}$ *is said to be an ANR-space (absolute neighborhood retract) if, for any closed subset* $\mathcal{B}$ *of any metric space* $\mathscr{X}$ *and any continuous mapping* $f\colon \mathcal{B} \to \mathscr{Y}$, *there exist a neighborhood* U *of the set* $\mathcal{B}$ *in* $\mathscr{X}$ *and a continuous extension* $\widetilde{f}\colon U \to \mathscr{Y}$ *of the mapping* f.

Definition 9. *A topological space* $\mathscr{T}$ *is said to be locally contractible at a point* $x_0 \in \mathscr{T}$ *if any neighborhood* U *of* x_0 *contains a neighborhood* U_0 *contractible to a point with respect to* U.

Definition 10. *A space is said to be locally contractible if this space is locally contractible at each of its points.*

Proposition 3. *A finite-dimensional compact set is an ANR-space if and only if it is locally contractible.*

Definition 11. *A compact nonempty set is said to be an* R_δ*-set if it can be expressed as the intersection of a decreasing sequence of compact contractible sets.*

Proposition 4. *Suppose* $\mathscr{Y}$ *is an ANR-space and* $\Sigma\colon \mathscr{X} \multimap \mathscr{Y}$ *is an upper semicontinuous set-valued mapping. Then* $\Sigma \in \mathrm{ASV}(\mathscr{X}, \mathscr{Y})$ *if at least one of the following conditions hold:*

- $\Sigma(x)$ *is a convex set, for any* $x \in \mathscr{X}$;
- $\Sigma(x)$ *is a contractible set, for any* $x \in \mathscr{X}$;
- $\Sigma(x)$ *is a* R_δ*-set, for any* $x \in \mathscr{X}$.

2.3. Continuous Single-Valued Approximations of Set-Valued Mappings

Let $\mathscr{X}$ and $\mathscr{Y}$ be metric spaces and let $\Sigma\colon \mathscr{X} \multimap \mathscr{Y}$ be a set-valued mapping.

Definition 12. *For a positive number* ε, *a continuous single-valued mapping* $\sigma_\varepsilon\colon \mathscr{X} \to \mathscr{Y}$ *is called an* ε*-approximation of the set-valued mapping* Σ *if, for any element* $x \in \mathscr{X}$, *there exists an element* $x' \in O_\varepsilon(x)$ *such that* $\sigma_\varepsilon(x) \in O_\varepsilon(\Sigma(x'))$.

By $\mathrm{appr}(\Sigma, \varepsilon)$ we denote the set of all ε-approximations of the set-valued mapping Σ.

In the next two lemmas, we summarize some important properties of ε-approximations (see [26] for details).

Lemma 2. *Let* $\Sigma\colon \mathscr{X} \multimap \mathscr{Y}$ *be an upper semicontinuous set-valued mapping. Then the following statements hold.*

(i) *For any compact subset* $\mathscr{X}_0$ *of* $\mathscr{X}$ *and for any positive number* ε*, there exists a positive number* δ *such that*
$$\sigma \in \operatorname{appr}(\Sigma,\delta) \implies \sigma|_{\mathscr{X}_0} \in \operatorname{appr}(\Sigma|_{\mathscr{X}_0},\varepsilon).$$

(ii) *Suppose* $\mathscr{X}$ *is a compact set and* $\psi\colon \mathscr{Y} \to \mathscr{X}'$ *is a continuous mapping. Then, for any* $\varepsilon > 0$*, there exists* $\delta > 0$ *such that*
$$\sigma \in \operatorname{appr}(\Sigma,\delta) \implies \psi \circ \sigma \in \operatorname{appr}(\psi \circ \Sigma,\varepsilon).$$

(iii) *Suppose* $\mathscr{X}$ *is a compact set and* $\Sigma_*\colon \mathscr{X} \times [0,1] \multimap \mathscr{Y}$ *is an upper semicontinuous set-valued mapping. Then, for any* $\lambda \in [0,1]$ *and* $\varepsilon > 0$*, there exists* $\delta > 0$ *such that*
$$\sigma_* \in \operatorname{appr}(\Sigma_*,\delta) \implies \sigma_*(\cdot,\lambda) \in \operatorname{appr}(\Sigma_*(\cdot,\lambda),\varepsilon).$$

Let $f\colon \mathscr{X} \to \mathscr{X}'$ be a single-valued mapping and let $\Lambda\colon \mathscr{X} \multimap \mathscr{X}'$ be a set-valued mapping. By $\operatorname{Coin}(f,\Lambda)$ we denote the solutions set for the inclusion $f(x) \in \Lambda(x)$, that is,
$$\operatorname{Coin}(f,\Lambda) := \{x \in \mathscr{X} : f(x) \in \Lambda(x)\}.$$

Lemma 3. *Suppose* $f\colon \mathscr{X} \to \mathscr{X}'$ *and* $\psi\colon \mathscr{Y} \to \mathscr{X}'$ *are continuous mappings and* $\Sigma\colon \mathscr{X} \multimap \mathscr{Y}$ *is an upper semicontinuous set-valued mapping. Let* $\mathscr{X}_0$ *be a compact subset of* $\mathscr{X}$ *such that*
$$\mathscr{X}_0 \cap \operatorname{Coin}(f,\psi \circ \Sigma) = \varnothing.$$
If $\varepsilon > 0$ *is sufficiently small and the inclusion* $\sigma_\varepsilon \in \operatorname{appr}(\Sigma,\varepsilon)$ *holds, then*
$$\mathscr{X}_0 \cap \operatorname{Coin}(f,\psi \circ \sigma_\varepsilon) = \varnothing.$$

In the paper [54], the following approximability properties of ASV-mappings have been established.

Proposition 5. *Suppose* $\mathscr{X}$ *is a compact ANR-space,* $\Sigma \in \operatorname{ASV}(\mathscr{X},\mathscr{Y})$*, then*

(i) *the set-valued mapping* Σ *is approximable, that is, for any* $\varepsilon > 0$ *there exists* $\sigma_\varepsilon \in \operatorname{appr}(\Sigma,\varepsilon)$*;*

(ii) *for any* $\varepsilon > 0$*, there exists* $\delta_0 > 0$ *such that, for any* δ $(0 < \delta < \delta_0)$ *and any* δ*-approximations* $\sigma_\delta, \sigma'_\delta \in \operatorname{appr}(\Sigma,\delta)$*, there exists a continuous mapping* $\tilde{\sigma}\colon \mathscr{X} \times [0,1] \to \mathscr{Y}$ *satisfying the following properties:*
   1) $\tilde{\sigma}(\cdot,0) = \sigma_\delta$ *and* $\tilde{\sigma}(\cdot,1) = \sigma'_\delta$*;*
   2) $\tilde{\sigma}(\cdot,\lambda) \in \operatorname{appr}(\Sigma,\varepsilon)$ *for any* $\lambda \in [0,1]$.

2.4. Leray–Schauder Lemma

Lemma 4 (see [55])**.** *Let* $\mathcal{D}$ *be a bounded open subset of* $\mathbb{R}^n$ *such that*
$$\mathcal{D}' := \mathcal{D} \cap \{x : x_n = 0\} \neq \varnothing.$$
Suppose that $\omega\colon \overline{\mathcal{D}} \to \mathbb{R}^n$ *is a continuous mapping such that*
$$\omega_n(x_1,\dots,x_n) \equiv x_n, \quad \forall (x_1,\dots,x_n) \in \mathcal{D},$$
$$\omega(x) \neq 0, \quad \forall x \subset \partial\mathcal{D}.$$
Then
$$\deg(\omega,\overline{\mathcal{D}},0) = \deg(\omega',\overline{\mathcal{D}}',0),$$

where the mapping $\omega' \colon \overline{\mathcal{D}}' \to \mathbb{R}^{n-1}$ *is defined by*

$$\omega'(x_1, \ldots, x_{n-1}) := \big(\omega_1(x_1, \ldots, x_{n-1}, 0), \ldots, \omega_{n-1}(x_1, \ldots, x_{n-1}, 0)\big).$$

3. Topological Degree for $(S)_+$-Operators with Set-Valued Perturbations

3.1. Construction of Topological Degree

Let X be a real separable reflexive Banach space and let $\mathscr{Y}$ be a metric space. Suppose $\mathcal{U}$ is a bounded open subset of X such that for any $\mathrm{E} \in \mathscr{F}(X)$, the set $\overline{\mathcal{U} \cap \mathrm{E}}$ is locally contractible.

We will construct the topological degree of a set-valued mapping $T - \Phi \colon \overline{\mathcal{U}} \multimap X^*$ that satisfies the following four conditions:

(H.1) the single-valued mapping $T \colon \overline{\mathcal{U}} \to X^*$ is strong-to-weak continuous and satisfies the condition $(S)_+$;
(H.2) the set-valued mapping $\Phi = \psi \circ \Sigma \colon \overline{\mathcal{U}} \multimap X^*$ belongs to the class C-ASV$(\overline{\mathcal{U}}, X^*)$;
(H.3) the set $\Phi(\overline{\mathcal{U}})$ is relatively compact in X^*;
(H.4) the equality $\mathrm{Coin}(T, \Phi) \cap \partial\mathcal{U} = \varnothing$ holds.

Let E be a finite-dimensional subspace of X with a basis $v_1, \ldots, v_m$ and let π_{E} be the mapping defined in (1).

For an arbitrary subset $\mathcal{S}$ of X, by $\mathcal{S}_{\mathrm{E}}$ we denote the intersection $\mathcal{S} \cap \mathrm{E}$.

Let us consider the three mappings:

$$\pi_{\mathrm{E}} \circ T \colon \overline{\mathcal{U}}_{\mathrm{E}} \to \mathrm{E}, \quad \pi_{\mathrm{E}} \circ \psi \colon \mathscr{Y} \to \mathrm{E}, \quad \pi_{\mathrm{E}} \circ \Phi \colon \overline{\mathcal{U}}_{\mathrm{E}} \multimap \mathrm{E}.$$

The following statement is true.

Lemma 5. *Suppose conditions* (H.1) *and* (H.3) *hold and* $\mathcal{V}$ *is a subset of* $\overline{\mathcal{U}}$ *such that*

(i) *the set* $\mathcal{V}$ *is closed;*
(ii) *the equality* $\mathrm{Coin}(T, \Phi) \cap \mathcal{V} = \varnothing$ *holds.*

Then there exists a space $\mathrm{E}_0 \in \mathscr{F}(X)$ *such that*

$$\mathrm{E} \in \mathscr{F}(X) \text{ and } \mathrm{E} \supset \mathrm{E}_0 \implies \mathrm{Coin}(\pi_{\mathrm{E}} \circ T,\, \pi_{\mathrm{E}} \circ \Phi) \cap \mathcal{V}_{\mathrm{E}} = \varnothing. \tag{2}$$

Proof. Following [37], we introduce the set $\mathfrak{A}(\mathrm{E}, \mathrm{E}_0)$ by

$$\mathfrak{A}(\mathrm{E}, \mathrm{E}_0) := \big\{x \in \mathcal{V}_{\mathrm{E}} : \text{ there exists } y \in \Phi(x) \text{ such that } \langle T(x) - y, x\rangle \leq 0 \\ \text{and } \langle T(x) - y, v\rangle = 0, \text{ for any } v \in \mathrm{E}_0\big\}.$$

First, we show there exists a subspace $\mathrm{E}_0 \in \mathscr{F}(X)$ such that

$$\mathrm{E} \in \mathscr{F}(X) \text{ and } \mathrm{E} \supset \mathrm{E}_0 \implies \mathfrak{A}(\mathrm{E}, \mathrm{E}_0) = \varnothing. \tag{3}$$

Assume the converse, that is, for any subspace $\mathrm{E} \in \mathscr{F}(X)$, there exists a subspace $\mathrm{E}_1 \in \mathscr{F}(X)$ such that

$$\mathrm{E}_1 \supset \mathrm{E} \text{ and } \mathfrak{A}(\mathrm{E}_1, \mathrm{E}) \neq \varnothing.$$

Let

$$\mathfrak{R}_{\mathrm{E}} := \bigcup_{\mathrm{E}' \supset \mathrm{E}} \mathfrak{A}(\mathrm{E}', \mathrm{E}), \text{ where } \mathrm{E}' \in \mathscr{F}(X).$$

By $\overline{\mathfrak{R}}_{\mathrm{E}}^{(\mathrm{weak})}$ we denote the weak closure of $\mathfrak{R}_{\mathrm{E}}$. We claim that the following system

$$\big\{\overline{\mathfrak{R}}_{\mathrm{E}}^{(\mathrm{weak})} : \mathrm{E} \in \mathscr{F}(X)\big\} \tag{4}$$

is centered.

Let $\overline{\mathfrak{R}}_{\mathrm{E}_1}^{(\mathrm{weak})}, \ldots, \overline{\mathfrak{R}}_{\mathrm{E}_p}^{(\mathrm{weak})}$ be an arbitrary finite subsystem of this system. By $\mathscr{L}(\mathrm{E}_1, \ldots, \mathrm{E}_p)$ we denote the linear hull of $\mathrm{E}_1, \ldots, \mathrm{E}_p$. By our assumption, there exists $\widetilde{\mathrm{E}} \in \mathscr{F}(X)$ such that

$$\mathfrak{A}(\widetilde{\mathrm{E}}, \mathscr{L}(\mathrm{E}_1, \ldots, \mathrm{E}_p)) \neq \varnothing.$$

Note that

$$\mathfrak{A}(\widetilde{\mathrm{E}}, \mathscr{L}(\mathrm{E}_1, \ldots, \mathrm{E}_p)) \subset \mathfrak{A}(\widetilde{\mathrm{E}}, \mathrm{E}_j) \subset \mathfrak{R}_{\mathrm{E}_j} \subset \overline{\mathfrak{R}}_{\mathrm{E}_j}^{(\mathrm{weak})}, \; j = 1, \ldots, p,$$

and hence

$$\bigcap_{j=1}^{p} \overline{\mathfrak{R}}_{\mathrm{E}_j}^{(\mathrm{weak})} \neq \varnothing,$$

which means that system (4) is centered.

Since the space X is reflexive and system (4) is centered, there exists an element u_0 such that

$$u_0 \in \bigcap_{\mathrm{E} \in \mathscr{F}(X)} \overline{\mathfrak{R}}_{\mathrm{E}}^{(\mathrm{weak})}.$$

Let us show that $u_0 \in \mathcal{V}$ and $T(u_0) \in \Phi(u_0)$.

Consider $\mathrm{E} \in \mathscr{F}(X)$ such that $u_0 \in \mathrm{E}$. Taking into account the inclusion $u_0 \in \overline{\mathfrak{R}}_{\mathrm{E}}^{(\mathrm{weak})}$, we see that there exist sequences $\{u_n\}_{n=1}^{\infty}$ and $\{y_n\}_{n=1}^{\infty}$ such that

$$u_n \in \mathfrak{A}(\mathrm{E}_n, \mathrm{E}), \quad \mathrm{E}_n \in \mathscr{F}(X), \quad \mathrm{E}_n \supset \mathrm{E}, \quad \forall n \in \mathbb{N},$$

$$u_n \rightharpoonup u_0 \text{ in X as } n \to \infty,$$

$$y_n \in \Phi(u_n) \subset \Phi(\overline{\mathcal{U}}), \quad \forall n \in \mathbb{N},$$

$$\langle T(u_n) - y_n, u_n \rangle \leq 0, \quad \langle T(u_n) - y_n, u_0 \rangle = 0, \quad \forall n \in \mathbb{N}, \tag{5}$$

$$\langle T(u_n) - y_n, w \rangle = 0, \quad \forall n \in \mathbb{N}, w \in \mathrm{E}. \tag{6}$$

Moreover, since the set $\Phi(\overline{\mathcal{U}})$ is relatively compact, we can assume without loss of generality that

$$y_n \to y_0 \text{ in } X^* \text{ as } n \to \infty,$$

for some $y_0 \in X^*$.

Note that the following representation of $\langle T(u_n), u_n - u_0 \rangle$ holds.

$$\begin{aligned} \langle T(u_n), u_n - u_0 \rangle = & \langle T(u_n) - y_n, u_n - u_0 \rangle \\ & + \langle y_n - y_0, u_n - u_0 \rangle + \langle y_0, u_n - u_0 \rangle, \quad \forall n \in \mathbb{N}. \end{aligned} \tag{7}$$

Clearly, the second and third terms in the right-hand side of equality (7) converge to zero.

From (5) it follows that

$$\langle T(u_n) - y_n, u_n - u_0 \rangle \leq 0, \quad \forall n \in \mathbb{N},$$

whence

$$\limsup_{n \to \infty} \langle T(u_n), u_n - u_0 \rangle \leq 0. \tag{8}$$

Since the operator T satisfies the condition $(S)_+$, inequality (8) and the inclusion

$$u_n \in \mathcal{V}_{\mathrm{E}_n} \subset \overline{\mathcal{U}}, \quad \forall n \in \mathbb{N},$$

holds, and $u_n \rightharpoonup u_0$ in X as $n \to \infty$, so we have $u_n \to u_0$ in X as $n \to \infty$. Therefore, recalling that the set $\mathcal{V}$ is closed, we obtain the inclusion $u_0 \in \mathcal{V}$.

Moreover, from the conditions

$$\begin{gathered} u_n \to u_0 \ \text{ in } X \text{ as } n \to \infty, \\ y_n \in \Phi(u_n), \quad \forall n \in \mathbb{N}, \\ y_n \to y_0 \ \text{ in } X^* \text{ as } n \to \infty, \end{gathered}$$

and the upper semicontinuity of the set-valued mapping Φ, it follows that $y_0 \in \Phi(u_0)$.

Further, we pass the limit $n \to \infty$ in equality (6); this gives

$$\langle T(u_0) - y_0, w \rangle = 0, \quad \forall w \in \mathrm{E}. \tag{9}$$

Therefore, for any space $\mathrm{E} \in \mathscr{F}(X)$ such that $u_0 \in \mathrm{E}$, there exists $y_0 \in \Phi(u_0)$ satisfying equality (9).

In view of the space in which X is separable, there exists a countable set $\mathcal{Q}$ such that $\mathcal{Q} \subset X$ and $\mathcal{Q}$ is dense in X. For the sake of being definite, let $\mathcal{Q} = \{x_i\}_{i=1}^{\infty}$.

Consider the sequence of spaces $\{\mathrm{F}_i\}_{i=1}^{\infty}$, where

$$\mathrm{F}_k := \operatorname{span}\{u_0, x_1, \dots, x_k\}, \quad \forall k \in \mathbb{N}.$$

From the above reasoning, it follows that, for any $\mathrm{F}_k \in \mathscr{F}(X)$, there exists $f_k \in \Phi(u_0)$ such that

$$\langle T(u_0) - f_k, w \rangle = 0, \quad \forall w \in \mathrm{F}_k. \tag{10}$$

Without loss of generality, it can be assumed that

$$f_k \to f_0 \in \Phi(u_0) \ \text{ in } X^* \text{ as } k \to \infty \tag{11}$$

because the set $\Phi(u_0)$ is compact.

Let us show that $T(u_0) = f_0$. Fix arbitrary $x \in X$ and $\varepsilon > 0$. Suppose C is a constant such that

$$\begin{aligned} \|T(u_0)\|_{X^*} &< C, \\ \|f_k\|_{X^*} &< C, \quad \forall k \in \mathbb{N}. \end{aligned} \tag{12}$$

Because the set $\mathcal{Q}$ is dense in X, there exists an element $x_m \in \mathcal{Q}$ such that

$$\|x - x_m\|_X < \frac{\varepsilon}{4C}. \tag{13}$$

Let us take a sufficiently large integer k such that $k \geq m$ and

$$|\langle f_k - f_0, x \rangle| < \frac{\varepsilon}{4}. \tag{14}$$

This is possible since the element x is fixed and convergence (11) holds.

We observe that $x_m \in \mathrm{F}_m \subset \mathrm{F}_k$. Therefore, from equality (10), it follows that

$$\langle T(u_0) - f_k, x_m \rangle = 0. \tag{15}$$

Using relations (12)–(15), we derive

$$\begin{aligned}
&|\langle T(u_0) - f_0, x\rangle| \\
&= |\langle T(u_0) - f_k, x_m\rangle + \langle T(u_0) - f_k, x - x_m\rangle + \langle f_k - f_0, x\rangle| \\
&\leq |\langle T(u_0) - f_k, x_m\rangle| + |\langle T(u_0) - f_k, x - x_m\rangle| + |\langle f_k - f_0, x\rangle| \\
&\leq \|T(u_0)\|_{X^*}\|x - x_m\|_X + \|f_k\|_{X^*}\|x - x_m\|_X + |\langle f_k - f_0, x\rangle| \\
&\leq C(\varepsilon/4C) + C(\varepsilon/4C) + \varepsilon/4 \\
&= 3\varepsilon/4 < \varepsilon,
\end{aligned}$$

whence,

$$\langle T(u_0) - f_0, x\rangle = 0, \tag{16}$$

since ε was taken arbitrarily.

Moreover, taking into account that x is an arbitrary element from the space X, we deduce from equality (16) the relation $T(u_0) = f_0 \in \Phi(u_0)$, and hence, $u_0 \in \mathrm{Coin}(T, \Phi)$. Combining this with $u_0 \in \mathcal{V}$, we obtain

$$u_0 \in \mathrm{Coin}(T, \Phi) \cap \mathcal{V},$$

which contradicts condition (ii).

Thus, we have proved the existence of a subspace $\mathrm{E}_0 \in \mathscr{F}(X)$ such that implication (3) holds for any $\mathrm{E} \in \mathscr{F}(X)$.

Now we will show that the subspace E_0 satisfies implication (2). Assume the converse. Then there exists a subspace $\mathrm{E}_1 \in \mathscr{F}(X)$ such that

$$\mathrm{E}_1 \supset \mathrm{E}_0 \ \text{ and } \ \mathrm{Coin}(\pi_{\mathrm{E}_1} \circ T,\ \pi_{\mathrm{E}_1} \circ \Phi) \cap \mathcal{V}_{\mathrm{E}_1} \neq \varnothing.$$

Let u_1 be an element satisfying

$$u_1 \in \mathrm{Coin}(\pi_{\mathrm{E}_1} \circ T,\ \pi_{\mathrm{E}_1} \circ \Phi) \cap \mathcal{V}_{\mathrm{E}_1}.$$

We show that $u_1 \in \mathfrak{A}(\mathrm{E}_1, \mathrm{E}_0)$. Due to the inclusion

$$u_1 \in \mathrm{Coin}(\pi_{\mathrm{E}_1} \circ T,\ \pi_{\mathrm{E}_1} \circ \Phi),$$

there exists $y_1 \in \Phi(u_1)$ such that

$$(\pi_{\mathrm{E}_1} \circ T)(u_1) = \pi_{\mathrm{E}_1}(y_1). \tag{17}$$

Let $v_1, \ldots, v_{m_1}$ be a basis of $\mathrm{E} \in \mathscr{F}(X)$. Then equality (17) is equivalent to

$$\langle T(u_1) - y_1, v_i\rangle = 0, \ \ i = 1, \ldots, m_1. \tag{18}$$

Since $u_1 \in \mathrm{E}_1$, we have the representation

$$u_1 = \sum_{i=1}^{m_1} \zeta_i v_i, \tag{19}$$

where $\zeta_1, \ldots, \zeta_{m_1}$ are some real numbers.

Using equality (18) and representation (19), we obtain

$$\langle T(u_1) - y_1, u_1\rangle = \sum_{i=1}^{m_1} \zeta_i \langle T(u_1) - y_1, v_i\rangle = 0.$$

Similarly, we derive

$$\langle T(u_1) - y_1, v\rangle = 0, \quad \forall v \in \mathrm{E}_0.$$

Thus, we have established $u_1 \in \mathfrak{A}(\mathrm{E}_1, \mathrm{E}_0)$. On the other hand, for the subspaces E_0 and E_1, we have $\mathfrak{A}(\mathrm{E}_1, \mathrm{E}_0) = \varnothing$. This contradiction proves Lemma 5. □

Now we can return to constructing the topological degree of the set-valued mapping $T - \Phi$. Note that for the set $\mathcal{V} = \partial\mathcal{U}$ conditions (i) and (ii) of Lemma 5 hold. Let us fix a subspace $\mathrm{E}_0 \in \mathscr{F}(X)$ such that

$$\mathrm{Coin}(\pi_{\mathrm{E}_0} \circ T,\ \pi_{\mathrm{E}_0} \circ \Phi) \cap \partial\mathcal{U}_{\mathrm{E}_0} = \varnothing. \tag{20}$$

From our assumptions on the geometrical properties of $\mathcal{U}$, it follows that the set $\overline{\mathcal{U}}_{\mathrm{E}_0} = \overline{\mathcal{U} \cap \mathrm{E}_0}$ is locally contractible. Therefore, applying Proposition 3, we see that $\overline{\mathcal{U}}_{\mathrm{E}_0}$ is a compact ANR-space. Thus, for $\Sigma|_{\overline{\mathcal{U}}_{\mathrm{E}_0}}$, all the conditions of Proposition 5 hold. This implies that, for any $\varepsilon > 0$, there exists a continuous ε-approximation $\sigma_\varepsilon \in \mathrm{appr}(\Sigma|_{\overline{\mathcal{U}}_{\mathrm{E}_0}}, \varepsilon)$.

From equality (20) and Lemma 3 it follows that there exists $\varepsilon_0 > 0$ such that, for any $\varepsilon \in (0, \varepsilon_0]$, we have

$$(\pi_{\mathrm{E}_0} \circ T - \pi_{\mathrm{E}_0} \circ \psi \circ \sigma_\varepsilon)(x) \neq 0, \quad \forall x \in \partial\mathcal{U}_{\mathrm{E}_0}. \tag{21}$$

Moreover, applying Proposition 5 (ii), we deduce that there exists $\delta_0 \in (0, \varepsilon_0)$ such that, for any $\varepsilon \in (0, \delta_0)$ and $\sigma_\varepsilon, \sigma'_\varepsilon \in \mathrm{appr}(\Sigma|_{\overline{\mathcal{U}}_{\mathrm{E}_0}}, \varepsilon)$, there exists a continuous mapping $\widetilde{\sigma}\colon \overline{\mathcal{U}}_{\mathrm{E}_0} \times [0,1] \to \mathscr{Y}$ satisfying the following conditions:

$$\widetilde{\sigma}(\cdot, 0) = \sigma_\varepsilon, \quad \widetilde{\sigma}(\cdot, 1) = \sigma'_\varepsilon, \tag{22}$$

$$\widetilde{\sigma}(\cdot, t) \in \mathrm{appr}(\Sigma|_{\overline{\mathcal{U}}_{\mathrm{E}_0}}, \varepsilon_0), \quad \forall t \in [0,1]. \tag{23}$$

Fix $\varepsilon \in (0, \delta_0)$. Assuming that conditions (H.1)–(H.4) hold, we give the next definition.

Definition 13. *The topological degree of a set-valued mapping $T - \Phi\colon \overline{\mathcal{U}} \multimap X^*$ with respect to $\overline{\mathcal{U}}$ and $0 \in X^*$ is defined by the equality*

$$\mathrm{Deg}(T - \Phi, \overline{\mathcal{U}}, 0) = \deg(\pi_{\mathrm{E}_0} \circ T - \pi_{\mathrm{E}_0} \circ \psi \circ \sigma_\varepsilon, \overline{\mathcal{U}}_{\mathrm{E}_0}, 0),$$

where $\deg(\pi_{\mathrm{E}_0} \circ T - \pi_{\mathrm{E}_0} \circ \psi \circ \sigma_\varepsilon, \overline{\mathcal{U}}_{\mathrm{E}_0}, 0)$ denotes the Brouwer degree of the mapping

$$\pi_{\mathrm{E}_0} \circ T - \pi_{\mathrm{E}_0} \circ \psi \circ \sigma_\varepsilon \colon \overline{\mathcal{U}}_{\mathrm{E}_0} \to \mathrm{E}_0$$

with respect to $\overline{\mathcal{U}}_{\mathrm{E}_0}$ and $0 \in \mathrm{E}_0$.

3.2. Well-Definedness of Topological Degree

Let us show that the topological degree $\mathrm{Deg}(T - \Phi, \overline{\mathcal{U}}, 0)$ is well defined, that is, its value depends neither on the choice of an ε-approximation σ_ε nor on the choice of a subspace E_0.

Step 1. First, we establish the independence of $\mathrm{Deg}(T - \Phi, \overline{\mathcal{U}}, 0)$ from the choice of an ε-approximation. More precisely, it is necessary to prove that, for any $\varepsilon \in (0, \delta_0)$ and $\sigma_\varepsilon, \sigma'_\varepsilon \in \mathrm{appr}(\Sigma|_{\overline{\mathcal{U}}_{\mathrm{E}_0}}, \varepsilon)$, the following equality holds:

$$\deg(\pi_{\mathrm{E}_0} \circ T - \pi_{\mathrm{E}_0} \circ \psi \circ \sigma_\varepsilon, \overline{\mathcal{U}}_{\mathrm{E}_0}, 0) = \deg(\pi_{\mathrm{E}_0} \circ T - \pi_{\mathrm{E}_0} \circ \psi \circ \sigma'_\varepsilon, \overline{\mathcal{U}}_{\mathrm{E}_0}, 0). \tag{24}$$

From relations (21) and (23) it follows that

$$(\pi_{\mathrm{E}_0} \circ T)(x) - (\pi_{\mathrm{E}_0} \circ \psi \circ \widetilde{\sigma})(x, t) \neq 0, \quad \forall (x, t) \in \partial\mathcal{U}_{\mathrm{E}_0} \times [0,1],$$

which together with (22) yield that the mappings

$$\pi_{E_0} \circ T - \pi_{E_0} \circ \psi \circ \sigma_\varepsilon : \overline{\mathcal{U}}_{E_0} \to E_0 \text{ and } \pi_{E_0} \circ T - \pi_{E_0} \circ \psi \circ \sigma'_\varepsilon : \overline{\mathcal{U}}_{E_0} \to E_0$$

are homotopic. Therefore, in view of the homotopy invariance property of the Brouwer degree, we arrive at equality (24).

Step 2. Now we will show the independence of $\mathrm{Deg}(T - \Phi, \overline{\mathcal{U}}, 0)$ from the choice of a subspace E_0.

Let us fix $E \in \mathscr{F}(X)$ such that $E \supset E_0$ and prove that the following equality is valid:

$$\deg(\pi_{E_0} \circ T - \pi_{E_0} \circ \psi \circ \sigma_\varepsilon, \overline{\mathcal{U}}_{E_0}, 0) = \deg(\pi_E \circ T - \pi_E \circ \psi \circ \sigma_\varepsilon, \overline{\mathcal{U}}_E, 0), \tag{25}$$

where $\sigma_\varepsilon \in \mathrm{appr}(\Sigma|_{\overline{\mathcal{U}}_E}, \varepsilon)$.

Let us choose a basis of $E \in \mathscr{F}(X)$ in the form $v_1, \ldots, v_m, w_1, \ldots, w_k$, where $v_1, \ldots, v_m$ is a basis of $E_0 \in \mathscr{F}(X)$, and consider the three finite-dimensional mappings:

$$(\pi_{E_0} \circ T - \pi_{E_0} \circ \psi \circ \sigma_\varepsilon)(x) := \sum_{i=1}^{m} \langle T(x), v_i \rangle v_i - \sum_{i=1}^{m} \langle (\psi \circ \sigma_\varepsilon)(x), v_i \rangle v_i,$$

$$\begin{aligned}(\pi_E \circ T - \pi_E \circ \psi \circ \sigma_\varepsilon)(x) := &\sum_{i=1}^{m} \langle T(x), v_i \rangle v_i - \sum_{i=1}^{m} \langle (\psi \circ \sigma_\varepsilon)(x), v_i \rangle v_i \\ &+ \sum_{i=1}^{k} \langle T(x), w_i \rangle w_i - \sum_{i=1}^{k} \langle (\psi \circ \sigma_\varepsilon)(x), w_i \rangle w_i,\end{aligned}$$

$$R_{\varepsilon,E}(x) := \sum_{i=1}^{m} \langle T(x), v_i \rangle v_i - \sum_{i=1}^{m} \langle (\psi \circ \sigma_\varepsilon)(x), v_i \rangle v_i + \sum_{i=1}^{k} \langle p_i, x \rangle w_i,$$

where $\sigma_\varepsilon \in \mathrm{appr}(\Sigma|_{\overline{\mathcal{U}}_E}, \varepsilon)$ and p_i is an element from the space X^* such that

$$\begin{aligned}\langle p_i, w_j \rangle &= \delta_{ij}, \quad i = 1, \ldots, k,\ j = 1, \ldots, k, \\ \langle p_i, v_j \rangle &= 0, \quad\ \ i = 1, \ldots, k,\ j = 1, \ldots, m,\end{aligned}$$

and δ_{ij} is the Kronecker delta.

In view of Lemma 4, we have

$$\deg(\pi_{E_0} \circ T - \pi_{E_0} \circ \psi \circ \sigma_\varepsilon, \overline{\mathcal{U}}_{E_0}, 0) = \deg(R_{\varepsilon,E}, \overline{\mathcal{U}}_E, 0). \tag{26}$$

Moreover, we will show that if $\varepsilon > 0$ is small enough, then

$$\deg(\pi_E \circ T - \pi_E \circ \psi \circ \sigma_\varepsilon, \overline{\mathcal{U}}_E, 0) = \deg(R_{\varepsilon,E}, \overline{\mathcal{U}}_E, 0). \tag{27}$$

Due to the homotopy invariance property of the Brouwer degree, it is sufficient to prove the next lemma.

Lemma 6. *There exists $\varepsilon_0 > 0$ such that, for any $\sigma_\varepsilon \in \mathrm{appr}(\Sigma|_{\overline{\mathcal{U}}_E}, \varepsilon)$ with $0 < \varepsilon < \varepsilon_0$, the following relation is true:*

$$t(\pi_E \circ T - \pi_E \circ \psi \circ \sigma_\varepsilon)(x) + (1-t)R_{\varepsilon,E}(x) \neq 0, \quad \forall (x,t) \in \partial\mathcal{U}_E \times [0,1].$$

Proof. Assume the converse. Then there exist sequences $\{\varepsilon_n\}_{n=1}^{\infty} \subset (0,\infty)$, $\{t_n\}_{n=1}^{\infty} \subset [0,1]$, and $\{x_n\}_{n=1}^{\infty} \subset \partial\mathcal{U}_E$ such that $\varepsilon_n \to 0$ as $n \to \infty$ and

$$t_n(\pi_E \circ T - \pi_E \circ \psi \circ \sigma_{\varepsilon_n})(x_n) + (1-t_n)R_{\varepsilon_n,E}(x_n) = 0, \tag{28}$$

for some $\sigma_{\varepsilon_n} \in \mathrm{appr}(\Sigma|_{\overline{\mathcal{U}}_E}, \varepsilon_n)$.

Equality (28) is equivalent to the two following relations:

$$\langle (T-\psi\circ\sigma_{\varepsilon_n})(x_n), v_i\rangle = 0, \quad i=1,\dots,m, \tag{29}$$
$$t_n\langle (T-\psi\circ\sigma_{\varepsilon_n})(x_n), w_i\rangle + (1-t_n)\langle p_i, x_n\rangle = 0, \quad i=1,\dots,k. \tag{30}$$

Without loss of generality, it can be assumed that

$$x_n \to x_* \in \partial\mathcal{U}_{\mathrm{E}} \text{ in } X \text{ as } n\to\infty,$$
$$t_n \to t_* \in [0,1] \text{ as } n\to\infty,$$
$$(\psi\circ\sigma_{\varepsilon_n})(x_n) \to y_* \in (\psi\circ\Sigma)(x_*) \text{ in } X^* \text{ as } n\to\infty,$$

Further, we pass to the limit $n\to\infty$ in equalities (29) and (30); this gives

$$\langle T(x_*)-y_*, v_i\rangle = 0, \quad i=1,\dots,m, \tag{31}$$
$$t_*\langle T(x_*)-y_*, w_i\rangle + (1-t_*)\langle p_i, x_*\rangle = 0, \quad i=1,\dots,k. \tag{32}$$

We claim that, in the last equality, $t_*\neq 0$. Assume the converse. Then

$$\langle p_j, x_*\rangle = 0, \quad j=0,\dots,k.$$

Since $x_*\in\partial\mathcal{U}_{\mathrm{E}}\subset \mathrm{E}$, we have the representation

$$x_* = \sum_{i=1}^{m} a_i v_i + \sum_{i=1}^{k} b_i w_i \tag{33}$$

with some $a_i, b_i\in\mathbb{R}$. Applying the functional $p_j\in X^*$ to both sides of equality (33), we obtain

$$\langle p_j, x_*\rangle = b_j \tag{34}$$

Recalling that $\langle p_j, x_*\rangle = 0$, we arrive at the equality $b_j = 0$. Therefore,

$$x_* = \sum_{i=1}^{m} a_i v_i \in \mathrm{E}_0,$$

and hence $x_*\in\partial\mathcal{U}_{\mathrm{E}_0}$.

Moreover, from the definition of the mapping $\pi_{\mathrm{E}_0}\circ T$ and equality (31), it follows that

$$\begin{aligned}(\pi_{\mathrm{E}_0}\circ T)(x_*) &= \sum_{i=1}^{m}\langle T(x_*), v_i\rangle v_i\\ &= \sum_{i=1}^{m}\langle y_*, v_i\rangle v_i\\ &= \pi_{\mathrm{E}_0}(y_*) \in (\pi_{\mathrm{E}_0}\circ\Phi)(x_*).\end{aligned}$$

This means that

$$x_*\in \mathrm{Coin}(\pi_{\mathrm{E}_0}\circ T,\ \pi_{\mathrm{E}_0}\circ\Phi),$$

whence, taking into account inclusion $x_*\in\partial\mathcal{U}_{\mathrm{E}_0}$, we deduce

$$x_*\in \mathrm{Coin}(\pi_{\mathrm{E}_0}\circ T,\ \pi_{\mathrm{E}_0}\circ\Phi)\cap\partial\mathcal{U}_{\mathrm{E}_0},$$

which contradicts equality (20). Thus, we have established that $t_*\neq 0$.

Further, let us estimate the value of $\langle T(x_*) - y_*, x_* \rangle$. Using relations (31)–(34), we derive

$$\begin{aligned} \langle T(x_*) - y_*, x_* \rangle &= \Big\langle T(x_*) - y_*, \sum_{i=1}^{m} a_i v_i \Big\rangle + \Big\langle T(x_*) - y_*, \sum_{j=1}^{k} b_j w_j \Big\rangle \\ &= \sum_{j=1}^{k} b_j \langle T(x_*) - y_*, w_j \rangle \\ &= -\frac{(1-t_*)}{t_*} \sum_{j=1}^{k} b_j \langle p_j, x_* \rangle \\ &= -\frac{(1-t_*)}{t_*} \sum_{j=1}^{k} b_j^2 \leq 0. \end{aligned}$$

Similarly, it can be shown that

$$\langle T(x_*) - y_*, v \rangle = 0, \quad \forall v \in \mathrm{E}_0.$$

From the relations established above, it follows that $x_* \in \mathfrak{A}(\mathrm{E}, \mathrm{E}_0)$. On the other hand, in the framework of the proof of Lemma 5, we have shown that $\mathfrak{A}(\mathrm{E}, \mathrm{E}_0) = \emptyset$. This contradiction proves Lemma 6. □

Combining (26) and (27), we obtain the required equality (25).

Thus, we have established that the introduced characteristic $\mathrm{Deg}(T - \Phi, \overline{\mathcal{U}}, 0)$ is well defined.

Remark 1. *The topological degree for mappings of class $(S)_+$ with maximal monotone perturbations has been developed in* [32,35].

4. Properties of Topological Degree for $(S)_+$-Operators with Set-Valued Perturbations

In this section, following [37], we show that the constructed characteristic possesses natural properties of a topological degree.

Theorem 1 (Additivity property). *Let $\mathcal{U}'$ and $\mathcal{U}''$ be disjoint open subsets of $\mathcal{U}$ such that*

- *the equality $\mathrm{Coin}(T, \Phi) \cap (\overline{\mathcal{U}} \setminus (\mathcal{U}' \cup \mathcal{U}'')) = \emptyset$ holds;*
- *the sets $\overline{\mathcal{U}' \cap \mathrm{E}}$ and $\overline{\mathcal{U}'' \cap \mathrm{E}}$ are local contractible, for any $\mathrm{E} \in \mathscr{F}(X)$.*

Then

$$\mathrm{Deg}(T - \Phi, \overline{\mathcal{U}}, 0) = \mathrm{Deg}(T - \Phi, \overline{\mathcal{U}}', 0) + \mathrm{Deg}(T - \Phi, \overline{\mathcal{U}}'', 0). \tag{35}$$

Proof. Note that the set $\mathcal{V} = \overline{\mathcal{U}} \setminus (\mathcal{U}' \cup \mathcal{U}'')$ satisfies the conditions of Lemma 5. Hence, there exists a subspace $\mathrm{E}_0 \in \mathscr{F}(X)$ such that

$$\mathrm{E} \in \mathscr{F}(X) \text{ and } \mathrm{E} \supset \mathrm{E}_0 \implies \mathrm{Coin}(\pi_{\mathrm{E}} \circ T, \pi_{\mathrm{E}} \circ \Phi) \cap (\overline{\mathcal{U}}_{\mathrm{E}} \setminus (\mathcal{U}'_{\mathrm{E}} \cup \mathcal{U}''_{\mathrm{E}})) = \emptyset, \tag{36}$$

where $\mathcal{U}'_{\mathrm{E}}$ and $\mathcal{U}''_{\mathrm{E}}$ stand for $\mathcal{U}' \cap \mathrm{E}$ and $\mathcal{U}'' \cap \mathrm{E}$, respectively.

Due to Proposition 5, there exists $\sigma_\varepsilon \in \mathrm{appr}(\Sigma|_{\overline{\mathcal{U}}_{\mathrm{E}}}, \varepsilon)$, for any $\varepsilon > 0$.

From equality (36) and Lemma 3 it follows that if $\varepsilon > 0$ is small enough, then

$$(\pi_{\mathrm{E}} \circ T - \pi_{\mathrm{E}} \circ \psi \circ \sigma_\varepsilon)(x) \neq 0, \quad \forall x \in \overline{\mathcal{U}}_{\mathrm{E}} \setminus (\mathcal{U}'_{\mathrm{E}} \cup \mathcal{U}''_{\mathrm{E}}).$$

Taking into account the additivity property of the Brouwer degree, we obtain

$$\begin{aligned} &\deg(\pi_{\mathrm{E}} \circ T - \pi_{\mathrm{E}} \circ \psi \circ \sigma_\varepsilon, \overline{\mathcal{U}}_{\mathrm{E}}, 0) \\ &= \deg(\pi_{\mathrm{E}} \circ T - \pi_{\mathrm{E}} \circ \psi \circ \sigma_\varepsilon, \overline{\mathcal{U}}'_{\mathrm{E}}, 0) + \deg(\pi_{\mathrm{E}} \circ T - \pi_{\mathrm{E}} \circ \psi \circ \sigma_\varepsilon, \overline{\mathcal{U}}''_{\mathrm{E}}, 0). \end{aligned} \tag{37}$$

On the other hand, according to Definition 13, we have

$$\begin{aligned}
\mathrm{Deg}(T-\Phi,\overline{\mathcal{U}},0) &= \deg(\pi_{\mathrm{E}}\circ T-\pi_{\mathrm{E}}\circ\psi\circ\sigma_{\varepsilon},\overline{\mathcal{U}}_{\mathrm{E}},0), &(38)\\
\mathrm{Deg}(T-\Phi,\overline{\mathcal{U}}',0) &= \deg(\pi_{\mathrm{E}}\circ T-\pi_{\mathrm{E}}\circ\psi\circ\sigma_{\varepsilon},\overline{\mathcal{U}}'_{\mathrm{E}},0), &(39)\\
\mathrm{Deg}(T-\Phi,\overline{\mathcal{U}}'',0) &= \deg(\pi_{\mathrm{E}}\circ T-\pi_{\mathrm{E}}\circ\psi\circ\sigma_{\varepsilon},\overline{\mathcal{U}}''_{\mathrm{E}},0). &(40)
\end{aligned}$$

Combining equalities (37)–(40), we arrive at relation (35). Thus, Theorem 1 is proved. □

Now, we will discuss the property of homotopy invariance of the constructed topological degree. Consider operators $T_i\colon\overline{\mathcal{U}}\to X^*$ and $\Phi_i=\psi_i\circ\Sigma_i\colon\overline{\mathcal{U}}\multimap X^*$, where $i=1,2$, satisfying conditions (H.1)–(H.3) with

$$T:=T_i,\quad \Phi:=\Phi_i,\quad \psi:=\psi_i,\quad \Sigma:=\Sigma_i.$$

Definition 14. *The set-valued mappings $T_0-\Phi_0$ and $T_1-\Phi_1$ are homotopic with respect to the set $\mathcal{U}$ if the following four conditions hold:*

- *There exists a strong-to-weak continuous mapping $\widetilde{T}\colon\overline{\mathcal{U}}\times[0,1]\to X^*$ such that*

$$\widetilde{T}(\cdot,0)=T_0,\quad \widetilde{T}(\cdot,1)=T_1,$$

  and, for any sequences $\{x_n\}_{n=1}^{\infty}\subset\partial\mathcal{U}$ and $\{t_n\}_{n=1}^{\infty}\subset[0,1]$, from $x_n\rightharpoonup x_0$ in X and

$$\limsup_{n\to\infty}\langle\widetilde{T}(x_n,t_n),x_n-x_0\rangle\le 0$$

  it follows that $x_n\to x_0$ in X as $n\to\infty$.
- *There exist a set-valued mapping $\widetilde{\Sigma}\in\mathrm{ASV}(\overline{\mathcal{U}}\times[0,1],\mathscr{Y})$ and a continuous single-valued mapping $\widetilde{\psi}\colon\mathscr{Y}\times[0,1]\to X^*$ such that*

$$\begin{aligned}
\widetilde{\Sigma}(\cdot,0)&=\Sigma_0, & \widetilde{\Sigma}(\cdot,1)&=\Sigma_1,\\
\widetilde{\psi}(\cdot,0)&=\psi_0, & \widetilde{\psi}(\cdot,1)&=\psi_1.
\end{aligned}$$

- *For the set-valued mapping $\widetilde{\Phi}\colon\overline{\mathcal{U}}\times[0,1]\multimap X^*$ defined by*

$$\widetilde{\Phi}(x,t):=\widetilde{\psi}(\widetilde{\Sigma}(x,t),t),\quad \forall(x,t)\in\overline{\mathcal{U}}\times[0,1],$$

  the set $\widetilde{\Phi}(\overline{\mathcal{U}}\times[0,1])$ is relatively compact in X^*.
- *The intersection of the sets $\mathcal{U}\times[0,1]$ and $\mathrm{Coin}(\widetilde{T},\widetilde{\Phi})$, where*

$$\mathrm{Coin}(\widetilde{T},\widetilde{\Phi}):=\{(x,t)\in\overline{\mathcal{U}}\times[0,1]:\ \widetilde{T}(x,t)\in\widetilde{\Phi}(x,t)\},$$

  is the empty set.

Theorem 2 (Invariance under homotopy). *If the set-valued mappings $T_0-\Phi_0$ and $T_1-\Phi_1$ are homotopic with respect to the set $\mathcal{U}$, then*

$$\mathrm{Deg}(T_0-\Phi_0,\overline{\mathcal{U}},0)=\mathrm{Deg}(T_1-\Phi_1,\overline{\mathcal{U}},0).$$

Proof. Taking into account the last condition in Definition 14, by the same arguments as in Lemma 5, one can prove the existence of a subspace $\mathrm{E}_0\in\mathscr{F}(X)$ such that

$$\mathrm{E}\in\mathscr{F}(X)\text{ and }\mathrm{E}\supset\mathrm{E}_0\implies\mathrm{Coin}(\pi_{\mathrm{E}}\circ\widetilde{T},\,\pi_{\mathrm{E}}\circ\widetilde{\Phi})\cap(\partial\mathcal{U}_{\mathrm{E}}\times[0,1])=\varnothing.\tag{41}$$

For the set-valued mapping $\widetilde{\Sigma}|_{\overline{\mathcal{U}}_{\mathrm{E}}\times[0,1]}$, all the conditions of Proposition 5. Therefore, there exists $\widetilde{\sigma}_{\varepsilon}\in\mathrm{appr}(\widetilde{\Sigma}|_{\overline{\mathcal{U}}_{\mathrm{E}}\times[0,1]},\varepsilon)$, for any $\varepsilon>0$.

Let $\sigma_{i\varepsilon} := \widetilde{\sigma}_\varepsilon(\cdot, i)$, where $i = 0, 1$. Clearly, if $\varepsilon > 0$ is small enough, then the mapping $\sigma_{i\varepsilon}$ can be used as a continuous approximation of the set-valued mapping $\Sigma_i|_{\overline{\mathcal{U}}_E}$ (see Lemma 2 (iii)) to calculate $\mathrm{Deg}(T_i - \Phi_i, \overline{\mathcal{U}}, 0)$. Namely, we have

$$\mathrm{Deg}(T_i - \Phi_i, \overline{\mathcal{U}}, 0) = \deg(\pi_E \circ T_i - \pi_E \circ \psi_i \circ \sigma_{i\varepsilon}, \overline{\mathcal{U}}_E, 0), \quad i = 0, 1.$$

Therefore, to prove Theorem 2, it is sufficient to establish the following equality

$$\deg(\pi_E \circ T_0 - \pi_E \circ \psi_0 \circ \sigma_{0\varepsilon}, \overline{\mathcal{U}}_E, 0) = \deg(\pi_E \circ T_1 - \pi_E \circ \psi_1 \circ \sigma_{1\varepsilon}, \overline{\mathcal{U}}_E, 0). \tag{42}$$

Let us use a one-parameter family of mappings $\{\widetilde{H}_t \colon \overline{\mathcal{U}}_E \to X^*\}_{t\in[0,1]}$ defined by

$$\widetilde{H}_t(x) := \widetilde{T}(x,t) - \widetilde{\psi}(\widetilde{\sigma}_\varepsilon(x,t), t), \quad \forall (x,t) \in \overline{\mathcal{U}}_E \times [0,1].$$

Clearly, we have

$$\widetilde{H}_i(x) = T_i(x) - (\psi_i \circ \sigma_{i\varepsilon})(x), \quad i = 0, 1. \tag{43}$$

Moreover, from equality (41) and Lemma 3 it follows that

$$\mathrm{Coin}(\pi_E \circ \widetilde{T},\ \pi_E \circ \widetilde{\psi} \circ \widetilde{\sigma}_\varepsilon) \cap (\partial\overline{\mathcal{U}}_E \times [0,1]) = \varnothing,$$

and hence,

$$(\pi_E \circ \widetilde{H}_t)(x) \neq 0, \quad \forall x \in \partial\overline{\mathcal{U}}_E,\ t \in [0,1].$$

Therefore, by the homotopy invariance property of the Brouwer degree, we obtain

$$\deg(\pi_E \circ \widetilde{H}_0, \overline{\mathcal{U}}_E, 0) = \deg(\pi_E \circ \widetilde{H}_1, \overline{\mathcal{U}}_E, 0). \tag{44}$$

Combining relations (43) and (44), we arrive at equality (42). This completes the proof of Theorem 2. □

One of the most important properties of the introduced degree is formulated in the following theorem.

Theorem 3 (Zero degree). *If conditions* (H.1)–(H.3) *hold and* $\mathrm{Coin}(T, \Phi) = \varnothing$, *then*

$$\mathrm{Deg}(T - \Phi, \overline{\mathcal{U}}, 0) = 0.$$

Proof. For the set $\mathcal{V} = \overline{\mathcal{U}}$, all the conditions of Lemma 5 are valid. Therefore, there exists a subspace $E_0 \in \mathscr{F}(X)$ such that

$$E \in \mathscr{F}(X) \text{ and } E \supset E_0 \implies \mathrm{Coin}(\pi_E \circ T,\ \pi_E \circ \Phi) \cap \overline{\mathcal{U}}_E = \varnothing. \tag{45}$$

In view of Proposition 5, there exists $\sigma_\varepsilon \in \mathrm{appr}(\Sigma|_{\overline{\mathcal{U}}_E}, \varepsilon)$, for any $\varepsilon > 0$.
From equality (45) and Lemma 3 it follows that if $\varepsilon > 0$ is small enough, then

$$(\pi_E \circ T - \pi_E \circ \psi \circ \sigma_\varepsilon)(x) \neq 0, \quad \forall x \in \overline{\mathcal{U}}_E,$$

whence, by the properties of the Brouwer degree and Definition 13, we obtain

$$\mathrm{Deg}(T - \Phi, \overline{\mathcal{U}}, 0) = \deg(\pi_E \circ T - \pi_E \circ \psi \circ \sigma_\varepsilon, \overline{\mathcal{U}}_E, 0) = 0.$$

Thus, Theorem 3 is proved. □

As a direct consequence, we obtain the following coincidence principle.

Theorem 4 (Existence solution property). *Suppose that conditions* (H.1)–(H.4) *hold and*

$$\mathrm{Deg}(T-\Phi,\overline{\mathcal{U}},0)\neq 0.$$

Then the coincidence set $\mathrm{Coin}(T,\Phi)$ *is nonempty; that is, the inclusion* $T(x)\in\Phi(x)$ *has at least one solution in the set* $\mathcal{U}$.

The last theorem shows that our degree theory can be used as a tool for checking the existence of solutions to operator inclusions. Moreover, arguing as in [40], one can establish the compactness of the coincidence set.

Theorem 5 (Compactness property). *Under the conditions of Theorem 4, the coincidence set* $\mathrm{Coin}(T,\Phi)$ *is compact.*

5. Application: Optimal Feedback Control for Generalized Navier–Stokes System

In this section, we apply the obtained results to studying the solvability of an optimal feedback control problem for generalized stationary Navier–Stokes equations in the weak formulation.

5.1. Statement of Optimal Control Problem

Consider the following optimal control problem for the model describing the steady flow of an incompressible generalized Newtonian fluid with shear-dependent viscosity:

$$\begin{cases} (\vec{v}\cdot\nabla)\vec{v}-\operatorname{div}\mathbb{S}+\nabla p=\vec{f}+\vec{u} & \text{in } \Omega,\\ \nabla\cdot\vec{v}=0 & \text{in } \Omega,\\ \mathbb{S}=\eta_0\mathbb{D}(\vec{v})+\eta(|\mathbb{D}(\vec{v})|)\mathbb{D}(\vec{v}) & \text{in } \Omega,\\ \vec{v}=\vec{0} & \text{on } \Gamma,\\ \vec{u}\in\Sigma(\vec{v}), & \\ J=J(\vec{v})\to\min, & \end{cases} \tag{46}$$

where

- Ω is a bounded Lipschitz domain in $\mathbb{R}^d$, $d=2$ or 3, representing the flow region;
- Γ denotes the boundary of the domain Ω;
- $\vec{v}=\vec{v}(\vec{x})$ is the velocity vector;
- $\mathbb{S}=(\mathrm{S}_{ij}(\vec{x}))_{i,j=1}^{d}$ is the stress tensor deviator;
- $p=p(\vec{x})$ is the pressure;
- $\vec{f}=\vec{f}(\vec{x})$ is the given external body force;
- $\vec{u}=\vec{u}(\vec{x})$ is the control vector function;
- the operators ∇ and "div" are the gradient and the divergence, respectively,

$$\nabla:=\left(\frac{\partial}{\partial x_1},\ldots,\frac{\partial}{\partial x_d}\right),\quad \operatorname{div}\mathbb{S}:=\left(\sum_{i=1}^{d}\frac{\partial \mathrm{S}_{i1}}{\partial x_i},\ldots,\sum_{i=1}^{d}\frac{\partial \mathrm{S}_{id}}{\partial x_i}\right);$$

- $\mathbb{D}(\vec{v})$ denotes the rate-of-strain tensor,

$$\mathbb{D}(\vec{v}):=\frac{1}{2}(\nabla\vec{v}+(\nabla\vec{v})^{\top});$$

- η_0 is the "Newtonian" viscosity, $\eta_0>0$;
- $\eta=\eta(|\mathbb{D}(\vec{v})|)$ is the "non-Newtonian" viscosity, $\eta(|\mathbb{D}(\vec{v})|)\geq 0$;
- $\Sigma=\Sigma(\vec{v})$ is the feedback control function (set-valued operator);
- $J=J(\vec{v})$ is the cost functional (real-valued function).

A feature of optimal control problem (46) is that values of the functional J are independent of $\vec{u}$. A control with such a cost functional is referred to as *rigid* [56].

Note that, in the particular case $\eta \equiv 0$, the first three equations in (46) reduce to the incompressible stationary Navier–Stokes system describing the steady motion of fluids with constant viscosity.

5.2. Function Spaces and Assumptions on Model Data

First, we introduce some notation and the function spaces used.

For $s \in [1, \infty)$ and $k \in \mathbb{N}$, by $L^s(\Omega)$ and $H^k(\Omega)$ we denote the Lebesgue and Sobolev spaces, respectively. The definitions and detailed descriptions of the properties of these spaces can be found in the monographs [57,58].

Let

$$L^s(\Omega)^d := \underbrace{L^s(\Omega) \times \cdots \times L^s(\Omega)}_{d \text{ times}},$$
$$H^k(\Omega)^d := \underbrace{H^k(\Omega) \times \cdots \times H^k(\Omega)}_{d \text{ times}}.$$

Furthermore, we introduce the three spaces:

$$\mathfrak{D}(\Omega)^d := \{\vec{\phi}\colon \Omega \to \mathbb{R}^d : \vec{\phi} \in C^\infty(\Omega)^d,\ \operatorname{supp} \vec{\phi} \subset \Omega\},$$
$$\mathfrak{D}_{\text{sol}}(\Omega)^d := \{\vec{\phi} \in \mathfrak{D}(\Omega)^d : \nabla \cdot \vec{\phi} = 0\},$$
$V(\Omega)$ is the closure of the set $\mathfrak{D}_{\text{sol}}(\Omega)^d$ in the space $H^1(\Omega)^d$.

Note that $V(\Omega)$ is a Hilbert space and, for $d = 2, 3$, the embedding $V(\Omega) \hookrightarrow L^4(\Omega)^d$ is compact.

For any matrices $\mathbb{A} = (\mathrm{A}_{ij})_{i,j=1}^d$ and $\mathbb{B} = (\mathrm{B}_{ij})_{i,j=1}^d$, by $\mathbb{A} : \mathbb{B}$ and $|\mathbb{A}|$ we denote their scalar product and the Euclidean norm of $\mathbb{A}$, respectively:

$$\mathbb{A} : \mathbb{B} := \sum_{i=1}^{d} \mathrm{A}_{ij}\mathrm{B}_{ij}, \qquad |\mathbb{A}| := (\mathbb{A} : \mathbb{A})^{1/2}.$$

Suppose that

(A.1) the vector function $\vec{f}\colon \Omega \to \mathbb{R}^d$ belongs to the space $L^2(\Omega)^d$;

(A.2) the function $\eta\colon \mathbb{R}_+ \to \mathbb{R}_+$, where $\mathbb{R}_+ := [0, \infty)$, is continuous and bounded;

(A.3) the inequality
$$(\eta(|\mathbb{X}|)\mathbb{X} - \eta(|\mathbb{Y}|)\mathbb{Y}) : (\mathbb{X} - \mathbb{Y}) \geq 0$$
holds for any symmetric $d \times d$-matrices $\mathbb{X}$ and $\mathbb{Y}$;

(A.4) the set-valued mapping $\Sigma\colon V(\Omega) \multimap L^2(\Omega)^d$ is upper-semicontinuous;

(A.5) for any vector function $\vec{v} \in V(\Omega)$, the set $\Sigma(\vec{v})$ is aspheric in the space $L^2(\Omega)^d$;

(A.6) for any bounded set $\mathcal{B} \subset V(\Omega)$, the set $\Sigma(\mathcal{B})$ is relatively compact in the space $L^2(\Omega)^d$;

(A.7) the set-valued mapping Σ is globally bounded; that is, there exists a constant $q_{\max}$ such that, for any vector function $\vec{v} \in V(\Omega)$, we have
$$\sup_{q \in \Sigma(\vec{v})} \|q\|_{L^2(\Omega)^d} \leq q_{\max};$$

(A.8) the functional $J\colon V(\Omega) \to \mathbb{R}$ is lower semicontinuous.

Note that condition (A.3), which is imposed for the viscosity function η, holds when the function $\widetilde{\eta}\colon \mathbb{R}_+ \to \mathbb{R}_+$, $\widetilde{\eta}(\tau) := \eta(\tau)\tau$ is non-decreasing. Indeed, using the Cauchy–Schwarz inequality $|\mathbb{X} : \mathbb{Y}| \leq |\mathbb{X}||\mathbb{Y}|$, we obtain

$$\begin{aligned}
&\{\eta(|\mathbb{X}|)\mathbb{X} - \eta(|\mathbb{Y}|)\mathbb{Y}\} : (\mathbb{X} - \mathbb{Y}) \\
&= \eta(|\mathbb{X}|)|\mathbb{X}|^2 - \eta(|\mathbb{X}|)\mathbb{X} : \mathbb{Y} - \eta(|\mathbb{Y}|)\mathbb{Y} : \mathbb{X} + \eta(|\mathbb{Y}|)|\mathbb{Y}|^2 \\
&\geq \eta(|\mathbb{X}|)|\mathbb{X}|^2 - \eta(|\mathbb{X}|)|\mathbb{X}||\mathbb{Y}| - \eta(|\mathbb{Y}|)|\mathbb{Y}||\mathbb{X}| + \eta(|\mathbb{Y}|)|\mathbb{Y}|^2 \\
&= \{\eta(|\mathbb{X}|)|\mathbb{X}| - \eta(|\mathbb{Y}|)|\mathbb{Y}|\}(|\mathbb{X}| - |\mathbb{Y}|) \\
&= \{\widetilde{\eta}(|\mathbb{X}|) - \widetilde{\eta}(|\mathbb{Y}|)\}(|\mathbb{X}| - |\mathbb{Y}|) \geq 0,
\end{aligned}$$

for any $d \times d$-matrices $\mathbb{X}$ and $\mathbb{Y}$.

Recall that materials whose viscosity increases with the rate of shear strain are called *dilatant* [59] (also termed *shear-thickening* [60,61]). As examples of dilatant fluids, we can mention highly concentrated suspensions: starch paste, a suspension of river sand, etc.

Typical examples of the cost functional J are

$$\begin{aligned}
J = J_1(\vec{v}) &:= \int_\Omega |\vec{v} - \vec{v}_*|^2 \, d\vec{x}, \\
J = J_2(\vec{v}) &:= \int_\Omega |\mathbb{D}(\vec{v})|^2 \, d\vec{x}, \\
J = J_3(\vec{v}) &:= \int_\Omega |\mathbb{W}(\vec{v})|^2 \, d\vec{x},
\end{aligned}$$

where $\vec{v}_*\colon \Omega \to \mathbb{R}^d$ is a given vector function representing the desired velocity distribution in the flow region Ω and $\mathbb{W}(\vec{v})$ denotes the spin tensor, $\mathbb{W}(\vec{v}) := (\nabla\vec{v} - (\nabla\vec{v})^\top)/2$. It is easy to see that each of these functionals satisfies condition (A.8).

5.3. Weak Formulation of Optimal Control Problem and Existence Theorem

Definition 15. *We will say that a vector function $\vec{v} \in V(\Omega)$ is an admissible weak solution of problem* (46) *if*

$$\begin{aligned}
-\sum_{k=1}^{d} \int_\Omega v_k\vec{v} \cdot \frac{\partial \vec{w}}{\partial x_k} \, d\vec{x} + \eta_0 \int_\Omega \mathbb{D}(\vec{v}) : \mathbb{D}(\vec{w}) \, d\vec{x} + \int_\Omega \eta(|\mathbb{D}(\vec{v})|)\mathbb{D}(\vec{v}) : \mathbb{D}(\vec{w}) \, d\vec{x} \\
= \int_\Omega \vec{u} \cdot \vec{w} \, d\vec{x} + \int_\Omega \vec{f} \cdot \vec{w} \, d\vec{x}, \quad \forall \vec{w} \in V(\Omega),
\end{aligned}$$

for some vector function $\vec{u} \in \Sigma(\vec{v})$.

By $\mathfrak{M}_{\mathrm{ad}}$ we denote the set of all admissible weak solutions of (46).

Definition 16. *We will say that a vector function $\vec{v}_* \in V(\Omega)$ is an optimal weak solution of problem* (46) *if this vector function belongs to the set $\mathfrak{M}_{\mathrm{ad}}$ and the following equality holds:*

$$J(\vec{v}_*) = \inf_{\vec{v} \in \mathfrak{M}_{\mathrm{ad}}} J(\vec{v}).$$

Let us introduce the operators ψ, T, and Φ by the following formulae:

$$\psi\colon L^2(\Omega) \to V^*(\Omega),$$
$$\langle \psi(\vec{u}), \vec{w} \rangle_{V^*(\Omega)\times V(\Omega)} := \int\limits_{\Omega} \vec{u} \cdot \vec{w}\, \mathrm{d}\vec{x}, \quad \forall \vec{u} \in L^2(\Omega)^d,\ \vec{w} \in V(\Omega),$$
$$T\colon V(\Omega) \to V^*(\Omega),$$
$$\langle T(\vec{v}), \vec{w} \rangle_{V^*(\Omega)\times V(\Omega)} := -\sum_{k=1}^{d} \int\limits_{\Omega} v_k \vec{v} \cdot \frac{\partial \vec{w}}{\partial x_k}\, \mathrm{d}\vec{x} + \eta_0 \int\limits_{\Omega} \mathbb{D}(\vec{v}) : \mathbb{D}(\vec{w})\, \mathrm{d}\vec{x}$$
$$+ \int\limits_{\Omega} \eta(|\mathbb{D}(\vec{v})|)\mathbb{D}(\vec{v}) : \mathbb{D}(\vec{w})\, \mathrm{d}\vec{x} - \int\limits_{\Omega} \vec{f} \cdot \vec{w}\, \mathrm{d}\vec{x}, \quad \forall \vec{v}, \vec{w} \in V(\Omega),$$

and

$$\Phi\colon V(\Omega) \to V^*(\Omega), \quad \Phi := \psi \circ \Sigma.$$

Clearly, the problem of finding an admissible weak solution of (46) is equivalent to the inclusion $T(\vec{v}) \in \Phi(\vec{v})$.

Using Proposition 1 and condition (A.3), one can show that the operator T is of class $(S)_+$. Moreover, due to conditions (A.4) and (A.5), the set-valued mapping Φ belongs to the class C-ASV.

Taking into account conditions (A.1)–(A.8), by Theorems 4 and 5, we establish the following result.

Theorem 6 (Existence of optimal weak solutions). *Under conditions* (A.1)–(A.8), *problem* (46) *has at least one optimal weak solution in the sense of Definition* 16.

Remark 2. *The proposed approach can also be applied to the investigation of various control problems arising in other models for fluid flows* [62–66], *as well as in heat and mass transfer models* [67–71].

6. Conclusions

This article develops the topological degree method for studying the operator inclusions of the form $T(x) \in \Phi(x)$, where T is a single-valued $(S)_+$-operator and Φ is a compact set-valued operator. Using the topological degree of $T - \Phi$, we have established sufficient conditions for the solvability of the inclusion $T(x) \in \Phi(x)$. This result is an important generalization of the known results from fixed point theory for set-valued mappings. A feature of our approach is that it successfully combines very different techniques such as the monotonicity method and the principle of continuous single-valued approximation of set-valued mappings. Moreover, unlike conventional approaches used in topological degree theory for set-valued operators, we do not require the convexity condition of values of Φ. This extends a range of possible applications. In particular, we give an example illustrating how the introduced topological degree can be used in the analysis of the solvability of a strongly nonlinear system of partial differential equations and inclusions describing feedback control with complex geometry of admissible controls sets. A natural extension of this work includes analyzing topological characteristics of monotone-type single-valued operators with non-compact (for example, T-condensing) set-valued perturbations and their real-world applications.

Author Contributions: Conceptualization, E.S.B.; methodology, E.S.B.; investigation, E.S.B. and M.A.A.; writing—original draft preparation, E.S.B.; visualization, E.S.B.; writing—review and editing, E.S.B. and M.A.A. All authors have read and agreed to the published version of the manuscript.

Funding: This research received no external funding.

Institutional Review Board Statement: Not applicable.

Informed Consent Statement: Not applicable.

Data Availability Statement: Data are contained within the article.

Conflicts of Interest: The authors declare no conflicts of interest.

References

1. Agarwal, R.P.; Meehan, M.; O'Regan, D. *Fixed Point Theory and Applications*; Cambridge University Press: Cambridge, UK, 2001. [CrossRef]
2. Granas, A.; Dugundji, J. *Fixed Point Theory*; Springer: New York, NY, USA, 2003. [CrossRef]
3. Farmakis, I.; Moskowitz, M. *Fixed Point Theorems and Their Applications*; World Scientific Publishing: Singapore, 2013. [CrossRef]
4. Pathak, H.K. *An Introduction to Nonlinear Analysis and Fixed Point Theory*; Springer: Singapore, 2018. [CrossRef]
5. Subrahmanyam, P.V. *Elementary Fixed Point Theorems*; Springer: Singapore, 2018. [CrossRef]
6. Pata, V. *Fixed Point Theorems and Applications*; Springer: Cham, Switzerland, 2019. [CrossRef]
7. Debnath, P.; Konwar, N.; Radenović, S. (Eds.) *Metric Fixed Point Theory. Applications in Science, Engineering and Behavioural Sciences*; Springer: Singapore, 2021. [CrossRef]
8. Firozjah, A.A.; Rahimi, H.; Rad, G.S. Fixed and periodic point results in cone b-metric spaces over Banach algebras; a survey. *Fixed Point Theory* **2021**, *22*, 157–168. [CrossRef]
9. Hutchinson, J.E. Fractals and self-similarity. *Indiana Univ. Math. J.* **1981**, *30*, 713–747. [CrossRef]
10. Kashyap, S.K.; Sharma, B.K.; Banerjee, A. On Krasnoselskii fixed point theorem and fractal. *Chaos Solit. Fractals* **2014**, *61*, 44–45. [CrossRef]
11. Ri, S. A new fixed point theorem in the fractal space. *Indag. Math.* **2016**, *27*, 85–93. [CrossRef]
12. Nazeer, W.S.; Kang, M.; Tanveer, M.; Shahid, A.A. Fixed point results in the generation of Julia and Mandelbrot sets. *J. Inequal. Appl.* **2015**, *2015*, 298. [CrossRef]
13. Petruşel, A.; Petruşel, G.; Wong, M.M. Fixed point results for locally contractions with applications to fractals. *J. Nonlinear Convex Anal.* **2020**, *21*, 403–411.
14. Antal, S.; Tomar, A.; Prajapati, D.J.; Sajid, M. Fractals as Julia sets of complex sine function via fixed point iterations. *Fractal Fract.* **2021**, *5*, 272. [CrossRef]
15. Choudhury, B.S.; Chakraborty, P. Strong fixed points of Φ-couplings and generation of fractals. *Chaos Solit. Fractals* **2022**, *163*, 112514. [CrossRef]
16. Navascués, M.A. Stability of fixed points of partial contractivities and fractal surfaces. *Axioms* **2024**, *13*, 474. [CrossRef]
17. Shaheryar, M.; Ud Din, F.; Hussain, A.; Alsulami, H. Fixed point results for Fuzzy enriched contraction in fuzzy Banach spaces with applications to fractals and dynamic market equillibrium. *Fractal Fract.* **2024**, *8*, 609. [CrossRef]
18. Barnsley, M. *Fractals Everywhere*, 2nd ed.; Academic Press: Cambridge, MA, USA, 2014. [CrossRef]
19. Qi, X. *Fixed Points, Fractals, Iterated Function Systems and Generalized Support Vector Machines*; Mälardalen University Press Licentiate Theses, No. 247; License Thesis, Mälardalen University, Västerås, Sweden, 2016.
20. Navascués, M.A. Approximation of fixed points and fractal functions by means of different iterative algorithms. *Chaos Solit. Fractals* **2024**, *180*, 114535. [CrossRef]
21. Buescu, J.; Serpa, C. Fractal and Hausdorff dimensions for systems of iterative functional equations. *J. Math. Anal. Appl.* **2019**, *480*, 123429. [CrossRef]
22. Mawhin, J. *Topological Degree Methods in Nonlinear Boundary Value Problems*; McGraw-Hill: New York, NY, USA, 1976.
23. Gaines, R.E.; Mawhin, J.L. *Coincidence Degree and Nonlinear Differential Equations*; Springer: Berlin/Heidelberg, Germany, 1977. [CrossRef]
24. Han, Z.-Q. Coincidence degree and nontrivial solutions of elliptic boundary value problems at resonance. *Nonlinear Anal.* **2004**, *56*, 739–750. [CrossRef]
25. O'Regan, D.; Cho, Y.J.; Chen, Y.Q. *Topological Degree Theory and Applications*; Chapman and Hall/CRC: New York, NY, USA, 2006. [CrossRef]
26. Górniewicz, L. *Topological Fixed Point Theory of Multivalued Mappings*; Kluwer: Dordrecht, The Netherlands; Boston, MA, USA; London, UK, 1999. [CrossRef]
27. Arutyunov, A.V.; Zhukovskiy, E.S.; Zhukovskiy, S.E. Coincidence points principle for mappings in partially ordered spaces. *Topol. Appl.* **2015**, *179*, 13–33. [CrossRef]
28. Benarab, S.; Zhukovskiy, E.S. Coincidence points of two mappings acting from a partially ordered space to an arbitrary set. *Russ. Math.* **2020**, *64*, 8–16. [CrossRef]
29. Sessa, S.; Akkouchi, M. Coincidence points for mappings in metric spaces satisfying weak commuting conditions. *Symmetry* **2022**, *14*, 504. [CrossRef]
30. Tarafdar, E.; Teo, S.K. On the existence of solutions of the equation $Lx \in Nx$ and a coincidence degree theory. *J. Austral. Math. Soc. Ser. A* **1979**, *28*, 139–173.
31. Pruszko, T. A coincidence degree for L-compact convex-valued mappings and its application to the Picard problem of orientor. *Bull. Acad. Pol. Sci. Sér. Sci Math.* **1979**, *27*, 895–902.
32. Browder, F.E. Fixed point theory and nonlinear problems. *Bull. Amer. Math. Soc.* **1983**, *9*, 1–39. [CrossRef]

33. Hu, S.C.; Papageorgiou, N.S. Generalizations of Browder's degree theory. *Trans. Amer. Math. Soc.* **1995**, *347*, 233–259. [CrossRef]
34. Gabor, D. The coincidence index for fundamentally contractible multivalued maps with nonconvex values. *Ann. Pol. Math.* **2000**, *75*, 143–166. [CrossRef]
35. Kobayashi, J.; Ôtani, M. Topological degree for $(S)_+$-mappings with maximal monotone perturbations and its applications to variational inequalities. *Nonlinear Anal.* **2004**, *59*, 147–172. [CrossRef]
36. Kartsatos, A.G.; Skrypnik, I.V. A new topological degree theory for densely defined quasibounded mathematical equation-perturbations of multivalued maximal monotone operators in reflexive Banach spaces. *Abstr. Appl. Anal.* **2005**, *2005*, 121–158. [CrossRef]
37. Baranovskii, E.S. Topological Degree for Multivalued Perturbations of $(S)_+$-Maps and Its Applications. Ph.D. Thesis, Voronezh State University, Voronezh, Russia, 2010.
38. Asfaw, T.M. A degree theory for compact perturbations of monotone type operators and application to nonlinear parabolic problem. *Abstr. Appl. Anal.* **2017**, *2017*, 7236103. [CrossRef]
39. Baranovskii, E.S. Optimal problems for parabolic-type systems with aspheric sets of admissible controls. *Russ. Math.* **2009**, *53*, 63–67. [CrossRef]
40. Baranovskii, E.S. Feedback optimal control problem for a network model of viscous fluid flows. *Math. Notes* **2022**, *112*, 26–39. [CrossRef]
41. Baranovskii, E.S.; Brizitskii, R.V.; Saritskaia, Z.Y. Optimal control problems for the reaction–diffusion–convection equation with variable coefficients. *Nonlinear Anal. Real World Appl.* **2024**, *75*, 103979. [CrossRef]
42. Browder, F.E. Nonlinear elliptic boundary value problems and the generalized topological degree. *Bull. Amer. Math. Soc.* **1970**, *76*, 999–1005. [CrossRef]
43. Skrypnik, I.V. *Nonlinear Elliptic Equations of Higher Order*; Naukova Dumka: Kiev, Ukraine, 1973.
44. Browder, F.E. Degree theory for nonlinear mapping. *Proc. Sympos. Pure Math. Soc.* **1986**, *45*, 203–226.
45. Granas, A. Sur la notion du degré topologique pour une certaine classe de transformations multivalentes dans les espaces de Banach. *Bull. Acad. Polon. Sci.* **1959**, *7*, 191–194.
46. Granas, A. Theorem on antipodes and theorems on fixed points for a certain class of multi-valued maps in Banach spaces. *Bull. Acad. Polon. Sci.* **1959**, *7*, 271–275.
47. Cellina, A; Lasota, A. A new approach to the definition of topological degree for multivalued mappings. *Atti Accad. Naz. Lincei Rend. Cl. Sci. Fis. Mat. Natur.* **1969**, *47*, 434–440.
48. Skrypnik, I.V. *Methods for Analysis of Nonlinear Elliptic Boundary Value Problems*; American Mathematical Society: Providence, RI, USA, 1994; Volume 139.
49. Kachurovskii, R.I. Non-linear monotone operators in Banach spaces. *Russ. Math. Surv.* **1969**, *23*, 117–165. [CrossRef]
50. Zeidler, E. *Nonlinear Functional Analysis and Its Applications*; Springer: New York, NY, USA, 1990; Volume II/B.
51. Dinca, G.; Mawhin, J. *Brouwer Degree: The Core of Nonlinear Analysis*; Birkhäuser: Cham, Switzerland, 2021. [CrossRef]
52. Myshkis, A.D. Generalizations of the theorem on a fixed point of a dynamical system inside of a closed trajectory. *Mat. Sb.* **1954**, *34*, 525–540.
53. Borsuk, K. *Theory of Retracts*; Monografie Matematyczne PWN: Warsaw, Poland, 1967; Volume 44.
54. Górniewicz, L.; Granas, A.; Kryszewski, W. On the homotopy method in the fixed point index theory for multi-mappings of compact absolute neighborhood retracts. *J. Math. Anal. Appl.* **1991**, *161*, 457–473. [CrossRef]
55. Leray, J.; Schauder, J. Topologie et équations fonctionnelles. *Ann. Sci. Ecole Norm. Sup.* **1934**, *51*, 45–78. [CrossRef]
56. Fursikov, A.V. *Optimal Control of Distributed Systems*; AMS: Providence, RI, USA, 2000.
57. Adams, R.A.; Fournier J.J.F. Sobolev Spaces. In *Pure and Applied Mathematics*; Elsevier: Amsterdam, The Netherlands, 2003; Volume 40.
58. Boyer, F.; Fabrie, P. *Mathematical Tools for the Study of the Incompressible Navier–Stokes Equations and Related Models*; Springer: New York, NY, USA, 2013. [CrossRef]
59. Astarita, G.; Marucci, G.; *Principles of Non-Newtonian Fluid Mechanics*; McGraw-Hill: New York, NY, USA, 1974.
60. Pak, J.; Sin, C.; Baranovskii, E.S. Regularity criterion for 3D shear-thinning fluids via one component of velocity. *Appl. Math. Optim.* **2023**, *88*, 48. [CrossRef]
61. Sin, C.; Baranovskii, E.S. A note on regularity criterion for 3D shear thickening fluids in terms of velocity. *Math. Ann.* **2024**, *389*, 515–524. [CrossRef]
62. Baranovskii, E.S. On steady motion of viscoelastic fluid of Oldroyd type. *Sb. Math.* **2014**, *205*, 763–776. . [CrossRef]
63. Baranovskii, E.S.; Artemov, M.A. Mixed boundary-value problems for motion equations of a viscoelastic medium. *Electron. J. Diff. Equ.* **2015**, *2015*, 252. https://ejde.math.txstate.edu/Volumes/2015/252/abstr.html
64. Ershkov, S.V. About existence of stationary points for the Arnold–Beltrami–Childress (ABC) flow. *Appl. Math. Comput.* **2016**, *276*, 379–383. [CrossRef]
65. Mallea-Zepeda, E.; Ortega-Torres, E.; Villamizar-Roa, É.J. An optimal control problem for the Navier–Stokes-α system. *J. Dyn. Control Syst.* **2023**, *29*, 129–156. [CrossRef]
66. Ershkov, S.V.; Leshchenko, D.D. Non-Newtonian pressure-governed rivulet flows on inclined surface. *Mathematics* **2024**, *12*, 779. [CrossRef]

67. Brizitskii, R.V.; Saritskaia, Z.Y. Analysis of inhomogeneous boundary value problems for generalized Boussinesq model of mass transfer. *J. Dyn. Control Syst.* **2023**, *29*, 1809–1828. [CrossRef]
68. Mallea-Zepeda, E.; Lenes, E.; Valero, E. Boundary control problem for heat convection equations with slip boundary condition. *Math. Probl. Eng.* **2018**, *2018*, 7959761. [CrossRef]
69. Baranovskii, E.S. Exact solutions for non-isothermal flows of second grade fluid between parallel plates. *Nanomaterials* **2023**, *13*, 1409. [CrossRef]
70. Brizitskii, R.V. Generalised Boussinesq model with variable coefficients. *Sib. El. Math. Rep.* **2024**, *21*, 213–227. [CrossRef]
71. Baranovskii, E.S.; Brizitskii, R.V.; Saritskaia, Z.Y. Boundary value and control problems for the stationary heat transfer model with variable coefficients. *J. Dynam. Control Syst.* **2024**, *30*, 26. [CrossRef]

fractal and fractional

MDPI

Article

Hausdorff Outer Measures and the Representation of Coherent Upper Conditional Previsions by the Countably Additive Möbius Transform

Serena Doria

Department of Engineering and Geology, University G.d'Annunzio, 66100 Chieti-Pescara, Italy; serena.doria@unich.it

Abstract: This paper explores coherent upper conditional previsions, a class of nonlinear functionals that generalize expectations while preserving consistency properties. The study focuses on their integral representation using the countably additive Möbius transform, which is possible if coherent upper previsions are defined with respect to a monotone set function of bounded variation. In this work, we prove that an integral representation with respect to a countably additive measure is also possible, on the Borel σ-algebra, even when the coherent upper prevision is defined by the Choquet integral with respect to a Hausdorff measure, which is not of bounded variation. It occurs since Hausdorff outer measures are metric measures, and therefore every Borel set is measurable with respect to them. Furthermore, when the conditioning event has a Hausdorff measure in its own Hausdorff dimension equal to zero or infinity, coherent conditional probability is defined via the countably additive Möbius transform of a monotone set function of bounded variation. The paper demonstrates the continuity of coherent conditional previsions induced by Hausdorff measures.

Keywords: coherent upper conditional previsions; countable additive Möbius transform; Hausdorff outer measures

1. Introduction

In classical decision theory and probabilistic modeling, preference orderings and equivalence classes over uncertain outcomes are often represented using linear expectation operators associated with countably additive probability measures. However, it has long been recognized that such linear representations are inadequate for capturing many forms of ambiguity, imprecision, and risk attitudes observed in practical decision-making scenarios [1–3].

To address these limitations, a variety of nonlinear functionals have been introduced, including coherent upper and lower conditional previsions, which generalize the notion of expectation [4,5] by relaxing linearity while preserving certain consistency properties. These functionals provide a richer and more flexible framework for representing preferences that are not necessarily expressible through a single probability measure. Monotone set functions [6–8] and nonlinear integral [9,10] have been investigated in the literature. This paper focuses on a specific class of such functionals—coherent upper conditional previsions—and investigates their integral representations in terms of the countably additive Möbius transform. This integral representation is possible when uncertainty is represented by a monotone set function of bounded variation, that is, when coherent upper conditional previsions are defined with respect to a coherent upper probability of bounded variation. A first issue we address in this work is whether it is possible to represent the Choquet integral [11], with respect to a monotone set function μ—not necessarily of bounded variation—using a countably additive measure, atleast on suitable domains. We investigate whether it is possible to find conditions under which the Choquet integral can be equivalently expressed through a countably additive measure, even when the underlying capacity lacks bounded variation. The answer to this question is affirmative, and a concrete example is provided by the framework of coherent conditional previsions constructed via Hausdorff outer measures.

In particular, the model of coherent conditional prevision based on Hausdorff outer measures illustrates how such a representation can be achieved, despite the absence of bounded variation in μ (Theorem 10).

This example demonstrates that under certain conditions, it is indeed possible to reconcile non-additive integration with classical measure theory. A central contribution of this work is the examination of the role played by Hausdorff outer measures in this context. We demonstrate that these outer measures provide a natural and powerful tool for defining coherent upper conditional previsions, which satisfy a Continuity Principle, particularly in settings where regularity conditions on the underlying space are relaxed. In fact, Hausdorff outer measures $\mathcal{H}^s$ for $0 < s < 1$ are proven to not be of bounded variation. Through this investigation, we aim to deepen the understanding of the interplay between non-additive measure theory and nonlinear expectation functionals, and to provide new mathematical foundations for applications in robust statistics, imprecise probabilities, and decision theory. A second result of this work is the introduction, on the Borel sigma-field, of a countably additive model of conditional prediction. This model is constructed by considering the countably additive Möbius transform of a monotone set function of bounded variation in cases where the conditioning event has a Hausdorff measure equal to 0 or ∞ in its Hausdorff dimension.

The continuity property of the conditional prediction depends on whether the monotone function is continuous from below. Given a monotone set function μ of bounded variation, defined on an algebra of events, it is possible to construct a sigma-additive probability on a suitable σ-algebra such that the Choquet integral defined with respect to μ is equal to an integral defined with respect to a σ-additive probability. This representation of the Choquet integral can be given by constructing a σ-additive representation of the monotone function μ using the σ-additive Möbius transform. Moreover, since the Choquet integrals are preserved under the Möbius transform, the two integral representations coincide. The construction of the σ-additive Möbius transform (see Lemma 6.1 and Theorem 6.2 of [12]) is obtained by considering the Möbius transform defined on an opportune σ-field where all finitely additive functions are continuous from above to the empty set and so countably additive. It is the same procedure used in [13] based on Theorem 2.3 of [14]. The construction of the Möbius transform is based on the Stone extension of a space $(\Omega, \mathcal{A})$, where $\mathcal{A}$ is a field, to the measurable space $(\mathcal{H}_p, \mathcal{D}'(\mathcal{A}))$ of all supermodular 0–1 valued set functions. In this measurable space, each finite additive function is countably additive since it is continuous from above to the empty set.

A different construction of the Möbius transform of a monotone set function is proposed by using a composition norm so that any monotone set function can be expressed as a combination of particular coherent lower probabilities as the canonical representation of a game by unanimity games investigated in [15,16].

In this paper, the σ-additive Möbius transform is considered to propose a model of coherent countably additive conditional probability on the Borel σ-field (Theorem 4); we also prove that coherent lower conditional previsions defined with respect to the Möbius transform of a coherent lower probability ν are continuous if ν is continuous from below (Theorem 8) so that the monotone convergence theorem for monotone set functions (Theorem 5) holds.

The integral representation with respect to the σ-additive Möbius transform of belief functions has been investigated in [17,18]. In this paper, the general case of the integral representation with respect to a σ-additive probability of the Choquet integral is considered.

2. Preliminaries

Given a non-empty set Ω and denoted by $\wp(\Omega)$, the family of all subsets of Ω, a monotone set function, also called capacity, $\mu : \wp(\Omega) \to \overline{\Re}_+ = \Re_+ \cup \{+\infty\}$, is such that $\mu(\emptyset) = 0$, and if A, $B \in \wp(\Omega)$ with $A \subset B$, then $\mu(A) \leq \mu(B)$.

Let $\mathcal{F}$ be a field of subsets of Ω, i.e., a collection of sets closed under finite unions, finite intersections, and relative complements. A monotone set function μ is supermodular or 2-monotone if

$$\mu(A \cup B) + \mu(A \cap B) \geq \mu(A) + \mu(B)$$

A set function μ is said to be *k-monotone* if for every collection of sets $A_1, A_2, \ldots, A_k \subseteq \Omega$, the following inequality holds:

$$\mu\left(\bigcup_{i=1}^{k} A_i\right) \geq \sum_{\emptyset \neq J \subseteq \{1,\ldots,k\}} (-1)^{|J|+1} \mu\left(\bigcap_{j \in J} A_j\right).$$

A set function μ is *totally monotone* if it is monotone and k-monotone for $k \geq 2$. A set function μ is a belief function if it is totally monotone and $\mu(\Omega) = 1$.

A set function $\mu : \mathcal{F} \to [0, \infty]$ is called a *measure* on the field $\mathcal{F}$ if it satisfies the following properties:

1. $\mu(\emptyset) = 0$.

2. Countable additivity:

For any disjoint sets $A_1, A_2, \cdots \in \mathcal{F}$ and $\bigcup_{n=1}^{\infty} A_n \in \mathcal{F}$, we have

$$\mu\left(\bigcup_{n=1}^{\infty} A_n\right) = \sum_{n=1}^{\infty} \mu(A_n).$$

μ is a probability measure on $\mathcal{F}$ if μ is a measure such that $\mu(\Omega) = 1$.

Let μ be a probability measure. Then, the following properties hold (Theorem 2.1 [14]):

1. *Continuity from below*: If $A_1 \subset A_2 \subset \ldots$ is an increasing sequence of events such that $\bigcup_{n=1}^{\infty} A_n \in \mathcal{F}$, then

$$\mu\left(\bigcup_{n=1}^{\infty} A_n\right) = \lim_{n \to \infty} \mu(A_n).$$

2. *Continuity from above*: If $B_1 \supset B_2 \supset \ldots$ is a decreasing sequence of events such that $\bigcap_{n=1}^{\infty} B_n \in \mathcal{F}$, then

$$\mu\left(\bigcap_{n=1}^{\infty} B_n\right) = \lim_{n \to \infty} \mu(B_n).$$

3. *Countable subadditivity*: For any countable sequence of events $A_1, A_2, A_3, \cdots \in \mathcal{F}$ pairwise disjoint

$$\mu\left(\bigcup_{n=1}^{\infty} A_n\right) \leq \sum_{n=1}^{\infty} \mu(A_n).$$

In the presence of finite additivity, a special case of continuity from above implies countable additivity.

Proposition 1. *If μ is a finitely additive measure that is continuous, from above to $\emptyset$ on the field $\mathcal{F}$, then μ is countably additive. That is, if $B_1 \supset B_2 \supset \ldots$ is a decreasing sequence of events such that $\bigcap_{n=1}^{\infty} B_n = \emptyset$ and $lim_{n\to\infty}\mu(B_n) = 0$, then μ is countably additive.*

One important condition that characterizes the countable additivity of finite measures is continuity from above to the empty set. The vanishing of the measure on decreasing sequences of sets tending to the empty set guarantees that μ behaves well under countable unions and disjoint decompositions, which are essential aspects of countable additivity. A countably additive probability measure can be defined on the σ-field generated by the field of all cylinders in the space of infinite sequences. This is achieved using a procedure based on Theorem 2.3 of [14], which proves that every finitely additive probability measure on the field of all cylinders in this space is, indeed, countably additive.

The key reason is that any sequence of non-empty cylinders converges to a non-empty set. Consequently, any finite probability measure is continuous from above to the empty set. According to Proposition 1, this implies countable additivity.

However, the same procedure cannot be applied to define a conditional probability in the continuous case. This is due to the fact that the σ-field generated by the field of all cylinders in the space of infinite sequences is closely related to the Borel σ-field on $[0, 1]$, though significant differences exist.

In particular, the field of cylinders is strictly smaller than the field of finite disjoint unions of intervals in $(0, 1]$, and in this case, Theorem 2.3 does not always apply. Specifically, there exist sequences of subsets that are not continuous from above to the empty set so that the countable additivity of a finitely additive probability measure is not guaranteed (see Proposition 1).

Given a monotone set function μ on $S \subset \wp(\Omega)$, the *outer set function* of μ is the set function μ^* defined on the whole power set $\wp(\Omega)$ by

$$\mu^*(A) = \inf\{\mu(B) : B \supset A; B \in S\}, A \in \wp(\Omega).$$

On a field S, the outer set function μ^* of μ is sub-additive if μ is ([19] Proposition 2.4). So the outer set function of a measure defined on a field S is sub-additive.

The inner set function of μ is the set function μ_* defined on the whole power set $\wp(\Omega)$ by

$$\mu_*(A) = \sup\{\mu(B)|B \subset A; B \in S\}, A \in \wp(\Omega).$$

In [20], a weaker definition of continuity is proposed, named *null continuity*. This property is related to how a monotone measure behaves when we have an increasing sequence of null sets. It ensures that the measure of the limit of the sequence is also zero.

Definition 1. *Let μ be a monotone set function defined on a measurable space $(\Omega, \mathcal{A})$. We say that μ is null continuous if for every sequence of sets A_n with $A_n \in \mathcal{A} \quad \forall n \in \mathbb{N}$ such that $A_1 \subseteq A_2 \subseteq A_3 \subseteq \cdots$ and $\mu(A_n) = 0$, it follows that*

$$\mu(\bigcup_{n=1}^{\infty} A_n) = 0.$$

Example 1. *The vacuous coherent upper prevision defined by*

$$\overline{P}(X) = \sup_{\omega \in \Omega} X(\omega).$$

is a monotone set function that is null continuous, and the conjugate, called vacuous coherent lower prevision, defined by

$$\underline{P}(I_A) = \inf_{\omega \in \Omega} I_A(\omega),$$

is not null continuous. Let $\Omega = [0, 1]$, and consider $A_n = [0, 1 - \frac{1}{n}]$; then, $\underline{P}(A_n) = 0$ but $\underline{P}(\bigcup_{n=1}^{\infty} A_n) = 1$.

In [21], theconvergence of sequences of measurable functions with respect to a null-continuous monotone set function is investigated. In particular, it is proven that for a monotone set function, continuity from below implies null continuity, but the converse is not true. Moreover, countably sub-additive monotone set functions are null continuous. Finally, a countably additive probability on a field need not be continuous from below. This is also important when discussing decision models because it can lead to complications mathematically, especially in the examples in this paper.

3. The Role of Functions of Bounded Variation Among Different Integration Concepts

3.1. Functions of Bounded Variation and Associated Measures

Let $f : \mathbb{R} \to \mathbb{R}$ be a real-valued function. We say that f is of **bounded variation** on an interval $[a, b]$ if its total variation

$$V_a^b(f) := \sup\left\{ \sum_{i=1}^{n} |f(x_i) - f(x_{i-1})| : a = x_0 < x_1 < \cdots < x_n = b \right\}$$

is finite. The space of such functions is denoted by $BV([a, b])$.

More generally, a function $f : \mathbb{R} \to \mathbb{R}$ is said to be of bounded variation on $\mathbb{R}$ if it is of bounded variation on every compact interval $[a, b] \subset \mathbb{R}$.

3.2. Characterization

A function $f \in BV([a, b])$ if and only if it can be written as the difference of two monotone increasing functions:

$$f(x) = f_1(x) - f_2(x),$$

where f_1, f_2 both increase on $[a, b]$.

The following example shows that there exists a finitely additive probability that may not be of bounded variation.

3.3. Associated Measures: The Lebesgue–Stieltjes Measure

To every function $f \in BV(\mathbb{R})$ (i.e., of bounded variation on every compact interval), we can associate a Borel measure μ_f called the **Lebesgue–Stieltjes measure** defined by

$$\mu_f((a,b]) := f(b) - f(a), \quad \text{for all } a < b.$$

This measure μ_f extends uniquely to a Radon measure on $\mathbb{R}$. If f is right-continuous and of bounded variation, the measure is uniquely determined and satisfies

$$\mu_f([a,b]) = f(b^+) - f(a^-),$$

where the limits from the right and left are used to handle jump discontinuities.

3.4. Properties

- If f is monotone increasing, then μ_f is a positive measure;
- If f is absolutely continuous, then μ_f is absolutely continuous with respect to the Lebesgue measure and can be written as $d\mu_f = f'(x)\,dx$;
- If f has jump discontinuities, then μ_f contains atomic parts (Dirac deltas) at those jumps.

3.5. Examples

1. *Monotone function:* If $f(x) = x$, then μ_f is the Lebesgue measure on $\mathbb{R}$;
2. *Step function:* Let

$$f(x) = \begin{cases} 0 & x < 0 \\ 1 & x \geq 0 \end{cases} \quad \Rightarrow \quad \mu_f = \delta_0,$$

   where δ_0 is the Dirac measure at $x = 0$;
3. *Absolutely continuous:* If $f(x) = \sin(x)$ on $[0, \pi]$, then $\mu_f = f'(x)\,dx = \cos(x)\,dx$.

Let $\mu : \mathcal{A} \to \mathbb{R}$ be a finitely additive set function defined on an algebra $\mathcal{A}$ of subsets of a set X.

We say that μ is of *bounded variation* if there exists a constant $M > 0$ such that for every finite collection of disjoint sets $\{A_i\}_{i=1}^n \subset \mathcal{A}$, the following inequality holds:

$$\sum_{i=1}^{n} |\mu(A_i)| \leq M.$$

Equivalently, the *total variation* of μ, defined as

$$\|\mu\| := \sup\left\{ \sum_{i=1}^{n} |\mu(A_i)| : \{A_i\}_{i=1}^n \text{ is a finite partition of some } A \in \mathcal{A} \right\},$$

is finite.

A purely finitely additive probability may not be of bounded variation. An example can be given by a non-principal ultrafilter.

Definition 2. *An ultrafilter $\mathcal{U}$ is a class of subsets of $\wp(B)$ such that the following applies:*

(a) $\emptyset \notin \mathcal{U}$;
(b) $A, B \in \mathcal{U} \Rightarrow A \cap B \in \mathcal{U}$;
(c) $A \in \mathcal{A}; A \subset B \subset \Omega \Rightarrow B \in \mathcal{U}$;
(d) $\forall A \in \wp(\Omega)$ *either* $A \in \mathcal{U}$ *or* $A^c \in \mathcal{U}$.

If the class $\mathcal{U}$ satisfies the conditions (a), (b), and (c), it is called a filter.

Given an ultrafilter $\mathcal{U} \subset \wp(\Omega)$, a 0–1-valued, finitely additive probability $m_{\mathcal{B}}$ on $\wp(\Omega)$ can be defined by $m_B(A) = 1$ if $A \in \mathcal{A}$ and $m_B(A) = 0$ if $A^c \in \mathcal{A}$.

Example 2. *Consider the ultrafilter $\mathcal{U}$ over the set Ω, comprising sets whose complements are finite. In this context, if A represents any finite set, then the value of $m_\Omega(A)$ is 0. The ultrafilter is one of those extending the Frechét filter.*

Example 3. *Consider the scenario where Ω is synonymous with $\mathcal{N}$. Let $\mathcal{U}$ represent the ultrafilter of Ω, which pertains to sets where the complement is finite. Take A to be the set $\{2n : n \in \mathcal{N}\}$. According to property d), as defined in Definition 3, we can infer that if $A \in \mathcal{U}$, then it follows that $m_\Omega(A) = 1$, and in cases where $A^c \in \mathcal{U}$, it holds that $m_\Omega(A) = 0$, or alternatively, $m_\Omega(A^c) = 1$.*

An ultrafilter $\mathcal{U}$ on X is called a principal if there exists an element $x_0 \in X$ such that

$$\mathcal{U} = \{A \subseteq X \mid x_0 \in A\}.$$

In this case, we say that $\mathcal{U}$ is generated by the point x_0. That is, $\mathcal{U}$ consists of all subsets of X that contain x_0.

Example 4. *Let $\mathcal{A}$ be the algebra of all subsets of $\mathbb{N}$, the natural numbers. Let $\mathcal{U}$ be a non-principal ultrafilter on $\mathbb{N}$. We define a set function $\mu : \mathcal{A} \to \mathbb{R}$ by*

$$\mu(A) := \lim_{n \to \mathcal{U}} \frac{|A \cap [1, n]|}{n}.$$

Here, the ultrafilter limit $\lim_{n \to \mathcal{U}} a_n$ of a bounded real sequence (a_n) is defined as the unique real number L such that

$$\forall \varepsilon > 0, \quad \{n \in \mathbb{N} : |a_n - L| < \varepsilon\} \in \mathcal{U}.$$

This is referred to as the ultrafilter limit density.

- *Finitely additive: For disjoint sets $A, B \subseteq \mathbb{N}$, we have*

$$\mu(A \cup B) = \mu(A) + \mu(B).$$

- *Not countably additive: Let $A_n = \{n\}$. Then, $\mu(A_n) = 0$ for all n, but*

$$\mu\left(\bigcup_{n=1}^{\infty} A_n\right) = \mu(\mathbb{N}) = 1 \neq \sum_{n=1}^{\infty} \mu(A_n) = 0.$$

- *Not of bounded variation: If the sequence is not bounded, then the limit could be infinity.*

According to the previous notions, for monotone set functions, the following definition has been introduced in [12].

Definition 3. *A monotone set function $v : \mathcal{A} \to \Re$ of bounded variation is such that there exist two monotone set functions v_1, v_2 such that $v = v_1 - v_2$. Let $V_b(\mathcal{A})$ be the class of set functions on $\mathcal{A}$ with bounded variation and with v_1 and v_2, which are totally monotone.*

3.6. Riemann Integral

Let $\Omega : [a,b] \to \mathbb{R}$ be a bounded function. The Riemann integral of X over $[a,b]$ is defined as

$$\int_a^b X(\omega)\,dx = \lim_{\|\mathcal{P}\| \to 0} \sum_{i=1}^{n} X(\omega_i^*)\Delta\omega_i,$$

where $\mathcal{P} = \{a = x_0 < x_1 < \cdots < x_n = b\}$ is a partition of $[a,b]$, $\Delta\omega_i = \omega_i - \omega_{i-1}$, and $\omega_i^* \in [\omega_{i-1}, \omega_i]$. The integral exists if the limit is the same, regardless of the choice of ω_i^*.

3.7. Riemann–Stieltjes Integral

Let $X : [a,b] \to \mathbb{R}$ be a bounded function and $g : [a,b] \to \mathbb{R}$ a function of bounded variation. The Riemann–Stieltjes integral of X with respect to g is defined as

$$\int_a^b X(\omega)\,dg(\omega) = \lim_{\|\mathcal{P}\| \to 0} \sum_{i=1}^{n} X(\omega_i^*)[g(\omega_i) - g(\omega_{i-1})],$$

where $\mathcal{P}$ is a partition of $[a,b]$ and $\omega_i^* \in [\omega_{i-1}, \omega_i]$. This generalizes the Riemann integral by integrating with respect to a function g instead of $g(\omega) = \omega$. The Riemann–Stieltjes integral provides a natural way to define the expectation of a real-valued random variable X with a cumulative distribution function (CDF) F_X. Specifically, if X is integrable, its expected value is given by

$$\mathbb{E}[X] = \int_{-\infty}^{\infty} x\,dF_X(x),$$

where the integral is understood in the Riemann–Stieltjes sense. This definition of expectation is very general. It applies whether X is any of the following:

- **Discrete** (e.g., F_X has jumps);
- **Absolutely continuous** (i.e., F_X has a density f_X such that $F_X(x) = \int_{-\infty}^{x} f_X(t)dt$);
- A **mixed-type** random variable.

In the special case where F_X is absolutely continuous with density function f_X, the expectation simplifies to the classical Riemann integral:

$$\mathbb{E}[X] = \int_{-\infty}^{\infty} x f_X(x)\,dx.$$

3.8. Lebesgue Integral

Let $(\Omega, \mathcal{A}, \mu)$ be a measure space and $X : \Omega \to [0,\infty]$ a measurable function. The Lebesgue integral of f is defined as

$$\int_\Omega X\,d\mu = \sup\left\{\int_\Omega \phi\,d\mu : 0 \le \phi \le X,\ \phi \text{ simple}\right\}.$$

If X takes both positive and negative values, write $X = X^+ - X^-$ and define

$$\int_\Omega X\,d\mu = \int_\Omega X^+\,d\mu - \int_O megaX^-\,d\mu,$$

provided that at least one of the terms is finite.

3.9. Choquet Integral

In situations where only partial information is available about a phenomenon, and the probability distribution of the underlying random variables is unknown or ill-defined, traditional probabilistic models may not be appropriate. Moreover, when stochastic independence among variables cannot be justifiably assumed, the classical framework of probability theory proves inadequate. In such cases, a more general and flexible approach is to represent degrees of belief using a monotone set function, such as a capacity. This allows for the modeling of uncertainty without committing to precise probabilities. Within this framework, expectations can be coherently defined using the Choquet integral, which extends the notion of expectation to non-additive measures and accommodates a wide range of uncertainty models, including belief functions and possibility measures.

Let Ω be a finite or measurable set, and let $\nu : \mathcal{P}(\Omega) \to [0, \infty]$ be a *capacity*, (i.e., a monotone set function with $\nu(\emptyset) = 0$). For a non-negative measurable function $f : X \to [0, \infty]$, the *Choquet integral* of f with respect to ν is defined as

$$\int_X f\, d\nu = \int_0^{\infty} \nu(\{x \in X : f(x) \geq t\})\, dt.$$

If $X \geq 0$ or $X \leq 0$, the integral always exists.

If X is bounded and $\mu(\Omega) = 1$, we have that

$$\int X d\mu = \int_{inff}^{0} (\nu(\{x \in X : f(x) \geq t\}) - 1) dx + \int_0^{supf} \nu(\{x \in X : f(x) \geq t\}) dx.$$

Given $X : \Omega \to \overline{R}$, the Choquet integral of X with respect to μ is defined if $\mu(\Omega) < \infty$ through

$$\int X d\mu = \int_{-\infty}^{0} (\nu(\{x \in X : f(x) \geq t\}) - \mu(\Omega)) dx + \int_0^{+\infty} \nu(\{x \in X : f(x) \geq t\}) dx.$$

The integral is in $\Re$ or can assume the values $-\infty$, ∞, and 'non-existing'.

In the case of finite $X = \{x_1, \ldots, x_n\}$, with $f(x_1) \geq f(x_2) \geq \cdots \geq f(x_n)$, this becomes

$$\int_X f\, d\nu = \sum_{i=1}^{n} (f(x_i) - f(x_{i+1})) \nu(\{x_1, \ldots, x_i\}),$$

where $f(x_{n+1}) := 0$.

So we can conclude the following:

- The **Riemann integral** is the classical approach to integration, suitable for well-behaved functions on closed intervals.
- The **Riemann–Stieltjes integral** generalizes the Riemann integral by integrating with respect to a function $g(x)$, not just dx.
- The **Lebesgue integral** generalizes both by allowing integration with respect to a *measure*, offering better convergence properties.
- The **Choquet integral** generalizes the Lebesgue integral to *non-additive measure* (capacities), often used in decision theory and fuzzy systems. Having continuity from below will also imply null continuity for a monotonic set function.

Relations among different types of integrals are shown in Figure 1. In the following, we consider examples of monotone set functions defined on algebras. These functions, under suitable conditions, can be extended to countably additive measures.

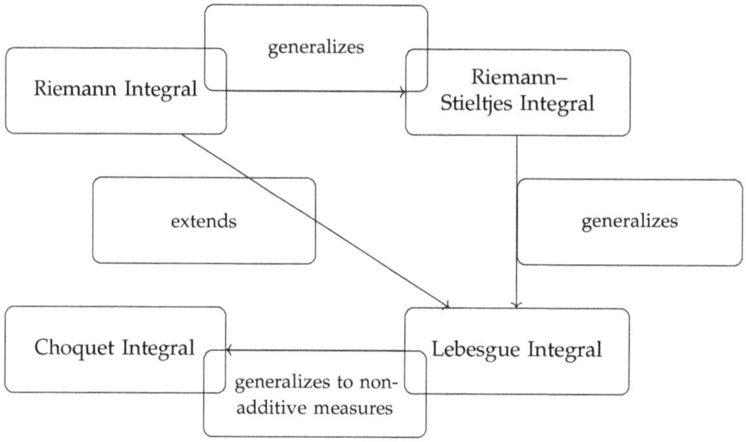

Figure 1. Relations among different types of integrals.

Our goal is to illustrate how certain set functions—initially defined in a limited context—can give rise to full measures once their additivity and continuity properties are verified.

4. Countable Additivity in Cylinder Set Algebras

In Theorem 2.3 of [14], it has been proved that any finitely additive probability measure defined on the field $\mathcal{C}_0$, which encompasses all cylinders in the space of infinite sequences S^∞, is, indeed, countably additive. It occurs because any sequence of non-empty cylinders converges from above to a non-empty set, so that there are no sequences converging from above to the empty set, and so Proposition 2.1 is trivially verified.

We recall from Example 3, Remark 1, and Example 4, the construction proposed in [14] (pp. 29–30) because a similar procedure is applied in [12] to prove the countable additivity of the Möbius transform.

Example 5. *Let S be a finite set, and let $\Omega = S^\infty$ be the space of all infinite sequences, that is*

$$\Omega = \{\omega = (z_1(\omega), z_2(\omega), \ldots)\}$$

such that $z_k(\omega) \in S$ for all $\omega \in S^\infty$. Consider S^n as the Cartesian product of n copies of the set S. This implies that S^n comprises sequences of length n composed of elements from S,

$$\{\omega : (z_1(\omega), z_2(\omega), \ldots z_n(\omega)) = u_1, \ldots u_n\}.$$

The set represents the event where the first n repetitions of the experiment result in the outcomes $u_1, u_2, \ldots, u_n$ occurring in sequence. For any $H \subset S^n$, a cylinder of rank n is a set of the form

$$A = \{\omega : (z_1(\omega), z_2(\omega), \ldots z_n(\omega)) \in H\}$$

A cylinder of order n is the set of ω that generates sequences whose first n components are in H. To clarify, for tossing a coin, we have $S = \{0, 1\}$, and each $\omega = \{(z_1(\omega), z_2(\omega), \ldots)\}$ can be viewed as the result of repeating infinitely often the simple experiment S.

Consider $\mathcal{C}_0$ as the field generated by cylinders with all finite ranks. Let p_u, where $u \in S$, be a probability distribution defined on S. We can define a probability measure P on $\mathcal{C}_0$ such that for a cylinder A, the probability P(A) is given by

$$P(A) = \sum_H p_{u_1} \cdots p_{u_n}.$$

According to Theorem 2.3 of [14], it follows that P is countably additive on $\mathcal{C}_0$. The proof of the theorem depends on the fact that if A_n is a sequence of non-empty cylinders converging to A, then A is non-empty since S is a finite set, and in the definition of a cylinder, the set H is non-empty.

A probability can be defined on the field $\mathcal{C}_0$ by the product rule and extended to the σ-field $\mathcal{F}$ generated by the field $\mathcal{C}_0$.

In the previous example, a key role in proving that the countable intersection of non-empty cylinders is non-empty is due to the fact that the alphabetic set S is finite.

The result can be generalized when different finite sets S_K of points, regarded as the possible outcomes of a simple experiment, are considered so that each component $z_k(\omega) \in S_K$.

Example 6. *Theorem 2.3 1 [14] holds even if we consider the space $\Omega = S_1 \times S_2 \times \ldots$ of sequences, where $z_k(\omega) \in S_k$, and the probability is defined by $P = \sum_H p_{u_1} \cdots p_{u_n}$, where the sum extending over all sequences in H is as in Example 3. Moreover, in this case, given any sequence of non-empty cylinders converging from above to a set A, then A is non-empty.*

If any of the sets S_K is infinite, it is not assured that for all sequences of non-empty cylinders converging from above to a set A that A is non-empty (see problem 2.20 of [14]).

Example 7. *Let S be a countable set, and let $\Omega = S^\infty$ be the space of all infinite sequences, that is*

$$\Omega = \{\omega = (z_1(\omega), z_2(\omega), \ldots)\}$$

such that $z_k(\omega) \in S$ for all $\omega \in S^\infty$. Consider S^n as the Cartesian product of n copies of the set S, and define a cylinder of rank n, as in Example 3

$$A = \{\omega : (z_1(\omega), z_2(\omega), \ldots z_n(\omega)) \in H\}.$$

Consider $\mathcal{C}_0$ as the field generated by cylinders with all having a finite rank. Let p_u, where $u \in S$, be a probability distribution defined on S. We can define a probability measure P on $\mathcal{C}_0$ such that for a cylinder A, the probability P(A) is given by

$$P(A) = \sum_H p_{u_1} \cdots p_{u_n}.$$

Since S is countable, we can consider a countable quantity of cylinders such that $\bigcap_{j=1}^{\infty} A_j = \emptyset$ but $\lim_{n\to\infty} P(\bigcap_{j=1}^{n} A_j) \neq 0$.

Remark 1. *We can observe that the approach proposed in Example 2 cannot be applied to define a probability measure in the continuous case. This discrepancy arises due to the relationship between the σ-field C and the Borel σ-field of the interval $[0,1]$. While the field $\mathcal{C}_0$ is smaller than the field $\mathcal{B}_0$ of finite disjoint unions of intervals in the range $(0,1]$, there are essential differences between them. One notable distinction is that non-empty sets in $\mathcal{B}_0$, such as $\left(\frac{1}{2}, \frac{1}{2} + \frac{1}{2^n}\right)$, have the potential to contract to the empty set. On the other hand, non-empty sets in $\mathcal{C}_0$ do not possess this property.*

As a result, a finitely additive probability defined on $\mathcal{B}_0$ may fail to be countably additive, whereas such a failure cannot occur in $\mathcal{C}_0$.

In the following example, we consider a finitely additive but not countably additive probability on the field $\mathcal{B}_0$.

Example 8. *Let $\mathcal{B}_0$ be the field of finite disjoint unions of intervals in the range $(0,1]$, and let P be a set function defined by*

$$P(A) = \begin{cases} 1 & \text{if exists} \quad \epsilon_A : \left(\frac{1}{2}, \frac{1}{2} + \epsilon_A\right] \subset A \\ 0 & \text{otherwise} \end{cases}$$

P is finitely but not countably additive on the σ-field generated by $\mathcal{B}_0$ since it is denoted by

$$A_n = \left(\frac{1}{2}, \frac{1}{2} + \frac{1}{n}\right]$$

and we have $\lim_{n\to\infty} P(A_n) = 1 \neq P(\lim_{n\to\infty} A_n) = 0$.

5. Countably Additive Representation of the Choquet Integral According to the Möbius Transform of a Monotone Set Function of Bounded Variation

Let $\mathcal{A}$ be an algebra of subsets of Ω properly contained in $\wp(\Omega)$, and let ν be a coherent lower probability. Let $\mathcal{H}(\mathcal{A})$ be the class of all normalized monotone set functions with values in $\{0,1\}$. Consider the two subsets of $\mathcal{H}(\mathcal{A})$

$$H_p(A) = \{\eta \in \mathcal{H}(\mathcal{A}) : \eta \quad \text{supermodalular}\}$$

$$H_u(A) = \{u_K \in \mathcal{H}(\mathcal{A}) : K \in \mathcal{A}; K \neq \emptyset\}$$

where u_K is defined on $\mathcal{A}$ for a fixed K subset of Ω, according to

$$u_K(A) = \begin{cases} 1 & \text{if} \quad K \subset A \\ 0 & \text{otherwise} \end{cases}$$

In combinatorics, depending on the two variables K and A, $u_K(A)$ is called the *zeta function*. It is continuous from above, whereas a general $\{0,1\}$-valued (even supermodular) set function continuous. $u_K(A)$ is supermodular, and it is a belief function since it is totally monotone. When Ω is finite, all filters have the form $\mathcal{A} = \{A : A \supset K\}$ for some non-empty set K, and so u_K is a coherent lower probability (Section 2.9.8 [22]). In game theory, u_K is called a unanimity game.

Definition 4. *Let $K \subseteq N$ be a coalition. The unanimity game on K is the game (N, u_K) where*

$$u_K(S) = \begin{cases} 1 & \text{if } K \subseteq S, \\ 0 & \text{if } K \nsubseteq S. \end{cases}$$

In other words, a coalition S has a worth of 1 (is winning) if it contains all players of K and a worth of 0 (is losing) if this is not the case.

We have

$$H_u(\mathcal{A}) \subset H_p(\mathcal{A}) \subset H(\mathcal{A})$$

and the equality $H_u(\mathcal{A}) = H_p(\mathcal{A})$ holds if Ω is finite.

Let the *tilde operator* be defined for an $\mathcal{A}$-measurable random variable X and with respect to any $\{0,1\}$-valued monotone set function $\eta \in \mathcal{H}(\mathcal{A})$:

$$\tilde{X} = \int X(\omega)\eta(\omega)$$

If X is the indicator function of an event $A \in \mathcal{A}$, then

$$\tilde{I_A} = I_{\tilde{A}}$$

where $\tilde{A} = \{\eta \in \mathcal{H}(\mathcal{A}) : \eta(A) = 1\}$.

Though $\mathcal{A}$ is a field, the set system $\tilde{\mathcal{A}} = \{\tilde{A} | A \in \mathcal{A}\}$ is not a field in $\wp(\mathcal{H}(\mathcal{A}))$, except for the trivial case $\tilde{A} = \{\emptyset, \Omega\}$.

We consider the field $\mathcal{D}(\tilde{\mathcal{A}})$ generated by $\tilde{\mathcal{A}}$ that is the smallest field containing $\tilde{\mathcal{A}}$.

If $(\Omega, \mathcal{F})$ is a measurable space and $\emptyset \neq E \subseteq \Omega$, then $\{E \cap A : A \in \mathcal{F}\}$ is a σ-field on E called the *trace σ-field.*

Let $\mathcal{D}'(\tilde{\mathcal{A}})$ and $\mathcal{D}''(\tilde{\mathcal{A}})$ be the trace σ fields generated by $\tilde{A}$, respectively, in $H_p(A)$ and $H_u(A)$.

Definition 5. *Given a monotone set function v on $\mathcal{A}$, the additive Möbius transform μ^v is uniquely determined on $(H_u(A), \mathcal{D}''(\tilde{\mathcal{A}}))$ by*

$$\mu^v(\tilde{A}) = v(A) \text{ for } A \in \mathcal{A}.$$

Moreover, in [12], it is proven that integrals are preserved under the Möbius transform, i.e.,

$$\int X dv = \int \tilde{X} d\mu^v$$

Example 9. *For a fixed non-empty set $K \in \wp(\Omega)$, the Choquet integral with respect to the set function u_K on $\wp(\Omega)$ is*

$$\tilde{X} = \int X(\omega) du_K(\omega) = \inf_{\omega \in K} X(\omega);$$

and the integral with respect to the restriction of u_K to a field $\mathcal{A}$ of an $\mathcal{A}$-measurable random variable X is

$$\tilde{X} = \int X(\omega) du_K(\omega) = \inf_{\omega \in K} X(\omega)$$

even if K does not belong to $\mathcal{A}$.

The Möbius transform of the monotone set function u_K is defined by $\mu^{u_K}(\tilde{A}) = u_K(A)$.

A set function v on an algebra $\mathcal{A} \subset \wp(\Omega)$ is totally monotone if and only if its Möbius transform μ^v is monotone, i.e., non-negative [23,24].

In Theorem 6.2 of [12], the following result has been proved

Theorem 1. *If $v \in V_b(\mathcal{A})$, the Möbius transform μ^v can be uniquely extended to $(H_p(A), D'(\tilde{A}))$, and it is σ-additive and named the σ-additive Möbius transform of v. It is a signed (i.e., it can assume real negative values) additive set function.*

The σ-additivity of the Möbius transform μ^{ν} on $(H_p(A), D'(\tilde{A}))$ is satisfied because μ^{ν} is finite additive and continuous from above to the empty set, and so, according Proposition 1, it is countably additive. Continuity from above to the empty set holds because for any $\mathcal{D}_n \in \mathcal{D}'(\tilde{A})$ such that $\mathcal{D}_n \downarrow \emptyset$, there exist $\overline{n} \in \mathbb{N}$ such that $\mathcal{D}_n = \emptyset$ for $n > \overline{n}$ (Lemma 6.1 of [12]). It implies that $\bigcap_n \mathcal{D}_n = \emptyset$. Theorem 3 holds because this lemma guarantees that the intersection of each decreasing sequence $\mathcal{D}_n$ is equal to the empty set so that any monotone set function defined on $\mathcal{D}'(\tilde{A})$ trivially is continuous from above to the empty set, and every finitely additive function is σ-additive (see Proposition 1).

Lemma 6.1 of [12] is proven by contradiction. It is proven that if we assume $D_n \neq \emptyset$ for large n, then it is possible to construct a sequence E_n, with $E_n \neq \emptyset$ for all n, such that there exists a set function $\eta \in \mathcal{H}'$ with $\eta \in \bigcap_n E_n$ so that we get the contradiction that $E_n \downarrow \emptyset$.

In Theorem 2.3 of [14], instead, every finitely additive probability is proven to be countably additive because any sequence of non-empty cylinders converges from above to a non-empty set so that there are no sequences converging, from above to the empty set, and so Proposition 1 is trivially verified.

We can observe that the finite probability P in Example 5 is not continuous from above to the empty set since $A_n \downarrow \emptyset$ but $\lim_{n\to\infty} P(A_n) = 1 \neq 0$. So P is finitely additive but not countably additive.

We can observe that the unanimity game u_K cannot be used in Theorems 1 and 2 to define coherent upper conditional previsions and probability because it is not finitely additive.

The following example [12] shows that Möbius transforms can differ on the two measurable spaces $(H_p, \mathcal{D}'(\tilde{A}))$ and $(H_u, \mathcal{D}''(\tilde{A}))$.

Example 10. *Let μ^{ν} be the Möbius transform defined on $\mathcal{D}'(\tilde{A})$ of the probability $\nu = P$ of Example 8, that is,*

$$\mu^{\nu}(D) = \begin{cases} 1 & \text{if exists} \quad \tilde{A}_n \subset D \quad \text{for some } n, \\ 0 & \text{otherwise} \end{cases}$$

We can observe that ν does not belong to H_u, that is, ν is not an unanimity game u_K for fixed K. The Möbius transform is the Dirac measure at the point $\eta = \nu$ on the measurable space $(H_p, \mathcal{D}'(\tilde{A}))$, and it is continuous from above, contrary to μ^{ν} on $(H_u, \mathcal{D}''(\tilde{A}))$ and ν. This can happen since, in H_p, we have $\nu \in \bigcap_{n=1}^{\infty} \tilde{A}$ so that any sequence $\tilde{A}_n$ does not converge to the empty set.

6. Hausdorff Outer Measure-Based Framework for Coherent Upper Conditional Previsions

Let **B** be a partition of a metric space (Ω, d). A *bounded random variable* is a function $X : \Omega \to \mathbb{R}$, where $\mathbb{R} = (-\infty, +\infty)$ denotes the real numbers. Let $L(\Omega)$ denote the set of all such bounded real-valued functions defined on Ω.

For each element $B \in \mathbf{B}$, we denote by $X|_B$ the restriction of the random variable X to the set B. The supremum of X over B is denoted by $\sup(X|_B)$, i.e., the least upper bound of the values that X takes on B. We define $L(B)$ as the collection of all bounded random variables restricted to B.

Given a subset $A \subseteq B$, the *indicator function* $I_A : B \to \{0,1\}$ is defined by

$$I_A(\omega) = \begin{cases} 1 & \text{if } \omega \in A, \\ 0 & \text{if } \omega \notin A. \end{cases}$$

For every $B \in \mathbf{B}$, we consider *coherent upper conditional expectations* (also known as *coherent upper conditional previsions*) $\overline{P}(\cdot|B)$, which are real-valued functionals defined on $L(B)$ [22].

Definition 6. *A functional $\overline{P}(\cdot|B) : L(B) \to \mathbb{R}$ is called a coherent upper conditional prevision if, for all $X, Y \in L(B)$ and every constant $\lambda > 0$, the following conditions hold:*

1. $\overline{P}(X|B) \leq \sup(X|B)$;
2. $\overline{P}(\lambda X|B) = \lambda\, \overline{P}(X|B)$ *(positive homogeneity);*
3. $\overline{P}(X + Y|B) \leq \overline{P}(X|B) + \overline{P}(Y|B)$ *(sub-additivity).*

A novel framework for defining coherent upper previsions has been proposed based on the Choquet integral with respect to Hausdorff outer measures. This approach provides a rich and flexible method for modeling upper expectations in settings with imprecise or non-additive probabilities.

6.1. Hausdorff Outer Measures

In this section sub-additive Hausdorff outer measures [25], [26] are recalled.

Let (Ω, d) be a metric space. The diameter of a non-empty set U of Ω is defined as $|U| = sup\left\{d(x,y) : x, y \in U\right\}$, and if a subset A of Ω is such that $A \subset \bigcup_i U_i$ and $0 < |U_i| < \delta$ for each i, the class $\left\{U_i\right\}$ is called a δ-cover of A. Let s be a non-negative number. For $\delta > 0$, we define $\mathcal{H}_{s,\delta}(A) = \inf \sum_{i=1}^{\infty} |U_i|^s$, where the infimum is over all δ-covers $\left\{U_i\right\}$. The *Hausdorff s-dimensional outer measure* of A [25,26], denoted by $\mathcal{H}^s(A)$, is defined as

$$\mathcal{H}^s(A) = lim_{\delta \to 0} \mathcal{H}_{s,\delta}(A).$$

This limit exists but may be infinite since $\mathcal{H}s, \delta(A)$ increases as δ decreases. The s-dimensional Hausdorff outer measure is submodular and continuous from below.

The property of being a metric outer measure ensures that if sets E and F are positively separated (i.e., $d(E,F) = \inf\left\{d(x,y) : x \in E, y \in F\right\} > 0$), then

$$\mathcal{H}^s(E \cup F) = \mathcal{H}^s(E) + \mathcal{H}^s(F).$$

According to Falconer's Theorem 1.5 [25], as Hausdorff outer measures are metric outer measures, all Borel subsets of Ω are measurable.

The *Hausdorff dimension* of a set A, $dim_H(A)$, is defined as the unique value, such that

$$\mathcal{H}^s(A) = \infty \text{ if } 0 \leq s < dim_H(A),$$
$$\mathcal{H}^s(A) = 0 \text{ if } dim_H(A) < s < \infty.$$

6.2. Hausdorff Measures and Bounded Variation Functions

A set $E \subset \mathbb{R}^n$ is said to be m-**rectifiable** if there exist countably many Lipschitz functions

$$f_i : \mathbb{R}^m \to \mathbb{R}^n, \quad i \in \mathbb{N},$$

such that

$$\mathcal{H}^m\left(E \setminus \bigcup_{i=1}^{\infty} f_i(\mathbb{R}^m)\right) = 0$$

where $\mathcal{H}^m$ denotes the m-dimensional Hausdorff measure.

Let $u \in L^1(\mathbb{R}^n)$. We say that the distributional derivative Du of u defines a (vector-valued) Radon measure μ on $\mathbb{R}^n$ if for every test function, $\varphi \in C_c^\infty(\mathbb{R}^n; \mathbb{R}^n)$,

$$\int_{\mathbb{R}^n} u \operatorname{div} \varphi \, dx = -\int_{\mathbb{R}^n} \varphi \cdot d\mu.$$

In this case, we write $Du = \mu$ in the sense of distributions, and μ is called the distributional (or weak) derivative of u.

A set $E \subset \mathbb{R}^n$ is said to be **purely m-unrectifiable** if for every Lipschitz map $f : \mathbb{R}^m \to \mathbb{R}^n$, the m-dimensional Hausdorff measure of $E \cap f(\mathbb{R}^m)$ is zero:

$$\mathcal{H}^m(E \cap f(\mathbb{R}^m)) = 0.$$

In other words, E does not contain any subset of positive $\mathcal{H}^m$-measure that is m-rectifiable.

In general, the s-dimensional Hausdorff measure $\mathcal{H}^s$ (for $0 < s < n$) on $\mathbb{R}^n$ cannot be derived from a function of bounded variation. That is, $\mathcal{H}^s$ is not a Lebesgue–Stieltjes measure associated with any real-valued function of bounded variation on $\mathbb{R}^n$.

Recall that a function $f : \mathbb{R}^n \to \mathbb{R}$ of bounded variation (i.e., $f \in BV(\mathbb{R}^n)$) defines a Radon measure μ_f via distributional derivatives. The measure μ_f is supported on countably $(n-1)$-rectifiable sets and satisfies the following:

- It is absolutely continuous with respect to the $(n-1)$-dimensional Hausdorff measure $\mathcal{H}^{n-1}$;
- It gives zero measure to purely unrectifiable sets (such as the classic Cantor set or many fractals).

However, many Hausdorff measures $\mathcal{H}^s$ (for $0 < s < n-1$) assign positive measure to purely unrectifiable sets, which contradicts the behavior of measures derived from BV functions.

Hence, no such f can exist, and $\mathcal{H}^s$ is not the distributional derivative of a function of bounded variation.

Example 11. *Let $C \subset [0,1]$ denote the classic middle-third Cantor set. It is totally disconnected and nowhere dense. It has zero Lebesgue measure and has a positive $\mathcal{H}^s$ measure for $s = \log 2 / \log 3$.*

Since C is purely unrectifiable, no BV function f can generate a measure μ_f such that $\mu_f(C) > 0$. Therefore, $\mathcal{H}^s|_C$ is not a BV-derived measure.

Example 12. *The von Koch snowflake curve is a fractal in $\mathbb{R}^2$ with a finite $\mathcal{H}^s$ measure for some $s > 1$, but it is nowhere differentiable and purely unrectifiable. Again, any BV function-derived measure must be concentrated on rectifiable sets, so it cannot capture $\mathcal{H}^s$ on the Koch curve.*

Hausdorff measures $\mathcal{H}^s$ with $s \notin \mathbb{N}$, especially when $s < n-1$ cannot be represented as distributional derivatives of functions of bounded variation. This is due to the fundamental difference in their support: BV-derived measures are concentrated on rectifiable sets, whereas Hausdorff measures can give full measure to purely unrectifiable sets.

Theorem 2. *Let $\mathcal{H}^s$ denote the s-dimensional Hausdorff outer measure on $\mathbb{R}^n$, with $s > 0$. Then, $\mathcal{H}^s$ is not, in general, derived from a function of bounded variation. In particular, there does not exist a function $F : \mathbb{R}^n \to \mathbb{R}$ of bounded variation such that $\mathcal{H}^s(E) = \int_E dF$ for all Borel sets $E \subseteq \mathbb{R}^n$.*

Proof. Suppose, for contradiction, that $\mathcal{H}^s$ is derived from a function F of bounded variation on $\mathbb{R}^n$. Then, by the Riesz Representation Theorem, $\mathcal{H}^s$ would define a finite Radon measure on compact subsets of $\mathbb{R}^n$, and in particular, would be regular and finite on all compact sets.

However, this contradicts the behavior of $\mathcal{H}^s$ for many sets of positive s-dimensional measure. For example, let $C \subseteq [0,1]$ be the standard middle-third Cantor set. It is known that C has Hausdorff dimension $\log 2/\log 3$, and its Hausdorff measure $\mathcal{H}^s(C)$ is finite and positive when $s = \log 2/\log 3$. □

6.3. Countably Additive Coherent Conditional Probability

We recall the model of conditional upper prevision based on Hausdorff outer measures, as introduced in [27–29]. In this framework, the conditional upper probability, which typically represents the probability of an event occurring, given that another is defined using the Hausdorff outer measure of order s, also known as the s-dimensional Hausdorff measure, when the conditioning event has a Hausdorff dimension equal to s.

Theorem 3. *Let (Ω, d) be a metric space, and let* **B** *be a partition of Ω. For every $B \in$* **B** *denote by s the Hausdorff dimension of the conditioning event B and by $\mathcal{H}^s$ the Hausdorff s-dimensional outer measure. Let m_B be a 0-1-valued, finitely additive, but not countably additive, probability on $\wp(B)$. Then, for each $B \in$* **B***, the functional $\overline{P}(X|B)$ defined on $L(B)$ by*

$$\overline{P}(X|B) = \begin{cases} \frac{1}{\mathcal{H}^s(B)} \int_B X dh^s & if \quad 0 < \mathcal{H}^s(B) < +\infty \\ \int_B X dm_B & if \quad \mathcal{H}^s(B) \in \{0, +\infty\} \end{cases}$$

is a coherent upper conditional probability.

The restriction to the class of all indicator functions of the coherent upper conditional prevision in Theorem 1 is the following coherent upper conditional probability:

Theorem 4. *Let (Ω, d) be a metric space, and let* **B** *be a partition of Ω. For every $B \in$* **B***, denote by s the Hausdorff dimension of the conditioning event B and by $\mathcal{H}^s$ the Hausdorff s-dimensional outer measure. Let m_B be a 0-1-valued, finitely additive, but not countably additive, probability on $\wp(B)$. Then, for each $B \in$* **B***, the functional $\overline{P}(A|B)$ defined on $\wp(B)$ by*

$$\overline{P}(X|B) = \begin{cases} \frac{\mathcal{H}^s(A \cap B)}{\mathcal{H}^s(B)} & if \quad 0 < \mathcal{H}^s(B) < +\infty \\ m_B & if \quad \mathcal{H}^s(B) \in \{0, +\infty\} \end{cases}$$

is a coherent upper conditional probability.

Let us consider a set $B \in$ **B** with a positive and finite Hausdorff outer measure corresponding to its Hausdorff dimension s. In this scenario, we define the monotone set function μ^*_B for every $A \in \wp(B)$ as follows: $\mu^*_B(A) = \frac{\mathcal{H}^s(AB)}{\mathcal{H}^s(B)}$. This function serves as a coherent upper conditional probability and exhibits properties such as submodularity and continuity from below. Furthermore, when we restrict it to the σ-field of all μ^*_B-measurable sets, it becomes a Borel regular countably additive probability. When considering $B \in$ **B** such that $\mathcal{H}^s(B)$ falls within the set $\{0, +\infty\}$, the consistent upper conditional probability is established through a finitely additive probability m_B on $\wp(B)$, which takes values of either 0 or 1 and is not countably additive. Notably, the realm of 0–1-valued, finitely additive probabilities is in direct bijective correspondence with ultrafilters, as outlined in the context of $\mathcal{A}$.

7. On the Continuity of Coherent Conditional Upper Previsions Induced by Hausdorff Measures

The σ-additive Möbius transform of a real supermodular monotone set function $v \in V_b(\mathcal{F})$ is considered to define coherent conditional probability when the conditioning event has a Hausdorff measure in its Hausdorff dimension equal to zero or infinity.

In the following theorem, a coherent countably additive conditional probability is defined on the Borel σ-field.

Theorem 5. *Let (Ω, d) be a metric space, and let $\mathcal{F}$ be the Borel σ-field. Let* **B** *be a Borel partition of Ω. For every $B \in \mathbf{B}$, denote by s the Hausdorff dimension of the conditioning event B and by $\mathcal{H}^s$ the Hausdorff s-dimensional outer measure. Let μ^v be the σ-additive Möbius transform of a finite additive probability $v \in V_b(\mathcal{F})$. Thus, for each $B \in \mathbf{B}$, the function defined on $\mathcal{F}$ by*

$$\overline{P}(A|B) = \begin{cases} \frac{\mathcal{H}^s(A\cap B)}{\mathcal{H}^s(B)} & if \quad 0 < \mathcal{H}^s(B) < +\infty \\ \mu^v_{\tilde{B}}(\tilde{A}) & if \quad \mathcal{H}^s(B) \in \{0, +\infty\} \end{cases}$$

is a coherent σ-additive conditional probability.

Proof. If $0 < \mathcal{H}^s(B) < +\infty$, the coherence of $\overline{P}(A|B)$ is proven in [28]. If $\mathcal{H}^s(B) \in \{0, +\infty\}$ $\overline{P}(A|B)$, it is a coherent conditional probability since it is countably additive, and the condition $\overline{P}(B|B) = 1$ is satisfied because (see Proposition 3.1 and Example 7.1 of [12])

$$\frac{\mu^v(\tilde{A} \cap \tilde{B})}{\mu^v(\tilde{B})} = \frac{\mu^v(\widetilde{A \cap B})}{\mu^v(\tilde{B})} = \frac{v(A \cap B)}{v(B)}. \quad (1)$$

□

Remark 2. *According to Theorem 6.2 of [12], if the additive probability is $v \in V_b(\mathcal{F})$, then there is a unique σ-additive Möbius transform.*

Example 13. *Let (Ω, d) be a metric space, and let $\mathcal{F}$ be the Borel σ-field. Let* **B** *be a Borel partition of Ω. For every $B \in \mathbf{B}$, denote by s the Hausdorff dimension of the conditioning event B and by $\mathcal{H}^s$ the Hausdorff s-dimensional outer measure. Let μ^v be the σ-additive Möbius transform defined on $\mathcal{D}'$ (see Example 6) of the additive function v of Example 4*

$$\mu^v(D) = \begin{cases} 1 & \text{if exists} \quad \tilde{A}_n \subset D \quad \text{for some } n, \\ 0 & \text{otherwise} \end{cases}$$

Then, the coherent conditional probability defined on $\mathcal{F}$ by

$$\overline{P}(A|B) = \begin{cases} \frac{\mathcal{H}^s(A\cap B)}{\mathcal{H}^s(B)} & if \quad 0 < \mathcal{H}^s(B) < +\infty \\ \mu^v_{\tilde{B}}(\tilde{A}) & if \quad \mathcal{H}^s(B) \in \{0, +\infty\} \end{cases}$$

is a coherent σ-additive conditional probability.

The model proposed in Theorem 5 can be used to assign a countably additive probability in the sequence space recalled in Example 4 when S is countable or, in Example 2, when at least one of the alphabetic sets S_k is infinite.

In [19], the monotone convergence theorem is proven for a monotone set function.

Theorem 6 (Monotone Convergence Theorem). *Let μ be a monotone set function on a σ field* **F** *properly contained in $\wp(\Omega)$, which is continuous from below. For an increasing sequence of non-negative,* **F***-measurable random variables X_n, the limit function $X = lim_{n\to\infty}X_n$ is* **F***-measurable and $lim_{n\to\infty} \int X_n d\mu = \int X d\mu$.*

Remark 3. *It is not restrictive to consider this in the monotone convergence theorem sequence of non-negative random variables, as any random variable X can be decomposed in its positive part X^+, and its negative part X^- given by*

$$X = X^+ - X^-; \quad X^+ = 0 \vee X; \quad X^- = (-X)^+$$

where $\vee$ is the maximum.

Theorem 7. *Let (Ω, d) be a metric space, and let* **B** *be a partition of Ω. For every $B \in$* **B***, denote by s the Hausdorff dimension of the conditioning event B and by $\mathcal{H}^s$ the s-dimensional Hausdorff outer measure. Let* **F** *be the σ-field of h^s-measurable sets, and let* **K** *be the class of all* **F***-measurable random variables. If B has a positive and finite Hausdorff outer measure in its dimension, then the functional defined as in Theorem 1 is continuous from below; that is, given an increasing sequence of non-negative random variables X_n of* **K** *converging point-wise to the random variable X, we have it that $lim_{n\to\infty}\overline{P}(Xn|B) = \overline{P}(X|B)$.*

Proof. If the set B has a positive and finite Hausdorff outer measure in its Hausdorff dimension s, then the conditional upper prevision is given by

$$\overline{P}(X \mid B) = \frac{1}{\mathcal{H}^s(B)} \int_B X \, d\mathcal{H}^s.$$

Since the s-dimensional Hausdorff outer measure is continuous from below, the monotone convergence theorem implies that the conditional upper prevision $\overline{P}(X \mid B)$ is also continuous from below. That is,

$$lim_{n\to\infty}\overline{P}(Xn|B) = lim_{n\to\infty}\tfrac{1}{\mathcal{H}^s(B)} \int_B X_n d\mathcal{H}^s = \tfrac{1}{\mathcal{H}^s(B)} \int_B X d\mathcal{H}^s = \overline{P}(X|B).$$

□

Theorem 8. *Let μ be a null-continuous monotone set function, and let X_n be an increasing sequence of functions converging to X, $X_n \uparrow X$ such that $X_n = 0$ μ a.e.; then, we have it that $lim_{n\to\infty}\overline{P}(Xn|B) = \overline{P}(X|B)$.*

In the following theorems, we consider the extension to the class of Borel measurable random variables of the countably additive conditional probability defined in Theorem 5; we prove that these extensions are continuous, linear previsions for each conditioning event B if the real monotone set function $\nu \in V_b(\mathcal{F})$ is countably additive.

Theorem 9. *If $\nu \in V_b(\mathcal{F})$ is a real coherent lower probability that is not continuous from below, then the functional defined by*

$$\underline{P}(X|B) = \int_{\tilde{B}} \tilde{X} d\mu^{\nu}_{\tilde{B}}$$

if $\mathcal{H}^s(B) \in \{0, +\infty\}$ is a coherent lower conditional prevision that is not continuous.

Proof. Since [12] the Choquet integrals are preserved under the Möbius transform, we have

$$\int_B X d\nu = \int_{\tilde{B}} \tilde{X} d\mu^{\nu}$$

and if ν is not continuous from below, then according to Theorem 8, we have it that the functional $\underline{P}(X|B)$ is not continuous. □

According to the previous theorems, we have

Theorem 10. *Let (Ω, d) be a metric space, and let $\mathcal{F}$ be the Borel σ-field. Let $\mathbf{B}$ be a partition of Ω. For every $B \in \mathbf{B}$, denote by s the Hausdorff dimension of the conditioning event B and by $\mathcal{H}^s$ the Hausdorff s-dimensional outer measure. Let μ^ν be the σ-additive Möbius transform of a finitely additive conditional probability ν of bounded variation. Then, for each $B \in \mathbf{B}$ with a positive and finite Hausdorff s-dimensional outer measure, the functional $\overline{P}(X|B)$ is defined on the class of all $\mathcal{F}$-measurable random variables by*

$$\overline{P}(X|B) = \begin{cases} \frac{1}{\mathcal{H}^s(B)} \int_B X d\mathcal{H}^s & if \quad 0 < \mathcal{H}^s(B) < +\infty \\ \int_{\tilde{B}} \tilde{X} d\mu^\nu_{\tilde{B}} & if \quad \mathcal{H}^s(B) \in \{0, +\infty\} \end{cases}$$

is a continuous linear conditional prevision.

It is important to observe that Theorem 8 holds because bounded random variables are considered. Extensions to unbounded random variables are investigated in [29].

Example 14. *Let Ω be an uncountable set and fixed $a \in \Omega$, and define the countable additive probability on the Borel σ-field by*

$$\nu(A) = \begin{cases} 1 & if \quad a \in A \quad , \\ 0 & otherwise \end{cases}$$

Then, $\tilde{X}(\nu) = X(a)$ and since

$$\int_B X d\nu = \int_{\tilde{B}} \tilde{X} d\mu^\nu,$$

then the Möbius transform is

$$\mu^\nu_{\tilde{B}}(\tilde{A}) = \begin{cases} 1 & if \quad a \in A \\ 0 & otherwise \end{cases}$$

Example 15. *Let the field $\mathcal{B}_0$ and the additive probability $\nu = P$ be as in Example 8, and consider the partition $\mathbf{B} = \left\{(0, \frac{1}{4}]; (\frac{1}{4}, 1]\right\}$. We have it that $P\left(0, \frac{1}{4}\right] = 0$ and $P\left(\frac{1}{4}, 1\right] = 1$.*

The Choquet integral representation of the extension of P to the class of all bounded random variables by the σ-additive Möbius transform μ^ν of Example 8 does not satisfy the monotone convergence theorem because $\nu = P$ is not continuous from below.

If the monotone set function ν is defined by a Hausdorff outer measure, as in Theorem 7, we have it that $\nu(A|B) = P(A|B) = \frac{\mathcal{H}^1(A \cap B)}{h^1(B)}$ since all sets in the partition $\mathbf{B}$ has a Hausdorff dimension equal to 1 and $\nu(A) = \frac{\mathcal{H}^1(A)}{\mathcal{H}^1(\Omega)}$. The outer Hausdorff measures are continuous from below (Lemma 1.3 [25]), so the monotone convergence theorem can be applied, and the extensions $P(X|B)$ and $P(X|\Omega)$ are continuous.

It is important to note that if the conditioning event has a Hausdorff measure in its Hausdorff dimension equal to zero, but it has a positive and finite packing measure in the same dimension (see Example 6 of [30]), we can define coherent upper previsions according to the packing outer measure; this outer measure is continuous from below, and it is a metric outer measure such that it is a measure on the Borel σ-field; this means that the monotone convergence theorem holds and the coherent previsions defined as in Theorem 6 are continuous. For this reason, other fractal outer measures have been introduced and investigated in [31–33].

Otherwise, if the conditioning event has a Hausdorff outer measure equal to infinity, as occurs if it is countable (see Example 8 in [30]), then to define a coherent conditional prevision, we have to consider the σ-additive Möbius transform of a 0–1-valued, finitely additive probability.

7.1. Weak Monotone Convergence Theorem

A sequence of random variables satisfies the weak monotone convergence theorem (WMCT) with respect to a monotone set function μ if the monotone convergence theorem is satisfied for sequences of random variables that are equal to zero almost everywhere with respect to μ

Theorem 11. *(WMCT) Let μ be a monotone set function on $\wp(\Omega)$, and let X_n be a sequence such that $X_n = 0$ μ, a.e., $\forall n \in \mathcal{N}$ and $X_n \uparrow X$, then $\lim_{n\to\infty} \int X_n d\mu = \int X d\mu$.*

Theorem 12. *(WMCT) Let μ be a null-continuous monotone set function on $\wp(\Omega)$, and let X_n be a sequence such that $X_n = 0$ μ, a.e., $\forall n \in \mathcal{N}$ and $X_n \uparrow X$, then the weak monotone convergence theorem holds.*

Proof. According to Proposition 5 and Proposition 11 of [21], we have it that $X = 0$ μ, a.e., and $\int X d\mu = 0$. □

7.2. Theoretical Contributions

In this subsection, the findings are contextualized within the broader mathematical literature so as to state, in evidence, their novelty and impact. The key points include the following:

- *Advancement of integration theory through countably additive representation:* The paper introduces a countably additive representation of the Choquet integral, which significantly advances existing integration theory. This representation enables a linear extension of a coherent upper prevision via a conditional probability under the condition that the conditioning event has a positive and finite Hausdorff outer measure in its Hausdorff dimension. This result relies on the metric and outer regular nature of Hausdorff outer measures, which ensures that every Borel set is measurable with respect to them.
- *Handling of degenerate conditioning events:* The proposed model offers a novel method to update partial knowledge, even when the conditioning event is unexpected or degenerate. This is achieved by employing the Hausdorff measure of the conditioning event's dimension to define the conditional probability, thereby enabling coherent updating in cases where traditional approaches fail.
- *σ-additive Möbius transforms and coherent conditional previsions:* The use of σ-additive Möbius transforms is shown to play a crucial role in constructing coherent conditional previsions. This enriches the theory of imprecise probabilities by bridging Möbius transforms with the structural properties of coherent assessments under uncertainty [17,18]. A future aim of this research is to investigate the optimal transport control of two monotone set functions by using the representation of the Choquet integral by the

countably additive Möbius transform. The transport problem has been formulated in terms of Möbius transform for non-additive measures, and in the finite case in [34], for a lower probability, which is the lower envelope of a particular type of credal sets (convex and weak*-closed set) [35], and for belief functions [36,37].

- *Connections to capacities and outer measures:* The results establish new connections and significant departures from foundational work on capacities and outer measures. In particular, the framework allows for a deeper understanding of the properties of monotone set functions, facilitating the selection of appropriate monotone functions based on specific modeling objectives.

8. Conclusions

In this work, we have addressed the problem of representing the Choquet integral with respect to a monotone set function—specifically, a Hausdorff outer measure that is not necessarily derived from a function of bounded variation—by means of a countably additive measure defined on suitable domains. We have shown that such a representation is indeed possible, thereby establishing a bridge between non-additive integration and classical measure theory.

A key contribution is the construction of a countably additive measure that coincides with the Choquet integral on a sufficiently rich class of integrable functions, despite the non-additivity of the original capacity. This construction is based on the continuity from below of Hausdorff outer measures and on identifying appropriate domains on which the additivity of the integral can be recovered.

Moreover, we have considered the countably additive Möbius transform associated with a monotone set function of bounded variation in order to define a coherent, countably additive conditional prevision. This framework is applicable, even when the conditioning event has a Hausdorff measure in its own dimension equal to zero or infinity—cases which are typically problematic within standard measure-theoretic conditioning. Coherent, countably additive conditional probabilities within a metric space framework are defined using the dimensional Hausdorff measures on the Borel σ-algebra. We demonstrated that when the conditioning event has a positive and finite s-Hausdorff measure, the conditional probability can be directly defined using this measure. When these conditions are not met, instead, we define the conditional probability through the σ-additive Möbius transform of a 0–1-valued, finitely additive probability of bounded variation.

We further extended our framework to include all Borel-measurable random variables and analyzed the conditions under which the monotone convergence theorem applies. Our findings show that the theorem holds when conditional previsions are defined via Hausdorff measures. This result follows from the continuity-from-below property of the outer measures associated with Hausdorff measures, which guarantees the necessary convergence behavior.

Additionally, we propose to consider alternative fractal outer measures, such as packing measures, which—like Hausdorff measures—are countably additive on the Borel σ-algebra and are continuous from below. Thus, if a conditioning event lies in its Hausdorff dimension but possesses a positive and finite packing measure, the conditional probability can be defined using the packing measure. In this setting, the monotone convergence theorem continues to hold.

Overall, the results contribute to a deeper understanding of the relationship between capacities, Hausdorff measures, and additive representations. They also provide a foundation for extending coherent inference in the presence of singular or degenerate conditioning events, with potential applications in the theory of imprecise probabilities and beyond.

Funding: This research received no external funding.

Data Availability Statement: No new data were created or analyzed in this study. Data sharing is not applicable to this article.

Conflicts of Interest: The author declare no conflicts of interest.

References

1. Gilboa, I.; Schmeidler, D. Maxmin expected utility with a non-unique prior. *J. Math. Econ.* **1989**, *18*, 141–153. [CrossRef]
2. Gilboa, I. *Theory of Decision Under Uncertainty*; Cambridge University Press: Cambridge, UK , 2009.
3. Gilboa, I.; Postlewaite, A.; Schmeidler, D. Probability and uncertainty in economic modeling. *J. Econ. Perspect.* **2008**, *22*, 173–188. [CrossRef]
4. de Finetti, B. *Probability, Induction and Statistics*; Wiley: Hoboken, NJ, USA, 1970.
5. de Finetti, B. *Theory of Probability*; Wiley: Hoboken, NJ, USA, 1974.
6. Mesiar, R.; Pap, E. Fuzzy Measures and Integrals in Decision Making and Fuzzy Systems. *Fuzzy Sets Syst.* **2000**, *114*, 205–220.
7. Mesiar, R.; Hajek, A. *Fuzzy Integrals: Theory and Applications*; Springer: Berlin/Heidelberg, Germany, 2007.
8. Mesiar, R.; Klement, J. Monotonicity Properties of Set Functions and Aggregation Operators. *Fuzzy Sets Syst.* **2009**, *160*, 2436–2447.
9. Mesiar, R.; Dombi, P.M. Nonlinear Aggregation Functions in Decision Making and Fuzzy Set Theory. *Fuzzy Sets Syst.* **2010**, *161*, 1055–1071.
10. Mesiar, R.; Nguyen, H.S. On Nonlinear Aggregation Operators in Information Fusion. *Inf. Fusion* **2014**, *17*, 125–133.
11. Choquet, G. *Theory of Capacities*; Annales de l'Institut Fourier: Brussels, Belgium , 1953.
12. Denneberg, D. Representation of the Choquet integral with the σ-additive Möbius transforms. *Fuzzy Sets Syst.* **1997**, *92*, 139–156. [CrossRef]
13. T'Joens, N.; de Bock, J.; de Cooman, G. A particular upper expectation as global belief model for discrete-time finite-state uncertain processes. *Int. J. Approx. Reason.* **2021**, *131*, 30–55. [CrossRef]
14. Billingsley, P. *Probability and Measure*, 3rd ed.; Wiley: Hoboken, NJ, USA, 1995.
15. Gilboa, I.; Schmeidler, D. Canonical representation of set functions. *Math. Oper. Res.* **1995**, *20*, 197–212. [CrossRef]
16. Marinacci, M. Decomposition and representation of coalitional games. *Math. Oper. Res.* **1996**, *21*, 1000–1015. [CrossRef]
17. Aouani, Z. Countably additive Möbius transforms for belief functions on Polish spaces. *Int. J. Approx. Reason.* **2013**, *54*, 1243–1251. [CrossRef]
18. Rébillé, Y. Integral representation of belief measures on compact spaces. *Int. J. Approx. Reason.* **2015**, *60*, 37–56. [CrossRef]
19. Denneberg, D. *Non-Additive Measure and Integral*; Wiley: Hoboken, NJ, USA, 1994.
20. Asahina, S.; Uchino, K.; Murofushi, T. Relationship among continuity conditions and null-additivity conditions in non-additive measure theory. *Fuzzy Sets Syst.* **2006**, *157*, 691–698. [CrossRef]
21. Li, J. On Null-Continuity of Monotone Measures. *Mathematics* **2020**, *8*, 205. [CrossRef]
22. Walley, P. *Statistical Reasoning with Imprecise Probabilities*; Chapman and Hall: London, UK , 1991.
23. Shaffer, G. Allocation of probability. *Ann. Probab.* **1976**, *4*, 827–839.
24. Dempster, A.P. Upper and lower probabilities induced by a multivalued mapping. *Ann. Math. Stat.* **1967**, *38*, 325–339. [CrossRef]
25. Falconer, K.J. *Fractal Sets*; Cambridge University Press: Cambridge, UK , 1985.
26. Rogers, C.A. *Hausdorff Measures*; Cambridge University Press: Cambridge, UK , 1970.
27. Doria, S. Probabilistic independence with respect to upper and lower conditional probabilities assigned by Hausdorff outer and inner measures. *Int. J. Approx. Reason.* **2007**, *46*, 617–635. [CrossRef]
28. Doria, S. Characterization of a coherent upper conditional prevision as the Choquet integral with respect to its associated Hausdorff outer measure. *Ann. Oper. Res.* **2012**, *195*, 33–48. [CrossRef]
29. Doria, S. Disintegration property of coherent upper conditional previsions with respect to Hausdorff outer measures for unbounded random variables. *Int. J. Gen. Syst.* **2021**, *50* , 262–280. [CrossRef]
30. Doria, S.; Selmi, B. *Defining Coherent Upper Conditional Previsions in a General Metric Space Using Distinct Dimensional Fractal Outer Measures*; Springer: Berlin/Heidelberg, Germany, 2024; pp. 45–75.
31. Achour, R.; Selmi, B. General fractal dimensions of typical sets and measures. *Fuzzy Sets Syst.* **2024**, *490*, 109039. [CrossRef]
32. Achour, R.; Doria, S.; Selmi, B.; Li, Z. Conditional aggregation operators defined by the Choquet integral and the Sugeno integral with respect to general fractal measures. *Fuzzy Sets Syst.* **2024**, *477*, 108811. [CrossRef]
33. Achour , R.; Li, Z.; Selmi, B.; Wang, T. General fractal dimensions of graphs of products and sums of continuous functions and their decompositions. *J. Math. Anal. Appl.* **2024**, *538*, 128400. [CrossRef]
34. Torra, V. The transport problem for non-additive measures. *Eur. J. Oper. Res.* **2023**, *311*, 679–689. [CrossRef]

35. Caprio, M. Optimal Transport for ϵ-Contaminated Credal Sets. *arXiv* **2025**, arXiv:2410.03267v2.
36. Bronevich, A.G.; Rozenberg, I.N. The measurement of relations on belief functions based on the Kantorovich problem and the Wasserstein metric. *Int. J. Approx. Reason.* **2021**, *131*, 108–135. [CrossRef]
37. Lorenzini, S.; Petturiti, D.; Vantaggi, B. Optimal Transport in Dempster-Shafer Theory and Choquet-Wasserstein Pseudo-Distances. In *Information Processing and Management of Uncertainty in Knowledge-Based Systems*; Lesot, M.-J., Vieira, S., Reformat, M.Z., Carvalho, J.P., Batista, F., Bouchon-Meunier, B., Yager, R.R., Eds.; IPMU 2024. Lecture Notes in Networks and Systems; Springer: Cham, Switzerland, 2025; Volume 1176.

fractal and fractional

MDPI

Review

Fractal Properties of the Cosmic Web

Jaan Einasto

Tartu Observatory, University of Tartu, Observatooriumi 1, 61602 Tõravere, Estonia; jaan.einasto@ut.ee

Abstract: The cosmic web is one of the most complex systems in nature, consisting of galaxies and clusters of galaxies joined by filaments and walls, leaving large empty regions called cosmic voids. The most common method of describing the web is a correlation function and its derivative, the fractal function. In this paper, I provide a review of the fractal properties of the cosmic web from the observational point of view within the Newtonian concordance ΛCDM Universe framework. I give a brief history of fractal studies of the Universe. I then describe the derivation of the fractal function from angular and spatial distributions of galaxies and their relations. Correlation functions are not sensitive to the shape of the galaxy distribution. To improve our quantitative understanding of properties of the web, statistics must be used which are sensitive to the pattern of the web.

Keywords: cosmic web; dark matter and galaxy clustering; fractal geometry; methods: numerical

1. Introduction

Long ago scientists noticed that many natural processes are self-similar over a large range of scales. Well-known examples are coastlines and mountain regions. The self-similarity of natural processes was discussed by Benoit Mandelbrot [1], who suggested the term *fractal* for this phenomenon. A similar phenomenon was observed in the distribution of galaxies, which are hierarchically clustered. This was noticed by Charlier [2] and studied in more detail by Carpenter [3], Kiang [4] Wertz [5,6], Haggerty and Wertz [7] and de Vaucouleurs [8,9]. Based on these observations a branch in physical cosmology, named fractal cosmology, was formed in the 1980s [10]. An important issue in the fractal cosmology is the fractal dimension and its dependence on the scale. The fractal dimension of a homogeneous spatial object is three, of a surface is two, and of a line is one. Actual objects can have non-integer values of the fractal dimension.

Studies of the fractal properties of the cosmic web are conducted using either the Newtonian framework or the relativistic approach. In the Newtonian framework, researchers use direct observational data and N-body simulations to describe large-scale structures, assuming gravity to be the dominant force, without accounting for relativistic effects. This approach treats cosmic structures within the concordant Lambda Cold Dark Matter (ΛCDM) universe model, relying on classical mechanics to model clustering patterns. The history of the formation of this model is given, among others, in books by Peebles [11,12] and Einasto [13].

In contrast, the relativistic approach incorporates general relativity, taking into account the expansion of the Universe and relativistic corrections to gravitational interactions. This perspective provides a more accurate description of cosmic evolution, particularly on a large scale, where relativistic effects influence the formation of the distribution of structures. Studies in this field examine how fractal-like properties emerge within the relativistic framework. This often involves the use of tensor-based models and relativistic perturbation theory. Relativistic approaches include, among other topics, theories of inflation [14,15], chaotic inflation (Linde [16,17], Linde and Riotto [18], Linde [19], and Nambu and Sasaki [20]), and quantum gravity (Ambjørn et al. [21] and Calcagni [22,23]).

In this review, I provide an overview of the fractal properties of the cosmic web in the Newtonian approximation of the Lambda Cold Dark Matter (ΛCDM) Universe. The review is based on the Newtonian approach for two reasons: (i) almost all fractal studies of real and simulated galaxies are conducted within the framework of the Lambda Cold Dark Matter universe, described in a new section; (ii) the relativistic approach is mostly related to the early stages of the evolution of the Universe, where some constraints of the concordant Lambda Cold Dark Matter Universe are invalid. The relativistic approach is a new and rapidly evolving field of study. It is outside the scope of the present observational review.

I begin with the description of the Lambda Cold Dark Matter (ΛCDM) Universe in Section 2. Next, I give a brief history of fractal studies of the cosmic web in Section 3. Section 3.1 discusses the angular distribution of galaxies and how this can be described by the angular correlation function. Section 4 discusses the statistical description of the cosmic web by measuring the correlation function and fractal dimension. In Sections 5 and 6, I discuss the correlation and fractal analysis of the web using spatial data. Section 7 is devoted to comparing angular and spatial distributions of galaxies. Here, I pay special attention to two aspects of fractal studies: the dependence of fractal characteristics on the scale from sub-megaparsec to hundreds of megaparsecs and the differences between 2D and 3D fractal characteristics. Section 8 is devoted to the study of the structure and evolution of the cosmic web, using combined spatial and velocity data. Section 9 discusses the scale of homogeneity of the cosmic web. The review concludes with a summary and outlook.

2. Basics of the Concordant ΛCDM Universe

In Section 2, I describe the concordant ΛCDM Universe, the basic framework of fractal studies of the cosmic web. The concordant ΛCDM model of the Universe is based on five pillars: the Big Bang model of the birth of the Universe, the Big Bang nucleosynthesis, data on the cosmic microwave background (CMB) radiation, data on the web-like distribution of galaxies in the present epoch, and the inflation hypothesis.

The Big Bang model is based on the general relativity theory by Einstein [24] and its extensions, developed by Friedmann [25] and Lemaître [26]. An alternative model of a Steady-state Universe by Hoyle [27] contradicts many astronomical data and is now rejected. The physics of the Big Bang is now well known. There exist variants that suggest that the Bang that created our Universe was actually only one event in the chaotic inflation, as discussed, among others, by Linde [16,19].

According to the Big Bang model, the Universe began in an extremely hot and dense state. After a few minutes, the Universe cooled to temperatures that allowed light chemical elements—hydrogen, helium and deuterium—to form. This process is called Big Bang nucleosynthesis and was studied first by Hoyle [28] and more recently by Cyburt et al. [29]. All heavier elements were synthesized in stars, as studied in detail by Burbidge et al. [30]. The results of these calculations are in good agreement with the observed distribution of chemical elements in stars and gas clouds.

The evolution of densities of various components of the Universe in units of the critical density is shown in Figure 1. The total density is equal to the critical density with very high accuracy, since even small deviations from the critical density increase during the evolution. The vertical dashed line corresponds to the present moment, and the gray shaded region represents the future. The vertical dotted lines show epochs of equality of radiation and matter, z_{eq}, recombination, z_{rec}, and equality of dark energy and matter, z_{eq}^{LM}. Solid colored lines show components of the standard ΛCDM, and dotted lines represent a model, where Λ is replaced by decaying dark energy, as suggested by recent DESI measurements [31].

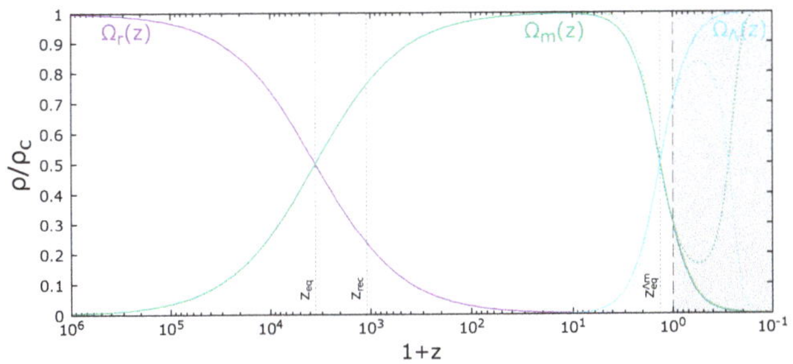

Figure 1. The evolution of radiation ($\Omega_{\rm R}(z)$), matter ($\Omega_{\rm m}(z)$), and dark energy ($\Omega_\Lambda(z)$) densities shown as a function of redshift z [32]. Reproduced with permission from Einasto, J.; Hütsi, G.; Szapudi, I.; Tenjes, P., Spinning the Cosmic Web; published by World Scientific, 2025.

The third important epoch in the cosmic history is the recombination of hydrogen at $z \approx 1000$ at temperatures around 3000° K. The emission from this epoch is observable as CMB radiation. As stressed by Sunyaev and Chluba [33], the physics at this epoch is very simple and well understood from laboratory experiments. The CMB radiation angular power spectrum depends on essential cosmological parameters. Modern CMB observations with the Planck satellite [34] yield for the spatial curvature of the Universe $\Omega_k = 0.0007 \pm 0.0019$. This means that the Planck data did not find any deviations from a spatial flat Universe with $\Omega_k = 0$ and $\Omega_{tot} = 1$. For the amount of matter, the Planck data give the following values: baryon density $\Omega_b h^2 = 0.02233 \pm 0.00015$, cold dark matter (CDM) density $\Omega_c h^2 = 0.1198 \pm 0.0012$, and dark energy density $\Omega_\Lambda = 0.6889 \pm 0.0056$. These density estimates are in good agreement with estimates from Big Bang nucleosynthesis for baryonic matter, dark matter (DM) in systems of galaxies, as found by Einasto et al. [35] and Ostriker et al. [36], and with the dark energy density value found from direct measurements of supernovas by Perlmutter et al. [37] and Riess et al. [38]. Planck and recent James Webb Space Telescope data yield for the Hubble constant $H_0 = 70.2 \pm 1.4$ km s^{-1}Mpc^{-1}, and the age of the Universe $t_0 = 13.77 \pm 0.12$ Gyr [39],

The inflation hypothesis of the early evolution of the Universe was suggested independently by Starobinsky [14] and Guth [15] and extended by Linde [16,19] to chaotic inflation. Possible problems of the concordant ΛCDM model were analyzed in detail by Di Valentino et al. [40].

3. A Short History of the Fractal Studies of the Cosmic Web

In this section, I give a short history of fractal studies of the cosmic web. First, I describe the angular distribution of galaxies and the discovery of the cosmic web. Discussion of the fractal character of the cosmic web follows.

3.1. Angular Distribution of Galaxies

In their studies, Carpenter [3] and de Vaucouleurs [8] observed that extragalactic entities establish a linear correlation between their characteristic density and radius when expressed in logarithmic terms, as illustrated in Figure 2. This correlation exhibits a slope of approximately −1.7 and aligns with the Schwarzschild limit. Furthermore, de Vaucouleurs [8] highlighted that Abell's rich clusters are not only clustered on the characteristic scale of superclusters but also extend to larger scales, indicating an ongoing clustering phenomenon among galaxies. More recently, Sankhyayan et al. [41] created a catalog of superclusters based on galaxy clusters identified in the Sloan Digital Sky Survey (SDSS) by York et al. [42]. The authors derived the relationship between density contrast and comoving size, discovering a slope of around ~ -2.

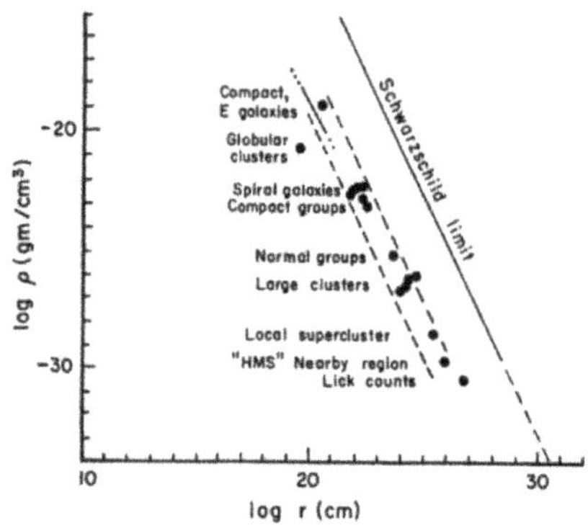

Figure 2. Density-radius relation of various systems of galaxies [8]. Reproduced with permission from AAAS, The Case for a Fierarchical Cosmology; published by Science, 1970.

The first deep catalog of galaxies, covering the whole northern hemisphere, was made in the Lick Observatory with the 20-inch Carnegie astrograph by Shane and Wirtanen [43]. Actual counts of galaxies were made in $10' \times 10'$ cells. Seldner et al. [44] used these actual counts and corrected the count for various errors and plate sensitivity differences. The final map of galaxies in the northern galactic hemisphere $b \geq 40^\circ$ is shown in the left panel of Figure 3. Several well-known clusters of galaxies are seen on the map. For example, the Coma cluster appears near the center of the map. The general impression is that field galaxies are distributed approximately randomly.

Soneira and Peebles [45] developed a fractal model Universe to match the character of the galaxy distribution in the Lick survey. The model assigns 'galaxy' positions in a three-dimensional clustering hierarchy, fixes absolute magnitudes, and projects angular positions of objects brighter than $m = 18.9$ onto sky. This procedure yields a galaxy map, shown in the right panel of Figure 3. Both the real Lick map and the computer generated map were used to calculate two-point angular correlation functions.

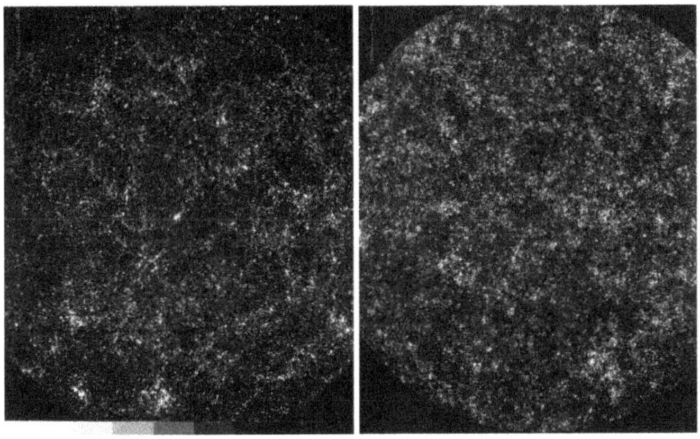

Figure 3. (**Left**): Map of Lick survey galaxies in the northern galactic hemisphere brighter than $m_B \leq 18.9$ and north of galactic latitude $b \geq 40°$ [45]. (**Right**): Simulated map of galaxies imitating the 2D distribution of Lick galaxies [45].

Peebles [46] proposed utilizing the correlation method for the analysis of distribution of galaxies, applying it to all significant catalogs of extragalactic objects, including works by Hauser and Peebles [47], Peebles and Hauser [48], Peebles [49], Peebles and Groth [50], and Peebles [51]. These investigations demonstrated that the angular distribution of galaxies could be characterized by a power law. When the estimated angular correlation function is converted to the spatial correlation function, it retains a power law form:

$$\xi(r) = (r/r_0)^{-\gamma}, \tag{1}$$

where $r_0 = 4.5 \pm 0.5\ h^{-1}$ Mpc is the correlation length, and $\gamma = 1.77$ is a characteristic power index [52]. This power law is valid in the scale interval $0.05 \leq r \leq 9\ h^{-1}$ Mpc, where distances are expressed in units of the dimensionless Hubble constant h ($H = 100$ h km/s per megaparsec). Groth and Peebles [52] showed that the angular correlation function is essentially zero at angular distances $\theta \geq 10$ degrees. The conclusion from these studies, based on the apparent (two-dimensional) distribution of galaxies and clusters on the sky, confirmed the picture that galaxies and clusters of galaxies are hierarchically clustered.

In 1970s and 1980s, British and Australian astronomers used Schmidt telescope plates to photograph the whole sky. The Automatic Plate Measuring (APM) machine in Cambridge was used to scan these plates. Special software was developed to separate galaxy and star images. The final catalog contains over two million galaxies brighter than $b_j = 20.5$. Maddox et al. [53] used APM galaxies to calculate the angular correlation function of galaxies, results are shown in Figure 4. We see that the power law relation, Equation (1), is valid over three decades of angular distances, $0.01 \leq \theta \leq 3$ degrees. The almost constant slope of the angular correlation function over a large range of angular scales was interpreted by Peebles [54] as evidence that the spatial correlation function is well represented by the law Equation (1) over the range of separations 10 kpc$\leq r \leq 10\ h^{-1}$ Mpc. As we see below in Section 7, this conclusion was influenced by the insensitivity of the two-dimensional correlation function to the spatial structure of the cosmic web.

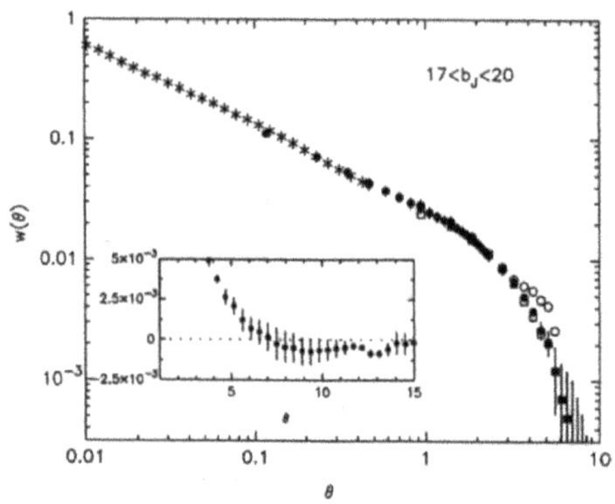

Figure 4. Average angular correlation function of APM catalog of galaxies in the magnitude range $17 \leq b_j \leq 20$. The inset shows the mean angular CF on a linear scale. As argument, the angular separation in degrees is used [53].

3.2. *Discovery of the Cosmic Web*

In late 1970s, the number of galaxies with measured redshifts allowed finding the distances of galaxies and studying the spatial three-dimensional (3D) distribution of galaxies. The first results of these analyses were reported in the IAU Symposium "Large Scale Structure of the Universe" in Tallinn, September 1977 [55]. Jõeveer et al. [56] presented the study of the structure of the Perseus–Pisces Supercluster and its surroundings and of the global network of superclusters and galaxy chains/filaments. Brent Tully and Fisher [57] presented a movie of the Local Supercluster. To obtain a spatial image of the supercluster, he used the simple trick of making the image rotate, which created a three-dimensional illusion. The movie showed that the Local Supercluster consists of a number of chains of galaxies that branch off from the supercluster's central cluster in the Virgo constellation as legs of a spider. William Tifft, in his talk, gave an overview of the recent study of the Coma supercluster and its environ by Gregory and Thompson [58].

The wedge diagram of galaxies in the 30–45° declination zone gives us a fascinating glimpse into the cosmic web. This diagram reveals how galaxies within the Perseus–Pisces Supercluster are arranged like a chain, with clusters and groups of galaxies appearing like pearls along a necklace. This structure is a prime example of the cosmic web's basic elements: clusters, filaments, sheets, and voids. Superclusters of galaxies are massive, but they occupy only about 4% of the Universe's total space. The remaining 96% is composed of vast voids. This large-scale geometry forms a continuous network that includes clusters, filaments, sheets, and the spaces between them. Interestingly, central galaxies in rich clusters are typically of the cD type and are often active radio sources.

Sergei Shandarin's early numerical simulations were groundbreaking in illustrating the evolution of particles through gravitational clustering, based on the theory developed by Zeldovich [59]. In the right panel of Figure 5, you can see a fascinating system of high- and low-density regions. High-density areas are compact and clumped together, forming a network of filaments that enclose expansive under-dense regions. This visualization was pivotal, as it gave the first glimpse into the Universe's structural patterns as predicted by the Zeldovich model.

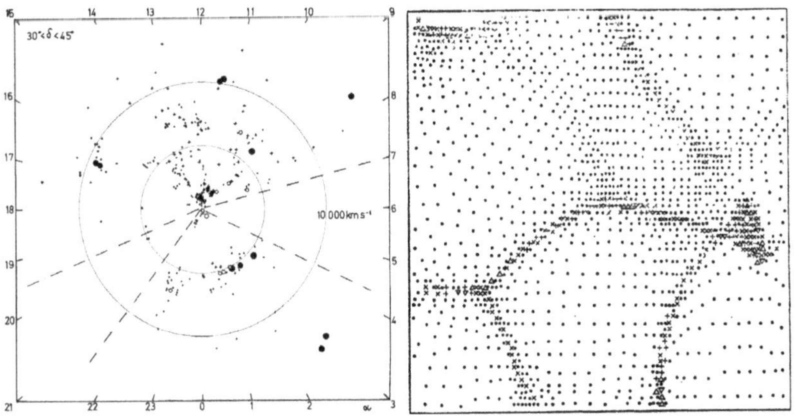

Figure 5. (**Left**): Wedge diagram for the 30°–45° declination zone. Filled circles show rich clusters of galaxies, open circles—groups, dots—galaxies, crosses—Markarian galaxies [60]. (**Right**): Distribution of particles in simulations by (Shandarin 1975, private communication), [61].

The origin of this filamentary structure was analyzed by Bond et al. [62], who introduced the term "cosmic web" to characterize this phenomenon. Analyses of galaxy distribution indicated that the correlation length of clusters significantly exceeds that of individual galaxies (see, for instance, Bahcall and Soneira [63], Klypin and Kopylov [64]). This observation was interpreted by Kaiser [65] as a form of bias affecting clusters in relation to galaxies. Szalay and Schramm [66] showed that, if the correlation function is in the form Equation (1), its index γ determines the fractal dimension of the sample: $D = 3 - \gamma = 1.23$.

3.3. Discussion of the Fractal Character of the Cosmic Web

The next step was made by Einasto et al. [67], who demonstrated that the correlation length is influenced not only by the luminosity of galaxies but also by the depth of the sample, as illustrated in Figure 6. This relationship between galaxy correlation length and sample depth was interpreted by Pietronero [10] as evidence for a fractal structure in the distribution of galaxies. Pietronero emphasized that the fractal nature of galaxy distribution extends to infinitely large distances, suggesting that the entire Universe exhibits fractal characteristics. Furthermore, Jones et al. [68] examined the galaxy distribution within the CfA redshift survey and in a simulation of the ΛCDM model conducted by Gramann [69,70], which is recognized as one of the first ΛCDM simulations featuring 64^3 particles within a 40 h^{-1} Mpc box. The authors concluded that both the galaxy distribution and the ΛCDM model can be effectively described using a multifractal approach, indicating that the fractals possess more than one scaling index. The dimensionality of this distribution varies between 1 and 3.

Fractal properties of the distribution of galaxies were discussed in the IAU Symposium "Large scale structures of the Universe", held in Balatonfured, Hungary, on 15–20 June 1987. Bernard Jones reported basic results by Jones et al. [68]. He started his talk showing the distribution of galaxies and declared *"this is a fractal"*. The distribution of both observed and model samples can be described by multifractals with varying fractal dimension. A further discussion of the fractal character of the large-scale distribution of galaxies was by Mandelbrot [71], who mentioned that he developed the multifractal concept long ago, between 1970 and 1976, as described in his books [1,72]. Further, he concentrated on the question: is the transition to homogeneity at the distance R_{cross} inside or outside of the limiting distance of data, R_{max}? If $R_{max} < R_{cross}$, we cannot make any decisions on the transition scale to homogeneity. After the Symposium, Alex Szalay invited a small group of interested people to Budapest to discuss in a relaxed atmosphere the fractal character of galaxy distribution: Benoit Mandelbrot, Yakov Zeldovich, Bernard Jones, and the author of the present review. In the discussion, we agreed that the limit of the validity of the power-law character of the correlation function with constant index $\gamma = 1.77$ is at least $2\,r_0 \approx 10\,h^{-1}$ Mpc. Available data go beyond this distance and show definitely a multifractal character. However, inside the limit of observational and model data, $R_{max} \approx 30\,h^{-1}$ Mpc, there is no evidence for the transition to homogeneity with fractal index $D = 3$. Thus, further studies are needed to find the value of R_{cross}. Zeldovich disliked the fractal description of the Universe for two reasons: (i) it gives no hint to the physics of the formation and evolution of the Universe, and (ii) it contradicts other data that show that the mean density of matter is not zero, as predicted by a simple fractal model.

Subsequent discussions of the fractal characteristics of the cosmic web have been undertaken by various research groups, employing diverse methodologies. The majority of these discussions have centered around the widely accepted concordant ΛCDM model. Key aspects of this model were presented at several IAU Symposia: in Tallinn in 1977 [55], Crete in 1982 [73], Hungary in 1987 [74], and again in Tallinn in 2014 [75]. The theoretical underpinnings of this model are rooted in the hierarchical clustering scenario proposed by Peebles and Yu [76], alongside the pancake model for cosmic web formation introduced by Zeldovich [59], and its extension through catastrophe theory as described by Arnold et al. [77]. Further advancements in methodology involved the application of statistical measures to investigate the fractal nature of galaxy distributions, as explored by Mandelbrot [72] and Martinez and Jones [78]. These methods encompass various definitions of fractal dimensions, including the Hausdorff dimension, capacity dimension, and correlation dimension (for definitions, refer to Martínez and Saar [79]).

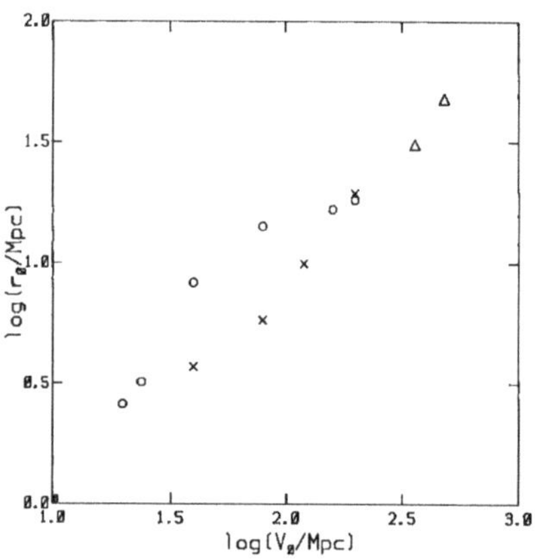

Figure 6. The different symbols (circles, crosses, triangles) highlight that different types of galaxy groupings have distinct clustering properties. Rich clusters, for example, might show a larger correlation length compared to galaxies [67].

In late 1970s, a burst of interest in the fractal character of the Universe emerged. Different authors had various styles in fractal studies: the Anglo-American style, Italian style, and a more neutral style, represented by Mandelbrot, Jones, Martinez, and Balian and Schaeffer [80,81]. The latter authors confirmed the bifractal character of galaxy distribution between scales from 0.1 to $10\,h^{-1}$ Mpc, with different fractal dimensions for dense clustered regions and for underdense regions. Song and Ruffini [82], Ruffini et al. [83] constructed a cellular fractal model of the early universe. The authors assumed that dark matter consisted of some 'inos', which become non-relativistic at epoch $1 + z_{nr}$, and calculated the main parameters of " elementary cells": characteristic Jeans masses are $4 \times 10^{17}\ M_{\odot}$, radii 100 h^{-1} Mpc, and epochs $1 + z_{nr} \approx 10^4$. The authors predicted that the cellular fractal model has an upper cutoff, and above this cutoff the mean density does not decrease with distance. This model was compared with observations by Calzetti et al. [84,85]. More recent investigations into the fractal properties of the cosmic web have been conducted by Gaite et al. [86] and Gaite [87,88].

The Anglo-American style of fractal studies was based essentially on the angular distribution of galaxies. The first steps in this approach were conducted by Peebles and Yu [76] and Peebles [46], who suggested the use of the correlation function to describe the distribution of galaxies. The next essential step was the application of a fractal model by Soneira and Peebles [45] to describe the angular distribution of galaxies. A further use of this approach was the study of the distribution of APM galaxies by Maddox et al. [53]. The fractal character of the cosmic web was analyzed by Peebles [89] and Peebles [90]. It is characteristic that authors of the Anglo-American style studies avoided in their publications the term "cosmic web".

The Italian style of fractal studies is essentially the continuation of earlier work by Charlier [2], Kiang [4], and de Vaucouleurs [8,9] on the hierarchical distribution of galaxies. This style is represented by Pietronero [10], Pietronero et al. [91], Pietronero and Sylos Labini [92], Sylos Labini et al. [93], and Borgani [94]. The focus of Italian-style studies was the fractal behavior of the Universe on large scales.

A dialogue between the Anglo-American and Italian views on fractal properties of the Universe took place during the celebration of the 250th anniversary of Princeton University [95]. Marc Davis [96] presented the Anglo-American group's view. His main arguments were as follows: (i) the constant value of the correlation length for 2D and 3D samples of various depths, $r_0 \approx 4\ h^{-1}$ Mpc; (ii) the mean density of galaxies is the same for nearby and more distant samples, and the scatter of densities decreases with distance. Luciano Pietronero [10] described the Italian vision. According to this view, the correlation length of samples increases with distance, and the mean density decreases with distance up to $\sim$1000 h^{-1} Mpc. Pietronero made a bet with Davis, over a case of Italian or Californian wine, Neil Turok was the referee—The correlation length for volume-limited samples, $M < -19.5$, is $r_0 \approx 5\ h^{-1}$ Mpc (Davis) or $r_0 \geq 50\ h^{-1}$ Mpc (Pietronero). These are fundamental questions, and I discuss these aspects of fractal studies in later sections.

4. Statistics of Galaxy Clustering

Differences between fractal studies of various styles start from variations in the methods to describe the fractal properties of the Universe. The three-dimensional distribution of galaxies and clusters of galaxies was described in the Tallinn 1977 symposium only qualitatively. In this section, I discuss some aspects of statistics related to the estimation of quantitative statistical parameters of the cosmic web.

4.1. Measuring Spatial Distribution of Galaxies

In the late 1970s, astronomers and cosmologists began to realize that the Universe's total density of matter was about 20% of what we call the "critical density"—the density needed for the Universe to be flat and perfectly balanced. Most intriguingly, they found that the majority of this mass was in a mysterious form: dark matter. This was highlighted by the pioneering work of Einasto et al. [35] and Ostriker et al. [36], who laid the groundwork for our understanding of this cosmic puzzle (for a discussion see de Swart [97]). Back then, scientists knew from Big Bang nucleosynthesis (the process that created the first atomic nuclei) that only about 5% of this critical density was made up of baryonic matter, which is the "normal" matter that makes up stars, planets, and us. The rest had to be something else. Given this gap, the scientific community began considering the possibility that dark matter was non-baryonic. The first candidate was massive neutrinos, which were then known as hot dark matter (HDM) because they moved at relativistic speeds.

The first quantitative comparison of Peebles' and Zeldovich's structure formation models was conducted by Zeldovich et al. [98]. The authors investigated the properties of the distribution of real galaxies in the Virgo–Coma region using CfA data (sample O), the distribution of particles in a 3D simulation by Klypin and Shandarin [99], calculated using the assumption that the dark matter particle population is made of neutrinos (sample A). The second model H was constructed according to the prescription described by Soneira and Peebles [45]. The two-dimensional view of this model is shown in the right panel of Figure 3. The authors used also the Poisson distribution of particles. Three tests were used: the spatial correlation function, percolation, and multiplicity tests.

The left panel of Figure 7 illustrates the spatial correlation functions for three different samples. This figure highlights a significant characteristic of the O and A samples: the presence of a distinct knee in their correlation function, which is notably absent in the hierarchical H and Poisson P models. At short distances, the correlation function is highly sensitive to the arrangement of galaxies or particles that are in close proximity to one another. In this range, most galaxies are found within clusters and groups that typically exhibit an almost spherical configuration. Conversely, at greater distances, the correlation function reflects the existence of galaxy filaments that are primarily one-dimensional in nature. Therefore, as we transition from small to large mutual distances among galaxies or particles, the geometric structure of the arrangement shifts. In contrast, the hierarchical and Poisson models lack filaments, resulting in a correlation function that appears featureless.

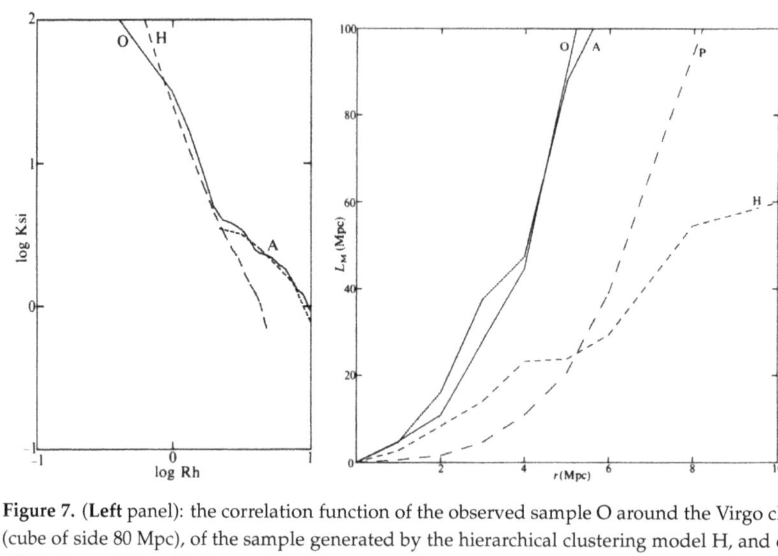

Figure 7. (**Left** panel): the correlation function of the observed sample O around the Virgo cluster (cube of side 80 Mpc), of the sample generated by the hierarchical clustering model H, and of the adiabatic model A. (**Right** panel): the maximal length L_M of connected regions as a function of neighbourhood radius r for four catalogs: O, A, H, and P (Poisson model). All distances are expressed for Hubble constant $h = 0.5$ [98]. Reproduced with permission from Zeldovich, Y.B.; Einasto, J.; Shandarin, S.F., Giant voids in the universe; published by Nature, 1982.

The percolation method enables the assessment of the largest system's length as a diagnostic tool. The right panel of Figure 7 illustrates the maximal lengths of galaxy and particle systems as a function of the neighborhood radius r. The neighborhood radius defines a range of distances around a galaxy or particle, where other elements are taken into account for analysis. Both galaxies and particles in simulations exhibit clustering behavior; consequently, at smaller radii r, the length of the longest system increases at a rate that surpasses that of a Poisson sample. However, at greater distances, the behavior of the samples diverges. In both the observed sample O and the model sample A, filaments connect clusters into a network. These filaments facilitate the formation of longer systems, resulting in a more rapid increase in the length of the longest system compared to the Poisson scenario. As depicted in Figure 7, the growth patterns of samples O and A are nearly identical. In contrast, for sample H, the rate of increase of length L with respect to radius r at larger distances is slower than that observed in the Poisson sample. This can be attributed to the lower density of field particles in sample H, as a significant portion of the particles is concentrated within clusters. Thus, this test proves to be sensitive to the existence of filaments that link clusters into a cohesive network.

The multiplicity test revealed distinct distributions of multiplicities across all samples. The observed sample exhibits a relatively balanced representation of systems with varying richness, indicating the presence of a detailed structure comprising galaxy systems of diverse richness levels. Notably, the majority of galaxies are concentrated within a single extensive structure—the Virgo supercluster. In contrast, the A sample features a prominent large system as well, but its distribution of smaller systems closely resembles that of a Poisson sample. This suggests a scarcity of systems with intermediate richness, such as small-scale filaments. Consequently, the A sample, derived from the neutrino-dominated Universe model, also appears to contradict the observational data.

The primary conclusion drawn from this analysis is that the hierarchical clustering model proposed by Soneira and Peebles [45] fails to perform adequately across all tests, while the adiabatic model struggles specifically in the multiplicity test. Additionally, the neutrino-based adiabatic model encounters a significant challenge: it predicts that structure forms too late. Observational data indicate that galaxies and rich clusters of galaxies formed earlier than this model suggests, as highlighted by van den Bergh [100]. Consequently, both conventional neutrino-dominated cosmology and the hierarchical clustering model exhibit shortcomings. To address the challenges associated with neutrinos as a candidate for dark matter, Peebles [101] proposed that dark matter consists of weakly interacting particles, known as Cold Dark Matter.

To evaluate the viability of the Cold Dark Matter (CDM) concept, Melott et al. [102] conducted an analysis of the pioneering 3D CDM simulation by Centrella and Melott [103]. This examination revealed that the CDM model aligns with all quantitative tests employed by Zeldovich et al. [98]. The formation of galaxies is initiated by the collapse of small-scale perturbations, consistent with the clustering scenario proposed by Peebles. In contrast, large-scale structures develop in accordance with Zeldovich's framework. The concept of the cosmic web was further refined by Bond et al. [62], whose study elucidated the mechanisms by which filaments are interconnected to create this intricate network. However, both structure formation scenarios require adjustments. Hierarchical clustering is not merely a random occurrence; rather, it represents a continuous flow of particles and galaxies directed toward attractors formed from the highest peaks of the primordial fluctuation field. The process of pancaking originates from these peaks, resulting in various types of caustics, as suggested by Arnold et al. [77].

4.2. Measuring the Correlation Function

Early studies of the distribution of galaxies were based on two-dimensional (2D) angular data as described in Section 3.1. To measure the distribution in a quantitative way, the correlation function was applied [46]. As discussed by Peebles [104], the angular correlation function of almost all samples of galaxies is well represented by a power-law function:

$$w(\theta) = A\theta^{1-\gamma}, \tag{2}$$

where A is a constant, and γ is a parameter, whose value for most samples studied was $\gamma \approx 1.7$. This power law can be inverted and has the solution:

$$\xi(r) = Br^{-\gamma}, \tag{3}$$

where B is a constant, depending on A. These equations show that the angular correlation function is a power law with index lower by one unit than the spatial correlation function $\xi(r)$.

When, in the 1980s, galaxy samples with known radial velocities were obtained, a question emerged: how to use these three-dimensional (3D) data to characterize the distribution in a quantitative way. Distances of galaxies, calculated from observed radial velocities, are influenced by the Kaiser [105] effect—an apparent contraction of the galaxy density field in the radial direction. To avoid this effect, Peebles [46] and Davis and Peebles [106] suggested the use of the angular position of galaxies to find first the two-dimensional correlation function. In this case, pair separations can be calculated parallel to the line of sight, π, and perpendicular to the line of sight, r_p. The angular correlation function, $w_p(r_p)$, can be found by integrating over the measured $\xi(r_p, \pi)$, using the equation

$$w_p(r_p) = 2\int_{r_{min}}^{r_{max}} \xi(r_p, \pi)d\pi, \tag{4}$$

where r_{min} and r_{max} are the minimum and maximum distances of the galaxies in the sample. This equation has the form of the Abel integral equation and can be inverted to recover the spatial correlation function [106]:

$$\xi(r) = -\frac{1}{\pi}\int_{r}^{r_{max}} \frac{w_p(r_p)}{\sqrt{r_p^2 - r^2}}dr_p. \tag{5}$$

If the correlation function is described as a power law function, angular and spatial functions have the forms of Equations (2) and (3), respectively. Davis and Peebles [106] made a correlation analysis of the CfA redshift survey with magnitude limit 14.5 and applied the procedure described above to find correlation function parameters. The authors found that the spatial correlation function can be well represented by a power law, Equation (1), with parameters $r_0 = 5.4 \pm 0.3\, h^{-1}$ Mpc, and $\gamma = 1.77$.

In subsequent years, this procedure was applied in most correlation analyses. Norberg et al. [107] investigated the luminosity dependence of galaxy clustering in the 2dF Galaxy Redshift Survey. To measure the correlation length, the authors used projected angular correlation functions as suggested by Davis and Peebles [106]. The authors found the real space correlation length $r_0 = 4.9 \pm 0.3\, h^{-1}$ Mpc and power law slope $\gamma = 1.71 \pm 0.06$. Zehavi et al. [108,109] studied the luminosity dependence of the SDSS galaxy correlation function and applied the standard procedure to measure the projected correlation function. Over the scales $0.1 < r_p < 10\, h^{-1}$ Mpc the power law approximation yields for correlation length of $L^\star$ galaxies with $M_r = 20.0$: $r_0 = 5.24 \pm 0.28\, h^{-1}$ Mpc and $\gamma = 1.87 \pm 0.03$.

The inversion Equation (5) assumes that spatial three-dimensional and projected two-dimensional density fields are statistically similar. As we see below in Section 7, this assumption is not valid.

4.3. Measuring the Fractal Dimension

The discovery of the dependence of the correlation length from the type of objects by Bahcall and Soneira [63], Klypin and Kopylov [64], and Einasto et al. [67] and the interpretation of this effect by Pietronero [10] in fractal terms initiated discussions on the following topic: what are the best methods to characterize fractal properties of the spatial distribution of galaxies? This problem was discussed also by Calzetti et al. [85], Coleman and Pietronero [110], and Borgani [94], who pointed to the fact that, in the usual correlation analysis, the observed galaxy distribution is normalized to the Poissonian distribution in a way that cannot be used to test the homogeneity of the sample.

The natural estimator to determine the two-point correlation function is

$$\xi_N(r) = \frac{DD(r)}{RR(r)} - 1, \tag{6}$$

where r is the galaxy pair separation (distance), and $DD(r)$ and $RR(r)$ are normalized counts of galaxy–galaxy and random–random pairs at a distance r of the pair members. Normalization equalizes the sum of all $DD(r)$ to the sum of all $RR(r)$. Galaxies are clustered; thus, at small distances, the number density of galaxies is enhanced, $DD(r) > RR(r)$, and $\xi(r) > 0$. At large distances, the density of galaxies is less than the mean galaxy density (a large fraction of galaxies is located in clusters), thus $DD(r) < RR(r)$, and by construction at large distances $\xi(r) < 0$, as found already by Calzetti et al. [85]. The relative volume of regions with $DD(r) < RR(r)$ is much larger than the relative volume of regions with $DD(r) > RR(r)$; thus, the correlation function on larger scales is only slightly negative, see Figure 4. The crossover at separation r_c, where $DD(r_c) = RR(r_c)$, is approximately proportional to the depth of the sample.

Pietronero [10], Calzetti et al. [85], and Coleman et al. [111] interpreted the increase in the galaxy correlation length with the sample size with this normalization effect and suggested that, instead of $\xi(r)$, an alternative clustering measure should be used: $\Gamma(r) = n\,(1 + \xi(r))$, where n is the mean density of galaxies. Another possibility is to use, instead of the correlation function $\xi(r)$, the structure function $g(r) = 1 + \xi(r)$, where $4\pi r^2 g(r) n dr$ is the mean number of galaxies lying in a shell of thickness dr at distance r from any other point. In a Poisson process, $g(r) = 1$. The structure function has a power law form on small scales, $r < 5\,h^{-1}$ Mpc, and approaches zero at large separations. In the following analysis, I use the structure function $g(r)$ to investigate fractal properties of the distribution of galaxies.

5. Correlation Analysis of the Cosmic Web

Historically, the quantitative analysis of the cosmic web has been dominated by correlation functions and their derivatives, the structure function and the fractal dimension function. It is well-known that the correlation function contains information on amplitudes of the density field but not on their phases. The importance of the phase information in the formation of the cosmic web has been understood long ago. To demonstrate the role of phase information, Coles and Chiang [112] extracted the simulated density field, Fourier transformed the density field, and randomized phases of all Fourier components. The modified field has on all wavenumbers k the same amplitudes as the original field, only the phases of waves are different. In the modified field, no structures are visible.

Over the years, a variety of statistical methods have been developed to analyze specific aspects of the spatial patterns in the large-scale Universe. Almost all these methods are borrowed from other branches of science such as image processing, mathematical morphology, computational geometry, and medical imaging. The richness of various methods to investigate the structure of the cosmic web is seen in proceedings of the IAU Symposium "The Zeldovich Universe: Genesis and Growth of the Cosmic Web" [75].

In the early years of the 21th century, new redshift surveys were published—the 2dF and the Sloan Digital Sky Survey (SDSS). The 2dF survey by Colless et al. [113] allowed finding angular correlation functions of 2dF galaxies [53], discussed in Section 3.1. Next, the SDSS was available [42,114,115], which allowed studying the distribution of galaxies in much larger volumes of space. It was used to calculate correlation functions and power spectra of SDSS galaxies by Tegmark et al. [116] and Zehavi et al. [109]. New large numerical simulations of the cosmic web were developed, which included hydrodynamical processes of formation and evolution of galaxies — the Millennium simulation by Springel et al. [117] and the Illustris The Next Generation (IllustrisTNG) simulation by Springel et al. [118]. These observational and modeling possibilities allowed studying the character of the distribution of dark matter and galaxies in much more detail.

As described above, various groups obtained very different pictures of the fractal characteristics of the cosmic web. Thus, it is evident that a new independent study is needed, using more recent observational data and simulations. This was conducted by Einasto et al. [119,120]. In this section, I describe the conventional correlation analysis of the cosmic web, using as tests SDSS galaxies and particles from several modern ΛCDM model simulations. First, I discuss the formation of galaxies in the cosmic web and the method, how to select particles in simulations to form samples of particles, comparable to samples of galaxies.

5.1. Formation of Galaxies in the Cosmic Web

By comparing spatial distributions of dark matter particles and galaxies, Jõeveer et al. [56] and Zeldovich et al. [98] found that there are almost no galaxies in voids, but voids are populated by a rarefied field of DM particles, see Figure 5. The authors emphasized from this difference that the galaxy formation is a threshold phenomenon. The analysis by White and Rees [121] confirmed this: the galaxy formation is a two-stage process: first, dark matter condenses to form heavy halos, where various hydrodynamical processes form visible galaxies. The first numerical simulations of galaxy formation with a hydrodynamical method by Cen and Ostriker [122] confirmed this model, verified by Springel et al. [118] by a much more detailed hydrodynamical simulation. In high-density regions the baryonic matter forms galaxies, and in low-density regions it remains in the pre-galactic diffuse form together with low-density field of dark matter.

Based on these arguments, it is natural to use particles in high-density regions to get a sample of DM particles that imitates samples of galaxies. We apply a sharp particle density limit, ρ_0, to select biased samples of particles. This method is similar to the Ising model, discussed by Repp and Szapudi [123]. Actually galaxy formation is a stochastic process; thus, the matter density limit, which divides unclustered and clustered matter, is fuzzy. However, a fuzzy density limit has little influence on the properties of correlation functions of biased and non-biased samples. Thus, we can accept a fixed threshold limit and select for biased model samples particles with density labels, $\rho \geq \rho_0$.

5.2. Correlation Functions of Galaxies and Matter

In early studies of the spatial distribution of galaxies, only samples with a rather low distance limit were available, which raised the question: how representative are these samples in terms of describing the whole cosmic web? As discussed in Section 3, various authors interpreted these early data in a very different way. To avoid these difficulties, I use in the following analysis only galaxy and model samples found in a large sample volume, as conducted by Einasto et al. [119,120].

Einasto et al. [119] used the luminosity-limited galaxy samples by Tempel et al. [124], selected from data release 10 of the SDSS galaxy redshift survey [125]. The catalog has a Petrosian r- band magnitude limit $m_r \leq 17.77$ and contains 489, 510 galaxies. The SDSS samples have $M_r - 5\log h$ magnitude limits -18.0, -19.0, -20.0, -21.0, and -22.0 and are referred to as SDSS.18t, SDSS.19t, SDSS.20t, SDSS.21t, and SDSS.22t. The effective size of the sample is 500 h^{-1} Mpc. One view of the SDSS density field is presented in Figure 8. We see here a complicated network of clusters, filaments, and voids. The rich complex of superclusters in the lower part of the Figure is the Sloan Great Wall, which actually consists of three superclusters [126].

To have both high spatial resolution and the presence of density perturbations in a large scale interval, Einasto et al. [119] used a series of simulations of the ΛCDM models with box sizes $L_0 = 256,\ 512,\ 1024\ h^{-1}$ Mpc with $N_{\rm grid} = 512$ and number of particles $N_{\rm part} = 512^3$. The cosmological parameters for all simulations are $(\Omega_m, \Omega_\Lambda, \Omega_b, h, \sigma_8, n_s)$ = (0.28, 0.72, 0.044, 0.693, 0.84, 1.00). In the present analysis, I use the model of size 512 h^{-1} Mpc. Additionally, I use the simulated galaxy sample of the Millennium simulation by [117] and Croton et al. [127], which has the box of size 500 h^{-1} Mpc, and the EAGLE simulation by McAlpine et al. [128]. EAGLE simulations were run in boxes of sizes 25, 50, and 100 h^{-1} Mpc.

In the Einasto et al. [119] simulation, the authors calculated local density values, ρ, at particle locations using the locations of the 27 nearest particles, and expressed the densities in units of the average density. The authors formed samples corresponding to the simulated galaxies, containing particles that exceeded a certain density limit, $\rho \geq \rho_0$. These samples are denoted as LCDM.i, where i denotes the particle density limit ρ_0. The full DM model covers all particles, corresponds to the particle density limit $\rho_0 = 0$, and is therefore denoted LCDM.00.

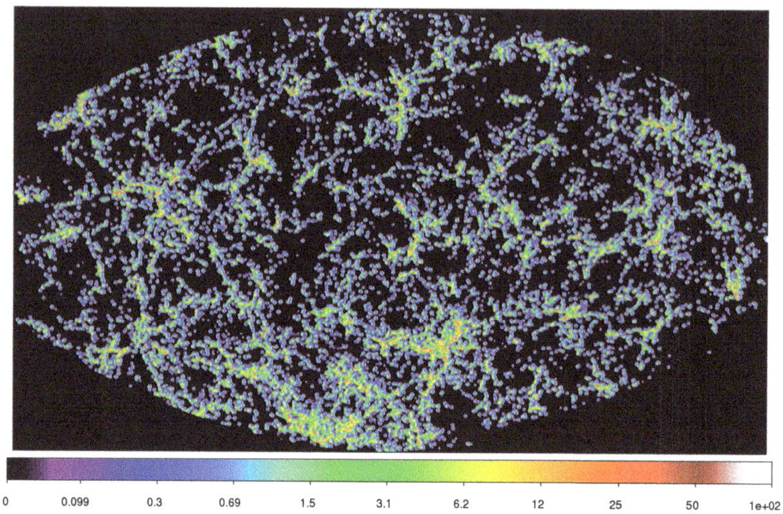

Figure 8. Slice of the density field from the Sloan Digital Sky Survey at a distance of 240 h^{-1} Mpc and thickness of 10 h^{-1} Mpc. At lower part of the figure, the Sloan Great Wall is seen [13]. Reproduced with permission from Einasto, J., Dark Matter and Cosmic Web Story; published by World Scientific, 2024.

Correlation functions of ΛCDM and SDSS samples are shown in the left and right panels of Figure 9, respectively. Figure 9 shows that samples with different galaxy luminosity and particle density limit form approximately parallel sequences, where the amplitude of the correlation functions increases with the increase in the luminosity/density limit. For galaxy samples, the amplitudes of the correlation functions are almost constant for low-luminosity samples and rise for samples brighter than approximately $M_r = -20$. The behavior of ΛCDM model particle density selected correlation functions is different—with increasing particle density threshold ρ_0, the amplitudes rise continuously. The luminosity dependence of the correlation functions is the principal factor of the biasing phenomenon, as shown by Kaiser [65]. A further discussion of the correlation length is given in the following subsection.

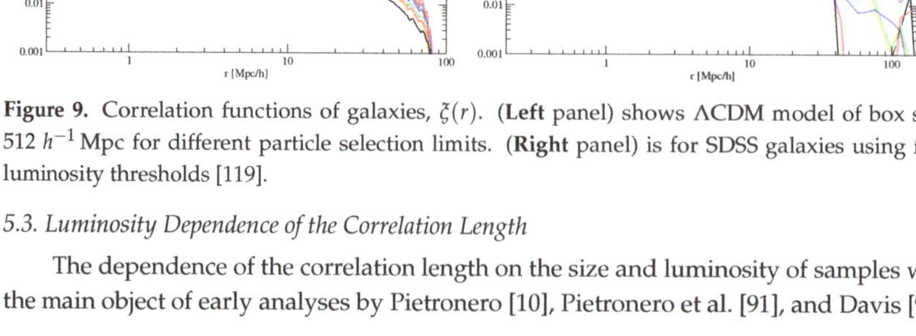

Figure 9. Correlation functions of galaxies, $\xi(r)$. (**Left** panel) shows ΛCDM model of box size 512 h^{-1} Mpc for different particle selection limits. (**Right** panel) is for SDSS galaxies using five luminosity thresholds [119].

5.3. Luminosity Dependence of the Correlation Length

The dependence of the correlation length on the size and luminosity of samples was the main object of early analyses by Pietronero [10], Pietronero et al. [91], and Davis [96].

Pietronero et al. [91] defended the view that the correlation length increases with the size of samples until very large scales, $r \approx 1000\ h^{-1}$ Mpc. Davis [96] argued that it remains constant, $r_0 \approx 5\ h^{-1}$ Mpc for all sample sizes. I use new analyses of the correlation length to have a fresh view of the problem.

The data presented above allow calculating the correlation lengths of observed SDSS samples and simulated Millennium and EAGLE samples. In Figure 10, I show the correlation lengths, r_0, of the SDSS, EAGLE, and Millennium samples as functions of magnitude M_r. We see that, for low and intermediate luminosities, all samples have correlation lengths $r_0 \approx 5\ h^{-1}$ Mpc, which rises to higher values for more luminous galaxies. The correlation length r_0 has a rather similar luminosity dependence for all samples. The luminosity dependence of the correlation functions is the principal factor of the biasing phenomenon, as discussed by Kaiser [65].

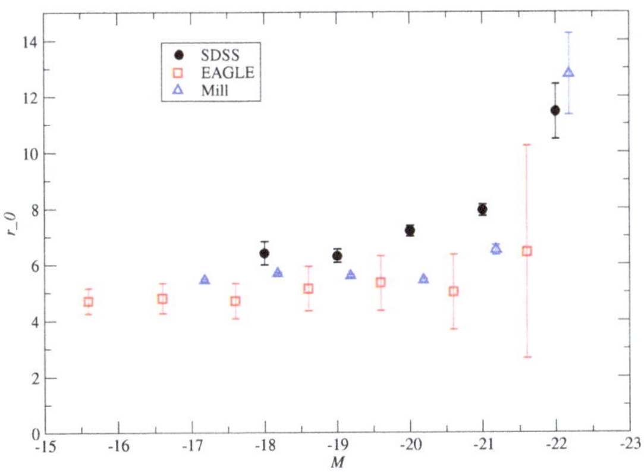

Figure 10. Correlation length r_0 in h^{-1} Mpc of SDSS galaxies as a function of their absolute magnitudes. For comparison, we also show the correlation lengths of the EAGLE and Millennium simulations for various magnitude bins [119].

SDSS and Millennium samples have sizes 500 h^{-1} Mpc, which is sufficiently large to consider them as representative for the whole cosmic web. Our analysis shows that correlation lengths of low and medium luminosity galaxies have the value $r_0 \approx 5\ h^{-1}$ Mpc, as predicted by Davis [96], and contrary to the prediction by Pietronero et al. [91]. But notice that the correlation length of the EAGLE sample at low luminosities, $r_0 \approx 4.5\ h^{-1}$ Mpc, is smaller than for the SDSS and Millennium samples. This can be the sample volume effect as discussed by Pietronero et al. [91], since the size of EAGLE samples is smaller than sizes of SDSS and Millennium samples.

A significant aspect of luminosity dependence is the observation that the correlation length remains nearly constant at low luminosities, $M \geq -20.0$. This phenomenon is evident in the SDSS.19 and SDSS.18 observational samples; however, it cannot be extrapolated to lower luminosities due to the lack of very faint galaxies in the luminosity-limited samples from SDSS. In the galaxy samples from the EAGLE and Millennium models, a gradual decline in r_0 with decreasing luminosity can be tracked down to very faint galaxies, with $M \approx -15.6$ in the EAGLE sample and $M \approx -17.2$ in the Millennium sample. Similar findings have been reported by Norberg et al. [107] and Zehavi et al. [109], indicating that the correlation lengths of low luminosity galaxies approach a specific limit as luminosity decreases. This trend suggests that very faint galaxies tend to follow the spatial distribution of their brighter counterparts, implying that faint galaxies often serve as satellites of more luminous galaxies.

6. Fractal Analysis of the Cosmic Web

To describe fractal properties of the cosmic web, most authors applied the correlation function and its derivatives, the structure function and the fractal dimension function. In this section, I describe how these functions can be used to analyze fractal properties of the cosmic web. In the fractal analysis, I use the same set of SDSS and model samples as discussed in the previous section. Model and SDSS samples have almost identical volumes; thus, the volume dependence of fractal properties is absent, and we see the luminosity (particle density limit) dependence of samples.

The natural estimator to determine the two-point spatial correlation function is given by the function Equation (6). Based on arguments discussed in Section 4.3, I use in the following analysis the structure function,

$$g(r) = 1 + \xi(r), \tag{7}$$

and its log–log gradient, the gradient function,

$$\gamma(r) = \frac{d \log g(r)}{d \log r}, \tag{8}$$

which I call the $\gamma(r)$ function.

Martínez and Saar [79] defined the correlation dimension

$$D_2 = 3 + d \log \hat{g}(r)/d \log r, \tag{9}$$

where $\hat{g}(r)$ is the average of the structure function,

$$\hat{g}(r) = 1/V \int_0^r g(r')dV. \tag{10}$$

The parameter D_2 is related to the effective fractal dimension function $D(r)$ of samples at mean separation of galaxies at r [10,78],

For our study, I prefer to use the local value of the structure function to define its gradient:

$$D(r) = 3 + \gamma(r). \tag{11}$$

Notice that the fractal dimension is defined for a range of scales r; thus, the definition (11) is only an approximation of the true fractal dimension. Also notice that the $\gamma(r)$ function has the opposite sign compared to the parameter γ in the correlation function, Equation (1).

In the previous section, we examined the correlation functions of our model alongside the observed samples. Figure 11 illustrates the structure functions, represented as $g(r) = 1 + \xi(r)$, while Figure 12 depicts the fractal dimension functions, denoted as $D(r) = 3 + \gamma(r)$. Notably, the last figure clearly indicates that the fractal dimension function features two distinct regions, with a transition occurring at a separation of approximately $r \approx 3\,h^{-1}$ Mpc. This phenomenon has been previously identified by Zeldovich et al. [98] and Zehavi et al. [129]. In the case of smaller mutual separations r, the correlation function effectively describes the distribution of matter within dark matter halos, whereas, at larger separations, it pertains to the distribution of the halos themselves.

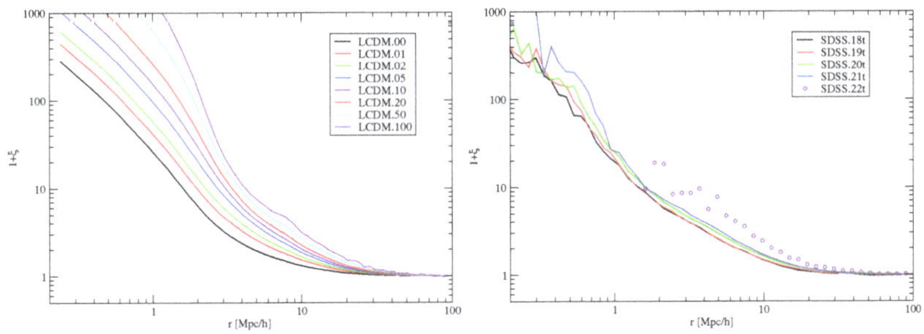

Figure 11. The structural functions are defined as $g(r) = 1 + \xi(r)$. The positioning of the panels remains consistent with what is illustrated in Figure 9 [119].

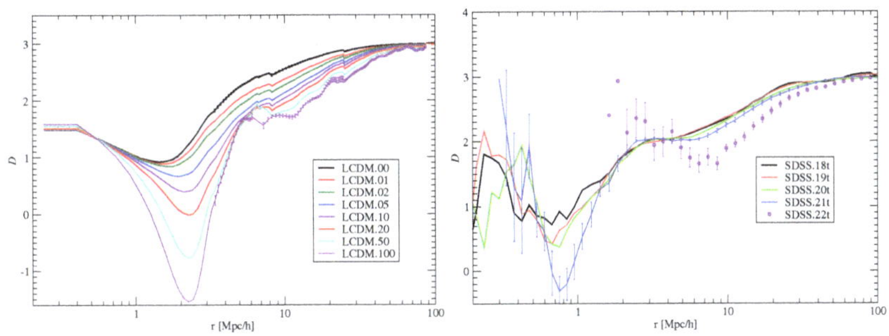

Figure 12. The fractal dimension functions are expressed as $D(r) = 3 + \gamma(r)$. The positioning of the panels corresponds to that depicted in Figure 9. Error values are provided for a selection of representative samples [119].

The fractal dimension function is a crucial concept in understanding the geometric properties of complex structures in cosmology, particularly in analyzing the distribution of particles in the Universe. In the context of ΛCDM (Lambda Cold Dark Matter) samples, this function provides insights into how matter is distributed on various scales. The parameter ρ_0 represents a particle density limit, which is essential when selecting particles for analysis. By adjusting this limit, researchers can examine how different densities affect the fractal characteristics of the sample. The left panel of Figure 12 illustrates that the fractal dimension function for the ΛCDM samples is influenced by the particle density threshold, ρ_0, employed in the selection of particles for the sample. All ΛCDM samples exhibit a uniform gradient function value of $\gamma(0.5) = -1.5$ at a distance of $r = 0.5\,h^{-1}$ Mpc, corresponding to a local fractal dimension of $D(0.5) = 1.5$. At approximately $2\,h^{-1}$ Mpc, the gradients reach a minimum that varies according to the particle density limit ρ_0 of the samples. The observed minimum in the gradients at around $2\,h^{-1}$ Mpc suggests a transition in the distribution of particles. This may imply that there are significant changes in the spatial arrangement of matter at this scale, reflecting the complexities of cosmic structures. After this point, the increase in the fractal dimension function signifies a return to a more regular distribution, culminating in the expected maximum value of $D(100) = 3.0$ at the largest distances. This value signifies a uniform and isotropic distribution of matter, consistent with the assumptions of the ΛCDM model at cosmological scales.

The equivalent values of the fractal dimension functions at $r = 0.5$ Mpc, succeeded by a minimum around $r \approx 2\,h^{-1}$ Mpc, can be attributed to the internal structure of dark matter (DM) halos. The extent of this minimum is influenced by the particle density threshold ρ_0.

Notably, DM halos exhibit nearly uniform density profiles, which can be characterized by both the Navarro–Frenk–White (NFW) profile [130] and the Einasto profile [13]:

$$\rho(a) = \rho_0 \exp\Big(-(a/a_c)^{1/N}\Big). \tag{12}$$

In this context, ρ_0 represents the central density, while a denotes the semi-major axis of the equidensity ellipsoid. The characteristic radius is indicated by a_c, and N serves as a structural parameter that allows for variations in the density profile's shape. Research by Wang et al. [131] demonstrated that the density profiles of halos across a diverse range of masses exhibit a consistent shape parameter value of $\alpha = 1/N = 0.16$, maintaining a similar form throughout a broad spectrum of halo masses. At the outer boundary of the halo, the gradient transitions to $d\log\rho/d\log r = -3.0$. It is important to highlight that the depth of the minimum in the ΛCDM model sample aligns with the local value of the $\gamma(r)$ function; thus, interpreting this as the fractal dimension $D(r)$ may not be entirely accurate.

Following the minimum observed at higher separation values r, the distribution of dark matter (DM) particles within filaments outside the halos becomes predominant. This shift contributes to an increase in the fractal dimension function. As illustrated in Figure 12 and Figure 2 of Zehavi et al. [129], the transition from individual DM halos to the broader cosmic web occurs at approximately $r \approx 2\,h^{-1}$ Mpc, which aligns well with the typical scales of DM halos. Thus, we can conclude that the correlation functions of ΛCDM models uniquely characterize the internal structure of DM halos, as well as the fractal dimensional properties of the entire cosmic web.

Figure 12 illustrates that the fractal dimension functions of SDSS galaxy samples closely resemble those of the ΛCDM sample, albeit with significantly greater scatter observed at small separations. The minor discrepancies in shape indicate that the internal structures of dark matter (DM) halos in the ΛCDM models are distinct from those found in actual and simulated galaxy clusters. In the ΛCDM model samples, all DM particles with density values $\rho \geq \rho_0$ are included, allowing for a comprehensive view of the density profile of the halos extending to their outer edges. Conversely, in real galaxy samples, only galaxies that exceed the selection threshold in brightness are represented. Consequently, in the most luminous galaxy samples, it is common for only one or a few of the brightest galaxies to fall within the observable range, leaving the true internal structures of the clusters, up to their outer boundaries, obscured.

7. Comparing Angular and Spatial Distributions of Galaxies

Redshifts are known to be influenced by the local movements of galaxies within clusters, a phenomenon referred to as the Finger-of-God (FoG) effect. Additionally, galaxies and clusters tend to move towards gravitational attractors, as described by the Kaiser effect [105]. To mitigate the impact of the Kaiser effect when computing correlation functions, Davis and Peebles [106] recommended utilizing galaxy position and velocity data independently, as detailed in Section 3.1. The inversion described in Equation (5) presupposes that the spatial three-dimensional (3D) and projected two-dimensional (2D) density fields exhibit statistical similarity. This premise has been widely accepted within the astronomical community, and the application of Equations (4) and (5) for the calculation of 3D correlation functions has become a standard practice.

A visual assessment of the 2D and 3D density fields, illustrated in Figures 3 and 8, reveals significant distinctions between the two. The 3D density field is primarily characterized by the filamentary structure of the cosmic web, while the 2D field exhibits a more random distribution. Consequently, the accuracy of the standard method for calculating correlation functions (CFs) in this context remains uncertain. To establish the relationship between the 2D and 3D CFs, it is essential to compare these functions using the same dataset. The findings from this comparison have been documented by Einasto et al. [120] and are presented in this work.

7.1. Relation Between 2D and 3D Correlation Functions

To compare 2D and 3D correlation functions, Einasto et al. [120] constructed the 2D density fields on a 2048^2 grid by integrating the 3D field,

$$\delta_2(x,y) = \int_{z_1}^{z_2} \delta(x,y,z)\mathrm{d}z. \tag{13}$$

In the next phase of their research, the authors segmented the cubic sample into n sequentially arranged 2D sheets, each measuring $L_0 \times L_0 \times L\, h^{-1}$ Mpc. Here, $L = L_0/n$ represents the thickness of each individual sheet, while n takes values of 1, 2, 4, and so forth, up to 2048, indicating the total number of sheets created. For each value of n, the authors computed the 2D correlation functions (CFs) for all n sheets and subsequently determined the average CF corresponding to each n.The sheet corresponding to $n = 1$ encompasses the entire sample along the z-direction, with a thickness of $L = L_0 = 512\, h^{-1}$ Mpc. For $n = 2$, the thickness reduces to $512/2 = 256\ h^{-1}$ Mpc, while for $n = 2048$, the thickness is $L = 512/2048 = 0.25\ h^{-1}$ Mpc. Through this methodology, the authors were able to calculate 2D correlation functions across a variety of particle density thresholds ρ_0 and 2D sample thickness L within the context of the ΛCDM model, as well as for different magnitude limits derived from the Millennium sample referenced by Springel et al. [117].

Two-dimensional correlation functions (CFs) are influenced by two key parameters: the thickness of the sheets, defined as $L = 512/n\ h^{-1}$ Mpc, and the particle density threshold for ΛCDM samples, denoted as ρ_0, or the magnitude limit M_r for Millennium samples. The analysis reveals that the 2D CFs exhibit a luminosity dependence that closely mirrors that of 3D CFs. This indicates that the correlation functions of 2D samples retain the luminosity dependence characteristic of their 3D counterparts. As luminosity increases, the amplitude of the correlation functions also rises, illustrating the well-established biasing effect described by Kaiser [65].

In our study, a key aspect is the relationship between the thickness of the samples and the 2D correlation functions. Figure 13 illustrates these correlation functions for a fixed particle density limit of $\rho_0 = 10$ in LCDM.10 samples, as well as for Millennium samples Mill.20.5 with a luminosity threshold of $M_r = -20.5$. These limits roughly align with L^* galaxies. In Figure 13, we present the 2D correlation functions across various sample thicknesses, represented as $L = L_0/n\ h^{-1}$ Mpc, with the number of sheets ranging from $n = 1$ to $n = 2048$. The case with $n = 1$ reflects the total sample thickness of $L = L_0$ and exhibits the lowest amplitude. Conversely, the final case corresponds to the average 2D correlation function of the thinnest sheets, each measuring $L = 0.25\ h^{-1}$ Mpc. Notably, the 2D correlation functions for the thinnest samples, where $n = 2048$, closely resemble the 3D correlation functions indicated by the dotted lines in Figure 13. This finding suggests that the structural information regarding dark matter halos and the overall cosmic web is comprehensively retained in the thin 2D correlation functions.

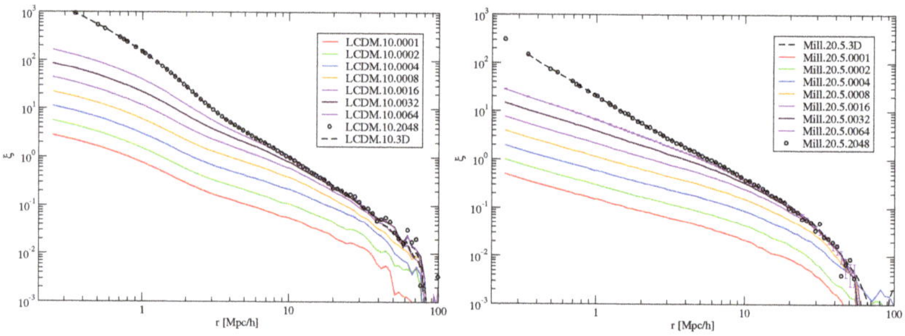

Figure 13. (**Left**): The two-dimensional correlation functions (CFs) of the ΛCDM model are presented with a particle density threshold of $\rho_0 = 10$, analyzed across various thicknesses of 2D samples. (**Right**): The two-dimensional CFs of the Millennium samples, constrained by a magnitude limit of $M_r = -20.5$, are displayed in real space. For our analysis, we define pair separations perpendicular to the line of sight as $r_p = \sqrt{(\Delta x)^2 + (\Delta y)^2}$. The sample thicknesses are represented by the parameter L. Different thicknesses of the 2D samples are denoted by lines of distinct colors. For reference, we include dotted lines representing the three-dimensional functions for samples with the same density threshold of $\rho_0 = 10$ and magnitude limit of $M_r = -20.5$ [120].

The relationship between luminosity and correlation functions, as discussed in this and the preceding section, is well established. This analysis reveals that the amplitudes of two-dimensional correlation functions (2D CFs) are also affected by an additional parameter: the sample thickness, denoted as L. The variation in the amplitudes of 2D CFs with respect to sample thickness is a consequence of the spatial configuration of the cosmic web. This cosmic web comprises galaxies arranged in a complex filamentary structure, leaving significant regions of space unoccupied by galaxies. In projected views, clusters and filaments occupy these voids, which varies with sample thickness. Consequently, the patterns of the cosmic web in two dimensions differ qualitatively from those in three dimensions, with the disparity becoming more pronounced as the thickness of the 2D sheets increases.

7.2. Fractal Analysis of the 2D Cosmic Web

In Figure 14, we illustrate the gradient functions for the ΛCDM model, utilizing a particle density limit of $\rho_0 = 10$, alongside the Millennium samples constrained by a magnitude limit of $M_r = -20.5$. The analysis employs pair separations that are perpendicular to the line of sight, defined as $r_p = \sqrt{(\Delta x)^2 + (\Delta y)^2}$. The parameter representing the thickness of the samples, denoted as L, is also incorporated. Different thicknesses of the 2D samples are indicated by lines of varying colors. For comparative purposes, we include 3D functions represented by dotted lines for samples with the same density and magnitude limits of $\rho_0 = 10$ and $M_r = -20.5$, respectively. Additionally, error bars are provided for the 2D samples where $n = 2048$.

The comparison of the gradient functions of two-dimensional samples with the fractal dimension functions of three-dimensional samples, as illustrated in Figure 12, indicates that the fine structure information at small scales is largely retained in the two-dimensional samples derived from the ΛCDM model. Conversely, in the Millennium samples, the details regarding the internal structure of clusters are diminished in the two-dimensional correlation functions (CFs). At the luminosity threshold of $M_r = -20.5$, the clusters are comprised of only a limited number of bright galaxies. The amplitudes of the two-dimensional CFs in the Millennium samples are relatively low, leading to the dominance of the first constant term in the gradient function $g(r) = 1 + \xi(r)$. As depicted in the right panel of Figure 14, for thicker samples, the slope of the two-dimensional CF exhibits a gradual variation over an extensive range of separations, specifically for $r_p > 1\,h^{-1}$ Mpc. This behavior supports the established observation that the two-dimensional CF can be effectively modeled using a simple power-law function, as demonstrated by Groth and Peebles [52], Davis and Peebles [106], and Maddox et al. [53]. Additionally, Figure 14 illustrates that the value of the two-dimensional gradient function is influenced by the thickness of the samples. When the thickness ranges from 64 to $128h^{-1}$ Mpc, the gradient achieves a value of approximately $\gamma(r) \sim -0.7$ at shorter distances, smoothly approaching $\gamma(r) = 0$ at $r = 100\,h^{-1}$ Mpc. This finding aligns with the results reported by Groth and Peebles [52], Davis and Peebles [106], and Maddox et al. [53] concerning the angular correlation function.

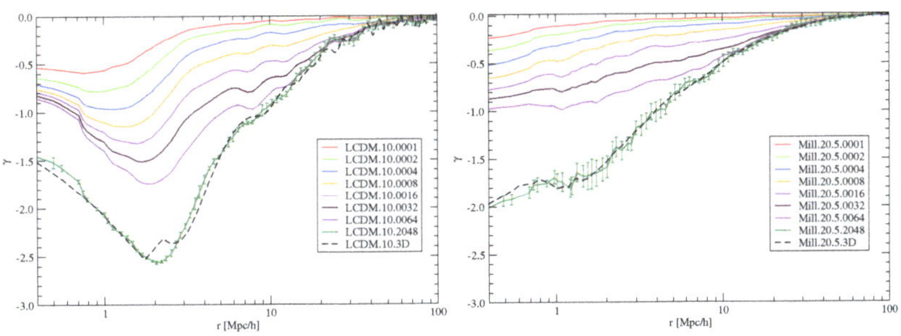

Figure 14. (**Left**): Two-dimensional gradient functions of the ΛCDM model, utilizing a particle density threshold of $\rho_0 = 10$, are presented for various thicknesses of 2D samples. (**Right**): Two-dimensional gradient functions of Millennium samples, constrained by a magnitude limit of $M_r = -20.5$, are displayed in real space [120].

The previous examination of the correlation study conducted by Groth and Peebles [52] and Peebles [54] revealed a flat profile of 2D correlation functions across an extensive separation range of $0.05 \leq r \leq 9\,h^{-1}$ Mpc. This analysis suggests that the broad range observed is primarily due to the 2D correlation functions' insensitivity to the presence of halos (clusters), rendering the actual structure at smaller separations undetectable. Additionally, the amplitude of the 2D correlation functions plays a significant role. As illustrated in Figure 13, the amplitude of the 2D correlation functions is notably lower than that of the 3D correlation functions, which varies with the thickness of the 2D samples. According to Norberg et al. [107] and Zehavi et al. [108], the correlation lengths for the faintest galaxies were measured at approximately $r_0 \approx 4.5\,h^{-1}$ Mpc, a value interpreted as representative of 3D samples. Figure 13 suggests that for these faint galaxies, the actual amplitude of the 3D correlation functions is greater, resulting in true 3D correlation lengths near $6\,h^{-1}$ Mpc. This finding aligns closely with our measurements of the correlation lengths of SDSS samples, as depicted in Figure 10.

8. Structure and Evolution of Cosmic Web from Combined Spatial and Velocity Data

The correlation function used in the study of fractal properties of the cosmic web uses only spatial data on the distribution of galaxies and dark matter. Modern numerical simulations and observational data allow the use of all phase–space data—spatial positions and velocities of particles and galaxies. In this section, I discuss the structure and evolution of the cosmic web using full phase–space data. Such combined data are very useful to study the hierarchy of the cosmic web in low-density regions—voids.

8.1. Void Hierarchy

One aspect of the hierarchical structure of the cosmic web is the hierarchy of voids. Already early studies showed that diameters of voids have a large scatter, from a few megaparsecs to hundred megaparsecs (Kirshner et al. [132], Pan et al. [133], Sutter et al. [134], Nadathur and Hotchkiss [135]). Sheth and van de Weygaert [136] studied the formation and evolution of voids, using numerical simulations of the evolution of the cosmic web. The authors showed that voids have a remarkable hierarchical structure—voids are filled with a complex web of tenuous filaments and low-mass haloes. During the evolution, larger voids grow by the mergers of smaller voids, which is analogous to how massive clusters form by merging less massive clusters and groups. Small voids, which are located on overdensity regions, disappear as the overdensity collapses around them.

In their study, Aragon-Calvo and Szalay [137] conducted a thorough examination of the hierarchical organization of cosmic voids through advanced numerical simulations. The large-scale fluctuations responsible for the formation of voids encompass smaller fluctuations that develop within regions resembling a locally low-density Universe. This phenomenon is evident at every level within the void hierarchy, as subvoids themselves harbor even smaller sub-subvoids, as illustrated in Figure 15. This observation highlights the hierarchical nature of the cosmic web, where low-density filamentary structures on smaller scales exhibit similarities to those on larger scales.

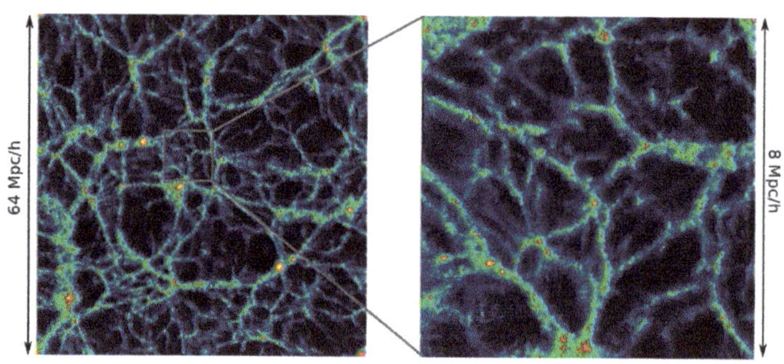

Figure 15. The hierarchy of structure within the cosmic web is illustrated in the provided visuals. The left panel displays the density field across a narrow slice of a 64 h^{-1} Mpc simulation based on the ΛCDM cosmology model. Meanwhile, the right panel focuses on a specific highlighted area within that slice. The density field for this zoomed-in region was derived from a high-resolution resimulation featuring $N_{part} = 1024^3$, centered in the void region [137].

Cosmic structures of varying scales can be analyzed by applying smoothing techniques to density fields with different smoothing parameters. The original density field retains all intricate details, while smoothing at a scale of 2 h^{-1} Mpc emphasizes structures characteristic of galaxy groups. In contrast, a smoothing scale of 4 h^{-1} Mpc brings out features such as the cores of superclusters and large voids. The top panels of Figure 16 illustrate the original density field at redshift $z = 0$ (left panel), alongside its smoothed versions at 2 and 4 h^{-1} Mpc (center and right panels, respectively). By comparing the panels with different smoothing scales, we can observe the hierarchical arrangement of filaments and voids. To capture the finer details of this cosmic web, the boundaries of voids were identified using the SpineWeb method, which is depicted in the bottom panels of Figure 16. The SpineWeb method, as described by Aragon-Calvo and Szalay [137], involves calculating the density and velocity fields, along with their respective gradients.

It is widely recognized that galaxies exclusively develop within dark matter halos, as void regions lack sufficient density for galaxy formation. Figure 17 illustrates the variations in the distribution of simulated galaxies (dark matter halos) alongside the density and velocity fields. The top-left panel displays a slice of the density field, highlighting halos within a 2 h^{-1} Mpc thick section. These halos are situated in high-density areas of the cosmic web, including filaments and clusters. The process of galaxy formation occurs in two stages: initially, dark matter aggregates to form halos, followed by the emergence of galaxies within these halos [121]. As depicted in Figure 17, halos containing galaxies occupy only a minor portion of the overall spatial volume.

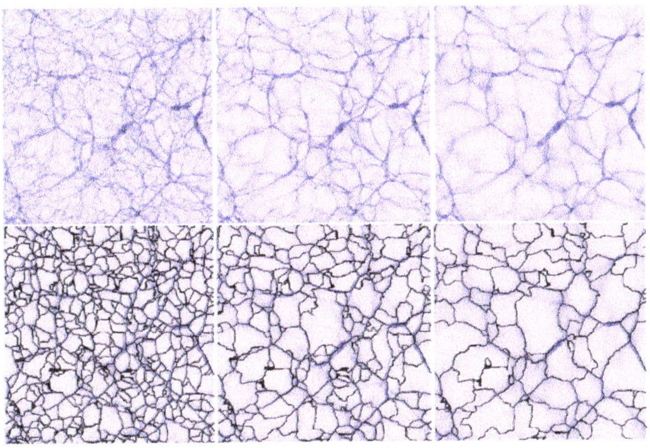

Figure 16. (**Top**): Density field across a thin slice of the simulation box at $z = 0$ for three cases: original field (**left** panel), after smoothing with 2 h^{-1} Mpc (**central** panel), and with 4 h^{-1} Mpc (**right** panel). (**Bottom**): Hierarchical cosmic web spine superimposed to its corresponding density field for the bottom, middle, and top levels (left, central, and right panels, respectively) [137].

The velocity fields depicted in the top right and bottom panels of Figure 17 are presented at smoothing scales of 4, 2, and 1 h^{-1} Mpc, alongside the same halos illustrated in the top left panel. This figure illustrates the hierarchy of voids nested within larger voids, where the largest voids are subdivided into progressively smaller ones. The local velocity fields in regions surrounding halos and voids exhibit significant differences. In halo regions, the velocity field is characterized by turbulence, which facilitates the condensation of matter into halos and subhalos. Conversely, at the larger smoothing scales of 4 and 2 h^{-1} Mpc, the velocity field surrounding the void halo is predominantly laminar and directed toward the halos. At the smaller scale of 1 h^{-1} Mpc, the velocity field approaches the halo from multiple directions. It is important to note that this intricate structure observed in low-density regions is composed of a sparse field of dark matter filaments and baryonic gaseous matter.

8.2. Evolution of Galaxies in the Void Hierarchy

Most galaxy formation models successfully replicate a diverse array of observations and shed light on the physical processes taking place within halos as distinct entities [121]. In reality, galaxies develop within the large-scale environment of the cosmic web. To comprehend how the cosmic environment influences galaxy characteristics, Aragon Calvo et al. [138] introduced the Cosmic Web Detachment (CWD) model. This model integrates multiple mechanisms that inhibit star formation and illustrates how galaxies acquire star-forming gas in their formative stages through a network of primordial filaments, as outlined in the preceding section.

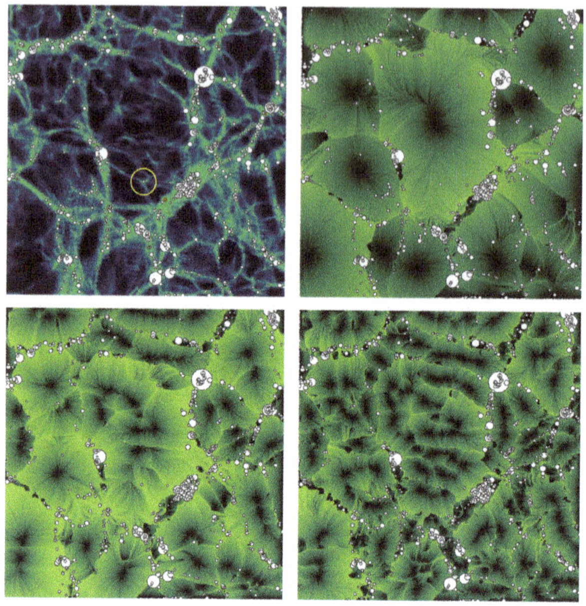

Figure 17. Dark matter haloes superimposed on the density and velocity fields. The (**top-left** panel) shows a slice of the density field and all the FoF haloes closer than 1 h^{-1} Mpc from the slice. The residual velocity field is shown at scales 4, 2, and 1 h^{-1} Mpc in the (**top-right**), (**bottom-left**), and (**bottom-right** panel), respectively. We show the same FoF haloes as in the density field slice [137].

The development and progression of hierarchical structures within the cosmic web are illustrated in Figure 18. The upper panels depict the density and velocity fields of the cosmic web at an early epoch, specifically at redshift $z = 5$, while the lower panels represent the current epoch at $z = 0$. The left panels showcase density fields spanning 32 h^{-1} Mpc, the central panels display the corresponding velocity fields, and the right panels provide a cross section of these fields. During the early epoch, the velocity field exhibits coherence, with star-forming cold gas being accreted through primordial coherent filamentary streams. Star formation occurs in conjunction with the accretion of cold gas and ceases once the gas supply is depleted. In contrast, at later epochs, the velocity field surrounding halos—indicated by red and white circles—becomes highly chaotic.

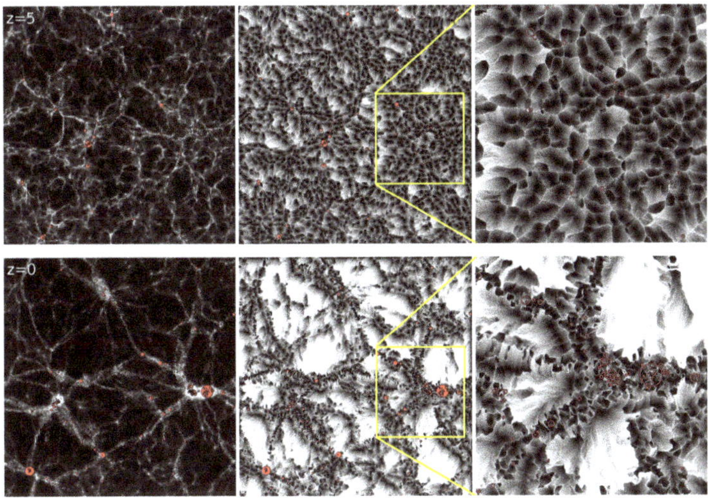

Figure 18. Coherent vs. chaotic velocity field around halos. For explanation see text [138].

9. Scale of Homogeneity

A key question in the fractal analysis of the cosmic web centers around the scale of homogeneity, where opinions among various authors diverge significantly. The Anglo-American school, as discussed in Section 3.1, has predominantly focused on utilizing only 2D data for their studies. According to the comprehensive findings of Maddox et al. [53], the fractal nature of galaxy distribution appears to be applicable within the distance range of 10 kpc $\leq r \leq 10\, h^{-1}$ Mpc, exhibiting a fractal dimension of approximately $D \approx 1.3$. This upper limit has been regarded as the scale of homogeneity.

The Italian School, as noted by Pietronero [10] and Sylos Labini et al. [93], established that the fractal nature of galaxy distribution, characterized by a fractal dimension of approximately $D \approx 1.7$, holds true from small scales up to the most extensive scales examined for visible matter. The most comprehensive samples studied by Sylos Labini et al. [93] encompass radio galaxies and quasars, spanning a magnitude range of $12 \leq m \leq 28$.

One method for determining the limit of a fractal structure involves calculating the fractal dimension function from the gradient function, as outlined in Section 6. The ΛCDM and SDSS fractal dimension functions, illustrated in Figure 12, converge towards the limit of $D = 3$, at a distance of approximately $r \approx 100\, h^{-1}$ Mpc, which represents just 1/5 of the sample size. Pan and Coles [139] examined the spatial distribution of IRAS sources from the PSC catalog and derived fractal dimensions across two distance ranges: $20 < r < 50\, h^{-1}$ Mpc and $r > 50\, h^{-1}$ Mpc. In the first range, the fractal dimension fluctuated between $2.05 \leq D \leq 2.83$, while in the second range, it remained constant at $D = 3.0$. Sarkar et al. [140] applied multifractal analysis to assess the scale of homogeneity within the range of 60 to 70 h^{-1} Mpc, utilizing SDSS DR6 spectroscopic galaxy data. Furthermore, Scrimgeour et al. [141] conducted a spectroscopic survey of blue galaxies within a cosmic volume of approximately $1h^{-1}$ Gpc and established a lower limit for the fractal dimension of $D_2 = 2.97$ on scales ranging from about 80 h^{-1} Mpc to $\sim$300 h^{-1} Mpc, with a confidence level of 99.99 percent.

One approach to determining the scale of homogeneity is to examine the structures of the largest astronomical objects, such as voids and superclusters. The recent catalog of superclusters from the SDSS survey compiled by Liivamägi et al. [126] includes objects identified using both adaptive and fixed density thresholds. The largest superclusters reach sizes of up to 120 h^{-1} Mpc for the primary galaxy superclusters and 200 h^{-1} Mpc for the LRG superclusters. Notably, the largest superclusters recorded in the Sankhyayan et al. [41] catalog of SDSS superclusters also measure 200 h^{-1} Mpc.

Independent insights into the structure of the cosmic web are derived from velocity data. In their analysis, Courtois et al. [142] examined the velocity field utilizing cosmic flow CF4 peculiar velocities. The research revealed that the bulk flow amplitude approaches zero at greater distances, suggesting an increasing homogeneity of the Universe. Within a range of 150 h^{-1} Mpc, the measured bulk flow is 230 ± 136 km/s. This indicates that the dynamic scale of homogeneity has not yet been attained within the 200–300 h^{-1} Mpc interval from the observer, signifying that the local Universe continues to display notable fluctuations in mass distribution and the dynamics of galaxy movements. Additionally, ref. [143] investigated a sample of quasars from the SDSS survey, discovering that this sample deviates from a random Poisson distribution. The authors concluded that the concept of a scale of homogeneity is not applicable. Instead, homogeneity is achieved only asymptotically as the observational scale increases, with no inherent characteristic scale in the Universe beyond which it can be considered homogeneous. Nevertheless, at scales exceeding 300 h^{-1} Mpc, the distribution of quasars approaches that of a homogeneous sample.

10. Summary and Outlook

The cosmic web is a complex geometric pattern. One of the aspects of the structure of the cosmic web is its fractal nature, which was recognized already in the introduction of the fractal concept by Mandelbrot [1,72]. In this review, I discussed various aspects of fractal properties of the cosmic web from an observational point of view. Our discussion can be summarized in following points.

Fractal properties from two-dimensional data . The first application of the fractal character of the distribution of galaxies was made by Soneira and Peebles [45] in the construction of the angular distribution of galaxies in a fractal way to mimic the Shane and Wirtanen [43] distribution of galaxies, as displayed in Figure 3. A deeper 2D distribution of APM galaxies was expressed by Maddox et al. [53] by a power-law correlation function, which has a constant slope -1.7 over the range of angular distances, $0.01 \leq \theta \leq 3$ degrees. This was interpreted as a hint that the power-law correlation function is valid in the range of separations 10 kpc$\leq r \leq 10\,h^{-1}$ Mpc [89].

Determining fractal dimension. As discussed in Section 4.3, Pietronero [10] noticed that the correlation function is normalized to a Poissonian distribution and is forced to vanish at large scales. For this reason, it is not suited for measuring large-scale homogeneity. To measure the fractal dimension, instead of the correlation function, its derivative, the structure function, $g(r) = 1 + \xi(r)$, and its log–log gradient, $\gamma(r) = \frac{d\log g(r)}{d\log r}$, should be used. The fractal dimension can be found from the gradient as follows: $D(r) = 3 + \gamma(r)$. In our analysis, we have used this definition of the fractal dimension.

Fractal properties from three-dimensional data. Essential fractal properties of the cosmic web are displayed in the fractal dimension function, Figure 12. The analysis was based on a ΛCDM model of size 512 h^{-1} Mpc, and a SDSS sample of similar volume. The fractal dimension function of both samples has two well separated regions: on small separations, $r \leq 3\,h^{-1}$ Mpc, the function characterizes the distribution of particles/galaxies in halos, and on larger separations, it characterizes the distribution of particles/galaxies in filaments. Fractal dimension functions depend on the magnitude (particle density) limits of samples. The minimum of the dimension function at scale $r \approx 2\,h^{-1}$ Mpc is deeper for samples of luminous galaxies. However, the depth of the minimum of the fractal dimension function is exaggerated, since it is based on the local value of the gradient of the structure function, $g(r) = 1 + \xi(r)$.

The gradient function from 2D data, presented in Figure 14, depends on the depth of the 2D sample. Very thin 2D samples behave similar to 3D samples. With increasing thickness of the samples, the information on the distribution of particles/galaxies in halos is gradually erased. This effect is very strong for SDSS and Millennium galaxy samples. Analyses of the relation between 2D and 3D correlation functions, presented in Section 7, shows that, in 2D distribution of galaxies, the information on the distribution of galaxies in clusters has been erased, and the division of the correlation function into two regions, halos and filaments, is not seen.

Fractal properties from velocity data. Velocity data yield essential additional information on the structure of the cosmic web. The combination of spatial and velocity data shows that the internal structure of voids is very complex. Inside voids there exist subvoids, sub-subvoids, etc., and the fractal character of the dark matter distribution continues to small scales.

Scale of homogeneity. Early 2D data emphasized that the fractal character of the distribution of galaxies extends only to $\sim 10\ h^{-1}$ Mpc and that, beyond this limit, the distribution of galaxies is homogeneous. Later analyses have shown that the correlation function $\xi(r)$ is not suited to find the limit of the fractal nature of the galaxy distribution; instead, the structure function $g(r) = 1 + \xi(r)$ can be applied. The scale of homogeneity has been studied by many authors, who found that the local Universe still has some fluctuations in the distribution of galaxies on distance $\approx 200\ h^{-1}$ Mpc. Homogeneity is only achieved asymptotically, as the scale of observation increases.

To conclude, we can say that the contemporary understanding of the fractal properties of the Universe includes the best aspects of both the Anglo-American and Italian approaches.

Funding: This work was supported by Tartu Observatory, University of Tartu.

Data Availability Statement: No new data were created or analyzed in this study. Data sharing is not applicable to this article.

Acknowledgments: Our special thanks to the anonymous referees for stimulating suggestions that greatly improved the paper and to colleagues in Tartu Observatory for discussions. Figures are reproduced by permission of the AAS, Monthly Notices of the Royal Astronomical Society, and EDPsciences. Permission is granted for the purpose of reuse in "Fractal properties of the cosmic web" and does not extend to any other forms of distribution or reproduction beyond what is customary for the journal's dissemination practices.

Conflicts of Interest: The author declares no conflicts of interest. The funders had no role in the design of the study; in the collection, analyses, or interpretation of data; in the writing of the manuscript; or in the decision to publish the results.

References

1. Mandelbrot, B.B. *The Fractal Geometry of Nature*; Echo Point Books & Media, LLC: Brattleboro, VT, USA, 1977.
2. Charlier, C.V.L. How an infinite world may be built up. *Medd. Fran Lunds Astron. Obs. Ser. I* **1922**, *98*, 1–37.
3. Carpenter, E.F. Some Characteristics of Associated Galaxies. I. a. Density Restriction in the Metagalaxy. *Astrophys. J.* **1938**, *88*, 344. [CrossRef]
4. Kiang, T. On the clustering of rich clusters of galaxies. *Mon. Not. R. Astron. Soc.* **1967**, *135*, 1–22. [CrossRef]
5. Wertz, J.R. Newtonian Hierarchical Cosmology. Ph.D. Thesis, University of Texas, Austin, TX, USA, 1970.
6. Wertz, J.R. A Newtonian Big-Bang Hierarchical Cosmological Model. *Astrophys. J.* **1971**, *164*, 227. [CrossRef]

7. Haggerty, M.J.; Wertz, J.R. On the redshift-magnituderelation in hierarchical cosmologies. *Mon. Not. R. Astron. Soc.* **1972**, *155*, 495. [CrossRef]
8. de Vaucouleurs, G. The Case for a Hierarchical Cosmology. *Science* **1970**, *167*, 1203–1213. [CrossRef]
9. de Vaucouleurs, G. The Large-Scale Distribution of Galaxies and Clusters of Galaxies. *Publ. Astron. Soc. Pacif.* **1971**, *83*, 113. [CrossRef]
10. Pietronero, L. The fractal structure of the universe: Correlations of galaxies and clusters and the average mass density. *Phys. A Stat. Mech. Its Appl.* **1987**, *144*, 257–284. [CrossRef]
11. Peebles, P.J.E. *Cosmology's Century: An Inside History of our Modern Understanding of the Universe*; Princeton University Press: Princeton, NJ, USA, 2020. [CrossRef]
12. Peebles, P.J.E. *The Whole Truth. A Cosmologist's Reflections on the Search for Objective Reality*; Princeton University Press: Princeton, NJ, USA, 2022.
13. Einasto, J. *Dark Matter and Cosmic Web Story*, 2nd ed.; World Scientific: Singapore, 2024.
14. Starobinsky, A.A. A new type of isotropic cosmological models without singularity. *Phys. Lett. B* **1980**, *91*, 99–102. [CrossRef]
15. Guth, A.H. Inflationary universe: A possible solution to the horizon and flatness problems. *Phys. Rev. D* **1981**, *23*, 347–356. [CrossRef]
16. Linde, A.D. Chaotic inflation. *Phys. Lett. B* **1983**, *129*, 177–181. [CrossRef]
17. Linde, A. Hybrid inflation. *Phys. Rev. D* **1994**, *49*, 748–754. [CrossRef]
18. Linde, A.; Riotto, A. Hybrid inflation in supergravity. *Phys. Rev. D* **1997**, *56*, R1841–R1844. [CrossRef]
19. Linde, A. Particle Physics and Inflationary Cosmology. *arXiv* **2005**, arXiv:hep-th/0503203. [CrossRef]
20. Nambu, Y.; Sasaki, M. Stochastic approach to chaotic inflation and the distribution of universes. *Phys. Lett. B* **1989**, *219*, 240–246. [CrossRef]
21. Ambjørn, J.; Jurkiewicz, J.; Loll, R. Reconstructing the Universe. *Phys. Rev. D* **2005**, *72*, 064014. [CrossRef]
22. Calcagni, G. Quantum field theory, gravity and cosmology in a fractal universe. *J. High Energy Phys.* **2010**, *2010*, 120. [CrossRef]
23. Calcagni, G. Fractal Universe and Quantum Gravity. *Phys. Rev. Lett.* **2010**, *104*, 251301. [CrossRef]
24. Einstein, A. Die Grundlage der allgemeinen Relativitätstheorie. *Ann. Der Phys.* **1916**, *354*, 769–822. [CrossRef]
25. Friedmann, A. Über die Möglichkeit einer Welt mit konstanter negativer Krümmung des Raumes. *Z. Phys.* **1924**, *21*, 326–332. [CrossRef]
26. Lemaître, G. Un Univers homogène de masse constante et de rayon croissant rendant compte de la vitesse radiale des nébuleuses extra-galactiques. *Ann. Soc. Scietifique Brux.* **1927**, *47*, 49–59.
27. Hoyle, F. A New Model for the Expanding Universe. *Mon. Not. R. Astron. Soc.* **1948**, *108*, 372–382. [CrossRef]
28. Hoyle, F. The synthesis of the elements from hydrogen. *Mon. Not. R. Astron. Soc.* **1946**, *106*, 343. [CrossRef]
29. Cyburt, R.H.; Fields, B.D.; Olive, K.A. Primordial nucleosynthesis in light of WMAP. *Phys. Lett. B* **2003**, *567*, 227–234. [CrossRef]
30. Burbidge, E.M.; Burbidge, G.R.; Fowler, W.A.; Hoyle, F. Synthesis of the Elements in Stars. *Rev. Mod. Phys.* **1957**, *29*, 547–650. [CrossRef]
31. Adame, A.G.; Aguilar, J.; Ahlen, S.; Alam, S.; Alexander, D.M.; Alvarez, M.; Alves, O.; Anand, A.; Andrade, U.; Armengaud, E.; et al. DESI 2024 VI: Cosmological constraints from the measurements of baryon acoustic oscillations. *J. Cosmol. Astropart. Phys.* **2025**, *2025*, 021. [CrossRef]
32. Einasto, J.; Hütsi, G.; Szapudi, I.; Tenjes, P. *Spinning the Cosmic Web*; World Scientific: Singapore, 2025.
33. Sunyaev, R.A.; Chluba, J. Signals from the epoch of cosmological recombination (Karl Schwarzschild Award Lecture 2008). *Astron. Nachrichten* **2009**, *330*, 657. [CrossRef]
34. Planck Collaboration; Aghanim, N.; Akrami, Y.; Ashdown, M.; Aumont, J.; Baccigalupi, C.; Ballardini, M.; Banday, A.J.; Barreiro, R.B.; Bartolo, N.; et al. Planck 2018 results. VI. Cosmological parameters. *Astron. Astrophys.* **2020**, *641*, A6. [CrossRef]
35. Einasto, J.; Kaasik, A.; Saar, E. Dynamic Evidence on Massive coronas of galaxies. *Nature* **1974**, *250*, 309–310. [CrossRef]
36. Ostriker, J.P.; Peebles, P.J.E.; Yahil, A. The size and mass of galaxies, and the mass of the universe. *Astrophys. J. Lett.* **1974**, *193*, L1–L4. [CrossRef]
37. Perlmutter, S.; Aldering, G.; Goldhaber, G.; Knop, R.A.; Nugent, P.; Castro, P.G.; Deustua, S.; Fabbro, S.; Goobar, A.; Groom, D.E.; et al. Measurements of Omega and Lambda from 42 High-Redshift Supernovae. *Astrophys. J.* **1999**, *517*, 565–586. [CrossRef]
38. Riess, A.G.; Filippenko, A.V.; Challis, P.; Clocchiatti, A.; Diercks, A.; Garnavich, P.M.; Gilliland, R.L.; Hogan, C.J.; Jha, S.; Kirshner, R.P.; et al. Observational Evidence from Supernovae for an Accelerating Universe and a Cosmological Constant. *Astron. J.* **1998**, *116*, 1009–1038. [CrossRef]
39. Komatsu, E.; Smith, K.M.; Dunkley, J.; Bennett, C.L.; Gold, B.; Hinshaw, G.; Jarosik, N.; Larson, D.; Nolta, M.R.; Page, L.; et al. Seven-year Wilkinson Microwave Anisotropy Probe (WMAP) Observations: Cosmological Interpretation. *Astrophys. J. Suppl.* **2011**, *192*, 18. [CrossRef]

40. Di Valentino, E.; Levi Said, J.; Riess, A.; Pollo, A.; Poulin, V.; Gómez-Valent, A.; Weltman, A.; Palmese, A.; Huang, C.D.; van de Bruck, C.; et al. The CosmoVerse White Paper: Addressing observational tensions in cosmology with systematics and fundamental physics. *arXiv* **2025**, arXiv:2504.01669. [CrossRef]
41. Sankhyayan, S.; Bagchi, J.; Tempel, E.; More, S.; Einasto, M.; Dabhade, P.; Raychaudhury, S.; Athreya, R.; Heinämäki, P. Identification of Superclusters and Their Properties in the Sloan Digital Sky Survey Using the WHL Cluster Catalog. *Astrophys. J.* **2023**, *958*, 62. [CrossRef]
42. York, D.G.; Adelman, J.; Anderson, J.E., Jr.; Anderson, S.F.; Annis, J.; Bahcall, N.A.; Bakken, J.A.; Barkhouser, R.; Bastian, S.; Berman, E.; et al. The Sloan Digital Sky Survey: Technical Summary. *Astron. J.* **2000**, *120*, 1579–1587. [CrossRef]
43. Shane, C.; Wirtanen, C. The distribution of galaxies. *Publ. Lick Obs.* **1967**, *22*.
44. Seldner, M.; Siebers, B.; Groth, E.J.; Peebles, P.J.E. New reduction of the Lick catalog of galaxies. *Astron. J.* **1977**, *82*, 249–256. [CrossRef]
45. Soneira, R.M.; Peebles, P.J.E. A computer model universe—Simulation of the nature of the galaxy distribution in the Lick catalog. *Astron. J.* **1978**, *83*, 845–849. [CrossRef]
46. Peebles, P.J.E. Statistical Analysis of Catalogs of Extragalactic Objects. I. Theory. *Astrophys. J.* **1973**, *185*, 413–440. [CrossRef]
47. Hauser, M.G.; Peebles, P.J.E. Statistical Analysis of Catalogs of Extragalactic Objects. II. the Abell Catalog of Rich Clusters. *Astrophys. J.* **1973**, *185*, 757–786. [CrossRef]
48. Peebles, P.J.E.; Hauser, M.G. Statistical Analysis of Catalogs of Extragalactic Objects. III. The Shane-Wirtanen and Zwicky Catalogs. *Astrophys. J. Suppl.* **1974**, *28*, 19. [CrossRef]
49. Peebles, P.J.E. Statistical Analysis of Catalogs of Extragalactic Objects. IV. Cross-Correlation of the Abell and Shane-Wirtanen Catalogs. *Astrophys. J. Suppl.* **1974**, *28*, 37. [CrossRef]
50. Peebles, P.J.E.; Groth, E.J. Statistical analysis of catalogs of extragalactic objects. V—Three-point correlation function for the galaxy distribution in the Zwicky catalog. *Astrophys. J.* **1975**, *196*, 1–11. [CrossRef]
51. Peebles, P.J.E. Statistical analysis of catalogs of extragalactic objects. VI—The galaxy distribution in the Jagellonian field. *Astrophys. J.* **1975**, *196*, 647–651. [CrossRef]
52. Groth, E.J.; Peebles, P.J.E. Statistical analysis of catalogs of extragalactic objects. VII. Two- and three-point correlation functions for the high-resolution Shane-Wirtanen catalog of galaxies. *Astrophys. J.* **1977**, *217*, 385–405. [CrossRef]
53. Maddox, S.J.; Efstathiou, G.; Sutherland, W.J.; Loveday, J. Galaxy correlations on large scales. *Mon. Not. R. Astron. Soc.* **1990**, *242*, 43. [CrossRef]
54. Peebles, P.J.E. The Galaxy and Mass N-Point Correlation Functions: A Blast from the Past. *Astron. Soc. Pac. Conf. Ser.* **2001**, *252*, 201.
55. Longair, M.S.; Einasto, J. (Eds.) *The Large Scale Structure of the Universe; Proceedings of the Symposium, Tallin, Estonian, USSR, September 12–16, 1977*; IAU Symposium; 1978; Volume 79. Available online: https://link.springer.com/book/10.1007/978-94-009-9843-8 (accessed on 21 August 2025).
56. Jõeveer, M.; Einasto, J.; Tago, E. The cell structure of the Universe. *Tartu Astr. Obs. Preprint* **1977**, *79*, 241.
57. Tully, R.B.; Fisher, J.R. A Tour of the Local Supercluster. In *Large Scale Structures in the Universe*; Longair, M.S., Einasto, J., Eds.; Symposium—International Astronomical Union; Cambridge University Press: Cambridge, UK, 1978; Volume 79, pp. 214–216. Available online: https://ui.adsabs.harvard.edu/abs/1978IAUS...79..214T/abstract (accessed on 21 August 2025).
58. Gregory, S.A.; Thompson, L.A. The Coma/A1367 supercluster and its environs. *Astrophys. J.* **1978**, *222*, 784–799. [CrossRef]
59. Zeldovich, Y.B. Gravitational instability: An approximate theory for large density perturbations. *Astron. Astrophys.* **1970**, *5*, 84–89.
60. Jõeveer, M.; Einasto, J. Has the universe the cell structure. In *Large Scale Structures in the Universe*; Longair, M.S., Einasto, J., Eds.; IAU Symposium; Cambridge University Press: Cambridge, UK, 1978; Volume 79, pp. 241–250. Available online: https://link.springer.com/chapter/10.1007/978-94-009-9843-8_25 (accessed on 21 August 2025).
61. Doroshkevich, A.G.; Kotok, E.V.; Poliudov, A.N.; Shandarin, S.F.; Sigov, I.S.; Novikov, I.D. Two-dimensional simulation of the gravitational system dynamics and formation of the large-scale structure of the universe. *Mon. Not. R. Astron. Soc.* **1980**, *192*, 321–337.
62. Bond, J.R.; Kofman, L.; Pogosyan, D. How filaments of galaxies are woven into the cosmic web. *Nature* **1996**, *380*, 603–606. [CrossRef]
63. Bahcall, N.A.; Soneira, R.M. The spatial correlation function of rich clusters of galaxies. *Astrophys. J.* **1983**, *270*, 20–38. [CrossRef]
64. Klypin, A.A.; Kopylov, A.I. The Spatial Covariance Function for Rich Clusters of Galaxies. *Sov. Astron. Lett.* **1983**, *9*, 41.
65. Kaiser, N. On the spatial correlations of Abell clusters. *Astrophys. J. Lett.* **1984**, *284*, L9–L12. [CrossRef]
66. Szalay, A.S.; Schramm, D.N. Are galaxies more strongly correlated than clusters? *Nature* **1985**, *314*, 718–719. [CrossRef]
67. Einasto, J.; Saar, E.; Klypin, A.A. Structure of superclusters and supercluster formation. V—Spatial correlation and voids. *Mon. Not. R. Astron. Soc.* **1986**, *219*, 457–478.

68. Jones, B.J.T.; Martinez, V.J.; Saar, E.; Einasto, J. Multifractal description of the large-scale structure of the universe. *Astrophys. J. Lett.* **1988**, *332*, L1–L5. [CrossRef]
69. Gramann, M. Formation of the structure in an axion Universe with a cosmological constant. *Tartu Astr. Obs. Publ.* **1987**, *52*, 216–255.
70. Gramann, M. Structure and formation of superclusters. VIII—Evolution of structure in a model with cold dark matter and cosmological constant. *Mon. Not. R. Astron. Soc.* **1988**, *234*, 569–582.
71. Mandelbrot, B.B. Discussion Panel: Fractal Large Scale Structures and Crossover to Homogeneity: The Mass-Radius Function versus the Correlations, and the Measurement of the Corrrelation Range. In *Large Scale Structures of the Universe*; Audouze, J., Pelletan, M.C., Szalay, A., Zel'dovich, Y.B., Peebles, P.J.E., Eds.; IAU Symposium; 1988; Volume 130, pp. 482–484. Available online: https://www.cambridge.org/core/journals/symposium-international-astronomical-union/article/discussion-panel/617AC4E14DDB6690A89E56AD0334A35A (accessed on 21 August 2025).
72. Mandelbrot, B.B. *The Fractal Geometry of Nature*; Freeman: San Francisco, CA, USA, 1982.
73. Abell, G.O.; Chincarini, G. (Eds.) *Early Evolution of the Universe and Its Present Structure*; IAU Symposium; D. Reidel Publishing Company: Dordrecht, The Netherlands, 1983; Volume 104.
74. Audouze, J.; Pelletan, M.C.; Szalay, A.; Zel'dovich, Y.B.; Peebles, P.J.E. (Eds.) *Large-Scale Structures in the Universe. Observational and Analytical Methods. Proceedings of the 130th Symposium of the International Astronomical Union, Dedicated to the Memory of Marc A. Aaronson (1950–1987), Held in Balatonfured, Hungary, 15–20 June 1987*; IAU Symposium; Kluwer Academic Publishers: Dordrecht, The Netherlands, 1988; Volume 130.
75. van de Weygaert, R.; Shandarin, S.; Saar, E.; Einasto, J. (Eds.) *The Zeldovich Universe: Genesis and Growth of the Cosmic Web*; IAU Symposium; Cambridge University Press: Cambridge, UK, 2016; Volume 308. [CrossRef]
76. Peebles, P.J.E.; Yu, J.T. Primeval Adiabatic Perturbation in an Expanding Universe. *Astrophys. J.* **1970**, *162*, 815–836. [CrossRef]
77. Arnold, V.I.; Shandarin, S.F.; Zeldovich, I.B. The large scale structure of the universe I. General properties. One-and two-dimensional models. *Geophys. Astrophys. Fluid Dyn.* **1982**, *20*, 111–130. [CrossRef]
78. Martinez, V.J.; Jones, B.J.T. Why the universe is not a fractal. *Mon. Not. R. Astron. Soc.* **1990**, *242*, 517–521.
79. Martínez, V.J.; Saar, E. *Statistics of the Galaxy Distribution*; Chapman & Hall/CRC: Boca Raton, FL, USA, 2002.
80. Balian, R.; Schaeffer, R. Galaxies: Fractal Dimensions, Counts in Cells, and Correlations. *Astrophys. J. Lett.* **1988**, *335*, L43. [CrossRef]
81. Balian, R.; Schaeffer, R. Scale-invariant matter distribution in the universe. II—Bifractal behaviour. *Astron. Astrophys.* **1989**, *226*, 373–414.
82. Song, D.J.; Ruffini, R. Determination of "inos" Masses Composing Galactic Halos. In *Observational Cosmology*; Hewitt, A., Burbidge, G., Fang, L.Z., Eds.; IAU Symposium; Cambridge University Press: Cambridge, UK, 1987; Volume 124, p. 723.
83. Ruffini, R.; Song, D.J.; Taraglio, S. The 'ino' mass and the cellular large-scale structure of the universe. *Astron. Astrophys.* **1988**, *190*, 1–9.
84. Calzetti, D.; Einasto, J.; Giavalisco, M.; Ruffini, R.; Saar, E. The Correlation Function of Galaxies in the Direction of the Coma Cluster. *Astrophys. Space Sci.* **1987**, *137*, 101–106. [CrossRef]
85. Calzetti, D.; Giavalisco, M.; Ruffini, R. The normalization of the correlation functions for extragalactic structures. *Astron. Astrophys.* **1988**, *198*, 1–15.
86. Gaite, J.; Domínguez, A.; Pérez-Mercader, J. The Fractal Distribution of Galaxies and the Transition to Homogeneity. *Astrophys. J. Lett.* **1999**, *522*, L5–L8. [CrossRef]
87. Gaite, J. Smooth halos in the cosmic web. *J. Cosmol. Astropart. Phys.* **2015**, *2015*, 020. [CrossRef]
88. Gaite, J. The Fractal Geometry of the Cosmic Web and Its Formation. *Adv. Astron.* **2019**, *2019*, 6587138. [CrossRef]
89. Peebles, P.J.E. The fractal galaxy distribution. *Phys. D Nonlinear Phenom.* **1989**, *38*, 273–278. [CrossRef]
90. Peebles, P.J.E. *Principles of Physical Cosmology*; Prinseton University Press: Prinseton, NJ, USA, 1993. [CrossRef]
91. Pietronero, L.; Montuori, M.; Sylos Labini, F. On the Fractal Structure of the Visible Universe. *arXiv* **1997**, arXiv:astro-ph/9611197. [CrossRef]
92. Pietronero, L.; Sylos Labini, F. Fractal Structures and the Large Scale Distribution of Galaxies. In *Current Topics in Astrofundamental Physics: The Cosmic Microwave Background*; Sánchez, N.G., Ed.; Springer: Dordrecht, The Netherlands, 2001; p. 391. [CrossRef]
93. Sylos Labini, F.; Gabrielli, A.; Montuori, M.; Pietronero, L. Finite size effects on the galaxy number counts: Evidence for fractal behavior up to the deepest scale. *Phys. A Stat. Mech. Its Appl.* **1996**, *226*, 195–242. [CrossRef]
94. Borgani, S. Scaling in the Universe. *Phys. Rep.* **1995**, *251*, 1–152. [CrossRef]
95. Turok, N. (Ed.) *Critical Dialogues in Cosmology*; World Scientific: Singapore, 1997.
96. Davis, M. Is the Universe Homogeneous on Large Scales? *arXiv* **1997**, arXiv:astro-ph/9610149. [CrossRef]
97. de Swart, J.G. Five decades of missing matter. *Phys. Today* **2024**, *77*, 24–43.

98. Zeldovich, Y.B.; Einasto, J.; Shandarin, S.F. Giant voids in the universe. *Nature* **1982**, *300*, 407–413. [CrossRef]
99. Klypin, A.A.; Shandarin, S.F. Three-dimensional numerical model of the formation of large-scale structure in the Universe. *Mon. Not. R. Astron. Soc.* **1983**, *204*, 891–907.
100. van den Bergh, S. Are Clusters of Galaxies Stable? *Astron. J.* **1962**, *67*, 285. [CrossRef]
101. Peebles, P.J.E. Large-scale background temperature and mass fluctuations due to scale-invariant primeval perturbations. *Astrophys. J. Lett.* **1982**, *263*, L1–L5. [CrossRef]
102. Melott, A.L.; Einasto, J.; Saar, E.; Suisalu, I.; Klypin, A.A.; Shandarin, S.F. Cluster analysis of the nonlinear evolution of large-scale structure in an axion/gravitino/photino-dominated universe. *Phys. Rev. Lett.* **1983**, *51*, 935–938. [CrossRef]
103. Centrella, J.; Melott, A.L. Three-dimensional simulation of large-scale structure in the universe. *Nature* **1983**, *305*, 196–198. [CrossRef]
104. Peebles, P.J.E. *The Large-Scale Structure of the Universe*; Princeton Series in Physics; Prinseton University Press: Prinseton, NJ, USA, 1980.
105. Kaiser, N. Clustering in real space and in redshift space. *Mon. Not. R. Astron. Soc.* **1987**, *227*, 1–21. [CrossRef]
106. Davis, M.; Peebles, P.J.E. A survey of galaxy redshifts. V. The two-point position and velocity correlations. *Astrophys. J.* **1983**, *267*, 465–482. [CrossRef]
107. Norberg, P.; Baugh, C.M.; Hawkins, E.; Maddox, S.; Peacock, J.A.; Cole, S.; Frenk, C.S.; Bland-Hawthorn, J.; Bridges, T.; Cannon, R.; et al. The 2dF Galaxy Redshift Survey: Luminosity dependence of galaxy clustering. *Mon. Not. R. Astron. Soc.* **2001**, *328*, 64–70. [CrossRef]
108. Zehavi, I.; Zheng, Z.; Weinberg, D.H.; Frieman, J.A.; Berlind, A.A.; Blanton, M.R.; Scoccimarro, R.; Sheth, R.K.; Strauss, M.A.; Kayo, I.; et al. The Luminosity and Color Dependence of the Galaxy Correlation Function. *Astrophys. J.* **2005**, *630*, 1–27. [CrossRef]
109. Zehavi, I.; Zheng, Z.; Weinberg, D.H.; Blanton, M.R.; Bahcall, N.A.; Berlind, A.A.; Brinkmann, J.; Frieman, J.A.; Gunn, J.E.; Lupton, R.H.; et al. Galaxy Clustering in the Completed SDSS Redshift Survey: The Dependence on Color and Luminosity. *Astrophys. J.* **2011**, *736*, 59. [CrossRef]
110. Coleman, P.H.; Pietronero, L. The fractal structure of the universe. *Phys. Rep.* **1992**, *213*, 311–389. [CrossRef]
111. Coleman, P.H.; Pietronero, L.; Sanders, R.H. Absence of any characteristic correlation length in the CfA galaxy catalogue. *Astron. Astrophys.* **1988**, *200*, L32–L34.
112. Coles, P.; Chiang, L. Characterizing the nonlinear growth of large-scale structure in the Universe. *Nature* **2000**, *406*, 376–378. [CrossRef]
113. Colless, M.; Peterson, B.A.; Jackson, C.; Peacock, J.A.; Cole, S.; Norberg, P.; Baldry, I.K.; Baugh, C.M.; Bland-Hawthorn, J.; Bridges, T.; et al. The 2dF Galaxy Redshift Survey: Final Data Release. *arXiv* **2003**, arXiv:astro–ph/0306581. [CrossRef]
114. Aihara, H.; Allende Prieto, C.; An, D.; Anderson, S.F.; Aubourg, É.; Balbinot, E.; Beers, T.C.; Berlind, A.A.; Bickerton, S.J.; Bizyaev, D.; et al. The Eighth Data Release of the Sloan Digital Sky Survey: First Data from SDSS-III. *Astrophys. J. Suppl.* **2011**, *193*, 29. [CrossRef]
115. Alam, S.; Albareti, F.D.; Allende Prieto, C.; Anders, F.; Anderson, S.F.; Anderton, T.; Andrews, B.H.; Armengaud, E.; Aubourg, É.; Bailey, S.; et al. The Eleventh and Twelfth Data Releases of the Sloan Digital Sky Survey: Final Data from SDSS-III. *Astrophys. J. Suppl.* **2015**, *219*, 12. [CrossRef]
116. Tegmark, M.; Blanton, M.R.; Strauss, M.A.; Hoyle, F.; Schlegel, D.; Scoccimarro, R.; Vogeley, M.S.; Weinberg, D.H.; Zehavi, I.; Berlind, A.; et al. The Three-Dimensional Power Spectrum of Galaxies from the Sloan Digital Sky Survey. *Astrophys. J.* **2004**, *606*, 702–740. [CrossRef]
117. Springel, V.; White, S.D.M.; Jenkins, A.; Frenk, C.S.; Yoshida, N.; Gao, L.; Navarro, J.; Thacker, R.; Croton, D.; Helly, J.; et al. Simulations of the formation, evolution and clustering of galaxies and quasars. *Nature* **2005**, *435*, 629–636. [CrossRef]
118. Springel, V.; Pakmor, R.; Pillepich, A.; Weinberger, R.; Nelson, D.; Hernquist, L.; Vogelsberger, M.; Genel, S.; Torrey, P.; Marinacci, F.; et al. First results from the IllustrisTNG simulations: Matter and galaxy clustering. *Mon. Not. R. Astron. Soc.* **2018**, *475*, 676–698. [CrossRef]
119. Einasto, J.; Hütsi, G.; Kuutma, T.; Einasto, M. Correlation function: Biasing and fractal properties of the cosmic web. *Astron. Astrophys.* **2020**, *640*, A47. [CrossRef]
120. Einasto, J.; Hütsi, G.; Einasto, M. Correlation functions in 2D and 3D as descriptors of the cosmic web. *Astron. Astrophys.* **2021**, *652*, A152. [CrossRef]
121. White, S.D.M.; Rees, M.J. Core condensation in heavy halos—A two-stage theory for galaxy formation and clustering. *Mon. Not. R. Astron. Soc.* **1978**, *183*, 341–358.
122. Cen, R.; Ostriker, J.P. A three-dimensional hydrodynamic treatment of the hot dark matter cosmological scenario. *Astrophys. J.* **1992**, *399*, 331–344. [CrossRef]
123. Repp, A.; Szapudi, I. A Gravitational Ising Model for the Statistical Bias of Galaxies. *arXiv* **2019**, arXiv:1904.05048.

124. Tempel, E.; Tamm, A.; Gramann, M.; Tuvikene, T.; Liivamägi, L.J.; Suhhonenko, I.; Kipper, R.; Einasto, M.; Saar, E. Flux- and volume-limited groups/clusters for the SDSS galaxies: Catalogues and mass estimation. *Astron. Astrophys.* **2014**, *566*, A1. [CrossRef]
125. Ahn, C.P.; Alexandroff, R.; Allende Prieto, C.; Anders, F.; Anderson, S.F.; Anderton, T.; Andrews, B.H.; Aubourg, É.; Bailey, S.; Bastien, F.A.; et al. The Tenth Data Release of the Sloan Digital Sky Survey: First Spectroscopic Data from the SDSS-III Apache Point Observatory Galactic Evolution Experiment. *Astrophys. J. Suppl.* **2014**, *211*, 17. [CrossRef]
126. Liivamägi, L.J.; Tempel, E.; Saar, E. SDSS DR7 superclusters. The catalogues. *Astron. Astrophys.* **2012**, *539*, A80. [CrossRef]
127. Croton, D.J.; Springel, V.; White, S.D.M.; De Lucia, G.; Frenk, C.S.; Gao, L.; Jenkins, A.; Kauffmann, G.; Navarro, J.F.; Yoshida, N. The many lives of active galactic nuclei: Cooling flows, black holes and the luminosities and colours of galaxies. *Mon. Not. R. Astron. Soc.* **2006**, *365*, 11–28. [CrossRef]
128. McAlpine, S.; Helly, J.C.; Schaller, M.; Trayford, J.W.; Qu, Y.; Furlong, M.; Bower, R.G.; Crain, R.A.; Schaye, J.; Theuns, T.; et al. The EAGLE simulations of galaxy formation: Public release of halo and galaxy catalogues. *Astron. Comput.* **2016**, *15*, 72–89. [CrossRef]
129. Zehavi, I.; Weinberg, D.H.; Zheng, Z.; Berlind, A.A.; Frieman, J.A.; Scoccimarro, R.; Sheth, R.K.; Blanton, M.R.; Tegmark, M.; Mo, H.J.; et al. On Departures from a Power Law in the Galaxy Correlation Function. *Astrophys. J.* **2004**, *608*, 16–24. [CrossRef]
130. Navarro, J.F.; Frenk, C.S.; White, S.D.M. A Universal Density Profile from Hierarchical Clustering. *Astrophys. J.* **1997**, *490*, 493. [CrossRef]
131. Wang, J.; Bose, S.; Frenk, C.S.; Gao, L.; Jenkins, A.; Springel, V.; White, S.D.M. Universal structure of dark matter haloes over a mass range of 20 orders of magnitude. *Nature* **2020**, *585*, 39–42. [CrossRef]
132. Kirshner, R.P.; Oemler, A., Jr.; Schechter, P.L.; Shectman, S.A. A million cubic megaparsec void in Bootes. *Astrophys. J. Lett.* **1981**, *248*, L57–L60. [CrossRef]
133. Pan, D.C.; Vogeley, M.S.; Hoyle, F.; Choi, Y.Y.; Park, C. Cosmic voids in Sloan Digital Sky Survey Data Release 7. *Mon. Not. R. Astron. Soc.* **2012**, *421*, 926–934. [CrossRef]
134. Sutter, P.M.; Lavaux, G.; Wandelt, B.D.; Weinberg, D.H. A Public Void Catalog from the SDSS DR7 Galaxy Redshift Surveys Based on the Watershed Transform. *Astrophys. J.* **2012**, *761*, 44. [CrossRef]
135. Nadathur, S.; Hotchkiss, S. A robust public catalogue of voids and superclusters in the SDSS Data Release 7 galaxy surveys. *Mon. Not. R. Astron. Soc.* **2014**, *440*, 1248–1262. [CrossRef]
136. Sheth, R.K.; van de Weygaert, R. A hierarchy of voids: Much ado about nothing. *Mon. Not. R. Astron. Soc.* **2004**, *350*, 517–538. [CrossRef]
137. Aragon-Calvo, M.A.; Szalay, A.S. The Hierarchical Structure and Dynamics of Voids. *Mon. Not. R. Astron. Soc.* **2013**, *428*, 3409–3424.
138. Aragon Calvo, M.A.; Neyrinck, M.C.; Silk, J. Galaxy Quenching from Cosmic Web Detachment. *Open J. Astrophys.* **2019**, *2*, 7. [CrossRef]
139. Pan, J.; Coles, P. Large-scale cosmic homogeneity from a multifractal analysis of the PSCz catalogue. *Mon. Not. R. Astron. Soc.* **2000**, *318*, L51–L54. [CrossRef]
140. Sarkar, P.; Yadav, J.; Pandey, B.; Bharadwaj, S. The scale of homogeneity of the galaxy distribution in SDSS DR6. *Mon. Not. R. Astron. Soc.* **2009**, *399*, L128–L131. [CrossRef]
141. Scrimgeour, M.I.; Davis, T.; Blake, C.; James, J.B.; Poole, G.B.; Staveley-Smith, L.; Brough, S.; Colless, M.; Contreras, C.; Couch, W.; et al. The WiggleZ Dark Energy Survey: The transition to large-scale cosmic homogeneity. *Mon. Not. R. Astron. Soc.* **2012**, *425*, 116–134. [CrossRef]
142. Courtois, H.M.; Mould, J.; Hollinger, A.M.; Dupuy, A.; Zhang, C.P. In search for the Local Universe dynamical homogeneity scale with CF4++ peculiar velocities. *arXiv* **2025**, arXiv:2502.01308. [CrossRef]
143. Park, C.; Song, H.; Einasto, M.; Lietzen, H.; Heinamaki, P. Large SDSS Quasar Groups and Their Statistical Significance. *J. Korean Astron. Soc.* **2015**, *48*, 75–82. [CrossRef]

fractal and fractional

MDPI

Article

Relational Contractions of Matkowski–Berinde–Pant Type and an Application to Certain Fractional Differential Equations

Doaa Filali [1], Faizan Ahmad Khan [2,*], Adel Alatawi [2], Esmail Alshaban [2], Montaser Saudi Ali [2] and Fahad M. Alamrani [2,*]

1 Department of Mathematical Science, College of Sciences, Princess Nourah bint Abdulrahman University, Riyadh 84428, Saudi Arabia; dkfilali@pnu.edu.sa

2 Department of Mathematics, Faculty of Science, University of Tabuk, Tabuk 71491, Saudi Arabia; amalatawi@ut.edu.sa (A.A.); ealshaban@ut.edu.sa (E.A.); mbarakat@ut.edu.sa (M.S.A.)

* Correspondence: fkhan@ut.edu.sa (F.A.K.); fm.alomrani@ut.edu.sa (F.M.A.)

Abstract: This paper concludes a few fixed-point outcomes involving almost Matkowski contraction-inequality of Pant type in a relational metric space. The findings established here enhance, expand, consolidate and develop several noted outcomes. In order to argue for our investigations, we construct some illustrative examples. We exploit our outcomes to analyze the availability of a (unique) positive solution to certain singular fractional differential equations.

Keywords: fixed point; binary relation; comparison function; singular fractional differential equations

MSC: 47H10; 34B15; 54H25

1. Introduction

Fractional-order derivatives offer several advantages over traditional integer-order derivatives, particularly in modeling and control systems. The concept of FDEs remains an expansion of the differential equations involving fractional-order derivatives. FDEs are characterized recently due to their impressive development and accuracy to the realm of fractional calculus. For a deep description of FDEs, we refer the works contained [1–5]. Zhou et al. [6] and Zhai and Hao [7] discussed the solvability of FDEs using fixed-point theorems in partially ordered MS. On the other hand, Liang and Zhang [8] subsequently investigated the unique positive solution for a three-point BVP of FDE. The singular three-point BVP associated to FDEs were proved by Cabrera et al. [9] using order-theoretic fixed point theorems. Karapınar et al. [10] employed fixed-point theorems for large contractions to discuss the solvability to nonlinear fractional differential equations. Very recently, Abdou [11] solved certain nonlinear FDEs using fixed-point theorems in orthogonal MS.

The classical fractional BVP with v as a dependent variable and θ as an independent variable is described as

$$-\mathbf{D}^{\mathrm{p}} v(\theta) = \hbar\Big(\theta, v(\theta), \mathbf{D}^{\alpha_1} v(\theta), \mathbf{D}^{\alpha_2} v(\theta), \ldots, \mathbf{D}^{\alpha_{r-1}} v(\theta)\Big)$$

$$\begin{cases} \mathbf{D}^{\alpha_i}\mathrm{v}(0) = 0, \quad 1 \le i \le r-1, \\ \mathbf{D}^{\alpha_{r-1}+1}\mathrm{v}(0) = 0, \\ \mathbf{D}^{\alpha_{r-1}}\mathrm{v}(1) = \sum_{j=1}^{m-2} e_j \mathbf{D}^{\alpha_{r-1}}\mathrm{v}(\delta_j), \end{cases} \tag{1}$$

The following definitions are used above:

- $r = 3, 4, 5, \ldots$ verifying $r - 1 < \mathrm{p} \le r$;
- $0 < \alpha_1 < \alpha_2 < \cdots < \alpha_{r-2} < \alpha_{r-1}$ and $r - 3 < \alpha_{r-1} < \mathrm{p} - 2$;
- $\mathbf{D}^{\mathrm{p}}$ refers the standard Riemann–Liouville derivative;
- $\hbar \in \mathcal{C}([0,1] \times \mathbb{R}^r; \mathbb{R}^+)$;
- $e_j \in \mathbb{R}$ and $0 < \delta_1 < \delta_2 < \cdots < \delta_{m-1} < 1$ with $0 < \sum_{j=1}^{m-2} e_j \delta_j^{\mathrm{p}-\alpha_{r-1}-1} < 1$.

The BCP serves as the cornerstone of metrical fixed-point theory. In accordance to this fundamental outcome, there is a contraction map on CMS. This finding also supplies a technique to predicate this (unique) fixed point. The vast majority of existing research contains a lot of generalizations of the BCP. Φ-contraction is a straightforward expanded contraction that was derived from conventional contraction by supplementing by the Lipschitz constant with a proper auxiliary function $\Phi : \mathbb{R}^+ \to \mathbb{R}^+$. Browder [12] established a first fixed-point finding under Φ-contractions. Subsequently, Matkowski [13] expanded the Browder fixed-point finding incorporating the concept of comparison functions.

Quite recently, Pant [14] expanded BCP by investigating the following non-unique fixed point finding.

Theorem 1. *Let $\mathcal{P}$ be a self-map CMS $(\mathbf{V}, \varpi)$. If $\exists\ \beta \in [0,1)$ with*

$$\varpi(\mathcal{P}z, \mathcal{P}w) \le \beta \cdot \varpi(z, w), \quad \forall\ z, w \in \mathbf{V} \text{ with } [z \ne \mathcal{P}(z) \text{ or } w \ne \mathcal{P}(w)],$$

then, $\mathcal{P}$ owns a fixed point.

A generalization of Theorem 1 for Φ-contraction was subsequently proven by Pant [15].

In 2015, Alam and Imdad [16] established one more interesting and core variant of BCP with endowing an arbitrary BR on underlying MS wherein the contraction map preserves the given BR. During the foregoing decades, various researchers have sharpened and improved the relation-theoretic contraction principle, e.g., [17–20]. In the same continuation, a few authors investigated such types of outcomes in solving some typical fractional differential equations (cf. [21,22]).

The idea of "almost contraction" was invented by Berinde [23], in 2004, as follows:

Definition 1 ([23])**.** *A self-map $\mathcal{P}$ on an MS $(\mathbf{V}, \varpi)$ is referred as an almost contraction if $\exists$ $\beta \in (0,1)$ and $\ell \in \mathbb{R}^+$ with*

$$\varpi(\mathcal{P}z, \mathcal{P}w) \le \beta \cdot \varpi(z, w) + \ell \cdot \varpi(w, \mathcal{P}z), \quad \forall\ z, w \in \mathbf{V}.$$

The above condition, by symmetry of ϖ, is equivalent to

$$\varpi(\mathcal{P}z, \mathcal{P}w) \le \beta \cdot \varpi(z, w) + \ell \cdot \varpi(z, \mathcal{P}w), \quad \forall\ z, w \in \mathbf{V}.$$

Theorem 2 ([23])**.** *Every almost contraction on a CMS enjoys a fixed point.*

The following subclass of almost contraction was established by Babu et al. [24] to investigate a uniqueness theorem associated with Theorem 2.

Definition 2 ([24]). *A self-map $\mathcal{P}$ on an MS $(\mathbf{V},\varpi)$ is referred to as a strict almost contraction if $\exists\, \beta \in (0,1)$ and $\ell \in \mathbb{R}^+$ with*

$$\varpi(\mathcal{P}z,\mathcal{P}w) \leq \beta \cdot \varpi(z,w) + \ell \cdot \min\{\varpi(z,\mathcal{P}z),\varpi(w,\mathcal{P}w),\varpi(z,\mathcal{P}w),\varpi(w,\mathcal{P}z)\}, \qquad \forall\, z,w \in \mathbf{V}.$$

Theorem 3 ([24]). *Every strict almost contraction on a CMS enjoys a unique fixed point.*

Berinde and Păcurar [25] proved continuity of almost contractions on a fixed-point set. Furthermore, Berinde [26] investigated some fixed-point findings for almost Matkowski contractions. Turinici [27] presented the nonlinear formulation of almost contraction maps and employed the same to enhance Theorem 2 (see also Alfuraidan et al. [28]). Recently, Khan [29], Filali et al. [30] and Alshaban et al. [31] investigated some fixed-point findings under almost contractions in the context of relational MS.

In the following lines, we summarize two certain families of control functions utilizing in the concept of Φ-contractions.

Definition 3 ([32]). *A monotonic increasing function $\Phi : \mathbb{R}^+ \to \mathbb{R}^+$ is termed as comparison function if*

$$\lim_{n\to\infty} \Phi^n(p) = 0, \quad \forall\, p \in \mathbb{R}^+\backslash\{0\}.$$

Definition 4 ([32]). *A monotonic increasing function $\Phi : \mathbb{R}^+ \to \mathbb{R}^+$ is termed as comparison function if*

$$\sum_{n=1}^{\infty} \Phi^n(p) < \infty, \quad \forall\, p \in \mathbb{R}^+\backslash\{0\}.$$

Obviously, each (c)-comparison function is a comparison function.

Remark 1. *Every comparison function Φ satisfies the following properties:*

(i) $\Phi(p) < p,\ \forall\, p \in \mathbb{R}^+\backslash\{0\}$;

(ii) $\lim\limits_{t\to 0^+} \Phi(t) = \Phi(0) = 0.$

In the continuation, Γ will denote the collection of comparison functions and Ω will denote the collection of functions $\varrho : \mathbb{R}^+ \to \mathbb{R}^+$ verifying $\lim\limits_{t\to 0^+} \varrho(t) = \varrho(0) = 0$. The class Ω presented was suggested by Turinici [27] and improved by Alfuraidan et al. [28].

In the present article, we expand the recent fixed-point findings of Alshaban et al. [31] from (c)-comparison functions to comparison functions. Indeed, the resultant contraction-inequality subsumes the earlier contraction conditions: Matkowski contraction, almost contraction, relational contraction and Pant contraction. In the process, we prove the assessments on fixed-points in a relational MS. Nonlinear contractions usually require a transitivity condition on underlying BR in order to ensure the existence of a fixed-point. Due to the restrictive nature of a transitivity requirement, we adopt an optimum condition of transitivity (locally $\mathcal{P}$-transitive). For illustration of our outcomes, we constructed two instances. We deduce a number of classical fixed-point assessments, especially owing to Matkowski [13], Pant [15], Arif et al. [19], Babu et al. [24], Berinde [26], Turinici [27], Khan [29], Filali et al. [30] and similar others. To depict our findings, we evaluate a (unique) positive solution of a BVP concerning a singular FDE.

2. Preliminaries

On a set $\mathbf{V}$, by a BR $\mathbf{S}$, we mean any subset of $\mathbf{V}^2$. In keeping with the aforementioned definitions, $\mathbf{V}$ is a set, $\mathcal{P} : \mathbf{V} \to \mathbf{V}$ is a map, $\mathbf{S}$ is a BR on $\mathbf{V}$, and ϖ is a metric on $\mathbf{V}$. We say that

Definition 5 ([16])**.** *Two elements $z, w \in \mathbf{V}$ are $\mathbf{S}$-comparative and denoted by $[z, w] \in \mathbf{S}$, if $(z, w) \in \mathbf{S}$ or $(w, z) \in \mathbf{S}$.*

Definition 6 ([33])**.** *The BR $\mathbf{S}^{-1} := \{(z, w) \in \mathbf{V}^2 : (w, z) \in \mathbf{S}\}$ is the inverse of $\mathbf{S}$.*

Definition 7 ([33])**.** *The BR $\mathbf{S}^s := \mathbf{S} \cup \mathbf{S}^{-1}$ is the symmetric closure of $\mathbf{S}$.*

Proposition 1 ([16])**.** $(z, w) \in \mathbf{S}^s \Longleftrightarrow [z, w] \in \mathbf{S}$.

Proof. The observation is straightforward as

$$\begin{aligned}
(z, w) \in \mathbf{S}^s &\Leftrightarrow (z, w) \in \mathbf{S} \cup \mathbf{S}^{-1} \\
&\Leftrightarrow (z, w) \in \mathbf{S} \text{ or } (z, w) \in \mathbf{S}^{-1} \\
&\Leftrightarrow (z, w) \in \mathbf{S} \text{ or } (w, z) \in \mathbf{S} \\
&\Leftrightarrow [z, w] \in \mathbf{S}.
\end{aligned}$$

□

Definition 8 ([16])**.** *A sequence $\{z_n\} \subset \mathbf{V}$ satisfying $(z_n, z_{n+1}) \in \mathbf{S}, \forall\, n \in \mathbb{N}$ is $\mathbf{S}$-preserving.*

Definition 9 ([16])**.** *$\mathbf{S}$ is ϖ-self-closed if for every convergent and $\mathbf{S}$-preserving sequence of $\mathbf{V}$, $\exists$ subsequence where the terms of this subsequence are $\mathbf{S}$-comparative with the limit.*

Definition 10 ([16])**.** *$\mathbf{S}$ is $\mathcal{P}$-closed if $(\mathcal{P}z, \mathcal{P}w) \in \mathbf{S}$, for every $(z, w) \in \mathbf{S}$.*

Proposition 2 ([18])**.** *$\mathbf{S}$ is $\mathcal{P}^n$-closed if it is $\mathcal{P}$-closed.*

Definition 11 ([34])**.** *A subset $\mathbf{W} \subseteq \mathbf{V}$ $\mathbf{S}$-directed if every pair $u, w \in \mathbf{W}$ admits an element $v \in \mathbf{V}$ with $(u, v) \in \mathbf{S}$ and $(w, v) \in \mathbf{S}$.*

Definition 12 ([17])**.** *$(\mathbf{V}, \varpi)$ is $\mathbf{S}$-complete if each Cauchy and $\mathbf{S}$-preserving sequence in $\mathbf{V}$ converges.*

Definition 13 ([17])**.** *$\mathcal{P}$ is $\mathbf{S}$-continuous if for each $z \in \mathbf{V}$ and for any $\mathbf{S}$-preserving sequence $\{z_n\} \subset \mathbf{V}$, we have*

$$z_n \xrightarrow{\varpi} z \Longrightarrow \mathcal{P}(z_n) \xrightarrow{\varpi} \mathcal{P}(z).$$

Definition 14 ([33])**.** *A BR, on a subset $\mathbf{W} \subseteq \mathbf{V}$, defined by*

$$\mathbf{S}|_{\mathbf{W}} := \mathbf{S} \cap \mathbf{W}^2$$

is the restriction of $\mathbf{S}$ on $\mathbf{W}$.

Definition 15 ([18])**.** *$\mathbf{S}$ is locally $\mathcal{P}$-transitive if for each $\mathbf{S}$-preserving sequence $\{w_n\} \subset \mathcal{P}(\mathbf{V})$ (with range-set $\mathbf{W} = \{w_n : n \in \mathbb{N}\}$), $\mathbf{S}|_{\mathbf{W}}$ is transitive.*

In response to the symmetric axiom of ϖ, we constitute the forthcoming claims.

Proposition 3. *If $\Phi \in \Gamma$ and $\varrho \in \Omega$, then two contraction-inequalities mentioned below are equivalent:*

(i) $\varpi(\mathcal{P}z, \mathcal{P}w) \leq \Phi(\varpi(z,w)) + \min\{\varrho(\varpi(w,\mathcal{P}z)), \varrho(\varpi(z,\mathcal{P}w))\}$,
$\forall\ (z,w) \in \mathbf{S}$ *with* $[z \neq \mathcal{P}(z)$ *or* $w \neq \mathcal{P}(w)]$;

(ii) $\varpi(\mathcal{P}z, \mathcal{P}w) \leq \Phi(\varpi(z,w)) + \min\{\varrho(\varpi(w,\mathcal{P}z)), \varrho(\varpi(z,\mathcal{P}w))\}$,
$\forall\ [z,w] \in \mathbf{S}$ *with* $[z \neq \mathcal{P}(z)$ *or* $w \neq \mathcal{P}(w)]$.

Proposition 4. *If $\Phi \in \Gamma$ and $\varrho \in \Omega$, then two contraction-inequalities mentioned below are equivalent:*

(i) $\varpi(\mathcal{P}z, \mathcal{P}w) \leq \Phi(\varpi(z,w)) + \min\{\varrho(\varpi(w,\mathcal{P}z)), \varrho(\varpi(z,\mathcal{P}w)), \varrho(\varpi(z,\mathcal{P}z)), \varrho(\varpi(w,\mathcal{P}w))\}$,
$\forall\ (z,w) \in \mathbf{S}$;

(ii) $\varpi(\mathcal{P}z, \mathcal{P}w) \leq \Phi(\varpi(z,w)) + \min\{\varrho(\varpi(w,\mathcal{P}z)), \varrho(\varpi(z,\mathcal{P}w)), \varrho(\varpi(z,\mathcal{P}z)), \varrho(\varpi(w,\mathcal{P}w))\}$,
$\forall\ [z,w] \in \mathbf{S}$.

3. Main Results

Hereby, we disclose the fixed-point findings in the structure of relational MS.

Theorem 4. *Assuming $(\mathbf{V},\varpi)$ is a MS comprising a BR $\mathbf{S}$ and $\mathcal{P}: \mathbf{V} \to \mathbf{V}$ is a map. Moreover, the following hold:*

(a) $(\mathbf{V},\varpi)$ *is* $\mathbf{S}$*-complete MS;*

(b) $\exists\ z_0 \in \mathbf{V}$ *with* $(z_0, \mathcal{P}z_0) \in \mathbf{S}$;

(c) $\mathbf{S}$ *is* $\mathcal{P}$*-closed and locally* $\mathcal{P}$*-transitive;*

(d) $\mathcal{P}$ *is* $\mathbf{S}$*-continuous or* $\mathbf{S}$ *is* ϖ*-self-closed;*

(e) $\exists\ \Phi \in \Gamma$ *and* $\varrho \in \Omega$ *satisfy*

$$\varpi(\mathcal{P}z, \mathcal{P}w) \leq \Phi(\varpi(z,w)) + \min\{\varrho(\varpi(w,\mathcal{P}z)), \varrho(\varpi(z,\mathcal{P}w))\},$$
$$\forall\ (z,w) \in \mathbf{S} \text{ with } [z \neq \mathcal{P}(z) \text{ or } w \neq \mathcal{P}(w)].$$

Then, $\mathcal{P}$ owns a fixed point.

Proof. The task will be finished in the following stages:
Step–1. Define the following sequence $\{z_n\} \subset \mathbf{V}$:

$$z_n = \mathcal{P}^n(z_0) = \mathcal{P}(z_{n-1}),\ \forall\ n \in \mathbb{N}. \tag{2}$$

Step–2. We will show that the sequence $\{z_n\}$ is $\mathbf{S}$-preserving. Utilizing (b), $\mathcal{P}$-closedness of $\mathbf{S}$ and Proposition 2, we conclude

$$(\mathcal{P}^n z_0, \mathcal{P}^{n+1} z_0) \in \mathbf{S}$$

which on utilizing (2) becomes

$$(z_n, z_{n+1}) \in \mathbf{S}, \quad \forall\ n \in \mathbb{N}. \tag{3}$$

Step–3. Define $\varpi_n := \varpi(z_n, z_{n+1})$. If for some $p \in \mathbb{N}_0$ with $\varpi_p = 0$, then from (2), we conclude that $w_p = w_{n_0+1} = \mathcal{P}(w_p)$; so $w_p \in \text{Fix}(\mathcal{P})$ and so, we are finished. Unless we have $\varpi_n > 0$, $\forall\ n \in \mathbb{N}_0$, so that we move to Step–4.
Step–4. We will show that the sequence $\{z_n\}$ is Cauchy. For each $n \in \mathbb{N}_0$, we conclude that $z_{n-1} \neq z_n$. By (e) and (2), we find

$$\varpi(z_n, z_{n+1}) \leq \Phi(\varpi(z_{n-1}, z_n)) + \varrho(\varpi(z_n, \mathcal{P}z_{n-1})) = \Phi(\varpi(z_{n-1}, z_n)) + \varrho(0),$$

i.e.,

$$\varpi_n \leq \Phi(\varpi_{n-1}),\ \forall\, n \in \mathbb{N}.$$

Using monotonicity of Φ, last relation reduces to

$$\varpi_n \leq \Phi^n(\varpi_0), \quad \forall\, n \in \mathbb{N}. \tag{4}$$

Applying $n \to \infty$ in (4) and using axiom (ii) of Φ, we conclude

$$\lim_{n\to\infty} \varpi_n = 0. \tag{5}$$

Choose $\varepsilon > 0$. Then by (5), we can determine $n \in \mathbb{N}_0$, verifying

$$\varpi_n < \varepsilon - \Phi(\varepsilon). \tag{6}$$

Next, we will show that $\{z_n\}$ is Cauchy. Due to the monotonic property of Φ, (4) and (6), we attain

$$\begin{aligned} \varpi(z_n, z_{n+2}) &\leq \varpi(z_n, z_{n+1}) + \varpi(z_{n+1}, z_{n+2}) = \varpi_n + \varpi_{n+1} \\ &\leq \varpi_n + \Phi(\varpi_n) < \varepsilon - \Phi(\varepsilon) + \Phi(\varepsilon - \Phi(\varepsilon)) \\ &\leq \varepsilon - \Phi(\varepsilon) + \Phi(\varepsilon) = \varepsilon \end{aligned}$$

so that

$$\varpi(z_n, z_{n+2}) < \varepsilon. \tag{7}$$

In lieu of (2), $\{z_n\} \subset \mathcal{P}(\mathbf{V})$. Now, (3) and the locally $\mathcal{P}$-transitivity of $\mathbf{S}$ yield that $(z_n, z_{n+2}) \in \mathbf{S}$. Hence, applying assumption (e), we conclude that

$$\varpi(z_n, z_{n+1}) = \varpi(\mathcal{P}z_n, \mathcal{P}z_{n+2}) \leq \Phi(\varpi(z_n, z_{n+2})),$$

which, making use of (7) and by monotonic property of Φ, reduces to

$$\varpi(z_n, z_{n+1}) \leq \Phi(\varepsilon). \tag{8}$$

Using triangular inequality, (6) and (8), we conclude

$$\begin{aligned} \varpi(z_n, z_{n+3}) &\leq \varpi_n + \varpi(z_{n+1}, z_{n+3}) \\ &< \varepsilon - \Phi(\varepsilon) + \Phi(\varepsilon) = \varepsilon. \end{aligned}$$

Using induction, we find

$$\varpi(z_n, z_{n+p}) < \varepsilon, \quad \forall\, p \in \mathbb{N}.$$

Thus, $\{z_n\}$ is Cauchy and $\mathbf{S}$-preserving. By condition (a), $\exists\, z^* \in \mathbf{V}$ with $z_n \xrightarrow{\varpi} z^*$.
Step–5. We will confirm that z^* is a fixed-point of $\mathcal{P}$. By (d), if $\mathcal{P}$ remains $\mathbf{S}$-continuous, then the $\mathbf{S}$-preserving property of the sequence $\{z_n\}$ and the fact $z_n \xrightarrow{\varpi} z^*$ yield that

$$z_{n+1} = \mathcal{P}(z_n) \xrightarrow{\varpi} \mathcal{P}(z^*)$$

implying thereby, $\mathcal{P}(z^*) = z^*$.

If **S** remains ϖ-self-closed, then $\{z_n\}$ admits a subsequence $\{z_{n_k}\}$ ensuring $[z_{n_k}, z^*] \in$ **S**, $\forall\, k \in \mathbb{N}$. Define $\sigma_n := \varpi(z^*, z_n)$. If $\mathcal{P}(z^*) = z^*$, then we are finished. If $\mathcal{P}(z^*) \neq z^*$, then by condition (e), Proposition 3 and $[z_{n_k}, z^*] \in$ **S**, we obtain

$$\begin{aligned}\varpi(z_{n_k+1}, \mathcal{P}z^*) &= \varpi(\mathcal{P}z_{n_k}, \mathcal{P}z^*)\\ &\leq \Phi(\varpi(z_{n_k}, z^*)) + \min\{\varrho(\varpi(z^*, \mathcal{P}z_{n_k})), \varpi(z_{n_k}, \mathcal{P}z^*)\}\\ &= \Phi(\sigma_{n_k}) + \min\{\varrho(\sigma_{n_k+1}), \varpi(z_{n_k}, \mathcal{P}z^*)\}. \end{aligned} \tag{9}$$

Now, $z_{n_k} \xrightarrow{\varpi} z^*$ implies that $\sigma_{n_k} \xrightarrow{\mathbb{R}^+} 0^+$, whenever $k \to \infty$. Letting $k \to \infty$ in (9) and using Remark 1 and the property of Ω, we find

$$\begin{aligned}\lim_{k\to\infty} \varpi(z_{n_k+1}, \mathcal{P}z^*) &\leq \lim_{k\to\infty} \Phi(\sigma_{n_k}) + \min\left\{\lim_{k\to\infty} \varrho(\sigma_{n_k+1}), \lim_{k\to\infty} \varpi(z_{n_k}, \mathcal{P}z^*)\right\}\\ &= \lim_{t\to 0^+} \Phi(t) + \min\left\{\lim_{t\to 0^+} \varrho(t), \lim_{k\to\infty} \varpi(z_{n_k}, \mathcal{P}z^*)\right\}\\ &= 0\end{aligned}$$

or, $z_{n_k+1} \xrightarrow{\varpi} \mathcal{P}(z^*)$ implying $\mathcal{P}(z^*) = z^*$. Thus, z^* is a fixed point of $\mathcal{P}$. □

Theorem 5. *Along with the conditions (a)–(d) of Theorem 4, if*
(f) $\quad \exists\, \Phi \in \Gamma$ and $\varrho \in \Omega$ with

$$\begin{aligned}\varpi(\mathcal{P}z, \mathcal{P}w) \leq\; & \Phi(\varpi(z, w)) + \min\{\varrho(\varpi(w, \mathcal{P}z)), \varrho(\varpi(z, \mathcal{P}w)), \varrho(\varpi(z, \mathcal{P}z)), \varrho(\varpi(w, \mathcal{P}w))\},\\ & \forall\, (z, w) \in \mathbf{S}\end{aligned}$$

and
(g) $\quad \mathcal{P}(\mathbf{V})$ is $\mathbf{S}^s$-directed,
then $\mathcal{P}$ enjoys a unique fixed point.

Proof. If (f) is valid, then (e) of Theorem 4 is valid. Employing Theorem 4, select two fixed points z, w of $\mathcal{P}$, i.e.,

$$\mathcal{P}^n(z) = z \text{ and } \mathcal{P}^n(w) = w, \quad \forall\, n \in \mathbb{N}. \tag{10}$$

As $z, w \in \mathcal{P}(\mathbf{V})$, by condition (g), $\exists\, v \in \mathbf{V}$ with $[z, v] \in \mathbf{S}$ and $[w, v] \in \mathbf{S}$. The $\mathcal{P}$-closedness of **S** along with Proposition 2 yields that

$$[\mathcal{P}^n z, \mathcal{P}^n v] \in \mathbf{S} \quad\text{and}\quad [\mathcal{P}^n w, \mathcal{P}^n v] \in \mathbf{S}, \quad \forall\, n \in \mathbb{N}. \tag{11}$$

Define $\varphi_n := \varpi(\mathcal{P}^n z, \mathcal{P}^n v)$. We will reveal that

$$\lim_{n\to\infty} \varphi_n = \lim_{n\to\infty} \varpi(\mathcal{P}^n z, \mathcal{P}^n v) = 0. \tag{12}$$

Using (10), (11), condition (f) and Proposition 4, we attain

$$\begin{aligned}\varpi(\mathcal{P}^{n+1}z, \mathcal{P}^{n+1}v) &\leq \Phi(\varpi(\mathcal{P}^n z, \mathcal{P}^n v)) + \min\{\varrho(\varpi(\mathcal{P}^n v, \mathcal{P}^{n+1}z)), \varrho(\varpi(\mathcal{P}^n z, \mathcal{P}^{n+1}v)),\\ &\quad \varrho(\varpi(\mathcal{P}^n z, \mathcal{P}^{n+1}z)), \varrho(\varpi(\mathcal{P}^n v, \mathcal{P}^{n+1}v))\},\\ &= \Phi(\varpi(\mathcal{P}^n z, \mathcal{P}^n v)), \qquad \text{as } \varpi(\mathcal{P}^n z, \mathcal{P}^{n+1}z) = \varpi(z, z) = 0\end{aligned}$$

i.e.,

$$\varphi_{n+1} \leq \Phi(\varphi_n). \tag{13}$$

If there is some $n_0 \in \mathbb{N}$ for which $\varphi_{n_0} = 0$, then we conclude that $\mathcal{P}^{n_0}(\mathsf{z}) = \mathcal{P}^{n_0}(\mathsf{v})$. This implies that $\mathcal{P}^{n_0+1}(\mathsf{z}) = \mathcal{P}^{n_0+1}(\mathsf{v})$. Thus, we find $\varphi_{n_0+1} = 0$. Using induction, we obtain $\varphi_n = 0,\ \forall\ n \geq n_0$, so that $\lim_{n\to\infty} \varphi_n = 0$. If $\varphi_n > 0,\ \forall\ n \in \mathbb{N}$, then by monotonic property Φ, (13) gives rise

$$\varphi_{n+1} \leq \Phi(\varphi_n) \leq \Phi^2(\varphi_{n-1}) \leq \cdots \leq \Phi^n(\varphi_1)$$

so that

$$\varphi_{n+1} \leq \Phi^n(\varphi_1).$$

Letting $n \to \infty$ in last relation and by a characteristic of Φ, we attain

$$\lim_{n\to\infty} \varphi_{n+1} \leq \lim_{n\to\infty} \Phi^n(\varphi_1) = 0.$$

Thus, (12) is proved. Likewise, we can find that

$$\lim_{n\to\infty} \varpi(\mathcal{P}^n\mathsf{w}, \mathcal{P}^n\mathsf{v}) = 0. \tag{14}$$

By (12) and (14), we obtain

$$\varpi(\mathsf{z},\mathsf{w}) = \varpi(\mathcal{P}^n\mathsf{z}, \mathcal{P}^n\mathsf{w}) \leq \varpi(\mathcal{P}^n\mathsf{z}, \mathcal{P}^n\mathsf{v}) + \varpi(\mathcal{P}^n\mathsf{w}, \mathcal{P}^n\mathsf{v}) \to 0 \quad \text{as} \quad n \to \infty$$

so $\mathsf{z} = \mathsf{w}$. The conclusion has thus been arrived. □

4. Consequences

In the following portion, we will implement our outcomes to figure out various known fixed-point findings.

Particularly, for $\Phi(\mathsf{p}) = \beta \cdot \mathsf{p}$ (where $\beta \in (0,1)$) and $\varrho(\mathsf{p}) = \ell \cdot \mathsf{p}$ (where $\ell \in \mathbb{R}^+$), Theorem 4 deduces the following outcome. However, in this case, the the condition of locally $\mathcal{P}$-transitivity can be relaxed.

Corollary 1 (Khan [29]). *Assuming $(\mathbf{V}, \varpi)$ is an MS comprising a BR $\mathbf{S}$ and $\mathcal{P} : \mathbf{V} \to \mathbf{V}$ is a map. Also,*

(a) *$(\mathbf{V}, \varpi)$ is $\mathbf{S}$-complete;*
(b) *$\exists\ z_0 \in \mathbf{V}$ with $(z_0, \mathcal{P}z_0) \in \mathbf{S}$;*
(c) *$\mathbf{S}$ is $\mathcal{P}$-closed;*
(d) *$\mathcal{P}$ is $\mathbf{S}$-continuous or $\mathbf{S}$ is ϖ-self-closed;*
(e) *$\exists\ \beta \in (0,1)$ and $\ell \in \mathbb{R}^+$ with*

$$\varpi(\mathcal{P}z, \mathcal{P}w) \leq \beta \cdot \varpi(z,w) + \ell \cdot \varpi(w, \mathcal{P}z), \quad \forall\ (z,w) \in \mathbf{S}.$$

Then, $\mathcal{P}$ owns a fixed point.

Under the restriction $\varrho(\mathsf{p}) = \ell \cdot \mathsf{p}$ (where $\ell \in \mathbb{R}^+$), Theorem 4 reduces to the following finding.

Corollary 2 (Filali et al. [30]). *Assuming $(\mathbf{V}, \varpi)$ is an MS comprising a BR $\mathbf{S}$ and $\mathcal{P} : \mathbf{V} \to \mathbf{V}$ is a map. Also,*

(a) $(\mathbf{V}, \varpi)$ *is* $\mathbf{S}$*-complete;*
(b) $\exists\, z_0 \in \mathbf{V}$ *with* $(z_0, \mathcal{P}z_0) \in \mathbf{S}$*;*
(c) $\mathbf{S}$ *is locally* $\mathcal{P}$*-transitive and* $\mathcal{P}$*-closed;*
(d) $\mathcal{P}$ *is* $\mathbf{S}$*-continuous or* $\mathbf{S}$ *is* ϖ*-self-closed;*
(e) $\exists\, \Phi \in \Gamma$ *and* $\ell \in \mathbb{R}^+$*, verifying*

$$\varpi(\mathcal{P}z, \mathcal{P}w) \leq \Phi(\varpi(z, w)) + \ell \cdot \min\{\varpi(w, \mathcal{P}z), \varpi(z, \mathcal{P}w)\}, \quad \forall\, (z, w) \in \mathbf{S}.$$

Then, $\mathcal{P}$ *owns a fixed point.*

If we take $\varrho(\mathsf{p}) = 0$ for all $\ell \in \mathbb{R}^+$ in Theorem 4, then we find the following result.

Corollary 3 (Arif et al. [19]). *Assuming* $(\mathbf{V}, \varpi)$ *is an MS comprised with a BR* $\mathbf{S}$ *and* $\mathcal{P} : \mathbf{V} \to \mathbf{V}$ *is a map. Also,*

(a) $(\mathbf{V}, \varpi)$ *is* $\mathbf{S}$*-complete;*
(b) $\exists\, z_0 \in \mathbf{V}$ *with* $(z_0, \mathcal{P}z_0) \in \mathbf{S}$*;*
(c) $\mathbf{S}$ *is locally* $\mathcal{P}$*-transitive and* $\mathcal{P}$*-closed;*
(d) $\mathcal{P}$ *is* $\mathbf{S}$*-continuous or* $\mathbf{S}$ *is* ϖ*-self-closed;*
(e) $\exists\, \Phi \in \Gamma$ *with*

$$\varpi(\mathcal{P}z, \mathcal{P}w) \leq \Phi(\varpi(z, w)), \quad \forall\, (z, w) \in \mathbf{S}.$$

Then, $\mathcal{P}$ *owns a fixed point.*

Under universal relation $\mathbf{S} = \mathbf{V}^2$, Theorem 4 deduces the following outcomes.

Corollary 4 (Turinici [27]). *Assuming* $(\mathbf{V}, \varpi)$ *is a CMS and* $\mathcal{P} : \mathbf{V} \to \mathbf{V}$ *is a map. If* $\exists\, \beta \in [0, 1)$ *and* $\varrho \in \Omega$*, verifying*

$$\varpi(\mathcal{P}z, \mathcal{P}w) \leq \beta \cdot \varpi(z, w)) + \varrho(\varpi(w, \mathcal{P}z)), \quad \forall\, z, w \in \mathbf{V},$$

then, $\mathcal{P}$ *owns a fixed point.*

Corollary 5 (Berinde [26]). *Assuming* $(\mathbf{V}, \varpi)$ *is a CMS and* $\mathcal{P} : \mathbf{V} \to \mathbf{V}$ *is a map. If* $\exists\, \Phi \in \Gamma$ *and* $\ell \in \mathbb{R}^+$*, verifying*

$$\varpi(\mathcal{P}z, \mathcal{P}w) \leq \Phi(\varpi(z, w)) + \ell \cdot \varpi(w, \mathcal{P}z), \quad \forall\, z, w \in \mathbf{V},$$

then, $\mathcal{P}$ *owns a fixed point.*

Corollary 6 (Pant [15]). *Assuming* $(\mathbf{V}, \varpi)$ *is a CMS and* $\mathcal{P} : \mathbf{V} \to \mathbf{V}$ *is a map. If* $\exists\, \Phi \in \Gamma$*, verifying*

$$\varpi(\mathcal{P}z, \mathcal{P}w) \leq \Phi(\varpi(z, w)), \quad \forall\, z, w \in \mathbf{V} \text{ with } [z \neq \mathcal{P}(z) \text{ or } w \neq \mathcal{P}(w)],$$

then, $\mathcal{P}$ *owns a fixed point.*

Under universal relation $\mathbf{S} = \mathbf{V}^2$, Theorem 5 deduces the following outcomes.

Corollary 7 (Babu et al. [24]). *Assume that* $(\mathbf{V}, \varpi)$ *is a CMS comprising a BR* $\mathbf{S}$ *and* $\mathcal{P}:\mathbf{V}\to\mathbf{V}$ *is a map. If* $\exists\ \beta\in[0,1)$ *and* $\ell\in\mathbb{R}^+$, *verifying*

$$\varpi(\mathcal{P}z,\mathcal{P}w)\leq\beta\cdot\varpi(z,w)+\ell\cdot\min\{\varpi(w,\mathcal{P}z),\varpi(z,\mathcal{P}w),\varpi(z,\mathcal{P}z),\varpi(w,\mathcal{P}w)\},\ \forall\, z,w\in\mathbf{V},$$

then, $\mathcal{P}$ *owns a unique fixed point.*

Corollary 8 (Matkowski [13]). *Assume that* $(\mathbf{V}, \varpi)$ *is a CMS and* $\mathcal{P}:\mathbf{V}\to\mathbf{V}$ *is a map. If* $\exists$ $\Phi\in\Gamma$, *verifying*

$$\varpi(\mathcal{P}z,\mathcal{P}w)\leq\Phi(\varpi(z,w)),\quad \forall\, z,w\in\mathbf{V},$$

then, $\mathcal{P}$ *owns a unique fixed point.*

5. Illustrative Examples

A number of examples concerning the Theorems 4 and 5 are offered in this part.

Example 1. *Consider* $\mathbf{V}=\mathbb{R}^+$ *under Euclidean metric* ϖ *and a BR* $\mathbf{S}:=\{(z,w)\in\mathbf{V}^2: z-w>0\}$. *Define the map* $\mathcal{P}:\mathbf{V}\to\mathbf{V}$ *by* $\mathcal{P}(z)=\frac{z}{z+1}$. *Clearly, the BR* $\mathbf{S}$ *is locally* $\mathcal{P}$*-transitive, the MS* $(\mathbf{V},\varpi)$ *is* $\mathbf{S}$*-complete and* $\mathcal{P}$ *is* $\mathbf{S}$*-continuous.*

Let $(z,w)\in\mathbf{S}$*; then we attain* $z-w>0$ *and so,*

$$\mathcal{P}(z)-\mathcal{P}(w)=\frac{z-w}{(z+1)(w+1)}>0,$$

which concludes that $(\mathcal{P}z,\mathcal{P}w)\in\mathbf{S}$ *so that* $\mathbf{S}$ *is* $\mathcal{P}$*-closed.*

Define $\Phi\in\Gamma$ *and* $\varrho\in\Omega$ *by* $\Phi(t)=\frac{t}{t+1}$ *and* $\varrho(t)=\ln(1+t)$. *Now, for all* $(z,w)\in\mathbf{S}$, *we have*

$$\begin{aligned}\varpi(\mathcal{P}z,\mathcal{P}w) &= \left|\frac{z}{z+1}-\frac{w}{w+1}\right|=\left|\frac{z-w}{1+z+w+zw}\right|\\ &\leq \frac{z-w}{1+(z-w)}=\frac{\varpi(z,w)}{1+\varpi(z,w)}\\ &\leq \Phi(\varpi(z,w))+\min\{\varrho(\varpi(w,\mathcal{P}z)),\varrho(\varpi(z,\mathcal{P}w)),\varrho(\varpi(z,\mathcal{P}z)),\varrho(\varpi(w,\mathcal{P}w))\}.\end{aligned}$$

It demonstrates that the argument (f) *of Theorem 5 is confirmed. Also,* $z_0=1$ *satisfies the condition* (b). *Finally,* $\mathcal{P}(\mathbf{V})$ *is* $\mathbf{S}^s$*-directed since for every pair* $z,w\in\mathcal{P}(\mathbf{V})$, *the element* $u:=(z+w)/2$ *satisfies* $[z,u]\in\mathbf{S}$ *and* $[w,u]\in\mathbf{S}$. *Therefore, all the assumptions of Theorem 5 hold and hence* $\mathcal{P}$ *owns a unique fixed point,* $\bar{z}=0$.

In above example Φ is not a (c)-comparison function. Therefore this example cannot be covered by corresponding theorems of Alshaban et al. [31]. This reveals that our results are more advantageous compared to the findings of Alshaban et al. [31].

Example 2. *Consider* $\mathbf{V}=[0,1]$ *under Euclidean metric* ϖ *and BR* $\mathbf{S}=\mathbb{R}\times\mathbb{Q}$. *Clearly,* $(\mathbf{V},\varpi)$ *is* $\mathbf{S}$*-complete MS. Let* $\mathcal{P}$ *be the identity map on* $\mathbf{V}$. *Then,* $\mathbf{S}$ *is* $\mathcal{P}$*-closed and* $\mathcal{P}$ *is* $\mathbf{S}$*-continuous.*

Fix $\beta\in[0,1)$ *and define* $\Phi\in\Gamma$ *and* $\varrho\in\Omega$ *with* $\Phi(t)=\beta t$ *and* $\varrho(t)=t-\beta t$. *For every* $(z,w)\in\mathbf{S}$, *the contraction-inequality of Theorem 4 is verified. In the same way, all the assertions of Theorem 4 hold; henceforth* $\mathcal{P}$ *owns a fixed point. In this example,* $Fix(\mathcal{P})=[0,1]$ *and hence Theorem 5 cannot be applied.*

6. Applications to Fractional Differential Equations

Consider the singular fractional BVP mentioned below

$$\begin{cases} \mathbf{D}^{\mathsf{p}}_{0+} v(\theta) + \hbar(\theta, v(\theta)) = 0, & \forall\, \theta \in (0,1), \\ v(0) = v'(0) = v''(0) = 0, & v''(1) = q v''(\delta), \end{cases} \tag{15}$$

in conjunction with the following presumptions:

- $3 < \mathsf{p} \leq 4$;
- $0 < \delta < 1$;
- $0 < q\delta^{\mathsf{p}-3} < 1$;
- $\hbar : [0,1] \times \mathbb{R}^+ \to \mathbb{R}^+$ is continuous;
- $\hbar$ retains singular at $\theta = 0$, indicating that $\lim_{\theta \to 0+} \hbar(\theta, \cdot) = \infty$.

Certainly, the BVP (15) is transformed into an integral equation given below:

$$v(\theta) = \int_0^1 \mathbf{G}(\theta,\tau)\hbar(\tau, v(\tau))d\tau + \frac{q\theta^{\mathsf{p}-1}}{(\mathsf{p}-1)(\mathsf{p}-2)(1-q\delta^{\mathsf{p}-3})} \int_0^1 \mathbf{H}(\delta,\tau)\hbar(\tau, v(\tau))d\tau \tag{16}$$

whereas Green function is

$$\mathbf{G}(\theta,\tau) = \begin{cases} \frac{\theta^{\mathsf{p}-1}(1-\tau)^{\mathsf{p}-3} - (\theta-\tau)^{\mathsf{p}-1}}{\Gamma(\mathsf{p})}, & 0 \leq \tau \leq \theta \leq 1, \\ \frac{\theta^{\mathsf{p}-1}(1-\tau)^{\mathsf{p}-3}}{\Gamma(\mathsf{p})}, & 0 \leq \theta \leq \tau \leq 1 \end{cases}$$

and its second derivative $\mathbf{H}(\theta,\tau) := \dfrac{\partial^2 \mathbf{G}(\theta,\tau)}{\partial \theta^2}$ becomes

$$\mathbf{H}(\theta,\tau) = \begin{cases} \frac{(\mathsf{p}-1)(\mathsf{p}-2)}{\Gamma(\mathsf{p})} \left[\theta^{\mathsf{p}-3}(1-\tau)^{\mathsf{p}-3} - (\theta-\tau)^{\mathsf{p}-3}\right], & 0 \leq \tau \leq \theta \leq 1, \\ \frac{(\mathsf{p}-1)(\mathsf{p}-2)}{\Gamma(\mathsf{p})} \theta^{\mathsf{p}-3}(1-\tau)^{\mathsf{p}-3}, & 0 \leq \theta \leq \tau \leq 1. \end{cases}$$

$\Gamma(\cdot)$ and $\beta(\cdot,\cdot)$ denote the gamma and beta functions, respectively. Inspired by [8,9], we will compute a (unique) positive solution of (15).

Proposition 5 ([9]). *If* $\mathbf{G}$ *and* $\mathbf{H}$ *are described as above, then the following hold:*

- $\mathbf{G}(\theta, 1) = 0$;
- $\mathbf{G}(\theta,\tau) \geq 0$ *and* $\mathbf{H}(\theta,\tau) \geq 0$;
- $\mathbf{G}$ *and* $\mathbf{H}$ *are continuous;*
- $\sup_{0 \leq \theta \leq 1} \int_0^1 \mathbf{G}(\theta,\tau)d\tau = \frac{2}{(p-2)\Gamma(p+1)}$;
- $\int_0^1 \mathbf{H}(\delta,\tau)d\tau = \frac{\delta^{p-3}(p-1)(1-\delta)}{\Gamma(p)}$.

Lemma 1. *If* $\rho \in (0,1)$, *then*

$$\sup_{0 \leq \theta \leq 1} \int_0^1 \mathbf{G}(\theta,\tau)\tau^{-\rho}d\tau = \frac{1}{\Gamma(p)}(\beta(1-\rho, p-2) - \beta(1-\rho, p)).$$

Proof. Observe that

$$\begin{aligned}
\int_0^1 \mathbf{G}(\theta,\tau)\tau^{-\rho}d\tau &= \int_0^\theta \mathbf{G}(\theta,\tau)\tau^{-\rho}d\tau + \int_\theta^1 \mathbf{G}(\theta,\tau)\tau^{-\rho}d\tau \\
&= \int_0^\theta \frac{\theta^{\mathrm{p}-1}(1-\tau)^{\mathrm{p}-3} - (\theta-\tau)^{\mathrm{p}-1}}{\Gamma(\mathrm{p})}\tau^{-\rho}d\tau + \int_\theta^1 \frac{\theta^{\mathrm{p}-1}(1-\tau)^{\mathrm{p}-3}}{\Gamma(\mathrm{p})}\tau^{-\rho}d\tau \\
&= \int_0^1 \frac{\theta^{\mathrm{p}-1}(1-\tau)^{\mathrm{p}-3}}{\Gamma(\mathrm{p})}\tau^{-\rho}d\tau - \int_0^\theta \frac{(\theta-\tau)^{\mathrm{p}-1}}{\Gamma(\mathrm{p})}\tau^{-\mathrm{p}}d\tau \\
&= \frac{\theta^{\mathrm{p}-1}}{\Gamma(\mathrm{p})}\int_0^1 (1-\tau)^{\mathrm{p}-3}\tau^{-\rho}d\tau - \frac{1}{\Gamma(\mathrm{p})}\int_0^\theta (\theta-\tau)^{\mathrm{p}-1}\tau^{-\rho}d\tau \\
&= \frac{\theta^{\mathrm{p}-1}}{\Gamma(\mathrm{p})}\beta(1-\rho,\mathrm{p}-2) - \frac{1}{\Gamma(\mathrm{p})}\aleph,
\end{aligned} \tag{17}$$

where

$$\aleph = \int_0^\theta (\theta-\tau)^{\mathrm{p}-1}\tau^{-\rho}d\tau = \int_0^\theta \left(1-\frac{\tau}{\theta}\right)^{\mathrm{p}-1}\theta^{\mathrm{p}-1}\tau^{-\rho}d\tau = \theta^{\theta-\rho}\int_0^\theta \left(1-\frac{\tau}{\theta}\right)^{\mathrm{p}-1}\left(\frac{\tau}{\theta}\right)^{-\rho}\theta d\tau.$$

Using the transformation $v = \tau/\theta$ (hence $\theta dv = d\tau$), the above integral gives rise

$$\aleph = \theta^{\theta-\rho}\int_0^\theta (1-v)^{\mathrm{p}-1}v^{-\rho}dv = \theta^{1-\rho}\beta(1-\rho,\mathrm{p}). \tag{18}$$

From (17) and (18), we conclude

$$\int_0^1 \mathbf{G}(\theta,\tau)\tau^{-\rho}d\tau = \frac{\theta^{\mathrm{p}-1}}{\Gamma(\mathrm{p})}\beta(1-\rho,\mathrm{p}-2) - \frac{\theta^{\mathrm{p}-\rho}}{\Gamma(\mathrm{p})}\beta(1-\rho,\mathrm{p}).$$

Define

$$\mathcal{F}(\theta) := \frac{\beta(1-\rho,\mathrm{p}-2)}{\Gamma(\mathrm{p})}\theta^{\mathrm{p}-1} - \frac{\beta(1-\rho,\mathrm{p})}{\Gamma(\mathrm{p})}\theta^{\mathrm{p}-\rho}$$

Finally, $\mathcal{F}(\theta)$ being increasing on $[0,1]$ yields that

$$\sup_{0\le\theta\le1}\int_0^1 \mathbf{G}(\theta,\tau)\tau^{-\rho}d\tau = \sup_{0\le\theta\le1}\mathcal{F}(\theta) = \mathcal{F}(1) = \frac{1}{\Gamma(\mathrm{p})}[\beta(1-\rho,\mathrm{p}-2) - \beta(1-\rho,\mathrm{p})].$$

□

Lemma 2. *If $\rho \in (0,1)$, then*

$$\int_0^1 \mathbf{H}(\delta,\tau)\tau^{-\rho}d\tau = \frac{(p-1(p-2)}{\Gamma(p)}\left(\delta^{p-3} - \delta^{p-\rho-2}\beta(1-\rho,p-2)\right).$$

Proof. Observe that

$$\int_0^1 \mathbf{H}(\delta,\tau)\tau^{-\rho}d\tau = \int_0^\delta \mathbf{H}(\delta,\tau)\tau^{-\rho}d\tau + \int_\delta^1 \mathbf{H}(\delta,\tau)\tau^{-\rho}d\tau$$
$$= \int_0^\delta \frac{(\mathsf{p}-1)(\mathsf{p}-2)}{\Gamma(\mathsf{p})}\left[\delta^{\mathsf{p}-3}(1-\tau)^{\mathsf{p}-3} - (\delta-\tau)^{\mathsf{p}-3}\right]\tau^{-\rho}d\tau + \int_\delta^1 \frac{(\mathsf{p}-1)(\mathsf{p}-2)}{\Gamma(\mathsf{p})}\delta^{\mathsf{p}-3}(1-\tau)^{\mathsf{p}-3}\tau^{-\rho}d\tau$$
$$= \int_0^1 \frac{(\mathsf{p}-1)(\mathsf{p}-2)}{\Gamma(\mathsf{p})}\delta^{\mathsf{p}-3}(1-\tau)^{\mathsf{p}-3}\tau^{-\rho}d\tau - \int_0^\delta \frac{(\mathsf{p}-1)(\mathsf{p}-2)}{\Gamma(\mathsf{p})}(\delta-\tau)^{\mathsf{p}-3}\tau^{-\rho}d\tau$$
$$= \frac{(\mathsf{p}-1)(\mathsf{p}-2)}{\Gamma(\mathsf{p})}\delta^{\mathsf{p}-3}\int_0^1 (1-\tau)^{\mathsf{p}-1}\tau^{-\rho}d\tau$$
$$- \frac{(\mathsf{p}-1)(\mathsf{p}-2)}{\Gamma(\mathsf{p})}\int_0^\delta (\delta-\tau)^{\mathsf{p}-3}\tau^{-\rho}d\tau$$
$$= \frac{(\mathsf{p}-1)(\mathsf{p}-2)}{\Gamma(\mathsf{p})}\delta^{\mathsf{p}-3}\beta(1-\rho,\mathsf{p}-2) - \frac{(\mathsf{p}-1)(\mathsf{p}-2)}{\Gamma(\mathsf{p})}\int_0^\delta (\delta-\tau)^{\mathsf{p}-3}\tau^{-\rho}d\tau.$$

Like the proof of Lemma 1, we attain

$$\begin{aligned}\int_0^1 \mathbf{H}(\delta,\tau)\tau^{-\rho}d\tau &= \frac{(\mathsf{p}-1)(\mathsf{p}-2)}{\Gamma(\mathsf{p})}\delta^{\mathsf{p}-3}\beta(1-\rho,\mathsf{p}-2)\\ &- \frac{(\mathsf{p}-1)(\mathsf{p}-2)}{\Gamma(\mathsf{p})}\delta^{\mathsf{p}-\rho-2}\beta(1-\rho,\mathsf{p}-2)\\ &= \frac{(\mathsf{p}-1)(\mathsf{p}-2)}{\Gamma(\mathsf{p})}(\delta^{\mathsf{p}-3}-\delta^{\mathsf{p}-\rho-2})\beta(1-\rho,\mathsf{p}-2).\end{aligned}$$

□

Remark 2. *Define*

$$\mu := \frac{1}{\Gamma(p)}\left[\left(1+\frac{\beta(\delta^{p-3}-\delta^{p-\rho-2})}{1-\beta\delta^{p-3}}\right)\beta(1-\rho,p-2) - \beta(1-\rho,p)\right].$$

Lastly, we will prove the prime outcomes.

Theorem 6. *Assume that the BVP (15) verifies above presumptions. Also, let $0 < \rho < 1$ and $\theta^\rho\hbar(\theta,\tau)$ be continuous. If $\exists\,\lambda \in (0, 1/\mu]$ and $\Phi \in \Gamma$ with*

$$\tau_1 \geq \tau_2 \geq 0 \text{ and } 0 \leq \theta \leq 1 \Longrightarrow 0 \leq \theta^\rho[\hbar(\theta,\tau_1) - \hbar(\theta,\tau_2)] \leq \lambda\Phi(\tau_1-\tau_2), \tag{19}$$

then BVP (15) admits a unique solution.

Proof. On $C[0,1]$, equip the following metric:

$$\varpi(v,w) = \sup_{0\leq\theta\leq 1}|v(\theta)-w(\theta)|.$$

Let

$$\mathbf{V} = \{v \in C[0,1] : v(\theta) \geq 0\}.$$

On $\mathbf{V}$, define a BR $\mathbf{S}$ and a self-map $\mathcal{P}$ given below:

$$\mathbf{S} = \{(v,w) \in \mathbf{V}^2 : v(\theta) \leq w(\theta), \text{ for each } \theta \in [0,1]\};$$

and

$$(\mathcal{P}v)(\theta) = \int_0^1 \mathbf{G}(\theta,\tau)\hbar(\tau,v(\tau))d\tau + \frac{q\theta^{\mathsf{p}-1}}{(\mathsf{p}-1)(\mathsf{p}-2)(1-q\delta^{\mathsf{p}-3})}\int_0^1 \mathbf{H}(\delta,\tau)\hbar(\tau,v(\tau))d\tau. \tag{20}$$

(*a*) Clearly, $(\mathbf{V},\varpi)$ remains $\mathbf{S}$-complete MS.

(*b*) Assume that $\mathbf{0}\in\mathbf{V}$ is a zero function. Then for each $\theta\in[0,1]$, we conclude $\mathbf{0}(\theta)\leq(\mathcal{P}\mathbf{0})(\theta)$ so that $(\mathbf{0},\mathcal{P}\mathbf{0})\in\mathbf{S}$.

(*c*) Clearly $\mathbf{S}$ being transitive is locally $\mathcal{P}$-transitive. Take $(v,w)\in\mathbf{S}$ implying $v(\theta)\leq w(\theta)$, for every $\theta\in[0,1]$. Hence, we conclude

$$\begin{aligned}(\mathcal{P}v)(\theta) &= \int_0^1 \mathbf{G}(\theta,\tau)\hbar(\tau,v(\tau))d\tau + \frac{q\theta^{\mathsf{p}-1}}{(\mathsf{p}-1)(\mathsf{p}-2)(1-q\delta^{\mathsf{p}-3})}\int_0^1 \mathbf{H}(\delta,\tau)\hbar(\tau,v(\tau))d\tau.\\ &= \int_0^1 \mathbf{G}(\theta,\tau)\tau^{-\rho}\tau^{\rho}\hbar(x,v(\tau))d\tau\\ &+ \frac{q\theta^{\mathsf{p}-1}}{(\mathsf{p}-1)(\mathsf{p}-2)(1-q\delta^{\mathsf{p}-3})}\int_0^1 \mathbf{H}(\delta,\tau)\tau^{-\rho}\tau^{\rho}\hbar(\tau,v(\tau))d\tau\\ &\leq \int_0^1 \mathbf{G}(\theta,\tau)\tau^{-\rho}\tau^{\rho}\hbar(\tau,w(\tau))d\tau\\ &+ \frac{q\theta^{\mathsf{p}-1}}{(\mathsf{p}-1)(\mathsf{p}-2)(1-q\delta^{\mathsf{p}-3})}\int_0^1 \mathbf{H}(\delta,\tau)\tau^{-\rho}\tau^{\rho}\hbar(\tau,w(\tau))d\tau\\ &= \int_0^1 \mathbf{G}(\theta,\tau)\hbar(\tau,w(\tau))d\tau + \frac{q^{\mathsf{p}-1}}{(\mathsf{p}-1)(\mathsf{p}-2)(1-q\delta^{\mathsf{p}-3})}\int_0^1 \mathbf{H}(\delta,\tau)\hbar(\tau,w(\tau))d\tau\\ &= (\mathcal{P}w)(\theta)\end{aligned}$$

yielding $(\mathcal{P}v,\mathcal{P}w)\in\mathbf{S}$. Therefore, $\mathbf{S}$ is $\mathcal{P}$-closed.

(*d*) We will confirm that $\mathbf{S}$ is ϖ-self-closed. Assume $\{v_n\}\subset\mathbf{V}$ ensuring $v_{\mathsf{n}}\to v$ and $(v_{\mathsf{n}},v_{\mathsf{n}+1})\in\mathbf{S}$, $\forall\,\mathsf{n}\in\mathbb{N}$. Then, $\{v_n(\theta)\}$ (where $\theta\in[0,1]$,) is increasing real sequence converging to $v(\theta)$; thereby, to each $n\in\mathbb{N}$, we obtain $v_n(\theta)\leq v(\theta)$. Thus, $(v_n,v)\in\mathbf{S}$, $\forall\,n\in\mathbb{N}$.

(*f*) For $(v,w)\in\mathbf{S}$, we have

$$\begin{aligned}\varpi(\mathcal{P}v,\mathcal{P}w) &= \sup_{0\leq\theta\leq1}|(\mathcal{P}v)(\theta)-(\mathcal{P}w)(\theta)| = \sup_{0\leq\theta\leq1}[(\mathcal{P}w)(\theta)-(\mathcal{P}v)(\theta)]\\ &= \sup_{0\leq\theta\leq1}\Bigg[\int_0^1 \mathbf{G}(\theta,\tau)(\hbar(\tau,w(\tau))-\hbar(\tau,v(\tau)))\,d\tau\\ &+ \frac{q\theta^{\mathsf{p}-1}}{(\mathsf{p}-1)(\mathsf{p}-2)(1-q\delta^{\mathsf{p}-3})}\int_0^1 \mathbf{H}(\delta,\tau)(\hbar(\tau,w(\tau))-\hbar(\tau,v)(\tau))d\tau\Bigg]\\ &\leq \sup_{0\leq\theta\leq1}\int_0^1 \mathbf{G}(\theta,\tau)\tau^{-\rho}\tau^{\rho}[\hbar(\tau,w(\tau))-\hbar(\tau,v(\tau))]d\tau\\ &+ \frac{q}{(\mathsf{p}-1)(\mathsf{p}-2)(1-q\delta^{\mathsf{p}-3})}\int_0^1 \mathbf{H}(\delta,\tau)\tau^{-\rho}\tau^{\rho}[\hbar(\tau,w(\tau))-\hbar(\tau,v)(\tau)]d\tau\\ &\leq \sup\int_0^1 \mathbf{G}(\theta,\tau)\tau^{-\rho}\lambda\Phi(w(\tau)-v(\tau))d\tau\\ &+ \frac{q}{(\mathsf{p}-1)(\mathsf{p}-2)(1-q\delta^{\mathsf{p}-3})}\int_0^1 \mathbf{H}(\delta,\tau)\tau^{-\rho}\lambda\Phi(w(\tau))-v(\tau)d\tau.\end{aligned}$$

By the monotonic property of Φ, the above inequality becomes

$$\begin{aligned}\varpi(\mathcal{P}v,\mathcal{P}w) \leq{}& \lambda\Phi(\varpi(v,w)) \sup_{0\leq\theta\leq 0}\int_0^1 \mathbf{G}(\theta,\tau)\tau^{-\rho}d\tau \\ &+ \frac{q}{(\mathrm{p}-1)(\mathrm{p}-2)(1-q\delta\mathrm{p}-3)}\lambda\Phi(\varpi(w,v))\int_0^1 \mathbf{H}(\delta,\tau)\tau^{\rho}d\tau \\ ={}& \lambda\Phi(\varpi(v,w))\left[\sup_{0\leq\theta\leq 0}\int_0^1 \mathbf{G}(\theta,\tau)\tau^{-\rho}d\tau\right. \\ &\left.+\frac{q}{(\mathrm{p}-1)(\mathrm{p}-2)(1-q\delta^{\mathrm{p}-3})}\int_0^1 \mathbf{H}(\delta,\tau)\tau^{-\rho}d\tau\right]. \end{aligned} \tag{21}$$

Using Lemmas 1 and 2, (21) reduces to

$$\begin{aligned}\varpi(\mathcal{P}v,\mathcal{P}w) \leq{}&\lambda\Phi(\varpi(v,w))\left[\frac{1}{\Gamma(\mathrm{p})}(\beta(1-\rho,\mathrm{p}-2)-\beta(1-\rho\mathrm{p}))+\frac{q}{(\mathrm{p}-1)(\mathrm{p}-2)(1-q\delta^{\mathrm{p}-3})}\right. \\ &\left.\times\frac{(\mathrm{p}-1)(\mathrm{p}-2)}{\Gamma(\mathrm{p})}\left(\delta^{\mathrm{p}-3}-\delta^{\mathrm{p}-\rho-2}\right)\right] \\ ={}& \lambda\Phi(\varpi(v,w))\left[\frac{1}{\Gamma(\mathrm{p})}(\beta(1-\rho,\mathrm{p}-2)-\beta(1-\rho,\mathrm{p}))\right. \\ &\left.+\frac{q(\delta^{\mathrm{p}-3}-\delta^{\mathrm{p}-\rho-2})}{(1-q\delta^{\mathrm{p}-3})\Gamma(\mathrm{p})}\beta(1-\rho,\mathrm{p}-2)\right] \\ ={}& \lambda\Phi(\varpi(v,w))\left[\frac{1}{\Gamma(\mathrm{p})}\left[\left(1+\frac{q(\delta^{\mathrm{p}-3}-\delta^{\mathrm{p}-\rho-2})}{1-q-q\delta^{\mathrm{p}-3}}\right)\beta(1-\rho,\mathrm{p}-2)-\beta(1-\rho,\mathrm{p})\right]\right] \\ ={}& \lambda\Phi(\varpi(v,w))\mu. \end{aligned}$$

As $0<\lambda\leq 1/\mu$, the above inequality reduces to

$$\varpi(\mathcal{P}v,\mathcal{P}w) \leq \lambda\Phi(\varpi(v,w))\mu \leq \Phi(\varpi(v,w))$$

yielding thereby

$$\varpi(\mathcal{P}\mathrm{z},\mathcal{P}\mathrm{w}) \leq \Phi(\varpi(\mathrm{z},\mathrm{w}))+\min\{\varrho(\varpi(\mathrm{w},\mathcal{P}\mathrm{z})),\varrho(\varpi(\mathrm{z},\mathcal{P}\mathrm{w})),\varrho(\varpi(\mathrm{z},\mathcal{P}\mathrm{z})),\varrho(\varpi(\mathrm{w},\mathcal{P}\mathrm{w}))\},$$

for every arbitrary choice of $\varrho\in\Omega$.

(g) For every pair $v,w\in\mathcal{P}(\mathbf{V})$, set $u:=\max\{v,w\}\in\mathbf{V}$. So, we find $(v,u)\in\mathbf{S}$ and $(w,u)\in\mathbf{S}$. Hence, $\mathcal{P}(\mathbf{V})$ is $\mathbf{S}^s$-directed.

Therefore, using Theorem 5, $\mathcal{P}$ owns a unique fixed point, which (owing to (16) and (20)) solves (15). □

Theorem 7. *Along-with the conditions of Theorem 6, BVP* (15) *admits a (unique) positive solution.*

Proof. Applying Theorem 6, assume that $\hat{\varpi}\in\mathbf{V}$ serves as the unique solution of (15). Since $\hat{\varpi}\in\mathbf{V}$, therefore, we attain $\hat{\varpi}(\theta)\geq 0$, $\forall\,\theta\in[0,1]$. It follows that the (unique) solution $\hat{\varpi}$ remains non-negative. We will prove that $\hat{\varpi}$ is positive, i.e., $\mathrm{p}(\mathrm{s})>0$, to each $\mathrm{s}\in(0,1)$. If there is a some $\theta^*\in(0,1)$ such that $\hat{\varpi}(\theta^*)=0$, then using (16), we obtain

$$\hat{\varpi}(\theta^*)=\int_0^1 \mathbf{G}(\theta^*,\tau)\hbar(\tau,\hat{\varpi}(\tau))d\tau+\frac{q\theta^{*\mathrm{p}-1}}{(\mathrm{p}-1)(\mathrm{p}-2)(1-q\delta^{\mathrm{p}-3})}\int_0^1 \mathbf{H}(\delta,\tau)\hbar(\tau,x(\tau))d\tau=0.$$

As $\hbar$ is non-negative, owing to Proposition 5, the two terms involved in RHS are non-negative. Thus, we conclude

$$\int_0^1 \mathbf{G}(\theta^*,\tau)\hbar(\tau,\hat{w}(\tau))d\tau = 0,$$
$$\int_0^1 \mathbf{H}(\delta,\tau)\hbar(\tau,\tau(\tau))d\tau = 0,$$

so that

$$\begin{cases} \mathbf{G}(\theta^*,\tau)\hbar(\tau,\hat{w}(\tau)) = 0, & a.e.\ (\tau), \\ \mathbf{H}(\delta,\tau)\hbar(\tau,\hat{w}(\tau)) = 0, & a.e\ (\tau). \end{cases} \tag{22}$$

Let $\kappa > 0$ be arbitrary. The singular property of $\hbar$ yields the existence of $R > 0$ with $\hbar(\tau,0) > \kappa, \forall\, \tau \in [0,1] \cap (0,R)$. Now, we have

$$[0,1] \cap (0,R) \subset \{\tau \in [0,1] : \hbar(\tau,\hat{w}(\tau)) > \kappa\},$$

and

$$\Lambda([0,1] \cap (0,R)) > 0,$$

where Λ is a Lebesque measure. Therefore, (22) implies that

$$\begin{cases} \mathbf{G}(\theta^*,\tau) = 0, & a.e.\ (\tau), \\ \mathbf{H}(\delta,\tau) = 0, & a.e.\ (\tau), \end{cases}$$

which contradicts the rationality of the functions $\mathbf{G}(\theta^*,\cdot)$ and $\mathbf{H}(\delta,\cdot)$. This concludes the proof. □

7. Conclusions and Future Directions

We have demonstrated the validity of fixed points and their uniqueness for a relation-theoretic almost Matkowski contraction of Pant type. Our outcomes expanded and unified a few known fixed-point findings. The contraction conditions in our investigations are imposed to the comparative elements only. To corroborate these findings, we presented a few examples. We also filled out an application to certain singular FDE to emphasize the worth of the theory and the depth of our findings.

As some possible future works, the readers can generalize our outcomes in the following ways:

1. To vary the features of auxiliary functions Φ and ϱ;
2. To enhance our findings over symmetric space, quasimetric space, cone MS, fuzzy MS, etc., composed with a BR;
3. To improve our finding for two maps by investigating common fixed-point findings;
4. To apply our finding in the area of nonlinear integral equations instead of fractional BVP.

Author Contributions: Conceptualization, D.F., F.A.K. and E.A.; Methodology, A.A. and F.M.A.; Formal analysis, M.S.A.; Investigation, F.M.A.; Resources, D.F., A.A. and M.S.A.; Writing—original draft, D.F., F.A.K. and F.M.A.; Writing—review and editing, A.A., E.A. and M.S.A.; Funding acquisition, D.F., E.A. and F.M.A.; Supervision, F.A.K. The earlier draft of the article is thoroughly examined and endorsed by all authors. All authors have read and agreed to the published version of the manuscript.

Funding: The first author acknowledges the Princess Nourah bint Abdulrahman University Researchers Supporting Project Number (PNURSP2025R174), Princess Nourah bint Abdulrahman University, Riyadh, Saudi Arabia.

Data Availability Statement: This paper contains the data produced during the current investigation. By an adequate request, further details can be accessed directly from corresponding authors.

Conflicts of Interest: Authors affirm that they possess no competing interests.

Notations and Abbreviations

The following acronyms and symbols were utilized in this assessment.

$\mathbb{R}^+$	the set of non-negative real numbers
$\mathbb{R}$	the set of real numbers
$\mathbb{N}$	the set of natural numbers
BR	binary relation
FDE	fractional differential equation(s)
BCP	Banach contraction principle
BVP	boundary value problems
MS	metric space
CMS	complete metric space
RHS	right hand side
iff	if and only if
$\mathcal{C}(A;B)$	the collection of all continuous functions from a set A to a set B.

References

1. Podlubny, I. *Fractional Differential Equations*, 1st ed.; Academic Press: San Diego, CA, USA, 1998; 340p.
2. Daftardar-Gejji, V. *Fractional Calculus and Fractional Differential Equations*; Springer: Singapore, 2019; 180p.
3. Kilbas, A.A.; Srivastava, H.M.; Trujillo, J.J. *Theory and Applications of Fractional Differential Equations*; North-Holland Mathematics Studies; Elsevier Science B.V.: Amsterdam, The Netherlands, 2006; Volume 204, pp. 1–523.
4. Cevikel, A.C.; Aksoy, E. Soliton solutions of nonlinear fractional differential equations with their applications in mathematical physics. *Rev. Mexicana Fís.* **2021**, *67*, 422–428. [CrossRef]
5. Aljethi, R.A.; Kiliçman, A. Analysis of fractional differential equation and its application to realistic data. *Chaos Solitons Fractals* **2023**, *171*, 113446. [CrossRef]
6. Zhou, X.; Wu, W.; Ma, H. A contraction fixed point theorem in partially ordered metric spaces and application to fractional differential equations. *Abstr. Appl. Anal.* **2012**, *2012*, 856302. [CrossRef]
7. Zhai, C.; Hao, M. Fixed point theorems for mixed monotone operators with perturbation and applications to fractional differential equation boundary value problems. *Nonlinear Anal.* **2012**, *75*, 2542–2551. [CrossRef]
8. Liang, S.; Zhang, J. Existence and uniqueness of strictly nondecreasing and positive solution for a fractional three-point boundary value problem. *Comput. Math. Appl.* **2011**, *62*, 1333–1340. [CrossRef]
9. Cabrera, I.J.; Harjani, J.; Sadarangani, K.B. Existence and uniqueness of positive solutions for a singular fractional three-point boundary value problem. *Abstr. Appl. Anal.* **2012**, *2012*, 803417. [CrossRef]
10. Karapınar, E.; Fulga, A.; Rashid, M.; Shahid, L.; Aydi, H. Large contractions on quasi-metric spaces with an application to nonlinear fractional differential equations. *Mathematics* **2019**, *7*, 444. [CrossRef]
11. Abdou, A.A.N. Solving a nonlinear fractional differential equation using fixed point results in orthogonal metric spaces. *Fractal Fract.* **2023**, *7*, 817. [CrossRef]
12. Browder, F.E. On the convergence of successive approximations for nonlinear functional equations. *Proc. K. Ned. Akad. Wet. Ser. A Indag. Math.* **1968**, *71*, 27–35. [CrossRef]
13. Matkowski, J. Integrable solutions of functional equations. *Diss. Math.* **1975**, *127*, 68.
14. Pant, R.P. Extended contraction mappings. *Filomat* **2024**, *38*, 1987–1990. [CrossRef]
15. Pant, R.P. Extended Φ-contraction mappings. *J. Anal.* **2024**, *32*, 1661–1670. [CrossRef]
16. Alam, A.; Imdad, M. Relation-theoretic contraction principle. *J. Fixed Point Theory Appl.* **2015**, *17*, 693–702. [CrossRef]
17. Alam, A.; Imdad, M. Relation-theoretic metrical coincidence theorems. *Filomat* **2017**, *31*, 4421–4439. [CrossRef]

18. Alam, A.; Imdad, M. Nonlinear contractions in metric spaces under locally T-transitive binary relations. *Fixed Point Theory* **2018**, *19*, 13–24. [CrossRef]
19. Arif, M.; Imdad, M.; Alam, A. Fixed point theorems under locally T-transitive binary relations employing Matkowski contractions. *Miskolc Math. Notes* **2022**, *23*, 71–83. [CrossRef]
20. Filali, D.; Khan, F.A. Relational strict almost contractions employing test functions and an application to nonlinear integral equations. *Mathematics* **2024**, *12*, 3262. [CrossRef]
21. Alamer, A.; Eljaneid, N.H.E.; Aldhabani, M.S.; Altaweel, N.H.; Khan, F.A. Geraghty type Contractions in relational metric space with applications to fractional differential equations. *Fractal Fract.* **2023**, *7*, 565. [CrossRef]
22. Khan, F.A.; Eljaneid, N.H.E.; Alamer, A.; Alshaban, E.; Alamrani, F.M.; Alatawi, A. Matkowski-type functional contractions under locally transitive binary relations and applications to singular fractional differential equations. *Fractal Fract.* **2024**, *8*, 72. [CrossRef]
23. Berinde, V. Approximating fixed points of weak contractions using the Picard iteration. *Nonlinear Anal. Forum.* **2004**, *9*, 43–53.
24. Babu, G.V.R.; Sandhy, M.L.; Kameshwari, M.V.R. A note on a fixed point theorem of Berinde on weak contractions. *Carpathian J. Math.* **2008**, *24*, 8–12.
25. Berinde, V.; Păcurar, M. Fixed points and continuity of almost contractions. *Fixed Point Theory* **2008**, *9*, 23–34.
26. Berinde, V. Approximating fixed points of weak ϕ-contractions using the Picard iteration. *Fixed Point Theory* **2003**, *4*, 131–142.
27. Turinici, M. Weakly contractive maps in altering metric spaces. *ROMAI J.* **2013**, *9*, 175–183.
28. Alfuraidan, M.R.; Bachar, M.; Khamsi, M.A. Almost monotone contractions on weighted graphs. *J. Nonlinear Sci. Appl.* **2016**, *9*, 5189–5195. [CrossRef]
29. Khan, F.A. Almost contractions under binary relations. *Axioms* **2022**, *11*, 441. [CrossRef]
30. Filali, D.; Eljaneid, N.H.E.; Alharbi, A.F.; Alshaban, E.; Khan, F.A.; Alruwaytie, M.Z. Solution of certain periodic boundary value problem in relational metric space via relational almost φ-contractions. *J. Appl. Anal. Comput.* **2025**, *15*, 1272–1283.
31. Alshaban, E.; Alatawi, A.; Alamrani, F.M.; Alamer, A.; Alrshidi, N.N.; Khan, F.A. Nonlinear almost contractions of Pant type under binary relations with an application to boundary value problems. *Mathematics* **2025**, *13*, 906. [CrossRef]
32. Rus, I.A. *Generalized Contractions and Applications;* Cluj University Press: Cluj-Napoca, Romania, 2001.
33. Lipschutz, S. *Schaum's Outlines of Theory and Problems of Set Theory and Related Topics;* McGraw-Hill: New York, NY, USA, 1964.
34. Samet, B.; Turinici, M. Fixed point theorems on a metric space endowed with an arbitrary binary relation and applications. *Commun. Math. Anal.* **2012**, *13*, 82–97.

fractal and fractional

MDPI

Article

A Short Note on Fractal Interpolation in the Space of Convex Lipschitz Functions

Fatin Gota and Peter Massopust *

Department of Mathematics, Technical University of Munich, Boltzmannstr. 3, 85747 Munich, Germany; fatingota1@hotmail.com
* Correspondence: massopust@ma.tum.de

Abstract: In this short note, we consider fractal interpolation in the Banach space $V^\theta(I)$ of convex Lipschitz functions defined on a compact interval $I \subset \mathbb{R}$. To this end, we define an appropriate iterated function system and exhibit the associated Read–Bajraktarević operator T. We derive conditions for which T becomes a Ratkotch contraction on a closed subspace of $V^\theta(I)$, thus establishing the existence of fractal functions of class $V^\theta(I)$. An example illustrates the theoretical findings.

Keywords: iterated function system (IFS); fractal interpolation; Read–Bajraktarević operator; Rakotch contraction; convex Lipschitz function

1. Introduction

Over the last few decades, the theory of fractal interpolation has been employed successfully to describe and model highly non-smooth functions naturally found in numerous applied situations. One of the main purposes of fractal interpolation or approximation is to describe intrinsically occurring complex geometric self-referential structures and to employ approximants that are well suited to be adapted to these types of structures. Usually, the approximants or interpolants belong to certain Banach spaces; see, for instance, reference [1] for a discussion of these issues in a (slightly) more general setting.

Many results in fractal interpolation come from the use of the Banach fixed point theorem, but recently, more general contraction-type results yielding a unique fixed point have been studied. Cf., for instance, references [2–6] for an albeit incomplete list of recent references. In [7], a review of such results is given in a convenient overall framework.

In this short note, we consider fractal interpolation in the Banach space of convex Lipschitz function using Rakotch contractions. Convex Lipschitz functions were introduced in [8] and play an important role in, for instance, optimization theory [9].

The organization of this paper is as follows. Section 2, introduces the fixed point theorems that are used in the sequel. Fractal interpolation is briefly presented in Section 3, and in Section 4, convex Lipschitz functions are introduced. In the final Section 5, the main result, namely fractal interpolation in the Banach space of convex Lipschitz functions, is discussed and the main theorem, namely the existence of fractal functions of class $V^\theta(I)$, is proven.

Throughout this paper, the following notations are employed: $\mathbb{N}$ denotes the set of positive integers; $\mathbb{N}_0$ is the set of non-negative integers; and $\mathbb{N}_n := \{1, \ldots, n\}$ and $\mathbb{N}_{0,n} := \{0, 1, \ldots, n\}$ are initial segments of $\mathbb{N}$ and $\mathbb{N}_0$, respectively.

2. Some Important Theorems in Fixed Point Theory

Undoubtedly, one of the most important theorems in fixed point theory is the Banach contraction principle proven by Stefen Banach in 1922. The immense applicability of this results lies in the existence of a unique fixed point of a contractive mapping $f : X \to X$, where (X, d) is a complete metric space. Numerous other contractive mappings have been introduced and studied over the last few decades. For a comparison of these generalized contractions, the interested reader may consult [10].

In this section, we introduce the Banach, the Rakotch, and the Matkowski fixed point theorem, with the later two being a generalization of the first.

Definition 1. *Let (X, d) be a complete metric space and let $f : X \to X$ be a map. If there exists a $\beta \in [0, 1)$ such that for all $x, y \in X$,*

$$d(f(x), f(y)) \leq \beta\, d(x, y), \tag{1}$$

then the map f is called a (d-)Banach contraction on X.

Theorem 1 (Banach Fixed Point Theorem). *Assume that (X, d) is a complete metric space and $f : X \to X$ is a contractive map in the sense of (1). Then, f has a unique fixed point.*

A more general contraction mapping is the following introduced in [11].

Definition 2 (Rakotch Contraction). *Let $\psi : [0, \infty) \to [0, \infty)$ be a map such that for all $t > 0$, we have $0 \leq \psi(t) < 1$ and $\psi(t)$ is non-increasing. If there exists a map $f : X \to X$ such thatthen f is called a ψ-Rakotch contraction or, when the map ψ is clear from the context, just a Rakotch contraction.*

Note that setting ψ = constant shows that every Banach contraction is a Rakotch contraction.

In the following, we also use an equivalent definition of Rakotch contraction presented in the theorem below. For a reference, see [4], p. 963.

Theorem 2 (Equivalent Definitions for Rakotch Contraction). *Let (X, d) be a complete metric space and $f : X \to X$ a map. Then, the following two definitions of Rakotch contractions are equivalent:*

1. *(a) There exists a $\psi : [0, \infty) \to [0, \infty)$;*
   - *(b)* $0 \leq \psi(t) < 1, \forall t > 0;$
   - *(c)* *ψ is non-increasing;*
   - *(d)* $d(f(x), f(y)) \leq \psi(d(x, y))\, d(x, y), \forall x, y \in X.$
2. *(a) There exists a non-decreasing $\tau : (0, \infty) \to (0, \infty)$;*
   - *(b)* $\tau(t) < t, \forall t > 0;$
   - *(c)* *The map $\frac{\tau(t)}{t}$ is non-increasing, $\forall t > 0$;*
   - *(d)* $d(f(x), f(y)) \leq \tau(d(x, y)), \forall x, y \in X.$

The next theorem whose proof can be found in [11] shows that a ψ-Rakotch contraction has a unique fixed point.

Theorem 3. *Let (X, d) be a complete metric space and $f : X \to X$ a ψ-Rakotch contraction. Then, f has a unique fixed point.*

Not every Banach contraction is a Rakotch contraction. The following example demonstrates this (see, also, reference [4]). Let $X := [0, \infty)$ and $f : X \to X$ be given by $f(x) := (1+x)^{-1}$. Then, using the usual metric d on $\mathbb{R}$ restricted to X, one has

$$d(f(x), f(y)) \le \psi(d(x,y))\, d(x,y),$$

where $\psi(t) := (1+t)^{-1}$. Hence, f is a Rakotch contraction but not a Banach (d-)contraction on $X \subset \mathbb{R}$.

Definition 3 (Matkowski Contraction [12]). *Let $\phi : \mathbb{R}^+ \to \mathbb{R}^+$ be a non-decreasing map such that for all $t > 0$, we have $\lim\limits_{n\to\infty} \phi^n(t) = 0$. If the map $f : X \to X$ satisfies*

$$d(f(x), f(y)) \le \phi(d(x,y)), \quad \textit{for all } x, y \in X,$$

then f is called a ϕ-Matkowski contraction or, when the map ϕ is clear from the context, just a Matkowski contraction.

For Matkowski contractions, we have the following result (see, e.g., [13]).

Theorem 4. *Let (X, d) be a complete metric space and $f : X \to X$ be a ϕ-Matkowski contraction. Then, the following properties hold:*

(i) For all $t > 0$, $\phi(t) < t$;
(ii) The map f is continuous;
(iii) The map f has a unique fixed point.

3. Fractal Interpolation

In this section, we give a very brief and compact introduction to iterated function systems, fractals, and fractal interpolation. The interested reader can find more details about these concepts in [14–17] and the references given therein.

Let (X, d) be a complete metric. Let $N > 1$ be an integer and, for $i \in \mathbb{N}_N$, consider Banach contractions $f_i : X \to X$. The collection $\{X; f_1, \dots, f_N\}$ is called an iterated function system (IFS) on X. Further, the collection of all nonempty compact subsets of X is denoted by $\mathcal{H}(X)$ and the Hausdorff–Pompeiu metric on $\mathcal{H}(X)$ is denoted by h_d, which are defined by

$$h_d(A, B) := \max\left\{ \max_{x\in A}\min_{y\in B} d(x,y),\ \max_{y\in B}\min_{x\in A} d(x,y) \right\}, \quad \forall A, B \in \mathcal{H}(X).$$

It is known that the completeness of (X, d) implies the completeness of $(\mathcal{H}(X), h_d)$. Define a set-valued mapping $\mathcal{F} : \mathcal{H}(X) \to \mathcal{H}(X)$ by

$$\mathcal{F}(E) := \bigcup_{i=1}^{N} f_i(E).$$

Then, $\mathcal{F}$ is contractive on $\mathcal{H}(X)$ with Lipschitz constant $\mathrm{Lip}\mathcal{F} := \max\{\mathrm{Lip} f_i : i \in \mathbb{N}_N\}$. Here, $\mathrm{Lip} f$ of a mapping $f : X \to X$ is defined by

$$\mathrm{Lip} f := \sup_{x,y\in X,\, x\neq y} \frac{d(f(x), f(y))}{d(x,y)}.$$

Hence, by the Banach fixed point theorem, there exists a unique $A \in \mathcal{H}(X)$, called the attractor of the IFS, such that $\mathcal{F}(A) = A$ or, equivalently,

$$A = \bigcup_{i=1}^{N} f_i(A).$$

This latter equation reflects the fact that the attractor A is self-referential, and thus, in general, a fractal set.

Next, we consider a special class of IFSs, namely those whose attractors are graphs of continuous functions passing through a prescribed set of interpolation points. Such functions are termed fractal interpolation functions (FIFs) and were first introduced in [14,16].

For this purpose, let $I := [x_0, x_N] \subset \mathbb{R}$, where N is an integer greater than one. Further, let $\Delta := \{(x_i, y_i) \in I \times \mathbb{R} : i \in \mathbb{N}_{0,N}\}$ be a given set of interpolation points with $x_0 < x_1 < \ldots < x_N$.

Define subintervals $I_i := [x_{i-1}, x_i]$ of I and contractive homeomorphisms $l_i : I \to I_i$, $i \in \mathbb{N}_N$, such that

$$l_i(x_0) = x_{i-1}, \quad l_i(x_N) = x_i, \tag{2}$$

and

$$|l_i(x) - l_i(x')| \leq a_i |x - x'|, \quad \text{for all } x, x' \in I \text{ and } 0 \leq a_i < 1.$$

Furthermore, let $K := I \times [a, b]$ where $a < b$ are finite numbers with $y_0, y_1, \ldots, y_N \in [a, b]$. Thus, $\Delta = \{(x_0, y_0), \ldots, (x_N, y_N)\} \subset K$. In addition, we require continuous maps $F_i : K \to [a, b]$ with the property that

$$F_i(x_0, y_0) = y_{i-1} \quad \text{and} \quad F_i(x_N, y_N) = y_i, \quad i \in \mathbb{N}_N.$$

Finally, define maps

$$w_i : K \to K,$$
$$w_i(x, y) := (l_i(x), F_i(x, y)).$$

If $G \in \mathcal{H}(K)$ is the (unique) attractor of the IFS $\{K; w_1, \ldots, w_n\}$ and also the graph of a continuous function $f : I \to [a, b]$ satisfying

$$f(x_i) = y_i, \quad i \in \mathbb{N}_{0,N},$$

then f is called a fractal interpolation function (FIF) as it passes through the interpolation points $\Delta := \{(x_i, y_i) : i \in \mathbb{N}_{0,N}\}$. This is, for instance, the case when for some $M \geq 0$ and $s \in [0, 1)$, each F_i satisfies

$$|F_i(x, y) - F_i(x', y')| \leq M|x - x'| + s|y - y'|, \tag{3}$$

for all $x, x' \in I$ and $y, y' \in [a, b]$.

A different approach to FIFs is given as follows. (Cf., for instance, [17].) To this end, define

$$C(I) := \{g : I \to [a, b] : g \text{ continuous}\},$$
$$C^*(I) := \{g \in C(I) : g(x_0) = y_0, g(x_N) = y_N\},$$
$$C^{**}(I) := \{g \in C^*(I) : g(x_i) = y_i, i \in \mathbb{N}_{N-1}\}.$$

When endowed with the norm $\| g \|_\infty^I := \sup\{|g(x)| : x \in I\}$, the spaces $\left(C(I), \| \cdot \|_\infty^I\right)$, $\left(C(I)^*, \| \cdot \|_\infty^I\right)$, and $\left(C(I)^{**}, \| \cdot \|_\infty^I\right)$ all become complete metric spaces.

Define the following operator, called a Read–Bajractarević (RB) operator:

$$
\begin{aligned}
&T : C^*(I) \to C(I), \\
&Tf(x) := F_i\left(l_i^{-1}(x), f\left(l_i^{-1}(x)\right)\right), \quad \text{for } x \in [x_{i-1}, x_i] \text{ and } i \in \mathbb{N}_N.
\end{aligned}
\tag{4}
$$

Lemma 1 ([18]). *For all $f \in C^*(I)$, $Tf \in C^{**}(I)$. Consequently, $T : C^*(I) \to C^{**}(I)$ and $T^n := \underbrace{T \circ \cdots \circ T}_{n-\text{times}} : C^{**}(I) \to C^{**}(I)$, for all integers $n \geq 2$.*

If the maps F_i in (4) satisfy condition (3), then T has a unique fixed point f^* in $C^*(I)$ and by Lemma (1), $f^* = Tf^* \in C^{**}(I)$. Hence, f^* interpolates the data set Δ. Moreover, the fixed point f^* satisfies the self-referential equation

$$
f^*(x) = F_i\left(l_i^{-1}(x), f^*\left(l_i^{-1}(x)\right)\right), \quad \text{for } x \in l_i(I) = [x_{i-1}, x_i], \quad i \in \mathbb{N}_N.
$$

It is worthwhile to point out that such fractal functions can also be constructed using more general contractivity conditions than (3); see, for instance, [4] for one of the first such constructions.

4. Convex Lipschitz Functions

In this section, we consider convex Lipschitz functions and prove that under a certain norm, they form a Banach space.

Definition 4 ([8]). *Let $\theta : \mathbb{R}^+ \to \mathbb{R}^+$ and let $f : [x_0, x_N] \to \mathbb{R}$. If there exists a constant M such that for $x_0 \leq x < x + y \leq x_N$ and $0 \leq \delta \leq 1$, inequality (5) holds, then f is called a convex Lipschitz of order θ on the interval $[x_0, x_N]$.*

$$
|\Delta(x, y, \delta)| := |f(x + \delta y) - (\delta f(x + y) + (1 - \delta) f(x))| \leq M\theta(y) \tag{5}
$$

By a change in variables, $z = x + y$, rearranging, and renaming variables again, the expression for $|\Delta(x, y, \delta)|$ in inequality (5) can be rewritten in the more geometrical form

$$
|f(\delta x + (1 - \delta) y) - (\delta f(x) + (1 - \delta) f(y))| \leq M\theta(x \quad y), \tag{6}
$$

where the difference appearing in the left-hand side expresses the difference between the line through $(x, f(x))$ and $(y, f(y))$ and the function f.

It is worth mentioning that if f belongs the the Zygmund class Λ_α ([19], Chapter 2, §3), then f is a convex Lipschitz of order $\theta(x) = x^\alpha$, $x > 0$.

Following [20], we denote by $V^\theta(I)$ the set of convex Lipschitz functions of order θ on the interval $I := [x_0, x_N]$. Clearly, $V^\theta(I)$ is an $\mathbb{R}$-vector space. A norm on $V^\theta(I)$ is defined by setting

$$
[f]^* := \sup_{x_0 \leq x < x + y \leq x_N} \frac{|f(x + \delta y) - (\delta f(x + y) + (1 - \delta) f(x))|}{\theta(y)}
$$

and then $\| f \|_{V^\theta} := \| f \|_\infty^I + [f]^*$.

The proof for the next result can be found in [20].

Theorem 5. *The space $\left(V^\theta(I), \| \cdot \|_{V^\theta}\right)$ is a Banach space.*

Now, let

$$V^\theta_*(I) := \left\{ f \in V^\theta(I) : f(x_0) = y_0,\ f(x_N) = y_N \right\},$$

and

$$V^\theta_{**}(I) := \left\{ f \in V^\theta_*(I) : f(x_i) = y_i,\ \text{ for } i \in \mathbb{N}_{0,N} \right\}.$$

Then, the above theorem implies the following corollary.

Corollary 1. *$(V^\theta_*(I), \|\cdot\|_{V^\theta})$ and $(V^\theta_{**}(I), \|\cdot\|_{V^\theta})$ are complete metric spaces.*

Proof. Let $\{f_n\}$ be a convergent sequence in $V^\theta_*(I)$ and assume that the limit of the sequence is $f \in V^\theta(I)$. Thus,

$$\forall \epsilon > 0\ \exists n_0\ \forall n \geq n_0 : \ \| f_n - f \|_{V^\theta} < \epsilon.$$

As $\| f \|_{V^\theta} = \| f \|^I_\infty + [f]^*$, this in particular means that

$$\forall \epsilon > 0\ \exists n_0\ \forall n \geq n_0 : \ \| f_n - f \|_\infty < \epsilon$$

If $f \in V^\theta(I) \setminus V^\theta_*(I)$, then either $f(x_0) \neq y_0$ or $f(x_N) \neq y_N$. Without loss of generality, assume that $f(x_0) \neq y_0$ and set $\epsilon_0 |f(x_0) - y_0| > 0$. Since $\{f_n\} \subset V^\theta_*(I)$, for all n, we have $f_n(x_0) = y_0$. Therefore, for all n, we must have $\| f_n - f \|_\infty \geq \epsilon_0$, which contradicts the fact that $\lim_{n\to\infty} f_n = f$. So, we must have $f \in V^\theta_*(I)$. As a result, $V^\theta_*(I)$ is a closed subset of $V^\theta(I)$. Therefore, $(V^\theta_*(I), \|\cdot\|_{V^\theta})$ is a complete metric space. Similarly, it can be shown that $(V^\theta_{**}(I), \|\cdot\|_{V^\theta})$ is a complete metric space. □

5. Fractal Interpolation in the Space $V^\theta(I)$

In this section, besides the assumptions made in the previous section, we will also assume that F_i are ρ-Matkowski contractions (with the same function ρ) with respect to the second variable, i.e., for some non-decreasing function $\rho : \mathbb{R}^+ \to \mathbb{R}^+$, where, for all $t > 0$, we have $\lim_{n\to\infty} \rho^n(t) = 0$, and every F_i satisfies the following condition:

$$\forall x \in I\ \ \forall y, y' \in [a,b] \quad |F_i(x,y) - F_i(x,y')| \leq \rho(|y - y'|).$$

It is worth pointing out the following theorem from [4].

Theorem 6. *Under the given conditions on l_i, F_i, and K, the operator $T : C^*(I) \to C^*(I)$ has a unique fixed point $f^* \in C^{**}(I)$. Furthermore, the graph $G := \{(x, f^*(x)) : x \in I\}$ of f^* is invariant with respect to the IFS $\{K; w_1, \ldots, w_N\}$, i.e., $G = \bigcup_{i=1}^{N} w_i(G)$.*

From now on, let us furthermore assume that

$$l_i(x) = a_i x + b_i \quad \text{and} \quad F_i(x,y) = \alpha_i(x) y + q_i(x),$$

where $\alpha_i : I \to \mathbb{R}$ is a multiplier in $V^\theta(I)$ and $q_i \in V^\theta(I)$. The a_i and b_i are determined by the conditions (2) imposed on l_i. We also set $|\alpha_i|_\infty := \sup\{|\alpha_i(x)| : x \in I\}$ and $|\alpha|_\infty := \max_{i\in\mathbb{N}_N} \sup\{|\alpha_i(x)| : x \in I\}$. Note that due to the specific structure of the mappings F_i, we have that $T : V^\theta(I) \to V^\theta(I)$.

Theorem 7. *For all $f \in V^\theta_*(I)$, we have that $Tf \in V^\theta_{**}(I)$. Therefore, $T : V^\theta_*(I) \to V^\theta_{**}(I)$.*

Proof. We already know that $T : V^\theta(I) \to V^\theta(I)$. Let $f \in V^\theta_*(I)$, which means that $f(x_0) = y_0$ and $f(x_N) = y_N$. On the other hand, we know that for all $x \in [x_{i-1}, x_i]$, we have $Tf(x) = F_i\left(l_i^{-1}(x), f\left(l_i^{-1}(x)\right)\right)$. Therefore,

$$\begin{aligned} Tf(x_i) &= F_i\left(l_i^{-1}(x_i), f\left(l_i^{-1}(x_i)\right)\right) \\ &= F_i(x_N, f(x_N)) \quad (\text{since } l_i : I \to I_i \text{ is a homeomorphism}) \\ &= F_i(x_N, y_N) \quad \left(\text{since } f \in V^\theta_*(I)\right) \\ &= y_i \quad (\text{property of } F_i\ ). \end{aligned}$$

Hence, $Tf(x_i) = y_i$ for $i \in \mathbb{N}_N$. Similarly, it can be seen that $Tf(x_0) = y_0$. We conclude that $Tf \in V^\theta_{**}(I)$. □

Theorem 8. *If* $max\left\{ |\alpha|_\infty, \max_{i \in \mathbb{N}_N}\{|\alpha_i|_\infty sup\{\frac{\theta(y)}{\theta(a_i y)} : y \in I\}\}\right\} < 1$, *then* $T : V^\theta_*(I) \to V^\theta_{**}(I) \subseteq V^\theta_*(I)$ *is a Banach contraction.*

This theorem was proven indirectly in [20] and the result appears in Theorem 2.7 under slightly different conditions. The proof provided there remains the same under the current setting including the extension to non-constant scaling factors $\alpha_i : I \to \mathbb{R}$. In addition, we corrected the statement in ([20], Theorem 2.7) as the term with the sup over $y \in I$ is missing, which would make the contractivity condition presented there dependent on y.

The following Theorem (9) provides conditions under which T becomes a Rakotch contraction.

Theorem 9. *Assume that*

$$|\beta|_\infty := \max_{i \in \mathbb{N}_N}\left\{ |\alpha_i|_\infty \sup_{x_0 \le y \le x_N} \frac{\theta(y)}{\theta(a_i y)} \right\} < 1.$$

Let the maps F_i be Rakotch contractions with respect to the second variable for the same function τ, i.e., for some non-decreasing function $\tau : \mathbb{R}^+ \to \mathbb{R}^+$ with $\tau(t) < t$ and $\frac{\tau(t)}{t}$ non-increasing for all $t > 0$, we have that

$$\forall x \in I\ \forall y, y' \in [a, b]: \quad |F_i(x, y) - F_i(x, y')| \le \tau(|y - y'|).$$

Then, the operator $T : V^\theta_*(I) \to V^\theta_{**}(I) \subseteq V^\theta_*(I)$ is a Rakotch contraction.

Proof. First, we show that for all $f, g \in V^{\theta}(I)$, $\| Tf - Tg \|_{\infty}^{I} \leq \tau(\| f - g \|_{\infty}^{I})$. To this end, let $f, g \in V^{\theta}(I)$. Then,

$$\begin{aligned}
\| Tf - Tg \|_{\infty}^{I} &= \sup_{x\in I}|Tf(x) - Tg(x)| \\
&= \max_{i\in\mathbb{N}_N}\sup_{x\in I_i}|Tf(x) - Tg(x)| \\
&= \max_{i\in\mathbb{N}_N}\sup_{x\in I_i}\left|F_i\left(l_i^{-1}(x), f\left(l_i^{-1}(x)\right)\right) - F_i\left(l_i^{-1}(x), g\left(l_i^{-1}(x)\right)\right)\right| \\
&\leq \max_{i\in\mathbb{N}_N}\sup_{x\in I_i}\tau(|f\left(l_i^{-1}(x)\right) - g\left(l_i^{-1}(x)\right)|) \\
&\leq \max_{i\in\mathbb{N}_N}\tau(\sup_{x\in I_i}|f\left(l_i^{-1}(x)\right) - g\left(l_i^{-1}(x)\right)|) \text{ (since } \tau \text{ is non} - \text{decreasing)} \\
&= \max_{i\in\mathbb{N}_N}\tau(\| f - g \|_{\infty}^{I}) = \tau(\| f - g \|_{\infty}^{I}).
\end{aligned}$$

where in the penultimate equality, we used $\sup_{x\in I_i}|f\left(l_i^{-1}(x)\right) - g\left(l_i^{-1}(x)\right)| = \| f - g \|_{\infty}^{I})$ for $i = 1, \ldots, N$.

Next, we show that for all $f, g \in V^{\theta}(I)$, $[Tf - Tg]^* \leq |\beta|_{\infty}[f - g]^*$ where $|\beta|_{\infty} := \max_{i\in\mathbb{N}_N}\left\{|\alpha_i|_{\infty} \sup_{x_0\leq y\leq x_N} \frac{\theta(y)}{\theta(a_i y)}\right\}$. Let $f, g \in V^{\theta}(I)$ and $0 \leq \delta \leq 1$. Then, setting $h := f - g$, we have for $i \in \mathbb{N}_N$,

$$[Th]^* = \sup_{x_{i-1}\leq\tilde{x}<\tilde{x}+\tilde{y}\leq x_i} \frac{|(Th)(\tilde{x}+\delta\tilde{y}) - (\delta(Th)(\tilde{x}+\tilde{y}) + (1-\delta)(Th)(\tilde{x}))|}{\theta(y)}.$$

Substituting the expression for the RB operator T into the above equation and using the fact that each l_i is bijective with $x := l_i^{-1}(\tilde{x}) \in I$ and $l_i^{-1}(\tilde{x} + \tilde{y}) = x + y \in I$ with $y := \tilde{y}/a_i$, yields

$$\begin{aligned}
[Th]^* \leq & \max_{i\in\mathbb{N}_N} \sup_{x_0\leq x<x+y\leq x_N} \\
& \left\{|\alpha_i(x)|\frac{|h(x+\delta y) - (\delta h(x+y) + (1-\delta)h(x))|}{\theta(y)} \cdot \frac{\theta(y)}{\theta(a_i y)}\right\} \\
\leq & |\beta|_{\infty}[f - g]^*.
\end{aligned}$$

Finally, we establish that T is a Rakotch contraction. To this end, let $f, g \in V^{\theta}(I)$. Then,

$$\begin{aligned}
\| Tf - Tg \|_{V^\theta} &= \| Tf - Tg \|_{\infty}^{I} + [Tf - Tg]^* \\
&\leq \tau(\| f - g \|_{\infty}^{I}) + [Tf - Tg]^* \\
&\leq \tau(\| f - g \|_{V^\theta}) + [Tf - Tg]^* \\
&\leq \tau(\| f - g \|_{V^\theta}) + |\beta|_{\infty}[f - g]^* \\
&\leq \tau(\| f - g \|_{V^\theta}) + |\beta|_{\infty}\| f - g \|_{V^\theta} \quad ([f - g]^* \leq \| f - g \|_{V^\theta}),
\end{aligned}$$

where proceeding from the first inequality to the second inequality above, we used the above since τ is non-decreasing and $\| f - g \|_{\infty}^{I} \leq \| f - g \|_{V^\theta}$.

Hence, for $\| f - g \|_{V^\theta} \neq 0$, we have

$$\begin{aligned} \| Tf - Tg \|_{V^\theta} &\leq \frac{\tau(\| f - g \|_{V^\theta})}{\| f - g \|_{V^\theta}} \| f - g \|_{V^\theta} + |\beta|_\infty \| f - g \|_{V^\theta} \\ &\leq \max\left\{ \frac{\tau(\| f - g \|_{V^\theta})}{\| f - g \|_{V^\theta}}, |\beta|_\infty \right\} \| f - g \|_{V^\theta} \end{aligned}$$

Now, for all $t > 0$, $\frac{\tau(t)}{t} < 1$ is non-increasing and $|\beta|_\infty < 1$. Define $\sigma(t) := t \max\left\{ \frac{\tau(t)}{t}, |\beta|_\infty \right\}$. Then, for all $t > 0$, the map $\frac{\sigma(t)}{t} < 1$ and is non-increasing. Therefore, T is a Rakotch contraction. □

Example 1. *The result in the Theorem 9 establishes the existence of fractal functions of class $V^\theta(I)$. Here, we provide an example for such functions. For illustrative purposes, we choose convex Lipschitz functions of order $0 < \alpha \leq 1$, i.e., elements of the Zygmund class Λ_α. Let $I := [0,1]$ and suppose $\Delta := \left\{ (0,0), \left(\frac{1}{2}, 1\right), (1,0) \right\}$. Further, we assume that the scaling factors α_i, $i = 1,2$, are given by the two Weierstrass functions*

$$\alpha_1 : I \to \mathbb{R}, x \mapsto \gamma \sum_{n=0}^{\infty} 2^{-\alpha n} \sin(2^n \pi x)$$

and

$$\alpha_2 : I \to \mathbb{R}, x \mapsto \gamma \sum_{n=0}^{\infty} 2^{-\alpha n} \sin(2^n \pi x + \pi),$$

respectively, for some positive constant $\gamma \leq 2^{-\alpha-1}$. It is known that α_1 and α_2 are convex Lipschitz of order α [8]. This choice ensures that for an $f \in \Lambda_\alpha$, the product $\alpha_i f$ is also in Λ_α. Moreover, set $q_1 : I \to \mathbb{R}$, $x \mapsto x^\alpha$, and $q_2 : I \to \mathbb{R}$, $x \mapsto (1-x)^\alpha$. It is straight-forward to verify that all joined-up conditions are satisfied and that the RB operator T as defined above maps $V_*^\theta(I) \to V_{**}^\theta(I)$ with $\beta = \frac{1}{2}$.

6. Conclusions

In this paper, we introduced the concept of fractal interpolation on the Banach space $V^\theta(I)$ of convex Lipschitz functions of order θ defined on a compact interval $I \subset \mathbb{R}$. To achieve fractal interpolation, we introduced a Read–Bajraktarević operator T on a closed subspace of $V^\theta(I)$ and—in order to establish a more general result—derived conditions such that T becomes a Rakotch contraction. This includes and also corrects the case of Banach contractions considered in [20]. Our result then proves the existence of fractal functions of class $V^\theta(I)$. A class of examples is also provided.

Author Contributions: Conceptualization, F.G. and P.M.; methodology, F.G. and P.M.; validation, F.G. and P.M.; formal analysis, F.G. and P.M.; investigation, F.G. and P.M.; writing—original draft preparation, F.G.; writing—review and editing, F.G. and P.M.; supervision, P.M. All authors have read and agreed to the published version of the manuscript.

Funding: This research received no external funding.

Data Availability Statement: The original contributions presented in this study are included in the article. Further inquiries can be directed to the corresponding author.

Acknowledgments: We thank the anonymous referees for the careful reading of the manuscript and their suggestions which helped to improve this paper.

Conflicts of Interest: The authors declare no conflicts of interest.

References

1. Massopust, P.R. Local fractal functions and function spaces. In *Fractals, Wavelets and their Applications*; Springer: Berlin/Heidelberg, Germany, 2014; Volume 92, pp. 245–270; Springer Proceedings in Mathematics & Statistics.
2. Navascués, M.; Pacurar, C.; Drakopoulos, V. Scale-free fractal interpolation. *Fractal Fract.* **2022**, *6*, 15. [CrossRef]
3. Pacurar, C.M. A countable fractal interpolation scheme involving Rakotch contractions. *Results Math.* **2021**, *76*, 19. [CrossRef]
4. Ri, S. A new idea to construct the fractal interpolation function. *Indag. Math.* **2018**, *29*, 962–971. [CrossRef]
5. Ri, S.; Drakopoulos, V.; Nam, S.; Kim, K. Nonlinear fractal interpolation functions on the Koch curve. *J. Fractal Geom.* **2022**, *9*, 261–271. [CrossRef]
6. Verma, M.; Priyadarshi, A. New type of fractal functions for general data sets. *Acta Appl. Math.* **2023**, *187*, 22. [CrossRef]
7. Pasupathi, R.; Miculescu, R. A very general framework for fractal interpolation functions. *J. Math. Anal. Appl.* **2024**, *534*, 128093. [CrossRef]
8. Mauldin, R.D.; Williams, S.C. On the Hausdorff dimension of some graphs. *Trans. Amer. Math. Soc.* **1986**, *298*, 793–803. [CrossRef]
9. Nesterov, Y. *Lecture on Convex Optimization*, 2nd ed.; Springer: Berlin/Heidelberg, Germany, 2018.
10. Roades, B.E. A comparison of various definitions of contractive mappings. *Trans. Am. Math. Soc.* **1977**, *226*, 257–290. [CrossRef]
11. Rakotch, E. A note on contractive mappings. *Proc. Am. Math. Soc.* **1962**, *13*, 459–465. [CrossRef]
12. Matkowski, J. *Integrable Solutions of Functional Equations*; Instytut Matematyczny Polskiej Akademi Nauk: Warszawa, Poland, 1975.
13. Reich, S.; Zaslavski, A.J. A fixed point theorem for Matkowski contractions. *Fixed Point Theory* **2007**, *8*, 303–307.
14. Barnsley, M.F. Fractal Functions and Interpolation. *Constr. Approx.* **1986**, *2*, 303–329. [CrossRef]
15. Barnsley, M.F. *Fractals Everywhere*; Dover Publications: Mineola, NY, USA, 2013.
16. Hutchinson, J. Fractals and Self SImilarity. *Indiana Univ. Math. J.* **1981**, *30*, 713–747. [CrossRef]
17. Massopust, P.R. *Fractal Functions, Fractal Surfaces, and Wavelets*, 2nd ed.; Academic Press: Cambridge, MA, USA, 2016.
18. Barnsley, M.F.; Massopust, P.R. Bilinear Fractal Interpolation and Box Dimension. *J. Approx. Theory* **2015**, *192*, 362–378. [CrossRef]
19. Zygmund, A. *Trigonometric Series*; Cambridge University Press: Cambridge, UK, 1968.
20. Chandra, S.; Abbas, S. On fractal dimensions of fractal functions using function spaces. *Bull. Austral. Math. Soc.* **2022**, *106*, 470–480. [CrossRef]

fractal and fractional

MDPI

Article

Common Attractors of Generalized Hutchinson–Wardowski Contractive Operators

Bilal Iqbal [1], Naeem Saleem [1,2,*], Iram Iqbal [3] and Maggie Aphane [2]

1 Department of Mathematics, University of Management and Technology, Lahore 54770, Pakistan; bimirza91@gmail.com
2 Department of Mathematics and Applied Mathematics, Sefako Makgatho Health Sciences University, Ga-Rankuwa, Medunsa, Pretoria 0204, South Africa
3 Department of Mathematics, Government Ambala Muslim Graduate College, Sargodha 40100, Pakistan
* Correspondence: naeem.saleem2@gmail.com

Abstract: The aim of this paper is to obtain a fractal set of $\Im$-iterated function systems comprising generalized $\Im$-contractions. For a variety of Hutchinson–Wardowski contractive operators, we prove that this kind of system admits a unique common attractor. Consequently, diverse outcomes are obtained for generalized iterated function systems satisfying various generalized contractive conditions. An illustrative example is also provided. Finally, the existence results of common solutions to fractional boundary value problems are obtained.

Keywords: $\Im$-generalized iterated function systems; fractals; common attractors; $\Im$-contractions; Hutchinson–Wardowski contractive operators

1. Introduction And Preliminaries

Hutchinson [1] introduced an important and basic concept of fractal theory called an iterated function system (in short, IFS) in 1981. The Hutchinson operator, created by a finite system of contraction mappings on a Euclidean space, has a closed and bounded fixed point known as the attractor of the IFS. This concept is further developed by Barnsley [2]. IFSs are useful in a variety of fields, including engineering, medicine, forestry, economics, human anatomy, physics, and fractal picture compression. The IFS is a versatile tool that can handle complex structures and patterns, making it useful across a variety of disciplines. Its modeling, compression, and representation properties provide strong reasons to employ it in both theoretical and applied contexts.

Further, in Refs. [3,4], Miculescu and Mihail introduced the generalized iterated function system (in short, GIFS), which is composed of a finite number of Banach contractions, each defined on the Cartesian product $\mathbb{U}^m$ and taking values in $\mathbb{U}$. Dumitru [5] and Strobin and Swaczyna [6] built upon the work of Miculescu and Mihail by exploring generalized iterated function systems (GIFSs) consisting of Meir–Keeler-type mappings and $\Im$-contractions, respectively. Additionally, Secelean [7] investigated IFSs comprising a countable family of contractive mappings, $\Im$-contractions, and Meir–Keeler-type mappings, further expanding on this area of research. In a recent study [8], Khumalo et al. identified common attractors by utilizing a finite collection of generalized contractive mappings within a particular class of mappings in a partial metric space. The noteworthy findings about IFSs and generalizations of their contractions in different metric spaces can be found, for example, in Refs. [9–13] and others.

The Banach Fixed Point Theorem (BFPT), also known as the Contraction Mapping Principle, is a cornerstone of classical functional analysis, holding a prominent place among the most crucial results in the discipline, which was developed and demonstrated in Banach's 1920 doctoral dissertation and published in 1922 [14]. A remarkable and important generalization of BFPT is stated by Wardowski [15]. He explained the concept of $\Im$-contraction in the following manner:

Definition 1. *Consider a metric space $(\mathbb{U}, d)$. A mapping $g : \mathbb{U} \to \mathbb{U}$ is classified as an $\Im$-contraction if it happens that there is $\Im \in \mathcal{F}$ and $\lambda > 0$ such that $\forall\ \kappa, \xi \in \mathbb{U}$ with $d(\kappa, \xi) > 0$*

$$\lambda + \Im(d(g\kappa, g\xi)) \leq \Im(d(\kappa, \xi)), \tag{1}$$

where $\mathcal{F}$ is the group of all mappings $\Im : (0, \infty) \to (-\infty, \infty)$ that meet the requirements listed below:
($\Im$1) $\Im(\kappa) < \Im(\xi)\ \forall\ \kappa < \xi$;
($\Im$2) $\lim_{\varepsilon \to +\infty} \mu_\varepsilon = 0$, if and only if $\lim_{\varepsilon \to +\infty} \Im(\mu_\varepsilon) = -\infty$, for all sequences $\{\mu_\varepsilon\} \subseteq (0, \infty)$;
($\Im$3) it happens that there is $0 < \jmath < 1$ such that $\lim_{\mu \to 0^+} \mu^\jmath \Im(\mu) = 0$.

In Ref. [16], Secelean demonstrated that criterion ($\Im$2) can be substituted with an equivalent and more convenient one:
($\Im 2'$)$\inf \Im = -\infty$.

For convenience, we will denote the collection of all mappings $\Im : (0, \infty) \to (-\infty, \infty)$ that satisfy ($\Im$1), ($\Im 2'$), and ($\Im$3) by $\nabla(\Im)$.

Proposition 1 ([16]). *Let $F, G, H : (0, \infty) \to (-\infty, \infty)$ be functions defined by $F := \min\{\Im_1, \Im_2, \cdots, \Im_N\}$, $G := \max\{\Im_1, \Im_2, \cdots, \Im_N\}$, and $H := \rho_1\Im_1 + \rho_2\Im_2 + \cdots + \rho_n\Im_N$, where $\Im_1, \Im_2, \cdots, \Im_N \in \nabla(\Im)$ and $\rho_1, \rho_2, \cdots, \rho_N \in (0, \infty)$ for some $N \in \mathbb{N}$. Then, $F, G, H \in \nabla(\Im)$.*

Proposition 2 ([16]). *Let $\varphi, \psi : (0, \infty) \to (0, \infty)$ be two mappings satisfying the following conditions:*
(a) φ is strictly increasing and $\inf \varphi = 0$;
(b) ψ is strictly increasing and there is $\eta \in (0, 1)$ such that $\lim_{t \searrow 0} t^\eta \psi(t) = 0$;
(c) there exists $\lambda \in (0, 1)$ such that $\lim_{t \searrow 0} t^\lambda \varphi(t) = 0$. In particular, this condition holds iff is differentiable and there are $\pi, \varrho \in (0, \infty)$ such that $t\varphi\prime(t) \leq \pi\varphi(t)$ for every $t \in (0, \varrho)$.
Then, the function $F : (0, \infty) \to (-\infty, \infty)$ defined by $\ln \varphi(t) + \psi(t)$ belongs to $\nabla(\Im)$.

Secelean also explored the IFSs composed of $\Im$-contractions extending some fixed point results from the traditional Hutchinson–Barnsley theory of IFS consisting of Banach contractions. Cosentino and Vetro [17] introduced the notion of an $\Im$-contraction of Hardy–Rogers type and obtained a fixed point theorem.

Definition 2 ([17]). *Let $(\mathbb{U}, d)$ be a metric space. A self-mapping g on $\mathbb{U}$ is called an $\Im$-contraction of Hardy–Rogers type If it happens that there are $\Im \in \mathcal{F}$ and $\lambda > 0$ such that*

$$\lambda + \Im(d(g(\kappa), g(\xi))) \leq \Im(\alpha d(\kappa, \xi) + \beta d(\kappa, g\kappa) + \gamma d(\xi, g\xi) + \delta d(\kappa, g\xi) + Ld(\xi, g\kappa)),$$

where $d(g(\kappa), g(\xi)) > 0$, $\alpha, \beta, \gamma, \delta, L \geq 0$, $\alpha + \beta + \gamma + 2\delta = 1$ and $\gamma \neq 1$.

To extend the theory of fractal sets, in this paper, we construct a fractal set of an $\Im$-iterated function system, a certain finite collection of generalized $\Im$-contractions. We prove that Hutchinson–Wardowski contractive operators defined with the help of a finite family of generalized $\Im$-contractions on a complete metric space themselves represent a generalized $\Im$-contraction mapping on a family of compact subsets. We obtain a final fractal via the successive application of a Hutchinson–Wardowski contractive operator in a metric space.

2. Fundamental Results

Let $(\mathbb{U}, d)$ be a metric space and $\mathcal{C}^d(\mathbb{U})$ be the collection of all nonempty compact subsets of $\mathbb{U}$. The function $H_d : \mathcal{C}^d(\mathbb{U}) \to \mathcal{C}^d(\mathbb{U})$ defined by

$$H_d(\mathcal{N}, \mathcal{M}) = \max\left\{\sup_{a\in\mathcal{N}} D(a, \mathcal{M}), \sup_{b\in\mathcal{M}} D(b, \mathcal{N})\right\}, \quad \text{for all} \quad \mathcal{N}, \mathcal{M} \in \mathcal{C}^d(\mathbb{U}),$$

where $D(a, \mathcal{M}) = \inf\{d(a, b) : b \in \mathcal{M}\}$ is called the Hausdorff–Pompeiu metric. The metric space $(\mathcal{C}^d(X), H_d)$ is complete provided that $(\mathbb{U}, d)$ is complete.

Lemma 1 ([18]). *Let $\mathcal{N}, \mathcal{M} \in \mathcal{C}^d(\mathbb{U})$, and then*

(1) $\mathcal{N} \subset \mathcal{M}$ if and only if $D(\mathcal{N}, \mathcal{M}) = 0$;
(2) $D(\mathcal{N}, S) \le D(\mathcal{N}, \mathcal{M}) + D(\mathcal{M}, S)$.

Lemma 2 ([18]). *Let $(\mathcal{N}_i)_{i\in\mathcal{I}}, (\mathcal{M}_i)_{i\in\mathcal{I}}$ be two finite collections of sets in $(\mathcal{C}^d(X), H_d)$, and then*

$$H_d\left(\bigcup_{i\in\mathcal{I}} \mathcal{N}_i, \bigcup_{i\in\mathcal{I}} \mathcal{M}_i\right) \le \sup_{i\in\mathcal{I}} H_d(\mathcal{N}_i, \mathcal{M}_i).$$

We begin by defining generalized $\Im$-contraction as

Definition 3. *Let $(\mathbb{U}, d)$ be a metric space and $g, \ell : \mathbb{U} \to \mathbb{U}$ be two mappings. A pair (g, ℓ) is called a generalized $\Im$-contraction if it happens that there are $\Im \in \nabla(\Im)$ and $\lambda > 0$ such that, for all $\kappa, \xi \in \mathbb{U}$,*

$$d(g(\kappa), \ell(\xi)) > 0, \quad \textit{implying} \quad \lambda + \Im(d(g(\kappa), \ell(\xi))) \le \Im(d(\kappa, \xi)). \tag{2}$$

For two mappings $g, \ell : \mathbb{U} \to \mathbb{U}$, we define for any $\mathcal{N} \in \mathcal{C}^d(\mathbb{U})$,

$$g(\mathcal{N}) = \{g(a) : a \in \mathcal{N}\} \quad \text{and} \quad \ell(\mathcal{N}) = \{\ell(a) : a \in \mathcal{N}\}.$$

Definition 4. *Let $(\mathbb{U}, d)$ be a metric space. If for each $\kappa = 1, 2, 3, \cdots, \varepsilon$, $g_\kappa, \ell_\kappa : \mathbb{U} \to \mathbb{U}$ are continuous mappings and the pair (g_κ, ℓ_κ) is generalized $\Im_\kappa$-contraction for $\Im_\kappa \in \nabla(\Im)$ and $\lambda_\kappa > 0$, then $\{Y; (g_\kappa, \ell_\kappa), \kappa = 1, 2, 3, \cdots, \varepsilon\}$ is called an $\Im$-iterated function system (in short, $\Im$-IFS). The functions $\Theta, \Omega : \mathcal{C}^d(\mathbb{U}) \to \mathcal{C}^d(\mathbb{U})$ defined by*

$$\Theta(\mathcal{N}) = \bigcup_{\kappa=1}^{\varepsilon} g_\kappa(\mathcal{N}) \quad \textit{and} \quad \Omega(\mathcal{M}) = \bigcup_{\kappa=1}^{\varepsilon} \ell_\kappa(\mathcal{M}) \quad \textit{for all} \quad \mathcal{N}, \mathcal{M} \in \mathcal{C}^d(\mathbb{U}) \tag{3}$$

are called associated Hutchinson operators.

Definition 5. *Let $\mathcal{N} \in \mathcal{C}^d(\mathbb{U})$, and then $\mathcal{N}$ is called a common attractor of $\Im$-IFS if*

(i) $\Theta(\mathcal{N}) = \Omega(\mathcal{N}) = \mathcal{N}$;
(ii) there exists an open set $V \subseteq \mathbb{U}$ such that $\mathcal{N} \subseteq V$ and $\lim_{\kappa\to+\infty} \Theta^\kappa(\mathcal{M}) = \lim_{\kappa\to+\infty} \Omega^\kappa(\mathcal{M})$ for any compact set $\mathcal{M} \subseteq V$,

where Θ and Ω are provided in (3). The maximal open set V such that (ii) is satisfied is known as a basin of common attraction.

Next, we prove two basic results that play a key role in converting a pair of Hutchinson operators into generalized $\Im$-contraction on $\mathcal{C}^d(\mathbb{U})$ and to ensure the existence of a common attractor for these operators.

Lemma 3. *Let $(\mathbb{U}, d)$ be a metric space and $g, \ell : \mathbb{U} \to \mathbb{U}$ be two continuous mappings. If the pair (g, ℓ) is a generalized $\Im$-contraction for $\Im \in \nabla(\Im)$ and $\lambda > 0$, then*

(1) $\mathcal{N} \in \mathcal{C}^d(\mathbb{U})$ *implies* $g(\mathcal{N}) \in \mathcal{C}^d(\mathbb{U})$ *and* $\ell(\mathcal{N}) \in \mathcal{C}^d(\mathbb{U})$ *for any* $\mathcal{N} \in \mathcal{C}^d(\mathbb{U})$;

(2) *the pair* (g, ℓ) *is a generalized* $\Im$*-type contraction on* $(\mathcal{C}^d(\mathbb{U}), H_d)$.

Proof.

(1) Since an image of a compact subset under a continuous mapping is compact, continuity of g and ℓ thus signifies that $\mathcal{N} \in \mathcal{C}^d(\mathbb{U})$ implies $g(\mathcal{N}) \in \mathcal{C}^d(\mathbb{U})$ and $\ell(\mathcal{N}) \in \mathcal{C}^d(\mathbb{U})$ for any $\mathcal{N} \in \mathcal{C}^d(\mathbb{U})$.

(2) Let $\mathcal{N}, \mathcal{M} \in \mathcal{C}^d(\mathbb{U})$ such that $H_d(g\mathcal{N}, \ell\mathcal{M}) > 0$. Assume that

$$H_d(g\mathcal{N}, \ell\mathcal{M}) = \sup_{\kappa\in\mathcal{N}} \inf_{\xi\in\mathcal{M}} d(g\kappa, \ell\xi), \tag{4}$$

which further implies that $d(g\kappa, \ell\xi) > 0$. So, there exists $\lambda > 0$ such that

$$\lambda + \Im(d(g(\kappa), \ell(\xi))) \leq \Im(d(\kappa, \xi)) \quad \text{for all} \quad \kappa, \xi \in \mathbb{U}. \tag{5}$$

Due to compactness of $\mathcal{N}$ and continuity of g & ℓ, we have $u \in \mathcal{N}$ such that $\inf_{\xi\in\mathcal{M}} d(gu, \ell\xi) > 0$ for all $\xi \in \mathcal{M}$. Therefore,

$$\lambda + \Im(\inf_{\xi\in\mathcal{M}} d(g(u), \ell(\xi))) \leq \lambda + \Im(d(g(u), \ell(\xi))) \leq \Im(d(u, \xi)) \quad \text{for all} \quad \xi \in \mathcal{M}. \tag{6}$$

Hence, by using (4) and (6), we obtain

$$\lambda + \Im(H_d(g\mathcal{N}, \ell\mathcal{M})) \leq \Im(d(u, \xi)), \quad \text{for all} \quad \xi \in \mathcal{M}. \tag{7}$$

Now, let $v \in \mathcal{M}$ such that $d(u, v) = \inf_{\xi\in\mathcal{M}} d(u, \xi)$, and then (7) yields

$$\begin{aligned} \lambda + \Im(H_d(g\mathcal{N}, \ell\mathcal{M})) \leq \Im(d(u, \xi)) &= \Im(\inf_{\xi\in\mathcal{M}} d(u, \xi)) \\ &\leq \Im(\sup_{\kappa\in\mathcal{N}} \inf_{\xi\in\mathcal{M}} d(u, \xi)) \\ &\leq \Im(H_d(\mathcal{N}, \mathcal{M})). \end{aligned} \tag{8}$$

If we assume that

$$H_d(g\mathcal{N}, \ell\mathcal{M}) = \sup_{\xi\in\mathcal{M}} \inf_{\kappa\in\mathcal{N}} d(g\kappa, \ell\xi),$$

then, by similar arguments as above, we obtain

$$\lambda + \Im(H_d(g\mathcal{N}, \ell\mathcal{M})) \leq \Im(H_d(\mathcal{N}, \mathcal{M})).$$

Consequently, we have the pair (g, ℓ), which is a generalized $\Im$-contraction on $(\mathcal{C}^d(\mathbb{U}), H_d)$. □

Remark 1. *By considering* $g = \ell$ *in Lemma 3, we return to Lemma 4.1 of [16] and Theorem 1.10 of [10].*

Lemma 4. *Let* $(\mathbb{U}, d)$ *be a metric space and* $g_\kappa, \ell_\kappa : \mathbb{U} \to \mathbb{U}$ *be continuous mappings for* $\kappa = 1, 2, 3, \cdots, \varepsilon$. *If for each* $\kappa = 1, 2, 3, \cdots, \varepsilon$ *there exist* $\Im_1, \Im_2, \cdots, \Im_\varepsilon \in \nabla(\Im)$ *and* $\lambda_1, \lambda_2, \cdots, \lambda_\varepsilon > 0$ *such that the pair* (g_κ, ℓ_κ) *satisfy*

$$d(g_\kappa(\kappa), \ell_\kappa(\xi)) > 0, \quad \text{implying} \quad \lambda + \Im_\kappa(d(g_\kappa(\kappa), \ell_\kappa(\xi))) \leq \Im_\kappa(d(\kappa, \xi)) \tag{9}$$

for all $\kappa, \xi \in \mathbb{U}$, *and the mapping* $\mathcal{G}_\kappa := \Im - \Im_\kappa$ *is nondecreasing. Then, the pair* (Θ, Ω) *is a generalized* $\Im$*-contraction on* $\mathcal{C}^d(\mathbb{U})$ *for* $\Im = \max_{1\leq\kappa\leq\varepsilon} \Im_\kappa$ *and* $\lambda = \min_{1\leq\kappa\leq\varepsilon} \lambda_\kappa$, *where* Θ *and* Ω *are defined in* (3).

Proof. By hypothesis, there exist $\Im_1, \Im_2, \cdots, \Im_\varepsilon \in \nabla(\Im)$ and $\lambda_1, \lambda_2, \cdots, \lambda_\varepsilon > 0$ such that the pair (g_κ, ℓ_κ) satisfy (9) for each $\kappa = 1, 2, 3, \cdots, \varepsilon$ and $\kappa, \xi \in \mathbb{U}$. Let $\Im - \max\{\Im_1, \Im_2, \cdots, \Im_\varepsilon\}$ and $\lambda = \min\{\lambda_1, \lambda_2, \cdots, \lambda_\varepsilon\}$, and then $\lambda > 0$, and, by using Proposition 1, we have $\Im \in \nabla(\Im)$.

Now, let $\mathcal{N}, \mathcal{M} \in \mathcal{C}^d(\mathbb{U})$ such that $H_d(\Theta\mathcal{N}, \Omega\mathcal{M}) > 0$. Then, due to Lemma 2, for some $\kappa_0 \in \{1, 2, \cdots, \varepsilon\}$, we obtain

$$0 < H_d(\Theta\mathcal{N}, \Omega\mathcal{M}) \leq \sup_{1 \leq \kappa \leq \varepsilon} H_d(g_\kappa(\mathcal{N}), \ell_\kappa(\mathcal{M})) = H_d(g_{\kappa_0}(\mathcal{N}), \ell_{\kappa_0}(\mathcal{M})). \tag{10}$$

With the aid of Lemma 3, we obtain

$$\begin{aligned} \lambda + \Im(H_d(\Theta\mathcal{N}, \Omega\mathcal{M})) &\leq \lambda + \Im(H_d(g_{\kappa_0}\mathcal{N}, \ell_{\kappa_0}\mathcal{M})) \\ &\leq \lambda_{\kappa_0} + \Im_{\kappa_0}(H_d(g_{\kappa_0}\mathcal{N}, \ell_{\kappa_0}\mathcal{M})) + G_{\kappa_0}(H_d(g_{\kappa_0}\mathcal{N}, \ell_{\kappa_0}\mathcal{M})) \\ &\leq \Im_{\kappa_0}(H_d(\mathcal{N}, \mathcal{M})) + G_{\kappa_0}(H_d(\mathcal{N}, \mathcal{M})) \\ &= \Im(H_d(\mathcal{N}, \mathcal{M})); \end{aligned} \tag{11}$$

that is, the pair (Θ, Ω) is a generalized $\Im$-contraction on $\mathcal{C}^d(\mathbb{U})$. □

3. Main Results

This section is devoted to proving the existence results of common attractors of Hutchinson–Wardowski contractive operators. We start with the following definition.

Definition 6. *Let $(\mathbb{U}, d)$ be a metric space and $\Theta, \Omega : \mathcal{C}^d(\mathbb{U}) \to \mathcal{C}^d(\mathbb{U})$ be mappings as defined in* (3)*. A pair (Θ, Ω) is called Hardy–Rogers-type Hutchinson–Wardowski contractive operator if there exist $\Im \in \nabla(\Im)$ and $\lambda > 0$ such that, for all $\mathcal{N}, \mathcal{M} \in \mathcal{C}^d(\mathbb{U})$, the following holds*

$$H_d(\Theta(\mathcal{N}), \Omega(\mathcal{M})) > 0, \quad \textit{implying} \quad \lambda + \Im(H_d(\Theta(\mathcal{N}), \Omega(\mathcal{M}))) \leq \Im(\mathbb{Q}^{H_d}_{\Theta,\Omega}(\mathcal{N}, \mathcal{M})), \tag{12}$$

where

$$\mathbb{Q}^{H_d}_{\Theta,\Omega}(\mathcal{N}, \mathcal{M}) = \alpha H_d(\mathcal{N}, \mathcal{M}) + \beta H_d(\mathcal{N}, \Theta\mathcal{N}) + \gamma H_d(\mathcal{M}, \Omega\mathcal{M}) + \delta H_d(\mathcal{N}, \Omega\mathcal{M}) + L H_d(\mathcal{M}, \Theta\mathcal{N})$$

with $\alpha, \beta, \gamma, \delta, L \geq 0$, $\alpha + \beta + \gamma + 2\delta = 1$ and $\gamma \neq 1$.

Definition 7. *Let $(\mathbb{U}, d)$ be a metric space and $\Theta, \Omega : \mathcal{C}^d(\mathbb{U}) \to \mathcal{C}^d(\mathbb{U})$ be mappings as defined in* (3)*. A pair (Θ, Ω) is called weak Hutchinson–Wardowski contractive operator if there exist $\Im \in \nabla(\Im)$ and $\lambda > 0$ such that, for all $\mathcal{N}, \mathcal{M} \in \mathcal{C}^d(\mathbb{U})$, the following holds*

$$H_d(\Theta(\mathcal{N}), \Omega(\mathcal{M})) > 0, \quad \textit{implying} \quad \lambda + \Im(H_d(\Theta(\mathcal{N}), \Omega(\mathcal{M}))) \leq \Im(\mathbb{P}^{H_d}_{\Theta,\Omega}(\mathcal{N}, \mathcal{M})), \tag{13}$$

where

$$\mathbb{P}^{H_d}_{\Theta,\Omega}(\mathcal{N}, \mathcal{M}) = \max\left\{ H_d(\mathcal{N}, \mathcal{M}), H_d(\mathcal{N}, \Theta\mathcal{N}), H_d(\mathcal{M}, \Omega\mathcal{M}), \frac{H_d(\mathcal{N}, \Omega\mathcal{M}) + H_d(\mathcal{M}, \Theta\mathcal{N})}{2} \right\}.$$

Remark 2. *From* ($\Im$1), (12), *and* (13)*, we deduce that every Hardy–Rogers-type Hutchinson–Wardowski contractive operator and weak Hutchinson–Wardowski contractive operator satisfy the following conditions, respectively:*

$$H_d(\Theta(\mathcal{N}), \Omega(\mathcal{M})) < \mathbb{Q}^{H_d}_{\Theta,\Omega}(\mathcal{N}, \mathcal{M}) \tag{14}$$

and

$$H_d(\Theta(\mathcal{N}), \Omega(\mathcal{M})) < \mathbb{P}^{H_d}_{\Theta,\Omega}(\mathcal{N}, \mathcal{M}). \tag{15}$$

Theorem 1. *Let* $(\mathbb{U}, d)$ *be a metric space,* $\{\mathbb{U}; (g_\kappa, \ell_\kappa), \kappa = 1, 2, 3, \cdots, \varepsilon\}$ *be an* $\Im$*-IFS, and* $\Theta, \Omega : C^d(\mathbb{U}) \to C^d(\mathbb{U})$ *be mappings as defined in (3). If the pair* (Θ, Ω) *is a Hardy–Rogers-type Hutchinson–Wardowski contractive operator, then* Θ *and* Ω *share a common attractor* $\mathcal{A} \in C^d(\mathbb{U})$*. If* $\alpha + \delta + L \leq 1$*, then this common attractor is unique.*

Moreover, for any initial compact set $\mathcal{N}_0$*, the sequence*

$$\{\mathcal{N}_0, \Theta(\mathcal{N}_0), \Omega\Theta(\mathcal{N}_0), \Theta\Omega\Theta(\mathcal{N}_0), \cdots\}$$

of compact sets generated by Θ *and* Ω *will converge to the common attractor* $\mathcal{A}$*.*

Proof. Let $\mathcal{N}_0 \in C^d(\mathbb{U})$ be an arbitrary point. Define the following sequence for initial point $\mathcal{N}_0$ as

$$\left.\begin{array}{l} \mathcal{N}_1 = \Theta(\mathcal{N}_0), \mathcal{N}_3 = \Theta(\mathcal{N}_2), \cdots, \mathcal{N}_{2r+1} = \Theta(\mathcal{N}_{2r}), \\ \mathcal{N}_2 = \Omega(\mathcal{N}_1), \mathcal{N}_4 = \Omega(\mathcal{N}_3), \cdots, \mathcal{N}_{2r+2} = \Omega(\mathcal{N}_{2r+1}), \end{array}\right\} \text{for } r \in \mathbb{N}_0 = \mathbb{N} \cup \{0\}. \tag{16}$$

If $\mathcal{N}_{2r+1} = \mathcal{N}_{2r}$ for some $r \in \mathbb{N}_0$, then $\mathcal{N}_{2r}$ is the common attractor of Θ and Ω. Assume that $\mathcal{N}_{2r+1} \neq \mathcal{N}_{2r}$ for all $r \in \mathbb{N}_0$. So, by using $\mathcal{N} = \mathcal{N}_{2r}$ and $\mathcal{M} = \mathcal{N}_{2r+1}$ in inequality (12), we have

$$\lambda + \Im(H_d(\mathcal{N}_{2r+1}, \mathcal{N}_{2r+2})) = \lambda + \Im(H_d(\Theta\mathcal{N}_{2r}, \Omega\mathcal{N}_{2r+1})) \leq \Im(\mathbb{Q}^{H_d}_{\Theta,\Omega}(\mathcal{N}_{2r}, \mathcal{N}_{2r+1})),$$

where

$$\begin{aligned} \mathbb{Q}^{H_d}_{\Theta,\Omega}(\mathcal{N}_{2r}, \mathcal{N}_{2r+1})) =& \alpha H_d(\mathcal{N}_{2r}, \mathcal{N}_{2r+1}) + \beta H_d(\mathcal{N}_{2r}, \Theta\mathcal{N}_{2r}) + \gamma H_d(\mathcal{N}_{2r+1}, \Omega\mathcal{N}_{2r+1}) \\ &+ \delta H_d(\mathcal{N}_{2r}, \Omega\mathcal{N}_{2r+1}) + L H_d(\mathcal{N}_{2r+1}, \Theta\mathcal{N}_{2r}) \\ \leq& (\alpha + \beta) H_d(\mathcal{N}_{2r}, \mathcal{N}_{2r+1}) + \gamma H_d(\mathcal{N}_{2r+1}, \mathcal{N}_{2r+2}) + \delta H_d(\mathcal{N}_{2r}, \mathcal{N}_{2r+2}) \\ \leq& (\alpha + \beta + \delta) H_d(\mathcal{N}_{2r}, \mathcal{N}_{2r+1}) + (\gamma + \delta) H_d(\mathcal{N}_{2r+1}, \mathcal{N}_{2r+2}). \end{aligned}$$

Thus,

$$\begin{aligned} &\lambda + \Im(H_d(\mathcal{N}_{2r+1}, \mathcal{N}_{2r+2})) \\ &\leq \Im((\alpha + \beta + \delta) H_d(\mathcal{N}_{2r}, \mathcal{N}_{2r+1}) + (\gamma + \delta) H_d(\mathcal{N}_{2r+1}, \mathcal{N}_{2r+2})). \end{aligned}$$

Similarly, by using $\mathcal{N} = \mathcal{N}_{2r+1}$ and $\mathcal{M} = \mathcal{N}_{2r+2}$ in inequality (12), we have

$$\lambda + \Im(H_d(\mathcal{N}_{2r+2}, \mathcal{N}_{2r+3})) = \lambda + \Im(H_d(\Theta\mathcal{N}_{2r+1}, \Omega\mathcal{N}_{2r+2})) \leq \Im(\mathbb{Q}^{H_d}_{\Theta,\Omega}(\mathcal{N}_{2r+1}, \mathcal{N}_{2r+2})),$$

where

$$\begin{aligned} \mathbb{Q}^{H_d}_{\Theta,\Omega}(\mathcal{N}_{2r+1}, \mathcal{N}_{2r+2})) =& \alpha H_d(\mathcal{N}_{2r+1}, \mathcal{N}_{2r+2}) + \beta H_d(\mathcal{N}_{2r+1}, \Theta\mathcal{N}_{2r+1}) + \gamma H_d(\mathcal{N}_{2r+2}, \Omega\mathcal{N}_{2r+2}) \\ &+ \delta H_d(\mathcal{N}_{2r+1}, \Omega\mathcal{N}_{2r+2}) + L H_d(\mathcal{N}_{2r+2}, \Theta\mathcal{N}_{2r+1}) \\ \leq& (\alpha + \beta) H_d(\mathcal{N}_{2r+1}, \mathcal{N}_{2r+2}) + \gamma H_d(\mathcal{N}_{2r+2}, \mathcal{N}_{2r+3}) + \delta H_d(\mathcal{N}_{2r+1}, \mathcal{N}_{2r+3}) \\ \leq& (\alpha + \beta + \delta) H_d(\mathcal{N}_{2r+1}, \mathcal{N}_{2r+2}) + (\gamma + \delta) H_d(\mathcal{N}_{2r+2}, \mathcal{N}_{2r+3}). \end{aligned}$$

Thus,

$$\lambda + \Im(H_d(\mathcal{N}_{2r+2}, \mathcal{N}_{2r+3})) \leq \Im((\alpha + \beta + \delta) H_d(\mathcal{N}_{2r+1}, \mathcal{N}_{2r+2}) + (\gamma + \delta) H_d(\mathcal{N}_{2r+2}, \mathcal{N}_{2r+3})).$$

In general, for all $r \in \mathbb{N}_0$, we have

$$\lambda + \Im(H_d(\mathcal{N}_{r+1}, \mathcal{N}_{r+2})) \leq \Im((\alpha + \beta + \delta) H_d(\mathcal{N}_r, \mathcal{N}_{r+1}) + (\gamma + \delta) H_d(\mathcal{N}_{r+1}, \mathcal{N}_{r+2})). \tag{17}$$

Since $\Im$ is strictly increasing, we deduce that

$$H_d(\mathcal{N}_{r+1}, \mathcal{N}_{r+2}) < (\alpha + \beta + \delta) H_d(\mathcal{N}_r, \mathcal{N}_{r+1}) + (\gamma + \delta) H_d(\mathcal{N}_{r+1}, \mathcal{N}_{r+2}),$$

which further implies that

$$(1-\gamma-\delta)H_d(\mathcal{N}_{r+1},\mathcal{N}_{r+2}) < (\alpha+\beta+\delta)H_d(\mathcal{N}_r,\mathcal{N}_{r+1}), \quad \text{for all} \quad r \in \mathbb{N}_0.$$

Since $\alpha+\beta+\gamma+2\delta = 1$ and $\gamma \neq 1, 1-\gamma-\delta > 0$ and thus

$$\begin{aligned} H_d(\mathcal{N}_{r+1},\mathcal{N}_{r+2}) &< \frac{(\alpha+\beta+\delta)}{(1-\gamma-\delta)}H_d(\mathcal{N}_r,\mathcal{N}_{r+1}) \\ &= H_d(\mathcal{N}_r,\mathcal{N}_{r+1}). \end{aligned}$$

Consequently,

$$\lambda + \Im(H_d(\mathcal{N}_{r+1},\mathcal{N}_{r+2})) \leq \Im(H_d(\mathcal{N}_r,\mathcal{N}_{r+1})), \quad \text{for all} \quad r \in \mathbb{N}_0. \tag{18}$$

Inequality (18) implies that

$$\begin{aligned} \Im(H_d(\mathcal{N}_r,\mathcal{N}_{r+1})) &\leq \Im(H_d(\mathcal{N}_{r-1},\mathcal{N}_r)) - \lambda \\ &\leq \Im(H_d(\mathcal{N}_{r-2},\mathcal{N}_{r-1})) - 2\lambda \\ &\vdots \\ &\leq \Im(H_d(\mathcal{N}_0,\mathcal{N}_1)) - r\lambda \end{aligned} \tag{19}$$

for all $r \in \mathbb{N}$; thus,

$$\lim_{r\to\infty} \Im(H_d(\mathcal{N}_r,\mathcal{N}_{r+1})) = -\infty. \tag{20}$$

By using ($\Im 2'$) and (20), we obtain that $H_d(\mathcal{N}_r,\mathcal{N}_{r+1}) \to 0$ as $r \to \infty$. Now, from ($\Im 3$), there exists $j \in (0,1)$ such that

$$\lim_{r\to\infty} [H_d(\mathcal{N}_r,\mathcal{N}_{r+1})]^j \Im(H_d(\mathcal{N}_r,\mathcal{N}_{r+1})).$$

Thus, by using (19), the following holds for all $r \in \mathbb{N}$,

$$\begin{aligned} &[H_d(\mathcal{N}_r,\mathcal{N}_{r+1})]^j \Im(H_d(\mathcal{N}_r,\mathcal{N}_{r+1})) - [H_d(\mathcal{N}_r,\mathcal{N}_{r+1})]^j \Im(H_d(\mathcal{N}_0,\mathcal{N}_1)) \\ \leq &[H_d(\mathcal{N}_r,\mathcal{N}_{r+1})]^j (\Im(H_d(\mathcal{N}_0,\mathcal{N}_1)) - r\lambda) - [H_d(\mathcal{N}_r,\mathcal{N}_{r+1})]^j \Im(H_d(\mathcal{N}_0,\mathcal{N}_1)) \\ = &- r\lambda [H_d(\mathcal{N}_r,\mathcal{N}_{r+1})]^j \leq 0 \end{aligned} \tag{21}$$

On letting limit as $r \to \infty$ in (21), we obtain

$$\lim_{r\to\infty} r[H_d(\mathcal{N}_r,\mathcal{N}_{r+1})]^j = 0$$

and hence

$$\lim_{r\to\infty} (r)^{\frac{1}{j}} H_d(\mathcal{N}_r,\mathcal{N}_{r+1}) = 0. \tag{22}$$

Equation (22) guarantees that the series $\sum_{r=1}^{\infty} H_d(\mathcal{N}_r,\mathcal{N}_{r+1})$ is convergent. This implies that $\{\mathcal{N}_r\}$ is a Cauchy sequence in $\mathcal{C}^d(\mathbb{U})$. Completeness of $(\mathcal{C}^d(\mathbb{U}), H_d)$ ensures the existence of $\mathcal{A} \in \mathcal{C}^d(\mathbb{U})$ such that

$$\lim_{r\to\infty} \mathcal{N}_r = \mathcal{A}, \tag{23}$$

which implies

$$\lim_{r\to\infty} H_d(\mathcal{N}_r,\mathcal{A}) = \lim_{r\to\infty} H_d(\mathcal{N}_r,\mathcal{N}_{r+1}) = H_d(\mathcal{A},\mathcal{A}),$$

so we have

$$\lim_{r\to\infty} H_d(\mathcal{N}_r, \mathcal{A}) = 0. \tag{24}$$

Next, assume that $\mathcal{A} \neq \Theta\mathcal{A}$, and then we can assume that $\Theta\mathcal{N}_r \neq \Theta\mathcal{A}$ for all $r \in \mathbb{N}_0$. Now, from (14), we have

$$\begin{aligned} H_d(\Theta\mathcal{A}, \mathcal{A}) &\leq H_d(\Theta\mathcal{A}, \mathcal{N}_{2r+2}) + H_d(\mathcal{N}_{2r+2}, \mathcal{A}) \\ &= H_d(\Theta\mathcal{A}, \Omega\mathcal{N}_{2r+1}) + H_d(\mathcal{N}_{2r+2}, \mathcal{A}) \\ &< \mathbb{Q}^{H_d}_{\Theta,\Omega}(\mathcal{A}, \mathcal{N}_{2r+1}) + H_d(\mathcal{N}_{2r+2}, \mathcal{A}), \end{aligned} \tag{25}$$

where

$$\begin{aligned} \mathbb{Q}^{H_d}_{\Theta,\Omega}(\mathcal{A}, \mathcal{N}_{2r+1}) =&\alpha H_d(\mathcal{A}, \mathcal{N}_{2r+1}) + \beta H_d(\mathcal{A}, \Theta\mathcal{A}) + \gamma H_d(\mathcal{N}_{2r+1}, \Omega\mathcal{N}_{2r+1}) \\ &+ \delta H_d(\mathcal{A}, \Omega\mathcal{N}_{2r+1}) + L H_d(\mathcal{N}_{2r+1}, \Theta\mathcal{A}) \\ =&\alpha H_d(\mathcal{A}, \mathcal{N}_{2r+1}) + \beta H_d(\mathcal{A}, \Theta\mathcal{A}) + \gamma H_d(\mathcal{N}_{2r+1}, \mathcal{N}_{2r+2}) \\ &+ \delta H_d(\mathcal{A}, \mathcal{N}_{2r+2}) + L H_d(\mathcal{N}_{2r+1}, \Theta\mathcal{A}). \end{aligned} \tag{26}$$

By letting limit as $r \to \infty$ in (26) and combining with (25), we obtain

$$H_d(\Theta\mathcal{A}, \mathcal{A}) < (\beta + L) H_d(\Theta\mathcal{A}, \mathcal{A}) < H_d(\Theta\mathcal{A}, \mathcal{A}),$$

a contradiction; hence, $\mathcal{A} = \Theta\mathcal{A}$.

Similarly, assume that $\mathcal{A} \neq \Omega\mathcal{A}$, and then we can assume that $\Omega\mathcal{N}_r \neq \Omega\mathcal{A}$ for all $r \in \mathbb{N}_0$. Now, from (14), we have

$$\begin{aligned} H_d(\mathcal{A}, \Omega\mathcal{A}) &\leq H_d(\mathcal{A}, \mathcal{N}_{2r+1}) + H_d(\mathcal{N}_{2r+1}, \Omega\mathcal{A}) \\ &= H_d(\mathcal{A}, \mathcal{N}_{2r+1}) + H_d(\Theta\mathcal{N}_{2r}, \Omega\mathcal{A}) \\ &< H_d(\mathcal{A}, \mathcal{N}_{2r+1}) + \mathbb{Q}^{H_d}_{\Theta,\Omega}(\mathcal{N}_{2r}, \mathcal{A}), \end{aligned} \tag{27}$$

where

$$\begin{aligned} \mathbb{Q}^{H_d}_{\Theta,\Omega}(\mathcal{N}_{2r}, \mathcal{A}) =&\alpha H_d(\mathcal{N}_{2r}, \mathcal{A}) + \beta H_d(\mathcal{N}_{2r}, \Theta\mathcal{N}_{2r}) + \gamma H_d(\mathcal{A}, \Omega\mathcal{A}) \\ &+ \delta H_d(\mathcal{N}_{2r}, \Omega\mathcal{A}) + L H_d(\mathcal{A}, \Theta\mathcal{N}_{2r}) \\ =&\alpha H_d(\mathcal{N}_{2r}, \mathcal{A}) + \beta H_d(\mathcal{N}_{2r}, \mathcal{N}_{2r+1}) + \gamma H_d(\mathcal{A}, \Omega\mathcal{A}) \\ &+ \delta H_d(\mathcal{N}_{2r}, \Omega\mathcal{A}) + L H_d(\mathcal{A}, \mathcal{N}_{2r+1}). \end{aligned} \tag{28}$$

By letting limit as $r \to \infty$ in (28) and combining with (27), we obtain

$$H_d(\mathcal{A}, \Omega\mathcal{A}) < (\gamma + \delta) H_d(\mathcal{A}, \Omega\mathcal{A}) < H_d(\mathcal{A}, \Omega\mathcal{A}),$$

a contradiction; hence, $\mathcal{A} = \Omega\mathcal{A}$. Thus, $\mathcal{A}$ is a common attractor of Θ and Ω.

Next, we prove the uniqueness of the common attractor. Let $\mathcal{B}$ be another common attractor of Θ and Ω such that $\mathcal{A} \neq \mathcal{B}$. Then, $H_d(\mathcal{A}, \mathcal{B}) > 0$, so (12) yields

$$\lambda + \Im(H_d(\mathcal{A}, \mathcal{B}) = \lambda + \Im(H_d(\Theta\mathcal{A}, \Omega\mathcal{B}) \leq \Im(\mathbb{Q}^{H_d}_{\Theta,\Omega}(\mathcal{A}, \mathcal{B})), \tag{29}$$

where

$$\begin{aligned} \mathbb{Q}^{H_d}_{\Theta,\Omega}(\mathcal{A}, \mathcal{B}) =&\alpha H_d(\mathcal{A}, \mathcal{B}) + \beta H_d(\mathcal{A}, \Theta\mathcal{A}) + \gamma H_d(\mathcal{B}, \Omega\mathcal{B}) + \delta H_d(\mathcal{A}, \Omega\mathcal{B}) + L H_d(\mathcal{B}, \Theta\mathcal{A}) \\ =&(\alpha + \delta + L) H_d(\mathcal{A}, \mathcal{B}). \end{aligned}$$

If $\alpha + \delta + L \leq 1$, inequality (29) yields a contradiction to the fact that $\lambda > 0$. Hence, $\mathcal{A} = \mathcal{B}$. □

Theorem 2. *Let $(\mathbb{U},d)$ be a metric space, $\{\mathbb{U};(g_\kappa,\ell_\kappa),\kappa=1,2,3,\cdots,\varepsilon\}$ be an $\Im$-IFS, and $\Theta,\Omega:\mathcal{C}^d(\mathbb{U})\to\mathcal{C}^d(\mathbb{U})$ be mappings as defined in (3). If the pair (Θ,Ω) is a weak Hutchinson–Wardowski contractive operator, then Θ and Ω share at most one common attractor $\mathcal{A}\in\mathcal{C}^d(\mathbb{U})$. Moreover, for any initial compact set $\mathcal{N}_0$, the sequence*

$$\{\mathcal{N}_0,\Theta(\mathcal{N}_0),\Omega\Theta(\mathcal{N}_0),\Theta\Omega\Theta(\mathcal{N}_0),\cdots\}$$

of compact sets generated by Θ and Ω will converge to the common attractor $\mathcal{A}$.

Proof. Let $\mathcal{N}_0\in\mathcal{C}^d(\mathbb{U})$ be an arbitrary point. Define the sequence as in (16) for initial point $\mathcal{N}_0$. If $\mathcal{N}_{2r+1}=\mathcal{N}_{2r}$ for some $r\in\mathbb{N}_0$, then $\mathcal{N}_{2r}$ is the common attractor of Θ and Ω. Assume that $\mathcal{N}_{2r+1}\neq\mathcal{N}_{2r}$ for all $r\in\mathbb{N}_0$; thus, by using $\mathcal{N}=\mathcal{N}_{2r}$ and $\mathcal{M}=\mathcal{N}_{2r+1}$ in inequality (13), we have

$$\lambda+\Im(H_d(\mathcal{N}_{2r+1},\mathcal{N}_{2r+2}))=\lambda+\Im(H_d(\Theta\mathcal{N}_{2r},\Omega\mathcal{N}_{2r+1}))\leq\Im(\mathbb{P}^{H_d}_{\Theta,\Omega}(\mathcal{N}_{2r},\mathcal{N}_{2r+1})),\tag{30}$$

where

$$\begin{aligned}\mathbb{P}^{H_d}_{\Theta,\Omega}(\mathcal{N}_{2r},\mathcal{N}_{2r+1})) &=\max\{H_d(\mathcal{N}_{2r},\mathcal{N}_{2r+1}),H_d(\mathcal{N}_{2r},\Theta\mathcal{N}_{2r}),H_d(\mathcal{N}_{2r+1},\Omega\mathcal{N}_{2r+1}),\\ &\quad\frac{H_d(\mathcal{N}_{2r},\Omega\mathcal{N}_{2r+1})+H_d(\mathcal{N}_{2r+1},\Theta\mathcal{N}_{2r})}{2}\Big\}\\ &=\max\left\{H_d(\mathcal{N}_{2r},\mathcal{N}_{2r+1}),H_d(\mathcal{N}_{2r+1},\mathcal{N}_{2r+2}),\frac{H_d(\mathcal{N}_{2r},\mathcal{N}_{2r+2})}{2}\right\}\\ &\leq\max\{H_d(\mathcal{N}_{2r},\mathcal{N}_{2r+1}),H_d(\mathcal{N}_{2r+1},\mathcal{N}_{2r+2}),\\ &\quad\frac{H_d(\mathcal{N}_{2r},\mathcal{N}_{2r+1})+H_d(\mathcal{N}_{2r+1},\mathcal{N}_{2r+2})}{2}\Big\}\\ &=\max\{H_d(\mathcal{N}_{2r},\mathcal{N}_{2r+1}),H_d(\mathcal{N}_{2r+1},\mathcal{N}_{2r+2})\}.\end{aligned}$$

Now, if $\mathbb{P}^{H_d}_{\Theta,\Omega}(\mathcal{N}_{2r},\mathcal{N}_{2r+1}))=H_d(\mathcal{N}_{2r+1},\mathcal{N}_{2r+2})$, then (30) reduces to

$$\lambda+\Im(H_d(\mathcal{N}_{2r+1},\mathcal{N}_{2r+2}))\leq\Im(H_d(\mathcal{N}_{2r+1},\mathcal{N}_{2r+2})),\tag{31}$$

which leads to contradiction because $\lambda>0$. Hence, $\mathbb{P}^{H_d}_{\Theta,\Omega}(\mathcal{N}_{2r},\mathcal{N}_{2r+1}))=H_d(\mathcal{N}_{2r},\mathcal{N}_{2r+1})$ and

$$\lambda+\Im(H_d(\mathcal{N}_{2r+1},\mathcal{N}_{2r+2}))\leq\Im(H_d(\mathcal{N}_{2r},\mathcal{N}_{2r+1})).\tag{32}$$

Similarly, by using $\mathcal{N}=\mathcal{N}_{2r+1}$ and $\mathcal{M}=\mathcal{N}_{2r+2}$ in inequality (13), we have

$$\begin{aligned}\lambda+\Im(H_d(\mathcal{N}_{2r+2},\mathcal{N}_{2r+3}))&=\lambda+\Im(H_d(\Theta\mathcal{N}_{2r+1},\Omega\mathcal{N}_{2r+2}))\\ &\leq\Im(\mathbb{P}^{H_d}_{\Theta,\Omega}(\mathcal{N}_{2r+1},\mathcal{N}_{2r+2})),\end{aligned}\tag{33}$$

where

$$\begin{aligned}\mathbb{P}^{H_d}_{\Theta,\Omega}(\mathcal{N}_{2r+1},\mathcal{N}_{2r+2}) &=\max\{H_d(\mathcal{N}_{2r+1},\mathcal{N}_{2r+2}),H_d(\mathcal{N}_{2r+1},\Theta\mathcal{N}_{2r+1}),H_d(\mathcal{N}_{2r+2},\Omega\mathcal{N}_{2r+2}),\\ &\quad\frac{H_d(\mathcal{N}_{2r+1},\Omega\mathcal{N}_{2r+2})+H_d(\mathcal{N}_{2r+2},\Theta\mathcal{N}_{2r+1})}{2}\Big\}\\ &=\max\left\{H_d(\mathcal{N}_{2r+1},\mathcal{N}_{2r+2}),H_d(\mathcal{N}_{2r+2},\mathcal{N}_{2r+3}),\frac{H_d(\mathcal{N}_{2r+1},\mathcal{N}_{2r+3})}{2}\right\}\\ &\leq\max\{H_d(\mathcal{N}_{2r+1},\mathcal{N}_{2r+2}),H_d(\mathcal{N}_{2r+2},\mathcal{N}_{2r+3}),\\ &\quad\frac{H_d(\mathcal{N}_{2r+1},\mathcal{N}_{2r+2})+H_d(\mathcal{N}_{2r+2},\mathcal{N}_{2r+3})}{2}\Big\}\\ &=\max\{H_d(\mathcal{N}_{2r+1},\mathcal{N}_{2r+2}),H_d(\mathcal{N}_{2r+2},\mathcal{N}_{2r+3})\}.\end{aligned}$$

Thus,

$$\lambda + \Im(H_d(\mathcal{N}_{2r+2}, \mathcal{N}_{2r+3})) \leq \Im(H_d(\mathcal{N}_{2r+1}, \mathcal{N}_{2r+2})).$$

In general, for all $r \in \mathbb{N}_0$, we have

$$\lambda + \Im(H_d(\mathcal{N}_{r+1}, \mathcal{N}_{r+2})) \leq \Im(H_d(\mathcal{N}_r, \mathcal{N}_{r+1})). \tag{34}$$

Inequality (34) implies that

$$\begin{aligned} \Im(H_d(\mathcal{N}_r, \mathcal{N}_{r+1})) &\leq \Im(H_d(\mathcal{N}_{r-1}, \mathcal{N}_r)) - \lambda \\ &\leq \Im(H_d(\mathcal{N}_{r-2}, \mathcal{N}_{r-1})) - 2\lambda \\ &\vdots \\ &\leq \Im(H_d(\mathcal{N}_0, \mathcal{N}_1)) - r\lambda, \end{aligned} \tag{35}$$

for all $r \in \mathbb{N}$; thus,

$$\lim_{r \to \infty} \Im(H_d(\mathcal{N}_r, \mathcal{N}_{r+1})) = -\infty. \tag{36}$$

By using ($\Im 2'$) and (36), we obtain that $H_d(\mathcal{N}_r, \mathcal{N}_{r+1}) \to 0$ as $r \to \infty$. Now, from ($\Im 3$), there exists $j \in (0,1)$ such that

$$\lim_{r \to \infty} [H_d(\mathcal{N}_r, \mathcal{N}_{r+1})]^j \Im(H_d(\mathcal{N}_r, \mathcal{N}_{r+1})).$$

Thus, by using (35), the following holds for all $r \in \mathbb{N}$,

$$\begin{aligned} &[H_d(\mathcal{N}_r, \mathcal{N}_{r+1})]^j \Im(H_d(\mathcal{N}_r, \mathcal{N}_{r+1})) - [H_d(\mathcal{N}_r, \mathcal{N}_{r+1})]^j \Im(H_d(\mathcal{N}_0, \mathcal{N}_1)) \\ \leq &[H_d(\mathcal{N}_r, \mathcal{N}_{r+1})]^j (\Im(H_d(\mathcal{N}_0, \mathcal{N}_1)) - r\lambda) - [H_d(\mathcal{N}_r, \mathcal{N}_{r+1})]^j \Im(H_d(\mathcal{N}_0, \mathcal{N}_1)) \\ = &- r\lambda [H_d(\mathcal{N}_r, \mathcal{N}_{r+1})]^j \leq 0 \end{aligned} \tag{37}$$

On setting limit as $r \to \infty$ in (37), we obtain

$$\lim_{r \to \infty} r[H_d(\mathcal{N}_r, \mathcal{N}_{r+1})]^j = 0$$

and hence

$$\lim_{r \to \infty} (r)^{\frac{1}{j}} H_d(\mathcal{N}_r, \mathcal{N}_{r+1}) = 0. \tag{38}$$

Equation (38) guarantees that the series $\sum_{r=1}^{\infty} H_d(\mathcal{N}_r, \mathcal{N}_{r+1})$ is convergent. This implies that $\{\mathcal{N}_r\}$ is a Cauchy sequence in $C^d(\mathbb{U})$. Completeness of $(C^d(\mathbb{U}), H_d)$ ensures the existence of $\mathcal{A} \in C^d(\mathbb{U})$ such that

$$\lim_{r \to \infty} \mathcal{N}_r = \mathcal{A}, \tag{39}$$

which implies

$$\lim_{r \to \infty} H_d(\mathcal{N}_r, \mathcal{A}) = \lim_{r \to \infty} H_d(\mathcal{N}_r, \mathcal{N}_{r+1}) = H_d(\mathcal{A}, \mathcal{A}),$$

so we have

$$\lim_{r \to \infty} H_d(\mathcal{N}_r, \mathcal{A}) = 0. \tag{40}$$

Next, assume that $\mathcal{A} \neq \Theta\mathcal{A}$, and then we can assume that $\Theta\mathcal{N}_r \neq \Theta\mathcal{A}$ for all $r \in \mathbb{N}_0$. Now, from (15), we have

$$\begin{aligned} H_d(\Theta\mathcal{A}, \mathcal{A}) &\leq H_d(\Theta\mathcal{A}, \mathcal{N}_{2r+2}) + H_d(\mathcal{N}_{2r+2}, \mathcal{A}) \\ &= H_d(\Theta\mathcal{A}, \Omega\mathcal{N}_{2r+1}) + H_d(\mathcal{N}_{2r+2}, \mathcal{A}) \\ &< \mathbb{P}^{H_d}_{\Theta,\Omega}(\mathcal{A}, \mathcal{N}_{2r+1}) + H_d(\mathcal{N}_{2r+2}, \mathcal{A}), \end{aligned} \tag{41}$$

where

$$\begin{aligned} \mathbb{P}^{H_d}_{\Theta,\Omega}(\mathcal{A}, \mathcal{N}_{2r+1}) &= \max\left\{ H_d(\mathcal{A}, \mathcal{N}_{2r+1}), H_d(\mathcal{A}, \Theta\mathcal{A}), H_d(\mathcal{N}_{2r+1}, \Omega\mathcal{N}_{2r+1}) \right. \\ &\qquad \left. \frac{H_d(\mathcal{A}, \Omega\mathcal{N}_{2r+1}) + H_d(\mathcal{N}_{2r+1}, \Theta\mathcal{A})}{2} \right\} \\ &= \max\left\{ H_d(\mathcal{A}, \mathcal{N}_{2r+1}), H_d(\mathcal{A}, \Theta\mathcal{A}), H_d(\mathcal{N}_{2r+1}, \mathcal{N}_{2r+2}) \right. \\ &\qquad \left. \frac{H_d(\mathcal{A}, \mathcal{N}_{2r+2}) + H_d(\mathcal{N}_{2r+1}, \Theta\mathcal{A})}{2} \right\}. \end{aligned} \tag{42}$$

By setting limit as $r \to \infty$ in (41) and combining with (42), we obtain

$$\begin{aligned} H_d(\Theta\mathcal{A}, \mathcal{A}) &< \max\left\{ H_d(\mathcal{A}, \Theta\mathcal{A}), \frac{H_d(\mathcal{A}, \Theta\mathcal{A})}{2} \right\} \\ &= H_d(\mathcal{A}, \Theta\mathcal{A}), \end{aligned} \tag{43}$$

a contradiction; hence, $\mathcal{A} = \Theta\mathcal{A}$.

Similarly, assume that $\mathcal{A} \neq \Omega\mathcal{A}$, and then we can assume that $\Omega\mathcal{N}_r \neq \Omega\mathcal{A}$ for all $r \in \mathbb{N}_0$. Now, from (15), we have

$$\begin{aligned} H_d(\mathcal{A}, \Omega\mathcal{A}) &\leq H_d(\mathcal{A}, \mathcal{N}_{2r+1}) + H_d(\mathcal{N}_{2r+1}, \Omega\mathcal{A}) \\ &= H_d(\mathcal{A}, \mathcal{N}_{2r+1}) + H_d(\Theta\mathcal{N}_{2r}, \Omega\mathcal{A}) \\ &< H_d(\mathcal{A}, \mathcal{N}_{2r+1}) + \mathbb{P}^{H_d}_{\Theta,\Omega}(\mathcal{N}_{2r}, \mathcal{A}), \end{aligned} \tag{44}$$

where

$$\begin{aligned} \mathbb{P}^{H_d}_{\Theta,\Omega}(\mathcal{N}_{2r}, \mathcal{A}) &= \max\left\{ H_d(\mathcal{N}_{2r}, \mathcal{A}), H_d(\mathcal{N}_{2r}, \Theta\mathcal{N}_{2r}), H_d(\mathcal{A}, \Omega\mathcal{A}) \right. \\ &\qquad \left. \frac{H_d(\mathcal{N}_{2r}, \Omega\mathcal{A}) + H_d(\mathcal{A}, \Theta\mathcal{N}_{2r})}{2} \right\} \\ &= \max\left\{ H_d(\mathcal{N}_{2r}, \mathcal{A}), H_d(\mathcal{N}_{2r}, \mathcal{N}_{2r+1}), H_d(\mathcal{A}, \Omega\mathcal{A}) \right. \\ &\qquad \left. \frac{H_d(\mathcal{N}_{2r}, \Omega\mathcal{A}) + H_d(\mathcal{A}, \mathcal{N}_{2r+1})}{2} \right\}. \end{aligned} \tag{45}$$

By setting limit as $r \to \infty$ in (44) and combining with (45), we obtain

$$\begin{aligned} H_d(\mathcal{A}, \Omega\mathcal{A}) &< \max\left\{ H_d(\mathcal{A}, \Omega\mathcal{A}), \frac{H_d(\mathcal{A}, \Omega\mathcal{A})}{2} \right\} \\ &= H_d(\mathcal{A}, \Omega\mathcal{A}), \end{aligned} \tag{46}$$

a contradiction; hence, $\mathcal{A} = \Omega\mathcal{A}$. Thus, $\mathcal{A}$ is a common attractor of Θ and Ω.

Next, we prove the uniqueness of the common attractor. Let $\mathcal{B}$ be another common attractor of Θ and Ω such that $\mathcal{A} \neq \mathcal{B}$. Then, $H_d(\mathcal{A}, \mathcal{B}) > 0$, so (13) yields

$$\lambda + \Im(H_d(\mathcal{A}, \mathcal{B}) = \lambda + \Im(H_d(\Theta\mathcal{A}, \Omega\mathcal{B}) \leq \Im(\mathbb{P}^{H_d}_{\Theta,\Omega}(\mathcal{A}, \mathcal{B})), \tag{47}$$

where

$$\begin{aligned}\mathbb{P}^{H_d}_{\Theta,\Omega}(\mathcal{A}, \mathcal{B}) =& \max\left\{H_d(\mathcal{A}, \mathcal{B}), H_d(\mathcal{A}, \Theta\mathcal{A}), H_d(\mathcal{B}, \Omega\mathcal{B}), \frac{H_d(\mathcal{A}, \Omega\mathcal{B}) + H_d(\mathcal{B}, \Theta\mathcal{A})}{2}\right\} \\ =& H_d(\mathcal{A}, \mathcal{B}).\end{aligned}$$

Inequality (47) yields a contradiction because $\lambda > 0$. Hence, $\mathcal{A} = \mathcal{B}$. □

4. Consequences

By considering $\alpha = 1, \beta = \gamma = \delta = L = 0$ in (12) and then by using Theorem 1, we obtain the following existence result for a pair of Hutchinson operators.

Corollary 1. *Let $(\mathbb{U}, d)$ be a metric space, $\{\mathbb{U}; (g_\kappa, \ell_\kappa), \kappa = 1, 2, 3, \cdots, \varepsilon\}$ be an $\Im$-IFS, and $\Theta, \Omega : \mathcal{C}^d(\mathbb{U}) \to \mathcal{C}^d(\mathbb{U})$ be mappings as defined in* (3)*. If there exist $\Im \in \nabla(\Im)$ and $\lambda > 0$ such that, for all $\mathcal{N}, \mathcal{M} \in \mathcal{C}^d(\mathbb{U})$, the pair (Θ, Ω) satisfies*

$$H_d(\Theta(\mathcal{N}), \Omega(\mathcal{M})) > 0, \quad \textit{implying} \quad \lambda + \Im(H_d(\Theta(\mathcal{N}), \Omega(\mathcal{M}))) \leq \Im(H_d(\mathcal{N}, \mathcal{M})), \tag{48}$$

then Θ and Ω have a unique common attractor $\mathcal{A} \in \mathcal{C}^d(\mathbb{U})$. Moreover, for an arbitrarily chosen initial set $\mathcal{N}_0 \in \mathcal{C}^d(\mathbb{U})$, the sequence $\{\mathcal{N}_0, \Theta(\mathcal{N}_0), \Omega\Theta(\mathcal{N}_0), \Theta\Omega\Theta(\mathcal{N}_0), \cdots\}$ of compact sets converges to the common attractor $\mathcal{A}$ of Θ and Ω.

Further, setting $\alpha = \delta = L = 0, \beta + \gamma = 1$ and $\beta \neq 0$ in Theorem 1, we obtain the following existence result of common attractors of Kannan-type Hutchinson–Wardowski contractive operator.

Corollary 2. *Let $(\mathbb{U}, d)$ be a metric space, $\{Y; (g_\kappa, \ell_\kappa), \kappa = 1, 2, 3, \cdots, \varepsilon\}$ be an $\Im$-IFS, and $\Theta, \Omega : \mathcal{C}^d(\mathbb{U}) \to \mathcal{C}^d(\mathbb{U})$ be mappings as defined in* (3)*. If there exist $\Im \in \nabla(\Im)$ and $\lambda > 0$, for all $\mathcal{N}, \mathcal{M} \in \mathcal{C}^d(\mathbb{U})$, the pair (Θ, Ω) satisfies*

$$\begin{aligned}&H_d(\Theta(\mathcal{N}), \Omega(\mathcal{M})) > 0, \quad \textit{implying} \\ &\qquad \lambda + \Im(H_d(\Theta(\mathcal{N}), \Omega(\mathcal{M}))) \leq \Im(\beta H_d(\mathcal{N}, \Theta\mathcal{N}) + \gamma H_d(\mathcal{M}, \Omega\mathcal{M})),\end{aligned} \tag{49}$$

where $\beta + \gamma = 1$ and $\beta \neq 0$. Then, Θ and Ω have a unique common attractor $\mathcal{A}$ in $\mathcal{C}^d(\mathbb{U})$. Moreover, for an arbitrarily chosen initial set $\mathcal{N}_0 \in \mathcal{C}^d(\mathbb{U})$, the sequence $\{\mathcal{N}_0, \Theta(\mathcal{N}_0), \Omega\Theta(\mathcal{N}_0), \Theta\Omega\Theta(\mathcal{N}_0), \cdots\}$ of compact sets converges to the common attractor $\mathcal{A}$ of Θ and Ω.

Next, if we choose $\alpha = \beta = \gamma = 0$ and $\delta = \frac{1}{2}$ in Theorem 1, we obtain the following result for Chatterjea-type Hutchinson–Wardowski contractive operator.

Corollary 3. *Let $(\mathbb{U}, d)$ be a metric space, $\{Y; (g_\kappa, \ell_\kappa), \kappa = 1, 2, 3, \cdots, \varepsilon\}$ be an $\Im$-IFS, and $\Theta, \Omega : \mathcal{C}^d(\mathbb{U}) \to \mathcal{C}^d(\mathbb{U})$ be mappings as defined in* (3)*. If there exist $\Im \in \nabla(\Im)$ and $\lambda > 0$ such that, for all $\mathcal{N}, \mathcal{M} \in \mathcal{C}^d(\mathbb{U})$, the pair (Θ, Ω) satisfies*

$$\begin{aligned}&H_d(\Theta(\mathcal{N}), \Omega(\mathcal{M})) > 0, \quad \textit{implying} \\ &\qquad \lambda + \Im(H_d(\Theta(\mathcal{N}), \Omega(\mathcal{M}))) \leq \Im\left(\frac{1}{2}H_d(\mathcal{N}, \Omega\mathcal{M}) + LH_d(\mathcal{M}, \Theta\mathcal{N})\right).\end{aligned} \tag{50}$$

Then, Θ and Ω have a common attractor $\mathcal{A} \in \mathcal{C}^d(\mathbb{U})$. If $L \leq \frac{1}{2}$, then common attractor of Θ and Ω is unique. Moreover, for an arbitrarily chosen initial set $\mathcal{N}_0 \subset \mathcal{C}^d(\mathbb{U})$, the sequence $\{\mathcal{N}_0, \Theta(\mathcal{N}_0), \Omega\Theta(\mathcal{N}_0), \Theta\Omega\Theta(\mathcal{N}_0), \cdots\}$ of compact sets converges to the common attractor $\mathcal{A}$ of Θ and Ω.

Finally, if we set $\delta = L = 0$ in Theorem 1, we obtain the following existence of common attractors of Reich-type Hutchinson–Wardowski contractive operator.

Corollary 4. *Let $(\mathbb{U}, d)$ be a metric space, $\{\mathbb{U}; (g_\kappa, \ell_\kappa), \kappa = 1, 2, 3, \cdots, \varepsilon\}$ be an $\Im$-IFS, and $\Theta, \Omega : \mathcal{C}^d(\mathbb{U}) \to \mathcal{C}^d(\mathbb{U})$ be mappings as defined in (3). If there exist $\Im \in \nabla(\Im)$ and $\lambda > 0$, for all $\mathcal{N}, \mathcal{M} \in \mathcal{C}^d(\mathbb{U})$, the pair (Θ, Ω) satisfies*

$$\begin{aligned} &H_d(\Theta(\mathcal{N}), \Omega(\mathcal{M})) > 0, \quad \textit{implying} \\ &\quad \lambda + \Im(H_d(\Theta(\mathcal{N}), \Omega(\mathcal{M}))) \leq \Im(\alpha H_d(\mathcal{N}, \mathcal{M}) + \beta H_d(\mathcal{N}, \Theta\mathcal{N}) + \gamma H_d(\mathcal{M}, \Omega\mathcal{M})), \end{aligned} \tag{51}$$

where $\alpha\beta + \gamma = 1$ and $\gamma \neq 1$. Then, Θ and Ω have a unique common attractor $\mathcal{A} \in \mathcal{C}^d(\mathbb{U})$. Moreover, for an arbitrarily chosen initial set $\mathcal{N}_0 \in \mathcal{C}^d(\mathbb{U})$, the sequence $\{\mathcal{N}_0, \Theta(\mathcal{N}_0), \Omega\Theta(\mathcal{N}_0), \Theta\Omega\Theta(\mathcal{N}_0), \cdots\}$ of compact sets converges to the common attractor $\mathcal{A}$ of Θ and Ω.

Now, if we consider in Theorems 1 and 2 $\mathcal{S}^d(\mathbb{U})$, the collection of all singleton subsets of the space $\mathbb{U}$, then $\mathcal{S}^d(\mathbb{U}) \subseteq \mathcal{C}^d(\mathbb{U})$. Furthermore, if we take a pair of mappings $(g_\kappa, \ell_\kappa) = (g, \ell)$ for each κ, where $g = g_1$ and $\ell = \ell_1$, then the pair of operators (Θ, Ω) becomes $(\Theta(a_1), \Omega(a_2)) = (g(a_1), \ell(a_2))$. As a result, the subsequent common fixed point results are attained, respectively.

Corollary 5. *Let $(\mathbb{U}, d)$ be a metric space, $\{\mathbb{U}; (g_\kappa, \ell_\kappa), \kappa = 1, 2, 3, \cdots, \varepsilon\}$ be an $\Im$-IFS, and $g, \ell : \mathbb{U} \to \mathbb{U}$ be mappings defined as $(g_\kappa, \ell_\kappa) = (g, \ell)$ for each κ, where $g = g_1$ and $\ell = \ell_1$. If there exist $\Im \in \nabla(\Im)$ and $\lambda > 0$, for all $a_1, a_1 \in \mathbb{U}$, the pair (g, ℓ) satisfies*

$$d(g(a_1), \ell(a_2)) > 0, \quad \textit{implying} \quad \lambda + \Im(d(g(a_1), \ell(a_2))) \leq \Im(\mathbb{Q}^d_{g,\ell}(a_1, a_2)), \tag{52}$$

where

$$\mathbb{Q}^d_{g,\ell}(a_1, a_2) = \alpha d(a_1, a_2) + \beta d(a_1, ga_1) + \gamma d(a_2, \ell a_2) + \delta d(a_1, \ell a_2) + L d(a_2, ga_1)$$

with $\alpha, \beta, \gamma, \delta, L \geq 0$, $\alpha + \beta + \gamma + 2\delta = 1$ and $\gamma \neq 1$. Then, g and ℓ have a common fixed point $u \in \mathbb{U}$. Moreover, if $\alpha + \delta + L \leq 1$, then the common fixed point is unique. Furthermore, for an arbitrarily chosen initial set $u_0 \in \mathbb{U}$, the sequence $\{u_0, g(u_0), \ell g(u_0), g\ell g(u_0), \cdots\}$ converges to the common fixed point u of g and ℓ.

Corollary 6. *Let $(\mathbb{U}, d)$ be a metric space, $\{\mathbb{U}; (g_\kappa, \ell_\kappa), \kappa = 1, 2, 3, \cdots, \varepsilon\}$ be an $\Im$-IFS, and $g, \ell : \mathbb{U} \to \mathbb{U}$ be mappings defined as $(g_\kappa, \ell_\kappa) = (g, \ell)$ for each κ, where $g = g_1$ and $\ell = \ell_1$. If there exist $\Im \in \nabla(\Im)$ and $\lambda > 0$, for all $a_1, a_1 \in \mathbb{U}$, the pair (g, ℓ) satisfies*

$$d(g(a_1), \ell(a_2)) > 0, \quad \textit{implying} \quad \lambda + \Im(d(g(a_1), \ell(a_2))) \leq \Im(\mathbb{P}^d_{g,\ell}(a_1, a_2)), \tag{53}$$

where

$$\mathbb{P}^d_{g,\ell}(a_1, a_2) = \max\left\{ d(a_1, a_2), d(a_1, ga_1), d(a_2, \ell a_2), \frac{d(a_1, \ell a_2) + H_d(a_2, ga_1)}{2} \right\}.$$

Then, g and ℓ have a unique common fixed point $u \in \mathbb{U}$. Moreover, for an arbitrarily chosen initial set $u_0 \in \mathbb{U}$, the sequence $\{u_0, g(u_0), \ell g(u_0), g\ell g(u_0), \cdots\}$ converges to the common fixed point u of g and ℓ.

By considering $g = \ell$ and $\Theta = \Omega$ in Theorem 2, we return to Theorem 2.1 of [10].

Corollary 7 ([10])**.** *Let $(\mathbb{U}, d)$ be a metric space, $\{\mathbb{U}; g_\kappa), \kappa = 1,2,3,\cdots,\varepsilon\}$ be an $\Im$-IFS, and $\Theta : C^d(\mathbb{U}) \to C^d(\mathbb{U})$ be mappings as defined in (3). If there exist $\Im \in \nabla(\Im)$ and $\lambda > 0$, for all $\mathcal{N}, \mathcal{M} \in C^d(\mathbb{U})$ with $H_d(\Theta(\mathcal{N}), \Theta(\mathcal{M})) > 0$, the following holds*

$$\begin{aligned}\lambda + \Im(H_d(\Theta(\mathcal{N}), \Theta(\mathcal{M}))) \leq & \Im\Bigg(\max\Bigg\{H_d(\mathcal{N}, \mathcal{M}), H_d(\mathcal{N}, \Theta\mathcal{N}), H_d(\mathcal{M}, \Theta\mathcal{M}), \\ & \frac{H_d(\mathcal{N}, \Theta\mathcal{M}) + H_d(\mathcal{M}, \Theta\mathcal{N})}{2}\Bigg\}\Bigg).\end{aligned} \tag{54}$$

Then, Θ has a unique attractor $\mathcal{A} \in C^d(\mathbb{U})$. Furthermore, for an arbitrarily chosen initial set $\mathcal{N}_0 \in C^d(\mathbb{U})$, the sequence $\{\mathcal{N}_0, \Theta(\mathcal{N}_0), \Theta^2(\mathcal{N}_0), \Theta^3(\mathcal{N}_0), \cdots\}$ of compact sets converges to the attractor $\mathcal{A}$ of Θ.

By defining $\Im(t) = \ln(t)$ for all $t \in (0, \infty)$ in Theorem 2, we obtain the following:

Corollary 8. *Let $(\mathbb{U}, d)$ be a metric space, $\{\mathbb{U}; (g_\kappa, \ell_\kappa), \kappa = 1,2,3,\cdots,\varepsilon\}$ be an $\Im$-IFS, and $\Theta, \Omega : C^d(\mathbb{U}) \to C^d(\mathbb{U})$ be mappings as defined in (3). If there exist $\kappa \in (0,1)$, for all $\mathcal{N}, \mathcal{M} \in C^d(\mathbb{U})$ with $H_d(\Theta(\mathcal{N}), \Theta(\mathcal{M})) > 0$, the following holds*

$$\begin{aligned}\Im(H_d(\Theta(\mathcal{N}), \Omega(\mathcal{M}))) \leq & \kappa\Bigg(\max\Bigg\{H_d(\mathcal{N}, \mathcal{M}), H_d(\mathcal{N}, \Theta\mathcal{N}), H_d(\mathcal{M}, \Omega\mathcal{M}), \\ & \frac{H_d(\mathcal{N}, \Omega\mathcal{M}) + H_d(\mathcal{M}, \Theta\mathcal{N})}{2}\Bigg\}\Bigg).\end{aligned} \tag{55}$$

Then, Θ and Ω share at most one common attractor $\mathcal{A} \in C^d(\mathbb{U})$. Moreover, for any initial compact set $\mathcal{N}_0$, the sequence $\{\mathcal{N}_0, \Theta(\mathcal{N}_0), \Omega\Theta(\mathcal{N}_0), \Theta\Omega\Theta(\mathcal{N}_0), \cdots\}$ of compact sets generated by Θ and Ω will converge to the common attractor $\mathcal{A}$.

With the aid of Lemma 4, Theorems 1 and 2 provide the following corollary:

Corollary 9. *Let $(\mathbb{U}, d)$ be a metric space and $\{\mathbb{U}; (g_\kappa, \ell_\kappa), \kappa = 1,2,3,\cdots,\varepsilon\}$ be an $\Im$-IFS. If there exist $\Im_1, \Im_2, \cdots, \Im_\varepsilon \in \nabla(\Im)$ and $\lambda_1, \lambda_2, \cdots, \lambda_\varepsilon > 0$ such that the pair (g_κ, ℓ_κ) satisfy (9) and the mapping $\mathcal{G}_\kappa := \Im - \Im_\kappa$ is nondecreasing for each $\kappa = 1,2,3,\cdots,\varepsilon$, then the mappings $\Theta, \Omega : C^d(\mathbb{U}) \to C^d(\mathbb{U})$ defined in (3) have a unique common attractor $\mathcal{A} \in C^d(\mathbb{U})$. Moreover, for an arbitrarily chosen initial set $\mathcal{N}_0 \in C^d(\mathbb{U})$, the sequence $\{\mathcal{N}_0, \Theta(\mathcal{N}_0), \Omega\Theta(\mathcal{N}_0), \Theta\Omega\Theta(\mathcal{N}_0), \cdots\}$ of compact sets converges to the common attractor $\mathcal{A}$ of Θ and Ω.*

Next, we provide a supporting example of Corollary 9.

Example 1. *Let $\mathbb{U} = [0, \infty)$ be endowed with the Euclidian metric $d(\kappa, \xi) = |\kappa - \xi|$. Define $g_\kappa, \ell_\kappa : \mathbb{U} \to \mathbb{U}$, $\Im : (0, \infty) \to \mathbb{R}$ and $\Im_\kappa : (0, \infty) \to \mathbb{R}$, $\kappa = 1, 2$ as*

$$g_1(\kappa) = \frac{\kappa}{2}, \quad g_2(\kappa) = \frac{\kappa}{4} \quad \textit{for all } \kappa \in \mathbb{U},$$

$$\ell_1(\kappa) = \frac{\kappa}{2} + \frac{1}{4}, \quad \ell_2(\kappa) = \frac{\kappa + 1}{4} \quad \textit{for all } \kappa \in \mathbb{U},$$

and

$$\Im(a) = \ln a + \eta a \quad \Im_\kappa(a) = \ln a + \eta_\kappa a \quad \textit{for all } a \in (0, \infty),$$

where $\eta, \eta_\kappa \in (0,\infty)$ for all $\kappa = 1,2$. Then, by Proposition 2, $\Im, \Im_\kappa \in \nabla(\Im)$ and $\mathcal{G}_\kappa := \Im - \Im_\kappa$ are nondecreasing for each κ. Now, we will prove that there exist $\lambda_1, \lambda_2 > 0$ such that the pair $(g_\kappa, \ell_\kappa); \kappa = 1,2$ satisfy (9), which is equivalent to

$$\frac{|g_\kappa \kappa - \ell_\kappa \xi|}{|\kappa - \xi|} e^{\eta_\kappa(|g_\kappa \kappa - \ell_\kappa \xi| - |\kappa - \xi|)} \leq e^{-\lambda}; \quad \kappa = 1,2. \tag{56}$$

Let $\kappa, \xi \in X$ such that $d(g_1, \ell_1) > 0$ and $\kappa \neq \xi$. Suppose that $\xi < \kappa$; then,

$$\begin{aligned}
\frac{|g_1 \kappa - \ell_1 \xi|}{|\kappa - \xi|} e^{\eta_1(|g_1 \kappa - \ell_1 \xi| - |\kappa - \xi|)} &= \frac{\left|\frac{1}{2}(\kappa - \xi) - \frac{1}{4}\right|}{|\kappa - \xi|} e^{\eta_1\left(\left|\frac{1}{2}(\kappa-\xi) - \frac{1}{4}\right| - |\kappa - \xi|\right)} \\
&\leq \frac{\left|\frac{1}{2}(\kappa - \xi)\right|}{|\kappa - \xi|} e^{\eta_1\left(\left|\frac{1}{2}(\kappa-\xi) - \frac{1}{4}\right| - |\kappa - \xi|\right)} \\
&= \frac{1}{2} e^{\eta_1\left(\left|\frac{1}{2}(\kappa-\xi) - \frac{1}{4}\right| - |\kappa - \xi|\right)} \\
&< \frac{1}{2} \\
&\leq e^{-0.2} = e^{-\lambda_1}.
\end{aligned}$$

Also, for $\kappa, \xi \in X$ such that $d(g_2, \ell_2) > 0$ and $\kappa \neq \xi$, suppose that $\xi < \kappa$; then,

$$\begin{aligned}
\frac{|g_2 \kappa - \ell_2 \xi|}{|\kappa - \xi|} e^{\eta_2(|g_2 \kappa - \ell_2 \xi| - |\kappa - \xi|)} &= \frac{\left|\frac{1}{4}(\kappa - \xi) - \frac{1}{4}\right|}{|\kappa - \xi|} e^{\eta_2\left(\left|\frac{1}{4}(\kappa-\xi) - \frac{1}{4}\right| - |\kappa - \xi|\right)} \\
&\leq \frac{\left|\frac{1}{4}(\kappa - \xi)\right|}{|\kappa - \xi|} e^{\eta_2\left(\left|\frac{1}{4}(\kappa-\xi) - \frac{1}{4}\right| - |\kappa - \xi|\right)} \\
&= \frac{1}{4} e^{\eta_2\left(\left|\frac{1}{4}(\kappa-\xi) - \frac{1}{4}\right| - |\kappa - \xi|\right)} \\
&< \frac{1}{4} \\
&\leq e^{-0.2} = e^{-\lambda_2}.
\end{aligned}$$

Consider the $\Im$-IFS $\{\mathbb{U}; (g_\kappa, \ell_\kappa), \kappa = 1,2\}$ with the mappings $\Theta, \Omega : C^d(\mathbb{U}) \to C^d(\mathbb{U})$ defined as

$$\Theta(\mathcal{N}) = g_1(\mathcal{N}) \bigcup g_2(\mathcal{N}) \quad \text{and} \quad \Omega(\mathcal{M}) = \ell_1(\mathcal{M}) \bigcup \ell_1(\mathcal{M}) \quad \text{for all} \quad \mathcal{N}, \mathcal{M} \in C^d(\mathbb{U})$$

From Lemma 4, for all $\mathcal{N}, \mathcal{M} \in C^d(\mathbb{U})$ such that $H_d(\Theta\mathcal{N}, \Omega\mathcal{M}) > 0$, we have

$$\lambda + \Im(H_d(\Theta\mathcal{N}, \Omega\mathcal{M})) \leq \Im(H_d(\mathcal{N}, \mathcal{M}))$$

for $\Im = \max\{\Im_1, \Im_2\}$ and $\lambda = \min\{\lambda_1, \lambda_2\} = 0.2$. Thus, all conditions of Corollary 9 are satisfied. Moreover, for an arbitrarily chosen initial set $\mathcal{N}_0 \in C^d(\mathbb{U})$, the sequence $\{\mathcal{N}_0, \Theta(\mathcal{N}_0), \Omega\Theta(\mathcal{N}_0), \Theta\Omega\Theta(\mathcal{N}_0), \cdots\}$ of compact sets is convergent and has a limit point that is the common attractor of Θ and Ω.

5. Application to Fractional Differential Equations

Let C_J be the space of all continuous real-valued functions on J, where $J = [0,1]$. Then, C_J is a complete metric space with respect to metric $d : C_J \times C_J \to [0,\infty)$ defined by

$$d(\omega, v) = \|\omega - v\|_\infty = \max_{\mu \in J} |\omega(\mu) - v(\mu)|, \quad \text{for all} \quad \omega, v \in C_J.$$

For a continuous function $q : [0, \infty) \to \mathbb{R}$, the Caputo–Fabrizio derivative of order σ, ${}^{c}\mathcal{D}^{\sigma}$, is defined as

$$ {}^{c}\mathcal{D}^{\sigma} q(\mu) = \frac{1}{\Gamma(n-\sigma)} \int_0^{\mu} (\mu - s)^{n-\sigma-1} q^{(n)}(s) ds, \quad n-1 < \sigma < n, \; n = [\sigma] + 1, \tag{57} $$

where $[\sigma]$ denotes the integer part of the real number σ and the Riemann–Liouville fractional integral of order σ is defined as

$$ I^{\sigma} q(\mu) = \frac{1}{\Gamma(\sigma)} \int_0^{\mu} (\ell - s)^{\sigma-1} q(s) ds, \quad \sigma > 0, \tag{58} $$

provided the integral exists.

In this part, we apply our findings to demonstrate the existence of common solutions to the following Caputo–Fabrizio fractional differential equations:

$$ \begin{cases} {}^{c}\mathcal{D}^{\sigma} q(\mu) = \mathbb{K}_1(\mu, q(\mu)) \\ q(0) = 0, Iq(1) = q'(0), \end{cases} \tag{59} $$

and

$$ \begin{cases} {}^{c}\mathcal{D}^{\sigma} \wp(\mu) = \mathbb{K}_2(\mu, \wp(\mu)) \\ \wp(0) = 0, I\wp(1) = \wp'(0), \end{cases} \tag{60} $$

where $\mu \in [0, 1]$ and $\mathbb{K}_1, \mathbb{K}_2 : [0, 1] \times \mathbb{R} \to \mathbb{R}$.

Lemma 5 **([19]).** *Given $\mu \in [0, 1]$, problem* (59) *is equivalent to the following integral equation:*

$$ q(\mu) = \frac{1}{\Gamma(\sigma)} \int_0^{\mu} (\mu - s)^{\sigma-1} \mathbb{K}_1(s, q(s)) ds + \frac{2\mu}{\Gamma(\sigma)} \int_0^1 \int_0^s (s - w)^{\sigma-1} \mathbb{K}_1(w, q(w)) dw ds. \tag{61} $$

Now, define the operators $\mathcal{L}_1, \mathcal{L}_2 : C_J \to C_J$ as follows:

$$ \mathcal{L}_1(q(\mu)) = \frac{1}{\Gamma(\sigma)} \int_0^{\mu} (\mu - s)^{\sigma-1} \mathbb{K}_1(s, q(s)) ds + \frac{2\mu}{\Gamma(\sigma)} \int_0^1 \int_0^s (s - w)^{\sigma-1} \mathbb{K}_1(w, q(w)) dw ds \tag{62} $$

and

$$ \mathcal{L}_2(\wp(\mu)) = \frac{1}{\Gamma(\sigma)} \int_0^{\mu} (\mu - s)^{\sigma-1} \mathbb{K}_2(s, \wp(s)) ds + \frac{2\mu}{\Gamma(\sigma)} \int_0^1 \int_0^s (s - w)^{\sigma-1} \mathbb{K}_2(w, \wp(w)) dw ds. \tag{63} $$

Note that a common fixed point of operators (62) and (63) is the common solution of (59) and (60).

Theorem 3. *Boundary value problems* (59) *and* (60) *have a common solution in C_J given that*

(H1) there exists $\lambda > 0$ such that, for all $q, \wp \in C_J$, we have

$$ |\mathbb{K}_1(\mu, q(\mu)) - \mathbb{K}_2(\mu, \wp(\mu))| \leq e^{-\lambda} \mathbb{Q}(q(\mu), \wp(\mu)), $$

where $\mathbb{Q}(q(\mu), \wp(\mu)) = \alpha|q(\mu) - \wp(\mu)| + \beta|q(\mu) - \mathcal{L}_1 q(\mu)) + \gamma|\wp(\mu) - \mathcal{L}_2 \wp(\mu)| + \delta|q(\mu) - \mathcal{L}_2 \wp(\mu)| + L|\wp(\mu) - \mathcal{L}_1 q(\mu)|$ with $\alpha, \beta, \gamma, \delta, L \geq 0$, $\alpha + \beta + \gamma + 2\delta = 1$ and $\gamma \neq 1$;

(H2) $\Upsilon < \Gamma(\sigma)$, where

$$ \Upsilon = \int_0^{\mu} (\mu - s)^{\sigma-1} ds + 2\mu \int_0^1 \int_0^s (s - w)^{\sigma-1} (e^{-\lambda} \mathbb{Q}(q(w), \wp(w))) dw ds. $$

Proof. Let $q, \wp \in C_J$; then, for all $\mu \in [0,1]$, we have

$$
\begin{aligned}
|\mathcal{L}_1 q(\mu) - \mathcal{L}_2 \wp(\mu)| =& \Bigg| \frac{1}{\Gamma(\sigma)} \int_0^{\mu} (\mu - s)^{\sigma-1} [\mathbb{K}_1(s, q(s)) - \mathbb{K}_2(s, \wp(s))] ds \\
&+ \frac{2\mu}{\Gamma(\sigma)} \int_0^1 \int_0^s (s-w)^{\sigma-1} [\mathbb{K}_1(w, q(w)) - \mathbb{K}_2(w, \wp(w))] dw ds \Bigg| \\
\leq& \frac{1}{\Gamma(\sigma)} \int_0^{\mu} (\mu - s)^{\sigma-1} |\mathbb{K}_1(s, q(s)) - \mathbb{K}_2(s, \wp(s))| ds \\
&+ \frac{2\mu}{\Gamma(\sigma)} \int_0^1 \int_0^s (s-w)^{\sigma-1} |\mathbb{K}_1(w, q(w)) - \mathbb{K}_2(w, \wp(w))| dw ds \\
\leq& \frac{1}{\Gamma(\sigma)} \int_0^{\mu} (\mu - s)^{\sigma-1} (e^{-\lambda} \mathbb{Q}(q(s), \wp(s))) ds \\
&+ \frac{2\mu}{\Gamma(\sigma)} \int_0^1 \int_0^s (s-w)^{\sigma-1} (e^{-\lambda} \mathbb{Q}(q(w), \wp(w))) dw ds \\
\leq& \frac{1}{\Gamma(\sigma)} (e^{-\lambda} \mathbb{Q}(q(s), \wp(s))) \int_0^{\mu} (\mu - s)^{\sigma-1} ds \\
&+ \frac{2\mu}{\Gamma(\sigma)} (e^{-\lambda} \mathbb{Q}(q(w), \wp(w))) \int_0^1 \int_0^s (s-w)^{\sigma-1} (e^{-\lambda} \mathbb{Q}(q(w), \wp(w))) dw ds \\
\leq& \frac{\Upsilon}{\Gamma(\sigma)} (e^{-\lambda} \mathbb{Q}(q(s), \wp(s))) \\
\leq& e^{-\lambda} \mathbb{Q}(q(s), \wp(s)).
\end{aligned}
$$

Hence, (52) is satisfied for $\Im(t) = \ln(t)$ for all $t \in (0, \infty)$. Thus, with the aid of Corollary (5), operators $\mathcal{L}_1$ and $\mathcal{L}_2$ admit a common fixed point, and therefore boundary value problems (59) and (60) have a common solution in J. □

6. Conclusions

This paper effectively creates a fractal set for an $\Im$-iterated function system consisting of generalized $\Im$-contractions, establishing the existence of a unique common attractor for a range of Hutchinson–Wardowski contractive operators. Our findings produce a wide range of results for generalized iterated function systems that meet a variety of generalized contractive requirements, contributing to the advancement of the field. The provided illustrative example further validates our results, offering a comprehensive understanding of the subject matter. Finally, the existence results of common solutions to fractional boundary value problems are obtained, further extending the applicability of our work to a broader range of mathematical problems.

Author Contributions: Conceptualization, B.I., N.S., and I.I.; formal analysis, N.S., M.A., and I.I.; supervision, N.S.; investigation, B.I., N.S., M.A., and I.I.; writing—original draft preparation, B.I. and N.S.; writing—review and editing, B.I., N.S., I.I., and M.A. All authors have read and agreed to the published version of the manuscript.

Funding: This research did not receive any external funding.

Data Availability Statement: The data used to support the findings of this study are available from the corresponding author upon request.

Acknowledgments: Authors are thankful to the editor and anonymous referees for their valuable comments and suggestions.

Conflicts of Interest: The authors declare no conflicts of interest.

References

1. Hutchinson, J. Fractals and self-similarity. *Indiana Univ. Math. J.* **1981**, *30*, 713–747. [CrossRef]
2. Barnsley, M.F. *Fractals Everywhere*; Academic Press: Boston, MA, USA, 1993.
3. Mihail, A.; Miculescu, R. Applications of fixed point theorems in the theory of generalized IFS. *Fixed Point Theory Appl.* **2008**, *2008*, 312876. [CrossRef]
4. Mihail, A.; Miculescu, R. Generalized IFSs on noncompact spaces. *Fixed Point Theory Appl.* **2010**, *2010*, 584215. [CrossRef]

5. Dumitru, D. Generalized iterated function systems containing Meir-Keeler functions. *An. Univ. Bucur. Math.* **2009**, *LVIII*, 3–15.
6. Strobin, F.; Swaczyna, J. On a certain generalization of the iterated function system. *Bull. Aust. Math. Soc.* **2013**, *87*, 37–54. [CrossRef]
7. Secelean, N.A. The existence of the attractor of countable iterated function systems. *Mediterr. J. Math.* **2012**, *9*, 61–79. [CrossRef]
8. Khumalo, M.; Nazir, T.; Makhoshi, V. Generalized iterated function system for common attractors in partial metric spaces. *AIMS Math.* **2022**, *7*, 13074–13103. [CrossRef]
9. Abraham, I.; Miculescu, R. Generalized iterated function systems on b-metric spaces. *Mathematics* **2023**, *11*, 2826. [CrossRef]
10. Nazir, T.; Silvestrov, S.; Abbas, M. Fractals of generalized F-Hutchinson operator. *Waves Wavelets Fractals Adv. Anal.* **2016**, *2*, 29–40.
11. Saleem, N.; Iqbal, I.; Iqbal, B.; Radenovic, S. Coincidence and fixed points of multivalued $F-$contractions in generalized metric space with application. *J. Fixed Point Theory Appl.* **2020**, *22*, 81. [CrossRef]
12. Saleem, N.; Vujakovic, J.; Baloch, W.U.; Radenovic, S. Coincidence Point Results for Multivalued Suzuki Type Mappings Using $\theta-$Contraction in $b-$Metric Spaces. *Mathematics* **2019**, *7*, 1017. [CrossRef]
13. Saleem, N.; Zhou, M.; Bashir, S.; Husnine, S.M. Some new generalizations of $F-$contraction type mappings that weaken certain conditions on Caputo fractional type differential equations. *Aims Math.* **2021**, *6*, 1–25. [CrossRef]
14. Banach, S. Sur les opérations dans les ensembles abstraits et leur application aux équations intégrales. *Fund. Math.* **1922**, *3*, 133–181. [CrossRef]
15. Wardowski, D. Fixed points of a new type of contractive mappings in complete metric spaces. *Fixed Point Theory Appl.* **2012**, *2012*, 94. [CrossRef]
16. Secelean, N.A. Iterated function systems consisting of F-contractions. *Fixed Point Theory Appl.* **2013**, *2013*, 277. [CrossRef]
17. Cosentino, V.; Vetro, P. Fixed point result for F-contractive mappings of Hardy-Rogers type. *Filomat* **2014**, *28*, 715–722. [CrossRef]
18. Secelean, N.A. *Countable Iterated Function Systems*; Lambert Academic Publishing: Colne, UK, 2013.
19. Nazam, M.; Park, C.; Arshad, M. Fixed point problems for generalized contractions with applications. *Adv. Differ. Equ.* **2021**, *2021*, 247. [CrossRef]

fractal and fractional

MDPI

Article

An Iterative Method for the Approximation of Common Fixed Points of Two Mappings: Application to Fractal Functions

María A. Navascués

Department of Applied Mathematics, Universidad de Zaragoza, 50018 Zaragoza, Spain; manavas@unizar.es

Abstract: This paper proposes an iterative algorithm for the search for common fixed points of two mappings. The properties of approximation and convergence of the method are analyzed in the context of Banach spaces. In particular, this article provides sufficient conditions for the strong convergence of the sequence generated by the iterative scheme to a common fixed point of two operators. The method is illustrated with some examples of application. The procedure is used to approach a common solution of two Fredholm integral equations of the second kind. In the second part of the article, the existence of a fractal function coming from two different Read–Bajraktarević operators is proved. Afterwards, a study of the approximation of fixed points of a fractal convolution of operators is performed, in the framework of Lebesgue or Bochner spaces.

Keywords: fixed point approximation; quasi-nonexpansive maps; fractal functions; fractal convolution; iterative methods

Key Contribution: Conceptualization, M.A.N.; methodology, M.A.N.; validation, M.A.N.; formal analysis, M.A.N.; writing—original draft preparation, M.A.N.; writing—review and editing, M.A.N.

1. Introduction

In this paper, we address the approximation of a common fixed point of a finite number of mappings through an iterative method, and its applications to the study of fractal functions involving two different operators. From a practical point of view, the problem of finding common fixed points of two mappings appears in mathematical applications such as convex optimization (see, for instance, [1]).

Das and Debata [2] extended the classical iteration proposed by Ishikawa [3] to find a critical point of a single operator, acting on a normed space, to the case of the approximation of a common fixed point of two maps S and T. The iterative scheme is the following:

$$y_n = (1-\alpha_n)x_n + \alpha_n S x_n, \tag{1}$$

$$x_{n+1} = (1-\beta_n)x_n + \beta_n T y_n, \tag{2}$$

for $\alpha_n, \beta_n \in [0,1]$. They considered quasi-nonexpansive maps defined on uniformly convex Banach spaces. Takahashi and Tamura [4] studied the same method in the nonexpansive case on a strictly convex Banach space. Khan and Takahashi [5] generalized the procedure to deal with asymptotically nonexpansive operators.

In reference [6], Yadav proposed a variant of the iteration considered by Sahu [7] for a single map, in order to include two different mappings. The recurrence is given by the following steps:

$$y_n = (1-\beta_n)Tx_n + \beta_n S x_n, \tag{3}$$

$$x_{n+1} = Ty_n, \tag{4}$$

for $\beta_n \in [0,1]$. This method was called Y-iteration by the author. He gave sufficient conditions on the space and the maps S and T in order to obtain weak and strong convergences of the sequence (x_n) to a common fixed point of both mappings, and presented some examples of the application of the algorithm.

The single operator case proves that not all the fixed point approximation methods are useful for all kind of mappings. The convergence of each procedure depends on the underlying space and the properties of the map involved. Thus, it is desirable to have a variety of algorithms to focus a given problem. We propose a different iterative method for the search for common fixed points of a finite family of quasi-nonexpansive mappings, based on an algorithm defined in [8].

One of the first results of common fixed point existence of a family of operators is due to Browder [9]:

Theorem 1. *Let X be a uniformly convex Banach space, and $C \subseteq X$ be nonempty, bounded, closed and convex. If $\{U_\lambda\}$ is a commuting family of nonexpansive mappings $U_\lambda : C \to C$, then the set $\{U_\lambda\}$ has a common fixed point.*

The proof of this theorem is based on the well-known fixed point result of the same author for nonexpansive mappings on uniformly convex Banach spaces [9]. Theorem 1 is an extension of of the Markov–Kakutani Theorem [10,11]. It is also a generalization of the Theorem of De Marr [12], where C is assumed to be compact.

Afterwards, a great number of researchers expanded this result. For instance, R.E. Bruck [13] considered this problem in a Banach space X and $C \subseteq X$ satisfying some fixed point conditions, given in the following definition.

Definition 1. *Let X be a Banach space; a subset $C \subseteq X$ has the fixed point property for nonexpansive mappings if every nonexpansive map $f : C \to C$ has a fixed point. C has the conditional fixed point property for nonexpansive mappings if every nonexpansive mapping $f : C \to C$ satisfies either that f has no fixed points or that f has a fixed point in every nonempty bounded, closed and convex f-invariant subset of C.*

Example 1. *If X is a uniformly convex Banach space, any subset C that is nonempty, bounded, closed and convex has the fixed point property for nonexpansive mappings.*

$C = X$, where X is a uniformly convex Banach space, has the conditional fixed point property for nonexpansive mappings.

Both are consequences of Browder's Theorem on the existence of fixed points (Theorem 1 of reference [9]).

Bruck's Theorem [13] states that if X is a real or complex Banach space and $C \subseteq X$ has the fixed point property and the conditional fixed point property for nonexpansive mappings, and C is either weakly compact or bounded and separable, then any commuting family of nonexpansive self-mappings of C has a common fixed point. This is a generalization of Browder's common fixed point Theorem 1.

The existence of common fixed points of two maps was then historically linked to their commutativity. There was a conjecture stating that if two maps $f, g : [0,1] \to [0,1]$ are continuous and commute, they need to have a common fixed point. This hypothesis was refuted by Boyce [14] and Huneke [15]. However, the fact is true if some additional conditions are added on the underlying space X and the maps, as seen in Browder's Theorem.

It is clear that commutativity and continuity are not necessary conditions for the existence of common fixed points, and current research on the topic tries to remove both conditions (see, for instance, [16,17]). A discussion and bibliography on this subject can be found in reference [18].

We avoid in this article the problem of the existence of common fixed points (except in the definition of fractal functions of Section 5), and focus on their search in case of existence. We give sufficient conditions on the space and the maps for the strong convergence of a new procedure to approximate a common fixed point of the mappings S and T (Sections 2 and 3). Through two examples, the algorithm is illustrated in the cases of the approximation of a commom fixed point of two real maps and the search for a common solution of two integral equations of Fredholm type (Section 4).

In a subsequent section we give conditions for the existence of a common fractal function coming from two different Read–Bajraktarević operators (Section 5). Finally, we consider an application to the approximation of fixed points of the fractal convolution of two operators by means of the algorithm proposed (Section 6).

2. An Algorithm for the Approximation of Common Fixed Points of Quasi-Nonexpansive Operators

In this section, we propose an algorithm for the approximation of a common fixed point of two mappings. We start with a normed space X and two operators $S, T : C \to C$, where $C \subseteq X$ is nonempty, closed and convex. The algorithm to find a simultaneous critical point of S and T is given by the following iterative scheme:

$$z_n = (1-\gamma_n)x_n + \gamma_n S x_n, \quad (5)$$

$$y_n = (1-\beta_n)x_n + \beta_n z_n, \quad (6)$$

$$x_{n+1} = (1-\alpha_n)y_n + \alpha_n T y_n, \quad (7)$$

where $\alpha_n, \beta_n, \gamma_n \in [0,1]$ for $n \in \mathbb{N}$, and $x_0 \in C$. This method will be called common N-iteration, and it generalizes the N-iteration proposed in [8] for a single map. Throughout the paper, F_S and F_T will denote the set of fixed points of S and T, respectively. We propose the following definitions.

Definition 2. *A sequence $(x_n) \subseteq C$ has the common limit existence property (CLE) with respect to S and T if $\lim_{n\to\infty} ||x_n - x^*|| = l \in \mathbb{R}$ for any $x^* \in F_S \cap F_T$, provided that $F_S \cap F_T \neq \varnothing$.*

Remark 1. *This definition can be generalized to a finite number of mappings $(T_1, T_2, \ldots, T_m)$.*

Definition 3. *A sequence $(x_n) \subseteq C$ has the approximate fixed point property (AF) with respect to S if $\lim_{n\to\infty} ||x_n - Sx_n|| = 0$.*

Definition 4. *Let X be a normed space. A map $U : C \subseteq X \to X$ is quasi-nonexpansive if $F_U \neq \varnothing$ and*

$$||Ux - x^*|| \leq ||x - x^*||, \quad (8)$$

for any $x \in C$ and $x^* \in F_U$.

Proposition 1. *Let X be a normed space and $C \subseteq X$ be nonempty, closed and convex. Let $S, T : C \to C$ be two quasi-nonexpansive operators such that $F_S \cap F_T \neq \varnothing$. The common N-iteration has the CLE property; that is to say, for (x_n) defined as in (5), (6) and (7), $\lim_{n\to\infty} ||x_n - x^*|| = l \in \mathbb{R}$ for any $x^* \in F_S \cap F_T$ and any $x_0 \in C$.*

Proof. Let $x^* \in F_S \cap F_T$ and $x_0 \in C$. According to (5),

$$||z_n - x^*|| \leq (1-\gamma_n)||x_n - x^*|| + \gamma_n||Sx_n - x^*|| \leq ||x_n - x^*||. \quad (9)$$

In the same way, using (6),

$$||y_n - x^*|| \leq (1-\beta_n)||y_n - x^*|| + \beta_n||z_n - x^*|| \leq ||x_n - x^*||. \quad (10)$$

Finally,

$$||x_{n+1} - x^*|| \leq (1-\alpha_n)||y_n - x^*|| + \alpha_n||Ty_n - x^*|| \leq ||y_n - x^*|| \leq ||x_n - x^*||. \quad (11)$$

Consequently, the sequence $(||x_n - x^*||)$ is non-increasing and bounded and thus $\lim_{n\to\infty} ||x_n - x^*|| = l$ exists and it is real. □

The next lemma can be consulted in reference [19].

Lemma 1. *Let X be a uniformly convex Banach space, and let a sequence $(\lambda_n) \subseteq X$ be such that there exist $p, q \in \mathbb{R}$ satisfying the condition $0 < p \leq \lambda_n \leq q < 1$ for all $n \in \mathbb{N}$. Let (x_n), (y_n) be sequences of X such that $\limsup_{n\to\infty} ||x_n|| \leq r$, $\limsup_{n\to\infty} ||y_n|| \leq r$, and $\limsup_{n\to\infty} ||\lambda_n x_n + (1-\lambda_n)y_n|| = r$ for some $r \geq 0$. Then, $\lim_{n\to\infty} ||x_n - y_n|| = 0$.*

Theorem 2. *Let X be a uniformly convex Banach space and $C \subseteq X$ be nonempty, closed and convex. If $S, T : C \to C$ are two quasi-nonexpansive operators such that $F_S \cap F_T \neq \varnothing$ and $0 < \inf \gamma_n \leq \sup \gamma_n < 1$, $0 < \inf \alpha_n \leq \sup \alpha_n < 1$, then*

- *The sequences (x_n), (y_n) and (z_n) defined in (5), (6) and (7) have the CLE property.*
- *(x_n) has the AF property with respect to S and (y_n) has the AF property with respect to T.*

Proof. Let $x^* \in F_S \cap F_T$. By the previous proposition, $l := \lim_{n\to\infty} ||x_n - x^*||$ exists and it is real. According to (10),

$$\limsup_{n\to\infty} ||y_n - x^*|| \leq l, \quad (12)$$

and

$$\limsup_{n\to\infty} ||Ty_n - x^*|| \leq \limsup_{n\to\infty} ||y_n - x^*|| \leq l. \quad (13)$$

Using Lemma 1 and the following equality

$$l = \lim_{n\to\infty} ||x_{n+1} - x^*|| = \lim_{n\to\infty} ||(1-\alpha_n)(y_n - x^*) + \alpha_n(Ty_n - x^*)||$$

we have that

$$\lim_{n\to\infty} ||y_n - Ty_n|| = 0.$$

Hence, (y_n) has the AF property with respect to T. Again, by the third step of the algorithm,

$$||x_{n+1} - x^*|| \leq ||y_n - x^*|| + \alpha_n||Ty_n - y_n||.$$

Then,

$$l \leq \liminf_{n\to\infty} ||y_n - x^*||. \quad (14)$$

By (12) and (14), $l = \lim_{n\to\infty} ||y_n - x^*||$. Let us consider now that

$$||y_n - x^*|| \leq (1-\beta_n)||x_n - x^*|| + \beta_n||z_n - x^*||,$$

$$||y_n - x^*|| - ||x_n - x^*|| \leq \beta_n(||z_n - x^*|| - ||x_n - x^*||) \leq ||z_n - x^*|| - ||x_n - x^*||.$$

Then,

$$||y_n - x^*|| \leq ||z_n - x^*||.$$

Consequently,

$$l = \lim_{n\to\infty} ||y_n - x^*|| \leq \liminf_{n\to\infty} ||z_n - x^*||.$$

By (9), $\limsup_{n\to\infty} ||z_n - x^*|| < l$ and hence $l = \lim_{n\to\infty} ||z_n - x^*||$. Consequently, the sequences (x_n), (y_n) and (z_n) have the CLE property, with the same limit:

$$\lim_{n\to\infty} ||x_n - x^*|| = \lim_{n\to\infty} ||y_n - x^*|| = \lim_{n\to\infty} ||z_n - x^*||,$$

for $x^* \in F_S \cap F_T$. The quasi-nonexpansiveness of S implies that

$$\limsup_{n\to\infty} ||Sx_n - x^*|| \leq l.$$

The equality

$$l = \lim_{n\to\infty} ||z_n - x^*|| = \lim_{n\to\infty} ||(1-\gamma_n)(x_n - x^*) + \gamma_n(Sx_n - x^*)||,$$

along with the inequality $\limsup_{n\to\infty} ||Sx_n - x^*|| \leq l$ imply, by Lemma 1, that

$$\lim_{n\to\infty} ||x_n - Sx_n|| = 0,$$

and (x_n) has the AF property with respect to S. □

According to Proposition 1 and Theorem 2, the approximation properties of the common N-iteration are true also for the two-step common N-iteration, given by the following recurrence:

$$y_n = (1-\gamma_n)x_n + \gamma_n Sx_n, \tag{15}$$

$$x_{n+1} = (1-\alpha_n)y_n + \alpha_n Ty_n. \tag{16}$$

where $0 < \inf \gamma_n \leq \sup \gamma_n < 1$ and $0 < \inf \alpha_n \leq \sup \alpha_n < 1$ (taking $\beta_n = 1$ for all n in (6)).

This iterative scheme can be generalized to a finite number of operators with common fixed points, in order to provide the following m-step common fixed point N-algorithm for the mappings $T_1, T_2, \ldots, T_m : C \to C$ such that $\cap_{i=1}^m F_{T_i} \neq \varnothing$:

$$x_n^1 = (1-c_n^1)x_n + c_n^1 T_1 x_n, \tag{17}$$

$$x_n^2 = (1-c_n^2)x_n^1 + c_n^2 T_2 x_n^1, \tag{18}$$

$$\ldots \qquad \ldots \tag{19}$$

$$x_n^i = (1-c_n^i)x_n^{i-1} + c_n^i T_i x_n^{i-1}, \tag{20}$$

$$\ldots \qquad \ldots \tag{21}$$

$$x_{n+1} = x_n^m = (1-c_n^m)x_n^{m-1} + c_n^m T_m x_n^{m-1}, \tag{22}$$

where $0 < \inf_n c_n^i \leq \sup_n c_n^i < 1$ for all $n \geq 1$, $i = 1, \ldots, m$, and $x_0 \in C$.

3. Convergence Theorems for the Common N-Iteration

Throughout this section, we will assume a normed space X, $C \subseteq X$, $C \neq \varnothing$, and $S, T : C \to C$, such that $F_S \cap F_T \neq \varnothing$. We will consider the common N-iteration given by (5), (6) and (7) with the conditions for α_n and γ_n given in Theorem 2.

Remark 2. *The notation Id will represent the identity operator.*

Theorem 3. *Let X be a uniformly convex Banach space and $C \subseteq X$ be compact and convex. If $S, T : C \to C$ are quasi-nonexpansive and closed, then the common N-iteration described converges strongly to a common fixed point of S and T.*

Proof. Since C is compact, the sequence (y_n) of the iteration has a convergent subsequence. Let $\lim_{j\to\infty} y_{n_j} = \overline{x} \in C$. Since (y_n) has the AF property with respect to T, then $||y_{n_j} - Ty_{n_j}||$ tends to zero. Since $Id - T$ is closed, then $0 = (Id - T)\overline{x}$, and $\overline{x} \in F_T$.

According to the third step of the algorithm,

$$||x_{n_j+1} - \overline{x}|| = ||\left(1 - \alpha_{n_j}\right)\left(y_{n_j} - \overline{x}\right) + \alpha_{n_j}\left(Ty_{n_j} - \overline{x}\right)|| \leq ||y_{n_j} - \overline{x}|| \to 0.$$

Consequently, $\lim_{j\to\infty} x_{n_j+1} = \overline{x}$.

Since $Id - S$ is closed and (x_n) has the AF property with respect to S, then $0 = (Id - S)\overline{x}$, and $\overline{x} \in F_S \cap F_T$. The CLE property of (x_n) implies that $\lim_{n\to\infty} ||x_n - \overline{x}|| = 0$. □

Corollary 1. *Let X be a uniformly convex Banach space, and let $C \subseteq X$ be compact andconvex. If $S, T : C \to C$ are nonexpansive, then the common N-iteration described converges strongly to a common fixed point of S and T.*

Proof. A nonexpansive mapping with a fixed point is quasi-nonexpansive and continuous, and we have the hypotheses of Theorem 3. □

Definition 5. *Let X be a normed space. A mapping $T : X \to X$, such that there exists $B \geq 0$ satisfying for any $f, g \in X$ the following inequality*

$$||Tf - Tg|| \leq ||f - g|| + B \min\{||f - Tf||, ||g - Tg||\}, \tag{23}$$

is a nonexpansive partial contractivity.

For $B = 0$, we have a nonexpansive mapping.

Corollary 2. *Let X be a uniformly convex Banach space, and let $C \subseteq X$ be compact andconvex. If $S, T : C \to C$ are closed nonexpansive partial contractivities, then the common N-iteration described converges strongly to a common fixed point of S and T.*

Proof. A nonexpansive partial contractivity with a fixed point is quasi-nonexpansive, and we are in the conditions of Theorem 3. □

Definition 6. *Let X be a normed space, and $C \subseteq X$. A map $T : C \to X$ is demicompact if a bounded sequence $(x_n) \subseteq C$, such that $(Tx_n - x_n)$ is convergent, has a convergent subsequence. If a sequence $(x_n) \subseteq C$, such that $(Tx_n - x_n)$ is convergent to zero, has a convergent subsequence (x_{n_j}), then T is demicompact at zero.*

Remark 3. *According to this definition, if T is demicompact at zero, (x_n) is bounded and it has the AF property with respect to T, then there exists a convergent subsequence (x_{n_j}).*

Proposition 2. *Let X be a uniformly convex Banach space, and let $C \subseteq X$ be closed andconvex. If $S, T : C \to C$ are quasi-nonexpansive and closed, and T is demicompact at zero, then the common N-iteration described converges strongly to a common fixed point of S and T.*

Proof. The CLE property of (y_n) implies that the sequence (y_n) is bounded. The AF property of (y_n) with respect to T implies that $||y_n - Ty_n||$ tends to zero. As T is demicompact, there is a convergent subsequence (y_{m_k}). Let $x^* := \lim_{n\to\infty} y_{m_k}$. Then, $(Id - T)y_{m_k} \to 0$. Since T is closed, then $0 = (Id - T)x^*$, and $x^* \in F_T$.

Regarding (x_n), according to the last step of the algorithm,

$$||x_{m_k+1} - x^*|| = ||(1-\alpha_{m_k})(y_{m_k} - x^*) + \alpha_{m_k}(Ty_{m_k} - x^*)|| \leq ||y_{m_k} - x^*|| \to 0.$$

As $(Id - S)x_{m_k+1}$ tends to zero due to the AF property of (x_n) and $Id - S$ is closed, then $0 = (Id - S)x^*$ and $x^* \in F_S \cap F_T$.

The CLE property of (x_n) implies that the common N-iteration converges strongly to x^* for any $x_0 \in C$. □

Corollary 3. *Let X be a uniformly convex Banach space, and let $C \subseteq X$ be closed and convex. If $S, T : C \to C$ are nonexpansive and T is demicompact at zero, then the common N-iteration described converges strongly to a common fixed point of S and T.*

Corollary 4. *Let X be a uniformly convex Banach space, and let $C \subseteq X$ be closed andconvex. If $S, T : C \to C$ are closed nonexpansive partial contractivities and T is demicompact at zero, then the common N-iteration described converges strongly to a common fixed point of S and T.*

Definition 7. *Let X, Y be Banach spaces. Then, $S : X \to Y$ is demiclosed (at $z \in Y$) if $y_n \rightharpoonup y$ and $Sy_n \to z$ imply that $Sy = z$.*

Remark 4. *The symbol $\rightharpoonup$ denotes the weak convergence of a sequence.*

The following demiclosedness principle for nonexpansive mappings can be consulted in reference [20], Theorem 10.4:

Theorem 4. *Let X be a uniformly convex Banach space, C a nonempty, closed and convex subset of X and $T : C \to X$ a nonexpansive mapping. Then, $Id - T$ is demiclosed on C.*

Definition 8. *Let X, Y be Banach spaces. Then, $S : X \to Y$ is completely continuous if $x_n \rightharpoonup x$ implies that $Sx_n \to Sx$.*

Remark 5. *A completely continuous mapping is demiclosed.*

Proposition 3. *Let X be a uniformly convex Banach space, and let $C \subseteq X$ be bounded, closed and convex. If $S, T : C \to C$ are nonexpansive and T is completely continuous, then the common N-iteration described converges strongly to a common fixed point of S and T.*

Proof. Since C is bounded, closed and convex in a uniformly convex space, there exists a weakly convergent subsequence (y_{n_j}) of (y_n). That is to say, $y_{n_j} \rightharpoonup \overline{x}$. The AF property of (y_n) with respect to T implies that $||y_{n_j} - Ty_{n_j}||$ tends to zero. According to Theorem 4, $Id - T$ is demiclosed and this implies that $0 = (Id - T)\overline{x}$, that is to say, $\overline{x} \in F_T$.

Since T is completely continuous, $\lim_{j\to\infty} Ty_{n_j} = T\overline{x} = \overline{x}$. Then,

$$y_{n_j} = \left(y_{n_j} - Ty_{n_j}\right) + Ty_{n_j} \to \overline{x}.$$

$$||x_{n_j+1} - \overline{x}|| \leq ||\left(1-\alpha_{n_j}\right)\left(y_{n_j} - \overline{x}\right) + \alpha_{n_j}\left(Sy_{n_j} - \overline{x}\right)|| \leq ||y_{n_j} - \overline{x}|| \to 0.$$

Since $\left((Id - S)x_{n_j+1}\right)$ tends to zero due to the AF property of (x_n) with respect to S, and $Id - S$ is continuous, then $0 = (Id - S)\overline{x}$ and $\overline{x} \in F_S \cap F_T$.

The CLE property of (x_n) implies its convergence to $\overline{x}$. □

Remark 6. *All the results obtained in this section are applicable to the case $S = T$, and the usual N-algorithm for a single map defined in reference [8].*

4. Some Applications of the Common N-Iteration

In this section, we present two examples of the application of the common N-iteration.

4.1. Approximation of a Common Fixed Point of Two Mappings

The maps $S, T : [0,1] \to [0,1]$ given by $S(x) = \left(\sqrt{1 - x^{2/3}}\right)^3$ and $T(x) = x$ have a common fixed point at $x^* \simeq 0.353553$. The common N-iteration with all the scalars equal to $1/2$ has been used to approach this point. Namely, we have computed the successive values of x_n by means of the iterative scheme:

$$z_n = \frac{x_n + Sx_n}{2},$$

$$y_n = \frac{x_n + z_n}{2},$$

$$x_{n+1} = \frac{y_n + Ty_n}{2}.$$

The abscissas $x_0 = 0.1$ and $x_0 = 1$ have been chosen as starting points of two performances of the algorithm. The subsequent errors, computed as $|x_n - x^*|$, are collected in Table 1. The left part gathers the errors for $x_0 = 0.1$ and the right part displays the case $x_0 = 1$.

Table 1. Approximation errors of the first values given by the N-algorithm for a common fixed point of two maps starting at $x_0 = 0.1$ (left) and $x_0 = 1$ (right).

Iteration	Error	Iteration	Error
0	0.25355	0	0.64645
1	0.10482	1	0.39645
2	0.04951	2	0.22717
3	0.02415	3	0.12388
4	0.01193	4	0.06521
5	0.00593	5	0.03355
6	0.00296	6	0.01703
7	0.00148	7	0.00858
8	0.00074	8	0.00431
9	0.00037	9	0.00216
10	0.00018	10	0.00108

4.2. Search for a Common Solution of Two Fredholm Integral Equations of the Second Kind

Let us consider the following integral equations of Fredholm type:

$$f(x) = h(x) + \int_a^b K(x,y) f(y) dy,$$

$$g(x) = h'(x) + \int_a^b K'(x,y) g(y) dy,$$

where we look for a common solution in $\mathcal{L}^2([a,b])$. This problem is equivalent to the search for a common fixed point of the operators $S, T : \mathcal{L}^2([a,b]) \to \mathcal{L}^2([a,b])$ defined as

$$Su(x) = h(x) + \int_a^b K(x,y) u(y) dy,$$

$$Tu(x) = h'(x) + \int_a^b K'(x,y)u(y)dy.$$

It is well known that if K and K' are such that $K, K' \in \mathcal{L}^2(I \times I)$, where $I = [a,b]$, then the operators S and T are linear and compact and consequently demicompact. They are nonexpansive if

$$\int_{I\times I} |K(x,y)|dxdy \leq 1,$$

$$\int_{I\times I} |K'(x,y)|dxdy \leq 1.$$

The following integral equations:

$$f(x) = (e^x - 1) + \int_0^1 yf(y)dy,$$

$$f(x) = (e^x + 1 - e) + \int_0^1 f(y)dy.$$

have a common exact solution at $f(x) = e^x$. Let us apply the two-step common N-algorithm ($\beta_n = 0$), and let us choose $\alpha_n = \gamma_n = 1/2$ for all $n \geq 1$. Thus, the N-iteration is given by the following scheme:

$$g_n(x) = \left(f_n(x) + (e^x - 1) + \int_0^1 yf_n(y)dy\right)/2,$$

$$f_{n+1}(x) = \left(g_n(x) + (e^x + 1 - e) + \int_0^1 g_n(y)dy\right)/2.$$

Let the starting function be $f_0(x) = x$. The error of every approximation is computed as

$$Err_n = \left(\int_0^1 |f_n(x) - f(x)|^2 dx\right)^{1/2},$$

where $f(x)$ is the exact solution. Table 2 collects the errors from the first to the twentieth iteration. Figure 1 represents the exact common solution (in yellow) along with the first, fourth, seventh and tenth approximations, respectively (in blue).

Table 2. Errors of the first twenty approximations given by the two-step N-algorithm for a common solution of two Fredholm integral equations.

Iteration	Error	Iteration	Error
1	0.94392	11	0.05539
2	0.71417	12	0.04041
3	0.53734	13	0.03031
4	0.40345	14	0.02273
5	0.30270	15	0.01705
6	0.22705	16	0.01279
7	0.17030	17	0.00960
8	0.12772	18	0.00719
9	0.09579	19	0.00539
10	0.07184	20	0.00405

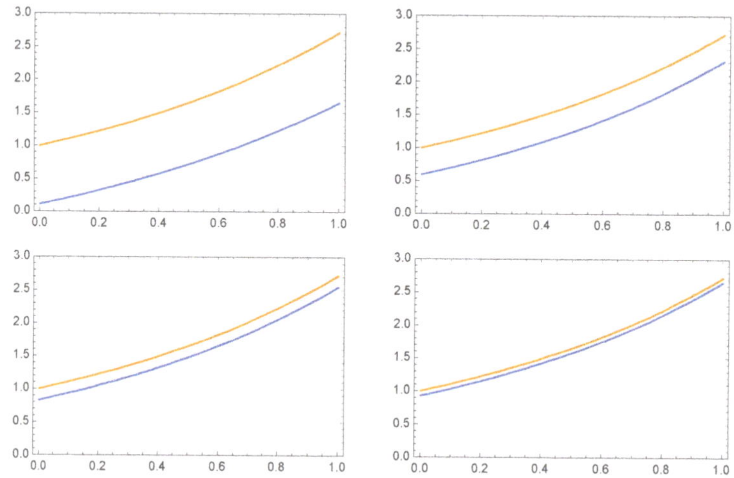

Figure 1. From upper left to bottom right, exact solution (yellow) along with the first, fourth, seventh and tenth approximations (f_1, f_4, f_7, f_{10}) (blue).

5. Fractal Functions as Common Fixed Points of Two Different Operators

In this section, we find a fractal function as a common fixed point of two different Read–Bajraktarević operators.

According to the formalism of these mappings, we consider a compact real interval $I = [a, b]$, and a partition of it $\Delta : a = t_0 < t_1 < t_2 \ldots < t_M = b$. Let us consider $I_m = [t_{m-1}, t_m)$, for $m = 1, 2, \ldots M-1$ and $I_M = [t_{M-1}, t_M]$ and define $L_m : I \to I_m$ such that $L_m(t) = a_m t + b_m$ and

$$L_m(t_0) = t_{m-1}, \qquad L_m(t_M) = t_m. \tag{24}$$

Let S_m, T_m be mappings on the space $\mathcal{L}^p(I)$, that is to say, $S_m, T_m : \mathcal{L}^p(I) \to \mathcal{L}^p(I)$, and let us assume that $1 < p < \infty$. Let us define the operators of Read–Bajraktarević type $S, T : \mathcal{L}^p(I) \to \mathcal{L}^p(I)$ given by

$$Sf(t) = S_m(f) \circ L_m^{-1}(t), \tag{25}$$

$$Tf(t) = T_m(f) \circ L_m^{-1}(t), \tag{26}$$

for $t \in I_m$. The next result gives sufficient conditions for the existence of a fractal function as a common fixed point of S and T. Let $||\cdot||_p$ denote the norm of the space $\mathcal{L}^p(I)$ for $1 < p < \infty$.

Theorem 5. *Let the operators S_m, T_m meet the following conditions for $m = 1, 2, \ldots, M$:*

1. *There exists $R > 0$ satisfying $||S_m f||_p \leq R$ and $||T_m f||_p \leq R$ for any $f \in \mathcal{L}^p(I)$ such that $||f||_p \leq R$.*
2. *S_m and T_m are nonexpansive.*
3. *$T_m\left(\sum_{i=1}^M \kappa_{I_i}(\cdot) S_i(f) \circ L_i^{-1}(\cdot)\right) = S_m\left(\sum_{i=1}^M \kappa_{I_i}(\cdot) T_i(f) \circ L_i^{-1}(\cdot)\right)$, where κ_{I_i} is the indicator map of I_i or, equivalently, $S_m\left(T_j f \circ L_j^{-1}(\cdot)\right) = T_m\left(S_j f \circ L_j^{-1}(\cdot)\right)$ where $L_j^{-1} : I_j \to I$, for $j = 1, \ldots, M$.*

Then, the operators S and T defined in (25) and (26) commute, they are nonexpansive and there exists a fractal function $\overline{f} \in \mathcal{L}^p(I)$ such that $\overline{f}$ is a common fixed point of S and T. This function *can be approached using the common N-iteration of the maps S and T whenever* $0 < \inf \alpha_n \leq \sup \alpha_n < 1$ *and* $0 < \inf \gamma_n \leq \sup \gamma_n < 1$.

Proof. The Hypothesis (1) of the theorem enables the restriction of the domain and codomain of the operators S and T to the closed ball with a center in the null function f_0 and radius R,$\overline{B}(f_0, R) \subseteq \mathcal{L}^p(I)$ since

$$||Sf||_p \leq R,$$

$$||Tf||_p \leq R,$$

for $f \in \overline{B}(f_0, R)$. Thus, S and T can be defined from and onto the bounded, closed and convex subset $\overline{B}(f_0, R)$ of the uniformly convex Banach space $\mathcal{L}^p(I)$. It is easy to check that S and T are nonexpansive, since

$$||Sf - Sf'||_p \leq \left(\sum_{m=1}^{M} a_m\right)^{1/p} ||S_m f - S_m f'||_p \leq ||f - f'||_p,$$

$$||Tf - Tf'||_p \leq \left(\sum_{m=1}^{M} a_m\right)^{1/p} ||T_m f - T_m f'||_p \leq ||f - f'||_p,$$

and $\sum_{m=1}^{M} a_m = 1$ due to conditions (24). Moreover,

$$(T \circ S)f(L_m t) = T(Sf)(L_m t) = T_m(Sf)(t),$$

and

$$(S \circ T)f(L_m t) = S(Tf)(L_m t) = S_m(Tf)(t),$$

where

$$T_m(Sf) = T_m\left(\sum_{i=1}^{M} \kappa_{I_i}(\cdot) S_i(f) \circ L_i^{-1}(\cdot)\right) = T_m\left(S_j f \circ L_j^{-1}(\cdot)\right)$$

and

$$S_m(Tf) = S_m\left(\sum_{i=1}^{M} \kappa_{I_i}(\cdot) T_i(f) \circ L_i^{-1}(\cdot)\right) = S_m\left(T_j f \circ L_j^{-1}(\cdot)\right)$$

where $L_j^{-1} : I_j \to I$. The last two equations are equal due to the Hypothesis (3) of the theorem, and, consequently, $S \circ T = T \circ S$. Then, we have the hypotheses of Browder's Theorem 1 for $C = B(f_0, R)$, and S and T have a common fixed point $\overline{f} \in \overline{B}(f_0, R) \subseteq \mathcal{L}^p(I)$. □

Example 2. *The operators defined as* $S_m f = c_m f$, $T_m f = c'_m f$ *for* $c_m, c'_m \in \mathbb{R}, |c_m|, |c'_m| \leq 1$, *and* $c_m c'_j = c'_m c_j$ *for* $m, j = 1, 2, \ldots, M$, *satisfy the hypotheses required.*

6. Fixed Points of the Fractal Convolution of Several Types of Operators

In this section, we consider a special type of operators defined in (26),

$$Tf(t) = T_m(f) \circ L_m^{-1}(t), \tag{27}$$

for $t \in I_m$ and

$$T_m f(t) = u \circ L_m(t) + k_m(f(t) - v(t)),$$

where $u, v \in \mathcal{L}^p(I)$ and $k_m \in \mathbb{R}$ are constant and such that $|k_m| < 1$ for $m = 1, 2, \ldots, M$. In this case, the operator T is a contraction since

$$||Tf - Tf'||_p \leq k||f - f'||_p,$$

for any $f, f' \in \mathcal{L}^p(I)$ and $k = \max\{|k_m|\} < 1$. Then, T has a fixed point, usually denoted as u^α, called α-fractal function in previous papers (see, for instance, [21] for the two-dimensional case). In other articles (see, for instance, [22]), u^α has been considered as the result of a binary internal operation in $\mathcal{L}^p(I)$, that is to say,

$$u^\alpha = u * v.$$

The operation $*$ has been called "fractal convolution". This operation has useful properties such as idempotency, namely, $u * u = u$ for any $u \in \mathcal{L}^p(I)$. Other features of the fractal convolution can be consulted in reference [22]. From this background, we have also defined a fractal convolution between operators on the same space defined, for $V, W : \mathcal{L}^p(I) \to \mathcal{L}^p(I)$, as

$$(V * W)f = (Vf) * (Wf),$$

for $f \in \mathcal{L}^p(I)$.

The fractal convolution of operators also has the property of idempotency, that is to say,

$$V * V = V.$$

A straightforward consequence of this characteristic is that, if F_V and F_W are the sets of fixed points of V and W, respectively, then

$$(F_V \cap F_W) \subseteq F_{V*W}.$$

Namely, a common fixed point of V and W is a fixed point of $V * W$.

In the following, we assume that V and W are such that $F_V \cap F_W \neq \emptyset$, and $V, W : C \to C$, where $C \subseteq \mathcal{L}^p(I)$ or $C \subseteq \mathcal{B}^p(I)$, where $\mathcal{B}^p(I)$ denotes the Bochner space of p-integrable maps $f : I \to B$, with B being a uniformly convex Banach space.

Let us consider $C \neq \emptyset$ and $1 < p < \infty$. For the common N-iteration algorithm, we will assume the following conditions on the scalars: $0 < \inf \alpha_n \leq \sup \alpha_n < 1$ and $0 < \inf \gamma_n \leq \sup \gamma_n < 1$.

The results obtained in previous sections for the common fixed points of two mappings and their approximation are applicable to the search for fixed points of $V * W$. A summary of these results, applied to $V * W$, is the following:

- If C is compact and convex and V, W are quasi-nonexpansive and closed, then the common N-iteration converges strongly to a fixed point of $V * W$.
- If C is compact and convex and V, W are nonexpansive, then the common N-iteration converges strongly to a fixed point of $V * W$.
- If C is compact and convex and V, W are closed nonexpansive partial contractivities, then the common N-iteration converges strongly to a fixed point of $V * W$.
- If C is closed and convex, V, W are quasi-nonexpansive and closed and W is demicompact at zero, then the common N-iteration converges strongly to a fixed point of $V * W$.
- If C is closed and convex, V, W are nonexpansive and W is demicompact at zero, then the common N-iteration converges strongly to a fixed point of $V * W$.
- If C is closed and convex, V, W are closed nonexpansive partial contractivities and W is demicompact at zero, then the common N-iteration converges strongly to a fixed point of $V * W$.
- If C is bounded, closed and convex, V, W are nonexpansive and W is completely continuous, then the common N-iteration converges strongly to a fixed point of $V * W$.

7. Conclusions

This article presents an iterative method to find common fixed points of two maps $S, T : C \to C$, where C is a nonempty, closed and convex subset of a normed space X. The recurrence is called common N-iteration, and it is given by the recurrence:

$$z_n = (1-\gamma_n)x_n + \gamma_n S x_n, \tag{28}$$

$$y_n = (1-\beta_n)x_n + \beta_n z_n, \tag{29}$$

$$x_{n+1} = (1-\alpha_n)y_n + \alpha_n T y_n. \tag{30}$$

for $\alpha_n, \beta_n, \gamma_n \in [0,1]$ and $x_0 \in C$.

It has been proved that (x_n), (y_n) and (z_n) have the CLE property, (x_n) has the AF property with respect to S, and (y_n) has the AF property with respect to T. This article provides sufficient conditions on X, C and the maps S and T for the strong convergence of the algorithm to a common fixed point of S and T, in case of existence.

The procedure has been applied to the approximation of a common fixed point of two maps defined in the interval $[0,1]$ and a common solution of two Fredholm integral equations of the second kind.

This paper has proved the existence of a fractal function that is a common fixed point of two different nonexpansive Read–Bajraktarević operators defined on $\mathcal{L}^p(I)$ or $\mathcal{B}^p(I)$. In the last section, the article gives sufficient conditions for the convergence of the algorithm to a fixed point of a fractal convolution of operators $V * W$, where $V, W : \mathcal{L}^p(I) \to \mathcal{L}^p(I)$ or $V, W : \mathcal{B}^p(I) \to \mathcal{B}^p(I)$. In both cases, the range of values of p is $1 < p < \infty$.

Funding: This research received no external funding.

Data Availability Statement: The original contributions presented in this study are included in the article. Further inquiries can be directed to the corresponding author.

Conflicts of Interest: The authors declare no conflicts of interest.

References

1. Takahashi, W. Iterative methods for approximation of fixed points and their applications. *J. Oper. Res. Soc. Jpn.* **2000**, *43*, 87–108. [CrossRef]
2. Das, G.; Debata, J.P. Fixed points of quasi-nonexpansive mappings. *Indian J. Pure Appl. Math.* **1986**, *17*, 1263–1269.
3. Ishikawa, S. Fixed points by a new iteration method. *Proc. AMS* **1974**, *44*, 147–150. [CrossRef]
4. Takahashi, W.; Tamura, T. Convergence theorems for a pair of nonexpansive mappings. *J. Convex Anal.* **1998**, *5*, 45–56.
5. Khan, S.H.; Takahashi, W. Approximating common fixed points of two asymptotically nonexpansive mappings. *Sci. Math. Jpn.* **2001**, *53*, 143–148.
6. Yadav, M.R. Two-step iteration scheme for nonexpansive mappings in Banach space. *Math. Moravica* **2015**, *19*, 95–105. [CrossRef]
7. Sahu, D.R. Applications of the S-iteration process to constrained minimization problems and split feasibility problems. *Fixed Point Theory* **2011**, *12*, 187–204.
8. Navascués, M.A. Approximation sequences for fixed points of non contractive operators. *J. Nonlinear Funct. Anal.* **2024**, *20*, 1–13.
9. Browder, F.E. Nonexpansive nonlinear operators in a Banach space. *Proc. Nat. Acad. Sci. USA* **1965**, *54*, 1041–1044. [CrossRef]
10. Markov, A. Quelques théorèmes sur les ensembles Abeliens. *Dokl. Akad. Nauk SSSR* **1936**, *10*, 311–314.
11. Kakutani, S. Two fixed point theorems concerning bicompact convex sets. *Proc. Imp. Acad.* **1938**, *14*, 242–245. [CrossRef]
12. De Marr, R. Common fixed points for commuting contraction mappings. *Pac. J. Math.* **1963**, *13*, 1139–1141. [CrossRef]
13. Bruck, R.E., Jr. A common fixed point theorem of a counting family of nonexpansive mappings. *Pac. J. Math.* **1974**, *53*, 59–71. [CrossRef]
14. Boyce, W.M. Commuting functions with no common fixed points. *Trans. AMS* **1969**, *137*, 77–92. [CrossRef]
15. Huneke, J.P. On common fixed points of commuting continuous function on an interval. *Trans. AMS* **1969**, *139*, 371–381. [CrossRef]
16. Pant, R.P. Common fixed points of noncommuting maps. *J. Math. Anal. Appl.* **1994**, *188*, 436–440. [CrossRef]
17. Pant, R.P. Discontinuity and fixed points. *J. Math. Anal. Appl.* **1999**, *240*, 284–289. [CrossRef]
18. Patel, D.K.; Kumam, P.; Gopal, D. Some discussion on the existence of common fixed points for a pair of maps. *Fixed Point Theory Appl.* **2013**, *187*, 187. [CrossRef]

19. Schu, J. Weak and strong convergence of fixed points of asymptotically nonexpansive mappings. *Bull. Aust. Math. Soc.* **1991**, *43*, 153–159. [CrossRef]
20. Goebel, K.; Kirk, W.A. *Topics in Metric Fixed Point Theory*; Cambridge University Press: Cambridge, UK, 1990.
21. Navascués, M.A.; Mohapatra, R.N.; Akhtar, M.N. Construction of fractal surfaces. *Fractals* **2019**, *28*, 2050033. [CrossRef]
22. Navascués, M.A.; Massopust, P. Fractal convolution: A new operation between functions. *Fract. Calc. Appl. Anal.* **2019**, *22*, 619–643. [CrossRef]

MDPI AG
Grosspeteranlage 5
4052 Basel
Switzerland
Tel.: +41 61 683 77 34

Fractal and Fractional Editorial Office
E-mail: fractalfract@mdpi.com
www.mdpi.com/journal/fractalfract

www.ingramcontent.com/pod-product-compliance
Lightning Source LLC
Chambersburg PA
CBHW061547210926
51850CB00009B/2030
* 9 7 8 3 7 2 5 8 5 4 0 3 5 *